The DEATH PENALTY

Constitutional Issues, Commentaries and Case Briefs

ROLANDO V. DEL CARMEN
Sam Houston State University

SCOTT VOLLUM
James Madison University

KELLY CHEESEMAN DIAL
University of Southern Mississippi

DURANT FRANTZEN
Texas A&M University-Kingsville

CLAUDIA SAN MIGUEL
Texas A&M International University

2nd **Edition**

 LexisNexis®

 anderson publishing
A member of the LexisNexis Group

The Death Penalty: Constitutional Issues, Commentaries, and Case Briefs, Second Edition

Copyright © 2005, 2008
Matthew Bender & Company, Inc., a member of the LexisNexis Group
Newark, NJ

ISBN: 978-1-59345-575-0

Phone: 877-374-2919
Web site: www.lexisnexis.com/anderson/criminaljustice

Library of Congress Cataloging-in-Publication Data

The death penalty : constitutional issues, commentary, and case briefs / Rolando V. del Carmen ... [et al.]. – 2nd ed.
    p. cm.
  Includes index.
  ISBN 978-1-59345-575-0 (softbound)
  1. Capital punishment–United States. I. Del Carmen, Rolando V.
KF9227.C2D4117 2008
345.73'0773—dc22

                                    2008041094

Cover design by Tin Box Studio, Inc./Cincinnati, OH

EDITOR Elisabeth Roszmann Ebben
ACQUISITIONS EDITOR Michael C. Braswell

Transferred to Digital Printing 2011

Preface and Introduction

Death as a form of punishment was used in the United States even before the American colonies became a republic. For a long time, the death penalty was—and still is—an option available to the state when dealing with serious offenders, and the public accepted it as such without many legal or political challenges. In recent times, however, issues have arisen concerning the constitutionality and wisdom of this ultimate sanction. This has spawned numerous court cases, decided over several decades, that have sought to declare this form of punishment unconstitutional, or that attempted to refine and polish some of its features. These cases and what they say are the focus of this book.

Constitutionality and the wisdom of imposing the death penalty are two separate issues, although they tend to be treated as one in some quarters. Constitutionality is an issue addressed and resolved by the courts, while the wisdom of imposing it is a political question to be resolved by political decisionmakers who represent the public. This book limits itself to the constitutionality issue. Whether the death penalty is wise or desirable as a form of punishment is for political entities to eventually determine and resolve.

Numerous books and articles have been written on the death penalty. This book seeks to add a legal dimension to existing literature by bringing together all the major cases decided by the United States Supreme Court on the death penalty. The first case decided by the Court on the death penalty was *Wilkerson v. Utah* in 1878. The cut-off date for the cases briefed in this book is July 1, 2008. A total of 64 cases are briefed here. As in any project in which choices are involved, subjectivity played a role in determining which cases from among the many decided by the Court are sufficiently important to justify inclusion among the briefed cases. That determination, including the "Top Ten Most Significant Death Penalty Cases," was made by the authors based on their familiarity over the years with death penalty cases.

The Book's Purpose and Audience

This text is written to fill a need for a book that brings together all the legal issues related to the death penalty. There is no such book available to the general public at present, except perhaps those used in law schools and in full case form. It classifies the death penalty cases according to legal issues, provides a commentary on the various subtopics, and then presents legal materials in an easy-to-digest and understandable form. The main audience of the book are undergraduates and criminal justice practitioners. The book should also prove useful, however, for anyone who has an interest in the legal issues surrounding the death penalty.

The Book's Content

The book consists of twelve chapters, subclassified into four parts.

Part I (Chapters 1 and 2) introduces the history of the death penalty and then discusses the foundation cases of *Furman v. Georgia* and *Gregg v. Georgia*.

Part II (Chapters 3, 4, and 5) focuses on constitutional issues and specific groups. These groups are those discriminated against because of race, mental impairment, or due to their having committed serious crimes at a young age. These offenders are treated differently by the Court.

Part III (Chapters 6, 7, 8, 9, 10, and 11) constitutes the major thrust of the book. It addresses constitutional issues such as the role of juries and jurors, the right to effective assistance of counsel, the right to due process, aggravating and mitigating circumstances, appeals, habeas corpus, and the concept of evolving standards of decency.

Part IV (Chapter 12) addresses the future of the death penalty and where the United States might go on this increasingly controversial issue.

Format

Every chapter starts with commentaries on the general case law on a subtopic, followed by a chart of the cases briefed in the chapter, and then the case briefs. The case brief approach to the study of law is deemed more effective for undergraduates and field practitioners who do not have the time or the inclination to go into a prolonged reading of United States Supreme Court cases. A case brief acquaints the reader with the case by summarizing its facts, issues, reasons, and holding. This is done in the interest of brevity, but hopefully not at the expense of accuracy.

A Word on Legal Referencing and Access to Original Cases

Every case briefed in this book contains a case citation. For those who may need some guidance in understanding case citations, the legal citation used in this book is similar to those used in general in law books and articles. To illustrate, let us use the following citation: *Gregg v. Georgia*, 428 U.S. 153 (1976).

> *Gregg v. Georgia* is the case title, 428 refers to the volume where the case starts, U.S. means the United States Reports (the official government publisher of United States Supreme Court cases), 153 refers to the page where the case starts, and 1976 refers to the year the case was decided.

Anyone who wants to read the case of *Gregg v. Georgia* as originally printed may therefore go to any law library, pull out Volume 428 of the United States Reports, then go to page 153, where the case starts. Some Supreme Court decisions are short, while others are very long.

The original decisions of the United States Supreme Court in these cases are readily available in various ways, particularly on the Internet. To find these cases, go to the Supreme Court's Web site at: www.supremecourtus.gov and click on "Opinions," then the year of the decision. If more research is desired on a case, perform an Internet search, then choose the U.S. Supreme Court decision from the many results. There will likely be many entries on that case, including the decisions of the lower courts that were appealed and commentaries on the case. Make sure the case is the U.S. Supreme Court decision and not that of the trial court, the court of appeals, or of a state supreme court.

Preface to the Second Edition

The death penalty, in the context of the United States Constitution and the Supreme Court, is constantly evolving. In this, the second edition of *The Death Penalty: Constitutional Issues, Commentaries, and Case Briefs*, we try to reflect this evolution by presenting the most recent Supreme Court cases and the issues inherent in them that have occurred in the years since we published the first edition of this book. As I write this preface, we have just come off the longest hiatus in executions since the death penalty was reinstated following the Supreme Court decision in *Gregg v. Georgia*. This informal moratorium resulted from the Court's decision to consider the constitutionality of the execution method of lethal injection. The case was *Baze v. Rees*, one of the most recent among the new cases analyzed and discussed in this book, and the Court held that lethal injection is a constitutionally permissible method of execution. The first execution since September 25, 2007, was carried out on May 6, 2008, when William Earl Lynd was executed in Georgia by lethal injection at 7:51 P.M. As I write this, Mark Schwab is scheduled to be executed by lethal injection in Florida for the rape and murder of an 11-year-old boy; It will be the tenth execution of the year. There are more than 20 executions scheduled to take place over the coming months.

Over the last several years executions have slowed, but the Supreme Court's consideration of constitutional issues pertaining to them certainly has not. During the four years since the first edition of this book was published, The Supreme Court has made significant decisions about, among other things, racial disparity in capital jury selection, mental impairment as a mitigating factor in capital sentencing, standards of effectiveness of legal representation for capital defendants, jury instructions pertaining to aggravating and mitigating evidence, evidence of actual innocence in habeas corpus petitions, and, most recently, the constitutionality of lethal injection as a method of execution and the constitutionality of the death penalty in cases of the rape of a child when the victim is not murdered. The makeup of the Court has also changed in the years since this book was first published. Chief Justice William H. Rehnquist has been succeeded by new Chief Justice John G. Roberts and Justice Sandra Day O'Connor has been succeeded by Justice Samuel Anthony

Alito Jr. Justice Alito's first death penalty opinion was in *Holmes v. South Carolina* (briefed in Chapter 8) and Chief Justice Roberts has written several opinions in death penalty cases and penned the plurality opinion in *Baze v. Rees* (briefed in Chapter 11).

Although the structure and much of the content in this second edition remains the same as in the original edition, there is much that is new and revised. There are 17 new cases briefed and many more new cases discussed throughout the book. The added case briefs are:

Chapter 3—Racial Discrimination and the Death Penalty

Cases Added:

Miller El v. Dretke (2005): Racially Disparate Questioning in Jury Selection
Snyder v. Louisiana (2008): Exclusion of Prospective Black Jurors without Racially Neutral Explanations

Chapter 4—The Mentally Impaired and the Death Penalty

Cases Added:

Singleton v. Norris (2003): Forcefully Medicating an Inmate for Competency in Order to be Executed
Tennard v. Dretke (2004): Mental Retardation as Mitigating Factor when Unrelated to Crime
Panetti v. Quarterman (2007): Mental Competency to Be Executed

Chapter 6—Juries, Jurors, and the Death Penalty

Case Added:

Uttecht v. Brown (2007): Trial Court Judge's Role in Death Qualification

Chapter 7—The Right to Effective Assistance of Counsel and the Death Penalty

Cases Added:

Rompilla v. Beard (2005): Counsel's Failure to Make a Reasonable Effort to Contest Evidence Supporting a Death Sentence
Schriro v. Landrigan (2007): Defendant's Interference with Counsel's Strategy and the Presentation of Mitigating Evidence

Chapter 8—Due Process and the Death Penalty

Cases Added:

Deck v. Missouri (2005): Shackling of a Capital Defendant During Sentencing Phase of Trial
Holmes v. South Carolina (2006): Introduction of Third-Party Guilt Evidence

Chapter 9—Aggravating and Mitigating Factors in Death Penalty Cases

Cases Added:

Kansas v. Marsh (2006): Death Sentence when Aggravating and Mitigating Factors are Equal in Weight
Brewer v. Quarterman (2007): Statutory Restrictions on Jury Instructions Regarding the Consideration of Mitigating Factors

Chapter 10—Appeals, Habeas Corpus, and the Death Penalty

Cases Added:

Nelson v. Campbell (2004): Right to Bring a Lawsuit Challenging the Method of Execution
House v. Bell (2007): Habeas Corpus Appeals on the Grounds of Actual Innocence
Lawrence v. Florida (2007): Suspension of AEDPA's Statute of Limitations While Awaiting Habeas Corpus Decision

Chapter 11—Evolving Standards of Decency and the Eighth Amendment's Ban on Cruel and Unusual Punishment

Case Added:

Baze v. Rees (2008): Constitutionality of Lethal Injection as a Method of Execution
Kennedy v. Louisiana (2008): Constitutionality of the Death Penalty for Non-Homicide Cases of Sexual Assault against a Child

Only one case brief has been removed (the 2003 case of *Miller-El v. Cockrell* has been replaced by the more recent 2005 case of *Miller-El v. Dretke*). Discussion surrounding past cases and the rich history and lineage of Supreme Court decisions in capital cases has been preserved but has been supplemented by numerous new decisions and updated information on the many related death penalty issues. In the end, we believe that the second edition of this book significantly strengthens and bolsters what was already a valuable and unique book and offers the reader the most comprehensive and up-to-date collection and consideration of constitutional issues and Supreme Court decisions pertaining to the death penalty.

Scott Vollum, Ph.D.
Harrisonburg, Virginia
July 1, 2008

About the Authors

Rolando V. del Carmen is Distinguished Professor of Criminal Justice (law) and Regents Professor at Sam Houston State University in Huntsville, Texas. He wrote Chapter 2 (The Foundation Cases: *Furman v. Georgia* and *Gregg v. Georgia*) and conceptualized and coordinated the writing and publication of the original edition of the book.

Scott Vollum is Assistant Professor of Justice Studies at James Madison University in Harrisonburg, Virginia. He wrote Chapter 6 (Juries, Jurors, and the Death Penalty), Chapter 9 (Aggravating and Mitigating Factors in Death Penalty Cases), and Chapter 11 (Evolving Standards of Decency and Cruel and Unusual Punishment). He conceptualized and coordinated the writing and revision of the book, and edited the various chapters.

Kelly Cheeseman Dial is Assistant Professor in the Department of Administration of Justice at the University of Southern Mississippi in Hattiesburg, Mississippi. She wrote Chapter 3 (Racial Discrimination and the Death Penalty) and Chapter 4 (The Mentally Impaired and the Death Penalty).

Durant Frantzen is Assistant Professor of Criminology at Texas A&M University-Kingsville, San Antonio System Center. He wrote Chapter 5 (Death Penalty for Juveniles), Chapter 7 (Right to Effective Counsel and the Death Penalty), and Chapter 8 (Due Process and the Death Penalty).

Claudia San Miguel is Assistant Professor of Criminal Justice and Director of the Criminal Justice Program at Texas A & M International University, in Laredo, Texas. She wrote Chapter 1 (The Death Penalty: Past and Present), Chapter 10 (Appeals, Habeas Corpus, and the Death Penalty) and Chapter 12 (Other Issues, Trends, and the Future of the Death Penalty).

Acknowledgments

The authors would like to thank the immediate members of their families, their faculty colleagues, their students, and others from whom they have learned so much in the course of their careers. They express deep gratitude to the staff at LexisNexis/Anderson Publishing, particularly Biz Ebben, who did the final edit of the book and saw it through—from inception to publication. Without her kind help and guidance this book would not have been possible.

Contents

Chapter 6
Juries, Jurors, and the Death Penalty   155

Chapter 7
The Right to Effective Assistance of Counsel
and the Death Penalty   189

Chapter 8
Due Process and the Death Penalty   229

Chapter 9
Aggravating and Mitigating Factors in Death Penalty Cases   259

Chapter 10
Appeals, Habeas Corpus, and the Death Penalty   301

Chapter 11
Evolving Standards of Decency and the Eighth Amendment's Ban on Cruel and Unusual Punishment   345

Chapter 12
Other Issues, Trends, and the Future of the Death Penalty   373

"Top Ten" Most Significant Death Penalty Cases

10. **Lockett v. Ohio**, 438 U.S. 586 (1978) — Death penalty statutes must allow for consideration of mitigating factors regarding the character or history of a defendant, as well as the circumstances of the offense.

9. **Payne v. Tennessee**, 495 U.S. 149 (1990) — Victim impact statements pertaining to characteristics of the victim and the emotional impact of the crime on the victim's family do not violate the Eighth Amendment and are admissible in the sentencing phase of the trial.

8. **Baze v. Rees**, 553 U.S. ___ (2008) — Lethal injection does not violate the Eighth Amendment's prohibition of cruel and unusual punishment and is thus a constitutionally permissible method of execution.

7. **Lockhart v. McCree**, 476 U.S. 162 (1986) — Prospective jurors whose opposition to the death penalty is so strong as to prevent or impair the performance of their duties as jurors at the sentencing phase of a trial may be removed for cause from jury membership.

6. **McCleskey v. Kemp**, 481 U.S. 279 (1987) — A statistical study suggesting racial discrimination in the imposition of death sentences does not make the death penalty unconstitutional. What is needed is that "petitioner must prove that decision-makers in his case acted with discriminatory purpose."

5. **Ring v. Arizona**, 536 U.S. 584 (2002) — "The decision whether or not to execute a defendant must be made by a jury. A judge may not alone make a determination of aggravating circumstances and thus elevate a punishment to death. Such aggravating circumstances are 'the functional equivalent of an element of a greater offense' and therefore must be determined by a jury as required by the Sixth Amendment."

4. **Atkins v. Virginia**, 536 U.S. 304 (2002) — "The execution of mentally retarded defendants is a violation of the Eighth Amendment's prohibition against cruel and unusual punishment."

3. **Roper v. Simmons**, 543 U.S. 551 (2005) — Imposing the death penalty on juveniles who commit crimes at age 16 or 17 constitutes cruel and unusual punishment prohibited by the Eighth Amendment.

2. **Furman v. Georgia**, 408 U.S. 238 (1972) — The death penalty is unconstitutional; it violates the Constitution's equal protection clause and the prohibition against cruel and unusual punishment.

1. **Gregg v. Georgia**, 428 U.S. 153 (1976) — Death penalty statutes that contain sufficient safeguards against arbitrary and capricious imposition are constitutional.

Chapter Outline

I. **Introduction**

II. **A Retrospective Analysis of the Death Penalty**
   A. The Colonial Period
   B. The Age of Enlightenment and the Early Movement to Abolish the Death Penalty
      1. From Europe to the Colonies: The Impact of Enlightenment
      2. Changes in the Death Penalty from 1790–1950

III. **Early Supreme Court Decisions on the Death Penalty**
   A. *Wilkerson v. Utah*: Death by Firing Squad
   B. *In re Kemmler*: Death by Electrocution
   C. *Louisiana ex rel. Francis v. Resweber*: The Constitutionality of Being Executed Twice
   D. Additional Changes in the Death Penalty Prior to 1972

IV. **In Summary, What Do these Cases Say?**

V. **Conclusion**

Cases Briefed in Chapter 1

Case Briefs
   Wilkerson v. Utah, 99 U.S. 130 (1878)
   In re Kemmler, 136 U.S. 436 (1890)
   Louisiana ex rel. Francis v. Resweber, 329 U.S. 459 (1947)

Internet Resources

Notes

Chapter 1

The Death Penalty: Past and Present

I. Introduction

The history of the death penalty in the United States may be divided into two historical periods—the period prior to the 1976 seminal decision in *Gregg v. Georgia* (1976)[1] and the period after *Gregg*. This chronological division, based on the two historical periods of the death penalty, reflects the most significant change made by the Supreme Court regarding the constitutionality of the death penalty. However, to fully appreciate the profoundness of the Court's decision in *Gregg* and to understand why *Gregg* is the point at which to differentiate between the two periods, an analysis of the historical roots of the death penalty must be undertaken.

This chapter presents a brief overview of the history of the death penalty from colonial times to 1971. Specifically, it first explores the virtual importation of the death penalty from England to the colonies and examines the early justifications for the death penalty. It also discusses early movements to abolish the death penalty that were inherently influenced by the Age of Enlightenment. Parts of this chapter examine the constitutional issues that were important prior to *Gregg*. Additionally, because of the Court's repeated use of the Eighth Amendment's proscription against cruel and unusual punishment in determining the constitutionality of state death penalty sentences, this chapter discusses the high court's early interpretation of the Eighth Amendment. The chapter also briefly explores the Court's decision to use the Eighth Amendment despite the fact that it was not made applicable to the states until 1962.[2]

II.   A Retrospective Analysis of the Death Penalty

A.   The Colonial Period

The first recorded execution in America occurred in 1608,[3] but the death penalty's formal and legal foundations were not firmly established until later in the seventeenth century, when European settlers formed permanent colonies in the New World after the 1620s. In colonial America, the penalty of death was typically imposed on those who engaged in crimes such as murder, adultery, bestiality, witchcraft, and blasphemy. Although each colony's codification of laws and accompanying penalties differed, most state codes were reflective of religious beliefs and thus the death penalty was justified on religious grounds. For instance, biblical arguments in favor of the death penalty were evident in the capital laws of the Massachusetts Bay Colony. Strongly influenced by the Mosaic Code of the Old Testament, known for the retributionist doctrine "an eye for an eye," the Bay Colony's 1641 *Body of Liberties* (the penal code) prescribed the penalty of death for violation of 12 laws, which included idolatry, witchcraft, blasphemy, murder, manslaughter, poisoning, bestiality, sodomy, adultery, man-stealing,[4] false witness in capital cases, conspiracy, and rebellion. Interestingly, the crimes listed in the Body of Liberties were accompanied by their biblical references in the Old Testament.[5]

The harshness that characterized the penal code of the Massachusetts Bay Colony was relatively lenient in comparison to the many crimes (more than 50) punishable by death in England during the same period. In addition, compared to the other colonies such as Virginia, Maryland, Georgia, and Carolina, which imposed the death penalty for crimes committed only by indentured slaves, the Bay Colony's capital laws were quite lax. However, by the eighteenth century, support for the death penalty in all of the colonies grew as immigration to the New World increased substantially and public order was threatened. The death penalty grew almost by necessity because the colonies lacked adequate long-term facilities to incarcerate offenders.[6] Despite such issues, the number of capital crimes increased because of the demands of the English Crown, which had renewed its control over the colonies during this time. The English Crown insisted that the colonies follow its example and revise their penal codes to include 200 crimes punishable by death.

B.   The Age of Enlightenment and the Early Movement to Abolish the Death Penalty

1.   From Europe to the Colonies: The Impact of Enlightenment

While the colonists were struggling to control the massive immigration movement to the New World during the eighteenth century, Europe was at the height of a philosophical and intellectual movement known as the Enlightenment. The Age of Enlightenment, which began a century before, was spurred by the writings of naturalistic philosophers who were instrumental in dispelling spiritualistic or religious notions that human beings were born with fixed or innate personality traits.[7] For example, John Locke, one of the most influential philosophers of the time, articulated the notion of sensationalism, which claimed that humans were shaped not by the spiritual world but rather by their sensory reactions to the external environment. In his book, *Two Treatises on Government* (1690), Locke also rejected the idea that government was the creation of God and instead supported the principle that the government derived its authority from the people.[8]

Locke's writings, and those of other philosophers such as Montesquieu and Voltaire, generated great changes in the intellectual and philosophical thinking in Europe by introducing the notion that humans had the mental capacity, or the rationality, to create a form of government that protected the rights of the people. The writings of these Enlightenment philosophers eventually generated changes in the administration of justice, particularly with regard to the death penalty. Their writings influenced Italian philosopher Cesare Beccaria to advocate for the abolition of the death penalty.people.[9] Beccaria, who wrote *An Essay On Crimes and Punishment* (1764), believed that a punishment should be proportionate to the crime committed or to the harm that was inflicted on society. He also believed that too severe a penalty, such as death, may provoke an individual to engage in lesser forms of crime simply to avoid capital punishment. Thus, rather than deterring punishment, the death penalty, according to Beccaria, may encourage lesser forms of crimes. In addition, he argued that "the death penalty served as an example of barbarity rather than a deterrent to it, because it sanctioned the taking of human life—the very act it was intended to deter."[10] As alternatives to the death penalty, Beccaria proposed incarceration among several humane and proportionate forms of punishment.

In the colonies, the Age of Enlightenment served as an impetus for revolution and independence. Influenced greatly by Locke's notion that a government should be altered or abolished by the people if it was not fulfilling its duty to protect natural rights such as life, liberty, and property, the colonists expressed their displeasure with the English Crown in the Declaration of Independence and subsequently declared war. However, with much concern about the beginning of the Revolutionary War, other Enlightenment ideals, such as those proposed by Beccaria, did not seep into the colonial mainstream until after the war. It was not until 1779 that Thomas Jefferson first advocated punishments in proportion to the crime committed. Jefferson, who advocated abolishing the death penalty for all crimes except for murder and treason, believed that imprisonment might be able to reform offenders. He also opposed the death penalty because executions would greatly decimate the number of able-bodied men who were needed for various laborious tasks. In *A Bill for Proportioning Crimes and Punishment* (1779), he proposed that:

> capital punishments, which exterminate instead of reforming . . . should be the last melancholy resource against those whose existence is become inconsistent with the safety of their fellow citizens . . . [capital punishments] also weaken the state by cutting off so many who, if reformed, might be restored sound members of society, who, even under a course of correction, might be rendered useful in various labors for the public, and would be living and long continued spectacles to deter others from committing the like offences.[11]

Several years after the Articles of Confederation were adopted in 1781, a few states began to slowly abolish the death penalty for certain offenses, such as robbery and rape, but continued to retain executions for offenders who committed murder or treason. Pennsylvania in 1786, for instance, no longer imposed the death penalty for crimes such as burglary, robbery, or sodomy.[12] The first true movement to completely abolish the death penalty, however, was spearheaded by Dr. Benjamin Rush in 1787. Rush, a signer of the Declaration of Independence, urged a reconsideration of the death penalty as well as punishments that were imposed for retributive or vengeful purposes. He declared that "laws which inflict death for murder, are . . . as unchristian as those which justify or tolerate revenge."[13] Because of a belief that jails and other penal facilities of the time were contributing to the corruption of offenders rather than deterring them from committing crime, Rush also argued in favor of the creation of a penal institution that not only incarcerated offenders in solitary cells but also allowed offenders an opportunity for reform through penance. Together with a group of Pennsylvania Quakers, Rush formed the Society for Alleviating the Miseries of Public Prisons in 1787, and in 1790 the first penitentiary was established in Pennsylvania.

2.   Changes in the Death Penalty from 1790–1950

The early abolitionist movement pioneered by Rush and the Pennsylvania Quakers prompted several states to modify their death penalty statutes. The first significant change was the introduction of statutes that distinguished first-degree murder from second-degree murder. Although the distinction between first- and second-degree murder was already in practice in England, the state of Pennsylvania in 1793 was the first to make such a distinction by executing only those who committed murder in the first degree. First-degree murder included crimes such as premeditated murder and the killing of a human being during the commission of a felony (arson, burglary, rape, robbery). Conversely, second-degree murder, which was punishable by imprisonment, included crimes such as manslaughter or the killing of another without malice or premeditation.[14]

The second significant change in the death penalty was the discontinuance of public executions. As a feature of the death penalty both in England and in the colonies, it was customary to execute an offender in public in order to achieve the greatest deterrent effect. However, the gathering of large crowds to witness an execution had the unintended effect of increasing crime. For instance, captivated groups of witnesses were suitable targets for petty thieves who found it convenient and easy to practice their trade. Additionally, executions had the effect of inciting riots and disorder, which not only placed a strain on limited law enforcement resources, but also contributed to a growing fear of crime.[15] Although public hangings provided lucrative business opportunities not only for thieves, but also for vendors who sold food and tickets for admission, witnesses were susceptible to injuries due to the unsafe conditions of viewing stands. In 1827, "one crowd was so dense at an execution in Cooperstown that several spectators were injured when a viewing stand collapsed."[16] Accordingly, several states found it prudent to execute offenders behind prison walls. The first state to end public executions was New York in 1834, followed by Pennsylvania and New Jersey. By 1845 almost every state had ended public executions.

Eliminating mandatory death sentences was the third significant change. A common feature in the colonies (and later the states) was for the death penalty to be automatically imposed when a defendant was found guilty of first-degree murder. Thus, no state allowed a jury to determine whether the penalty of death was justified. However, in the 1830s, the abolitionist movement urged a reconsideration of mandatory death sentences. In 1838, Tennessee was the first state to end mandatory death sentences. Tennessee was also the first state to allow a jury the option of imposing the death penalty for a convicted murderer. In the years following the decision made by the state of Tennessee, other states slowly began to abolish mandatory death sentences. By the end of the nineteenth century, 20 additional jurisdictions had eliminated mandatory death sentences.[17]

The fourth significant change in the death penalty was the method used to execute offenders. From England to the first European settlement in the colonies, hanging was the preferred method of execution. Undoubtedly, both in England and the colonies, its popularity could be attributed to the fact that it was the most inexpensive and easiest way to punish offenders who committed capital crimes.[18] However, hanging was also preferred because of its deterrent effect. The belief was that:

> Hanging inflicted a signal indignity on the victim in a uniquely conspicuous fashion. It displayed the victim to the onlookers in a most ignominious and abject of postures and would thus be likely to enhance the deterrent effect of his punishment on anyone who might be tempted to do what he had done.[19]

In the 1840s, abolitionists began to campaign for more humane forms of execution. Although they would have favored the complete abolition of the death penalty, many abolitionists were content with modifying torturous and painful deaths, especially when there was evidence that "numerous botched attempts and many cases of lingering death"[20] plagued so many hangings. The first state to look into a more humane form of execution was New York. In 1899, New York, which was also the first state to legally sanction hanging as a method of execution, introduced a new and more humane form of execution— the electric chair. The quest for a painless death eventually led to the use of lethal gas, or the gas chamber, as a form of execution. In 1921, execution by lethal gas became another acceptable form of execution.

In addition to these four significant changes in the death penalty, several other notable events occurred during this time. The Bill of Rights was ratified in 1791 and the Fifth and Eighth Amendments affirmed the colonial practice of executing capital offenders. In 1847, prior to the Civil War, Michigan became the first state to abolish the death penalty, except for the crime of treason. In 1852, Rhode Island outlawed capital punishment for all crimes, including treason, and in 1853 Wisconsin followed the example set by Rhode Island. In the mid-nineteenth century, the abolitionist movement that was started by Benjamin Rush had diminished in support due to preoccupation with the Civil War. However, after the Civil War, the abolition movement again gained momentum. Between 1907 and 1917 six states completely abolished the death penalty (Kansas, 1907; Minnesota, 1911; Washington, 1913; Oregon, 1914; South Dakota, 1915; Missouri, 1917)[21] and three other states (Tennessee, 1915; North Dakota, 1915; Arizona, 1916) modified their statutes to limit executions to offenders who committed either treason or the killing of a law enforcement officer or prison official. The beginning of World War I and intensified fears about the emerging war caused five out of the six states that had previously abolished the death penalty to reinstate it by 1920. From 1920 to 1940, the death penalty received unprecedented support. In the 1930s, more offenders were executed than in any other decade in American history—an average of 167 deaths per year.[22]

III. Early Supreme Court Decisions on the Death Penalty

The Bill of Rights has not been found to prohibit the practice of executing offenders found guilty of capital offenses, except for during a brief period from 1972 to 1976 as a result of the *Furman v. Georgia* (1972)[23] decision. The Bill of Rights, principally the Fifth Amendment, apparently permits the use of the death penalty as long as "no person shall be held to answer for a capital or otherwise infamous crime, unless on a presentment or indictment of a Grand Jury" and as long as no person is "deprived of life, liberty, or property without due process of law." The Eighth Amendment does not clearly bar the use of the death penalty per se but only prohibits the imposition of cruel and unusual punishments. Because both the Fifth and Eighth Amendments do not expressly prohibit the use of the death penalty, legal scholars contend that the inclusion of these two amendments in the Bill of Rights was necessary to prevent judicial arbitrariness in imposing the death penalty—a common practice in England before and during the time of the writing of the Constitution.

Because the death penalty was an acceptable form of punishment, there was little need for the Supreme Court to address the issue of its constitutionality. Thus, the Supreme Court refrained from making any declarations regarding the constitutionality of the death penalty until 1878. When the Supreme Court finally broke its silence, its decisions reinforced prevailing concepts that the death penalty was constitutional. These early decisions included interpretations of the Eighth Amendment's prohibition against cruel and unusual punishments and marked the beginning of a long series of cases addressing legal issues involving the death penalty.

A.   Wilkerson v. Utah: *Death by Firing Squad*

The first death penalty case ever to be decided by the Supreme Court was *Wilkerson v. Utah* (1878).[24] In *Wilkerson*, the issue before the Court was not the constitutionality of the death penalty per se, but rather its method of execution—in this case, death by firing squad. Although executions by firing squad were common under military law,[25] Utah was the first territory in the United States to include this method of execution in its death penalty statute. Since 1851, prior to Utah becoming a state, the General Assembly of the territory of Utah had decreed that "when a person shall be found guilty of murder . . . and sentenced to die, he, she or they shall suffer death by being shot, hung, or beheaded."[26] The inclusion of three forms of execution was distinctive for its time because most of the other states preferred to execute offenders only by hanging. Although Utah resorted to hanging convicted murderers, the first execution by firing squad was not carried out until 1861. By the time Utah became a state in 1896, it had executed 14 offenders, 11 of whom were executed by firing squad.

When Wallace Wilkerson was convicted of a capital offense (premeditated murder) and sentenced by the court to be executed by firing squad, Utah had not yet been granted statehood. Moreover, when Wilkerson was sentenced to be executed, Utah had repealed the law that had allowed for three forms of execution. In 1876, Utah repealed the section of its death penalty statute that offered three methods of execution and the newly adopted statute did not provide any guidance as to which specific method of execution should be imposed on those found guilty of capital offenses. However, the new statute included a provision that authorized the court to decide such issues. Convinced that the repeal of the law prevented Utah from using a firing squad to execute him, Wilkerson petitioned the Court to overturn his sentence, arguing that death by firing squad violated the Eighth Amendment's cruel and unusual punishment clause. The Court disagreed and ruled that "in view of the fact that the laws of the Territory contain no other specific regulation as the mode of executing such a sentence, the court here is of the opinion that the assignment [of death by firing squad] . . . is no grounds for reversal of the judgment of the court below."[27] The Court noted that because executions by firing squad were common practice in the territory of Utah, there was nothing unusual about Wilkerson's sentence.

The Court's decision to uphold the use of a firing squad to execute capital offenders was significant because it marked the beginning of the high court's death penalty jurisprudence. Although the decision was expected in light of the overwhelming support for the death penalty, the Court's use and interpretation of the Eighth Amendment was interesting. Historically, the Eighth Amendment only applied to federal sentencing practices, because the Bill of Rights was initially introduced for the sole purpose of curtailing the power of the federal government, but not the power of the states. Consequently, the states at the time of the *Wilkerson* decision were not bound by the first 10 amendments to the Constitution. The applicability of the provisions of the Bill of Rights to the states was not an issue until after the ratification of the Fourteenth Amendment in 1868, which holds that "no state shall make or enforce any law which shall abridge the privileges and immunities of citizens of the United States; nor shall any state deprive any person of life, liberty, or property without due process of law; nor shall deny to any person within the jurisdiction, the equal protection of the laws." In the 1920s the Court approved the applicability of some of the provisions of the Bill of Rights to the states and did so by carefully selecting which amendments to incorporate. It was not until 1962 that the Eighth Amendment was held binding on the states via the Fourteenth Amendment's due process clause.

Because the Eighth Amendment was not applicable to the states until 1962, *Wilkerson* represented a unique legal paradox because the Court opined that the amendment's prohibition against cruel and unusual punishment applied to the states and even to territories of the United States. The Court declared that although each state and territory "may define offenses and prescribe the punishment of offenders," all states and territories were "subject to the prohibition of the Constitution that cruel and unusual punishments shall not be inflicted [emphasis added]."[28] The Court also stated, however, that "cruel and unusual punishments are forbidden by the Constitution, but . . . the punishment of shooting as a mode of executing the death penalty for the crime of murder in the first degree is not included in that category, within the meaning of the Eighth Amendment."[29] By 1890, the Court reconsidered its rationale of using the Eighth Amendment in death penalty cases.

B. In re Kemmler: *Death by Electrocution*

In 1890, the Court addressed the constitutionality of using electrical current to execute capital offenders in *In re Kemmler* (1890).[30] Unlike its decision in *Wilkerson*, the Court in *Kemmler* explicitly said that the Eighth

Amendment was not applicable to the states. The Court therefore did not use the Eighth Amendment (cruel and unusual punishment) but instead used the Fourteenth Amendment (due process clause) to uphold the constitutionality of using the electric chair. The Court ruled that the amendment "was not designed to interfere with the power of the state to protect the lives, liberties, and property of its citizens, and to promote their health, peace, morals, education and good order."[31] Therefore, the Court held that the state of New York did not violate Kemmler's due process rights under the Fourteenth Amendment when it sentenced him to die by electrocution because it was merely preserving the lives of other citizens.

The constitutionality of using electrocution as a method of execution in *Kemmler* was challenged as a violation of the due process clause of the Fourteenth Amendment. But when Kemmler first appealed his death sentence, the legal issue used in state court was not the due process clause. Instead, it was the cruel and unusual punishment clause of the Eighth Amendment and a similar provision in the New York constitution. A change in legal strategy was employed after unsuccessfully trying to prove that electrocution was a form of cruel and unusual punishment under both the U.S. Constitution and the state's constitution.

Kemmler's difficulty in proving that electrocution was a form of cruel and unusual punishment may have been partly attributable to several reasons. First, at the time of his death sentence, electrocution was believed to be the most humane way to execute capital offenders. Electrocution as a method of execution was instituted by New York in 1888 when it adopted the Electrocution Act to overcome the cruelty and inhumanity of executing capital offenders through hanging. Several years prior to the formal adoption of the electric chair, the governor of New York argued before the legislature that "the present mode of executing criminals by hanging has come down to us from the dark ages, and it may well be questioned whether the science of the present day cannot provide a means for taking the life of such as are condemned to die in a less barbarous manner."[32]

Other reasons for Kemmler's failure to prove that electrocution was cruel and unusual may have been the politics and financial forces in New York at the time of Kemmler's first appeals. When Kemmler appealed his death sentence, a battle over the appropriate electrical current (AC—alternating current or DC—direct current) to use in bringing about the death of a convicted capital offender had intensified. Direct current was discovered by Thomas Edison in 1880 and used for the first time to provide electricity for a small residential area in New York. The current, although considered safe, was deemed to be limited in its capacity to provide electricity to the entire city of New York. Experimentations in alternating current, performed by George Westinghouse, began in 1884. With a lower cost to consumers, alternating current was gaining popularity over direct current.[33] Alternating current was also more powerful in that it was capable of providing more electricity to the entire city.

When debates ensued about which current to use in electrocutions, direct current was disfavored because it was believed to lack the potency needed to bring about instantaneous death. Because alternating current was more powerful, it was chosen as the appropriate current for use in electrocutions. However, "compelling evidence suggests that the commission's ultimate recommendation of electrocution as the most humane method of effecting death was influenced heavily by the financial competition between Thomas Edison and George Westinghouse concerning whose current would dominate the electrical industry."[34] Alternating current's cost-effectiveness and its powerful ability to provide electricity to the city may have swayed the commission's decision.

A more significant reason Kemmler did not succeed in overturning his death sentence was the state judiciary's refusal to invalidate a state law. Kemmler lost his legal battle primarily because he failed to meet the stringent burden of proving that the Electrocution Act was unconstitutional. In his first appeal, the county court was unconvinced that Kemmler had proven beyond a reasonable doubt that alternating current was a form of cruel and unusual punishment, and thus the court preserved the constitutionality of the Act. The Court further emphasized that:

> (1) every legislative act is presumed to be constitutional; (2) in a doubtful case, no act should be annulled by the judiciary since mere conflict of interpretation between the legislative and judicial powers is not a sufficient basis for determining that the legislature had erred; and (3) a single judge should declare a law to be invalid on constitutional grounds only when his duty to do so is entirely clear.[35]

The court also noted that the Eighth Amendment was not applicable to the states. In fact, it stated that "the Eighth Amendment did not refer to punishments provided in state courts for crimes against the State, but was addressed solely to the national government, as a constraint on its power."[36] The court further noted that "it had no duty to attempt to interpret any accurate and comprehensive definition"[37] of the cruel and unusual punishment clause of the Eighth Amendment. Thus, relying on the state's constitutional provision against cruel and unusual punishment as a guide, the court concluded that electrocution was not cruel or unusual and that "electricity would produce immediate and painless death, thereby preventing the unsightly and horrifying spectacles which now not infrequently attend executions by hanging."[38]

In a subsequent appeal to the New York Supreme Court, Kemmler faced similar obstacles. The court concluded that Kemmler had not met the burden of proving beyond a reasonable doubt that electrocution would be a cruel form of punishment. The court refrained from casting doubt on the constitutionality of the Electrocution Act, thus refusing to invalidate an act by the state legislature. The court said that "nothing in the Constitution or in the nature of things suggested that the court's judgment was superior to the legislature's in determining a mere question of fact involved in legislation."[39] Because the New York Court of Appeals affirmed the decision of the New York Supreme Court, Kemmler appealed to the United States Supreme Court, but the Court did not overturn his death sentence.

C.   Louisiana ex rel. Francis v. Resweber: *The Constitutionality of Being Executed Twice*

In 1947, the Court was presented with another case regarding the method of execution of a capital offender—Willie Francis.[40] Francis, who was convicted of murder and sentenced to death by electrocution in the state of Louisiana, was seated in the electric chair waiting to be executed. However, because of a mechanical malfunction, the electric current was not strong enough to cause his death. He was returned to prison and a new death warrant was issued by the governor. In his appeal to the Louisiana Supreme Court, Francis contended that a second attempt to execute him would violate the cruel and unusual punishment clause of the Eighth Amendment as well as the double jeopardy clause of the Fifth Amendment. The Louisiana Supreme Court denied his appeal, primarily holding that no current of sufficient intensity to cause death had passed through to Francis's body, and therefore no pain was inflicted.

On appeal, the Supreme Court was asked to determine whether the state of Louisiana could legally execute Francis after the electric chair had malfunctioned. The Court answered yes, saying that the second attempt to execute Francis would not violate the cruel and unusual punishment clause of the Eighth Amendment because "the fact that the petitioner has already been subjected to a current of electricity does not make his subsequent execution any more cruel in the constitutional sense than any other execution."[41] The Court also stated that the Eighth Amendment only prohibits the "infliction of unnecessary pain," not simply pain suffered as a result of an "unforeseeable accident."[42] The Fifth Amendment affirms that "no person shall be subject for the same offense to be twice put in jeopardy of life or limb," but the Court held that "when an accident, with no suggestion of malevolence, prevents the consummation of a sentence, the state's subsequent course in the administration of its criminal law is not affected on that account by any requirement of due process."[43]

The holding that a second attempt to execute Francis would not violate the Eighth or Fifth Amendments was supported by only four justices of the Court and therefore was a plurality decision. Justice Frankfurter, who wrote a concurring opinion, disagreed with the Court but only with respect to its use of the Eighth Amendment. Justice Frankfurter argued that when the Fourteenth Amendment was ratified, it was not meant to disrupt state criminal justice systems. Although the amendment prohibited states from infringing on the "privileges and immunities of citizens" and constrained them by affirming that no state "shall deprive any person of life, liberty, or property, without due process of law . . . ," Justice Frankfurter opined that the amendment did not place any restraints upon the states in the formulation or administration of their criminal law. Thus, the states were "free to carry out their own notions of criminal justice . . . unless in doing so offends some principles of justice so rooted in the traditions and conscience of our people as to be ranked fundamental."[44] Justice Frankfurter concluded by saying that because the first attempt to execute Francis did not cause his death and because such accident was unforeseeable, there was no miscarriage of justice grave enough to violate the Eighth Amendment.

The four dissenting justices said that the Court should have barred the state of Louisiana from executing Francis and should have required the state to conduct an investigation of the electrical current and voltage that was used during the first failed attempt at electrocution. However, they also said that to allow Francis to be subjected to a second electrocution, regardless of whether the first attempt was an accident or due to mechanical failure, would violate the due process clause of the Fourteenth Amendment and the cruel and unusual clause of the Eighth Amendment. Thus, according to the dissent, the Eighth Amendment applied to the states regardless of the original applicability of the Bill of Rights, because subjecting a person to electric shocks in intervals of several days "shocks the most fundamental instincts of civilized man."[45] The justices added that it was the duty of state officials to ensure that the current used to electrocute capital offenders was of sufficient intensity to cause a painless and instantaneous death. Because such precautions were not taken, Francis's death sentence should have been overturned.

D. Additional Changes in the Death Penalty Prior to 1972

Before the ruling in *Francis*, the Court had criticized the imposition of the death penalty in the case of *Powell v. Alabama* (1932).[46] Although the case was mainly decided on the issue of ineffective counsel (Sixth Amendment), the Court overturned the death sentences of seven black youths who were charged with the rapes of two white girls. The youths, who became known as the "Scottsboro Boys" due to the location of their arrest, were poor and illiterate. Arraigned the same day as their arrest, the youths were never told of their right to have appointed or retained counsel for their defense and were eventually given counsel on the day of their separate trials. Because of such flagrant violations of the Sixth Amendment, the Court ruled that "a defendant should be afforded a fair opportunity to secure counsel of his own choice. Not only was that not done here, but such designation of counsel as was attempted was either so indefinite or so close upon trial as to amount to a denial of effective and substantial aid in that regard."[47]

In *Patton v. Mississippi* (1947),[48] the Court was asked to determine the constitutionality of eliminating capital jurors solely on the basis of their race. The Court ruled that it was unconstitutional to systematically exclude blacks from trial juries. Specifically, the Court stated, "when a jury selection plan, whatever it is, operates in such way as always to result in the complete and long-continued exclusion of any representative at all from a large group of negroes, or any other racial group, indictments and verdicts returned against them by juries thus selected cannot stand."[49] In 1968, the Court was presented with another issue regarding jurors in death penalty cases. In *Witherspoon v. Illinois* (1968),[50] William Witherspoon had been sentenced to death for the murder of a police officer. He appealed his conviction and subsequent death sentence, stating that an Illinois law that allowed the prosecution to exclude all jurors who were opposed to or had mere reservations about the death penalty violated his Sixth Amendment right to a fair trial. The Court agreed and ruled that when a state excluded "from the jury all who expressed conscientious or religious scruples against capital punishment and all who opposed it in principle, the state crossed the line of neutrality. In its quest for a jury capable of imposing death, the state produced a jury uncommonly willing to condemn a man to die."[51]

Five years prior to *Gregg v. Georgia* (1976),[52] the Court issued rulings with regard to capital jurors in two cases: *McGautha v. California* (1971)[53] and *Crampton v. Ohio* (1971).[54] In both cases, defendants petitioned the Court for a reversal of their death sentences on grounds that jurors were given absolute or unguided discretion in deciding whether to impose the death penalty or a life sentence and that such unguided discretion violated the due process clause of the Fourteenth Amendment. An additional issue was raised in *Crampton*—the use of unitary trial, in which jurors decided both guilt and punishment during the same criminal proceeding. In a 6-to-3 decision, the Court ruled that "the absence of standards to guide the jury's discretion on the punishment issue is constitutionally tolerable."[55] With respect to a unitary trial, the Court did not find it to be unconstitutional.

IV.   In Summary, What Do these Cases Say?

Because the death penalty was an acceptable form of punishment during colonial times, jurisprudence on its constitutionality was nonexistent until the late nineteenth century. When the Supreme Court finally entered the arena of debate about the death penalty in 1878, it merely affirmed the public's attitude on this issue. In the few early cases decided by the Court prior to 1972, constitutionality of the death penalty was never an issue. The only issues presented before the high court were methods of execution and the constitutionality of certain procedural rules, such as jury selection. There appeared to be an assumption that the death penalty itself was constitutional.

Of significance in these early cases was the Court's use of the Eighth Amendment's proscription against cruel and unusual punishment despite the fact that this amendment was not held binding on the states until 1962. Although the states were not bound to follow the mandates of the Eighth Amendment, the Court nonetheless used this amendment to uphold the constitutionality of several methods of execution. For instance, in *Wilkerson*, the Court held that all capital punishments, even those imposed by territories of the United States, must be in accord with the Eighth Amendment. It also held that death by firing squad did not fall within the meaning of "cruelty" as prohibited by the Constitution. In *Kemmler*, the Court hesitated to use the Eighth Amendment and conceded that states were not bound by this federal constitutional amendment. The decision however, did not prevent the Court from using the Eighth Amendment 57 years later in *Louisiana ex rel. Francis v. Resweber*, when it used the Eighth Amendment to rule on the constitutionality of being executed twice. In totality, these cases on the death penalty dealt with methods of execution and demonstrate the degree of respect given to state court decisions as well as to laws enacted by the states.

Prior to the Court's ruling in *Louisiana ex rel. Francis v. Resweber*, the Court issued a surprising ruling in *Powell v. Alabama*. The Court's ruling was unexpected because prior to 1932, the Court's customary position was merely to rubber-stamp capital sentences issued by the states. However, in *Powell* the Court overturned several death sentences on grounds that they violated the Sixth Amendment's right to counsel. In the late 1940s the Court took issue with the systematic and prejudicial exclusion of jurors in *Patton v. Mississippi* and ruled that such practice violated the Constitution. By the late 1960s, the Court resolved issues of unguided discretion, which it had previously supported, and ruled that such discretion violated the due process class of the Fourteenth Amendment. It also ruled that the absence of jury standards in death penalty cases violated the Constitution. These latter cases are significant because they set the stage for the most important rulings issued by the Supreme Court in the cases of *Furman v. Georgia* (1972) and *Gregg v. Georgia* (1976).

V. Conclusion

The history of the death penalty in the United States dates back to the early seventeenth century, a time when European settlers were beginning to establish the first permanent colonies in the New World. The cultural heritage of these first permanent settlers, coupled with the subsequent waves of immigrants from Europe during the 1600s, influenced the administration of justice in the colonies, including the use of the death penalty. As was customary in Europe, the death penalty in colonial America was imposed for a variety of crimes. Analyses of early colonial criminal codes reveal that the death penalty was imposed for many crimes, including witchcraft, blasphemy, idolatry, poisoning, adultery, and murder. Also, analyses of these early criminal codes reflect that religious doctrine, principally based on the Mosaic Code of the Old Testament, served as the primary justification for imposing the death penalty.

Although the cultural heritage of the first European settlers contributed to the virtual importation of the death penalty to colonial America, the Age of

Enlightenment, which began in Europe during the seventeenth century, greatly influenced movements to abolish the death penalty. In addition to serving as the impetus for revolution and independence, the Age of Enlightenment swayed several states to abolish the death penalty for some crimes. It also influenced notable figures such as Thomas Jefferson and Benjamin Rush to advocate for the abolition of the death penalty for all crimes except for treason, and murder, and for solitary confinement as an alternative to the death penalty, respectively. Because of the Age of Enlightenment and the fervor of Rush and other death penalty abolitionists, significant changes in the use of this ultimate sanction occurred. From 1790 to 1950, several states modified their death penalty statutes to: (1) distinguish between first- and second-degree murder; (2) discontinue public executions; (3) eliminate mandatory death sentences; and (4) modify the methods used to execute offenders.

In 1791, when the Bill of Rights was adopted, the Framers of the Constitution affirmed the use of the death penalty by establishing procedural safeguards in both the Fifth and Eighth Amendments. The Bill of Rights has not been found to prohibit the practice of executing offenders found guilty of capital offenses, except for a brief period from 1972 to 1976, as a result of the Court's decision in *Furman v. Georgia* (1972).[56] Accordingly, the constitutionality of the death penalty was not a legal matter that required the attention of the Court. In 1879, when the Court first entered the arena of debate about the death penalty, executions, particularly by firing squad, became a constitutionally justifiable form of punishment. The following year, the Court upheld executions by electric chair. In 1932, in *Powell v. Alabama*,[57] the Court was critical of the imposition of the death penalty for seven black youths and for the first time overturned their death penalties because the youths were denied the right to effective counsel. However, the Court did not mandate the abolition of the death penalty. From 1947 to 1971, the Court issued several more rulings on the death penalty but again refrained from debating its constitutionality.

Since the Court's first ruling regarding the death penalty in 1879, the legal landscape of this ultimate penal sanction has changed dramatically. Until very recently, however, one legal aspect of the death penalty that had remained virtually unaltered was the constitutionality of the method used to execute capital offenders. Since *Louisiana ex rel. Francis v. Resweber* (1947),[58] the Court had not heard another case regarding the constitutionality of a method of execution, despite a steady flow of death penalty cases appealed on this basis. But in 2008 the Court considered the constitutionality of lethal injection in the case of *Baze v. Rees*.[59] The Court ruled, however, that the combination of drugs was not violative of the Eighth Amendment's ban on cruel and unusual punishment; thus, lethal injection remains an acceptable form of execution.

Because the Court has in the past refused to hear these types of cases, legal scholars had contended that the Court had closed any further arguments regarding the constitutionality of methods of execution. Thus, they opined that it was highly unlikely that the Court would hold any of the existing methods used to execute offenders unconstitutional. According to one scholar who commented on the use of the electric chair, "Since *Francis*, every challenge to the constitutionality of electrocution has been rejected. The prisoner's arguments are usually summarily dismissed without even an examination of evidence of electrocution's effects."[60] With regard to the use of firing squads, which may be considered the most violent method used to execute capital offenders, Utah, Idaho, and Oklahoma continue to make this method of execution available, although Utah is the only state that has recently intended to use a firing squad to execute a capital offender. Since *Wilkerson v. Utah* (1878),[61] very few challenges have been made regarding the constitutionality of firing squads.

Cases Briefed in Chapter 1

Case	Issue	Holding
Wilkerson v. Utah 99 U.S. 130 (1878)	Does the failure to include a specific method of execution prohibit the court from imposing death by firing squad?	The failure to include a specific provision concerning the method of execution does not forbid the court from imposing death by firing squad.
	Is the imposition of death by firing squad in violation of the Eighth Amendment?	The imposition of death by firing squad does not violate the Eighth Amendment.
In re Kemmler 136 U.S. 436 (1890)	Is the Electrocution Act of 1888, which authorizes electrocution as a method of execution, in violation of the due process clause of the Fourteenth Amendment?	Electrocution is not a punishment that is cruel and unusual within the meaning of the due process clause of the Fourteenth Amendment.
Louisiana ex rel. Francis 329 U.S. 459 (1947)	Is carrying out the execution of a criminal after a failed first attempt a violation of the Eight Amendment and the Fifth Amendment?	Carrying out a second execution after a failed first attempt due to mechanical malfunction does not violate the cruel and unusual clause or the double jeopardy clause of the Constitution.

Case Briefs

Wilkerson v. Utah
99 U.S. 130 (1878)

CAPSULE: The failure to include a specific method of execution in a Utah statute did not bar the court from imposing death by firing squad, nor was this method of execution a violation of the laws of Utah or the Eighth Amendment to the Constitution.

FACTS: Wallace Wilkerson, who was indicted by a grand jury in the territory of Utah for the willful, malicious, and premeditated murder of William Baxter, was tried and convicted of murder in the first degree. The trial judge ordered that Wilkerson be safely confined until December 14 and transferred to "some place within the district . . . to be publicly shot until . . . dead." Since 1851, prior to Utah becoming a state, the General Assembly of the territory of Utah decreed that capital offenders, who were found guilty of murder and sentenced to die, "shall suffer death by being shot, hung, or beheaded." Because Utah had repealed the section of its death penalty statute offering three methods of execution (firing squad, hanging, or beheading) in 1876, Wilkerson petitioned the court on grounds that his particular mode of execution violated the Eighth Amendment's proscription against cruel and unusual punishment.

ISSUES:
1. Does the failure to include a specific method of execution in a Utah statute bar the court from imposing death by firing squad? NO.
2. Is the imposition of death by firing squad a violation of the Eighth Amendment to the U.S. Constitution? NO.

HOLDING:
1. The failure to include a specific statutory provision regarding the mode of execution does not bar a court from imposing death by firing squad because the statute authorized the court to choose the method of execution most fitting for the crime committed.
2. The imposition of death by firing squad did not violate the Eighth Amendment because in the territory of Utah this method of execution was common practice and thus not unusual. Furthermore, death by firing squad is not considered cruel within the meaning of the Eighth Amendment.

REASON: "The law of Utah provided that whenever any person was convicted of a capital offense, he should suffer death by being shot, hanged or beheaded, as the court should direct. This law was repealed by the Code, which provided that every person guilty of murder should suffer death, but did not provide the mode of executing the sentence, but which devolved a duty upon the court authorized to pass sentence for the crimes declared the punishment therein, to determine and impose the punishment prescribed. Construed as that provision must be in connection with the enactment that every person guilty of murder in the first degree shall suffer death, and in view of the fact that the laws of the Territory contain no other specific regulation as to the mode of executing such a sentence, the court here is of the opinion that the assignment of error shows no legal ground for reversing the judgment of the court below."

"The Territories are invested with legislative power which extends to all rightful subjects of legislation not inconsistent with the Constitution and the laws of the United States. By virtue of that power the legislative branch of the Territory may define offenses and prescribe the punishment of offenders, subject to the prohibition of the Constitution that cruel and unusual punishment shall not be inflicted."

"Cruel and unusual punishments are forbidden by the Constitution, but . . . the punishment of shooting as a mode of executing the death penalty for the crime of murder in the first degree is not included in that category, within the meaning of the Eighth Amendment."

CASE SIGNIFICANCE: The significance of this case is twofold. First, this case marks the beginning of the Court's death penalty jurisprudence. Although the Court's decision was not surprising in light of the overwhelming support for the death penalty during the colonial period, this case ended almost a decade of silence by the Court regarding the constitutionality of any matter regarding the death penalty. Second, this case represents a unique judicial problem because at the time the Court issued its ruling, the Eighth Amendment had not yet been incorporated to the states (the Eighth Amendment was not incorporated to the states until 1962 in the case of *Robinson v. California*, 370 U.S. 666) much less to a territory of the United States (Utah did not become a state until 1896). Nonetheless, the Court used this amendment to uphold the constitutionality of death by firing squad. The Court held that although the legislative branch of the territory of Utah may prescribe the specific punishment for offenders, such punishment must be in accord with the mandate of the cruel and unusual punishment clause of the Eighth Amendment. However, because Utah had originally used death by firing squad, in addition to hanging and beheading, to execute capital offenders, the Court held that the imposition of death by firing squad was not an unusual form of punishment.

In re Kemmler
136 U.S. 436 (1890)

CAPSULE: The Electrocution Act of 1888, which prescribed the use of electrical current (electric chair) to execute a capital offender, did not violate the due process clause of the Fourteenth Amendment.

FACTS: In 1889, William Kemmler was tried and convicted of the murder of his mistress in the state of New York. Rather than being sentenced to die by hanging, Kemmler was sentenced to die by electrocution—the prescribed method of execution under the recently enacted Electrocution Act of 1888. On appeal to the county court, Kemmler then petitioned to have his death sentence overturned on grounds that the method of execution violated the Eighth Amendment's proscription against cruel and unusual punishment and also violated New York law banning similar punishments. The county court, which held an evidentiary hearing to determine the constitutionality of the Electrocution Act, ruled that Kemmler failed to prove beyond a reasonable doubt that the act was unconstitutional. Based upon testimonial evidence that electrocution was a reliable method of execution as well as a method that would cause instantaneous and painless death, the court concluded that electrocution was not violative of state constitutional law barring cruel and unusual punishment. Because the Eighth Amendment was not applicable to the states, the court refrained from issuing a ruling in this regard.

Kemmler appealed to both the Supreme Court of New York and the New York Court of Appeals, but failed. Because the appellate courts had both ruled that the Electrocution Act did not violate either the cruel and unusual punishment clause of the Eighth Amendment or state law, Kemmler changed his legal strategy and filed a petition with the Court saying that the act violated the due process clause of the Fourteenth Amendment.

ISSUE: Does the Electrocution Act of 1888, which authorizes electrocution as a method of execution, violate the due process clause of the Fourteenth Amendment? NO.

HOLDING: Electrocution is not a punishment that is cruel and unusual within the meaning of the due process clause of the Fourteenth Amendment, because it is neither inhumane nor barbarous, nor does it involve torture or lingering death. Electrocution does not "involve more than the mere extinguishment of life."

REASON: "Section 5 of article 1 of the Constitution of the State of New York provides that excessive bail shall not be required, nor excessive fines imposed, nor shall cruel and unusual punishments be inflicted, nor shall witnesses be unreasonably detained. The Eighth Amendment to the Federal Constitution reads: excessive bail shall not be required, nor excessive fines imposed, nor cruel and unusual punishments inflicted. By the Fourteenth Amendment it is provided that: all persons born or naturalized in the United States, and subject to the jurisdiction thereof, are citizens of the United States and of the State wherein they reside. No state shall make or enforce any law which shall abridge the privileges or immunities of citizens . . . nor shall any state deprive any person of life, liberty or property without due process of law . . . The enactment of this statute [the Electrocution Act] was in itself within the legitimate sphere of the legislative power of the state, and in the observance of those general rules prescribed by our systems of jurisprudence; and the legislature of New York determined that it did not inflict cruel and unusual punishment and its courts have sustained that determination. We cannot perceive that the state has thereby abridged the privileges or immunities of the petitioner, nor deprived him of due process of law."

"Punishments are cruel when they involve torture or lingering death; but the punishment of death is not cruel within the meaning of that word as used in the Constitution. It implies there is something inhumane and barbarous, something more than the mere extinguishment of life. Electrocution did not involve more than the mere extinguishment of life."

CASE SIGNIFICANCE: This case is significant for several reasons. First, unlike the ruling in *Wilkerson v. Utah*, the Court specifically stated that the cruel and unusual punishment clause of the Eighth Amendment was not applicable to the states. Second, and more importantly, this case is significant because it demonstrated the deference afforded to the legislative branch and subsequently to statutory laws. Every law is presumed to be constitutional on its face. Thus, petitioners challenging the constitutionality of any law, such as the Electrocution Act of 1888, must prove that the law is unconstitutional by presenting evidence to that effect. At the time of Kemmler's appeals, the required burden of proof was reasonable doubt. Therefore, Kemmler needed to prove beyond a reasonable doubt that the Act was unconstitutional. However, because the state of New York passed the Electrocution Act specifically to end torturous deaths and cruelty, Kemmler had a difficult time proving that the act was unconstitutional. In addition, Kemmler faced a difficult burden because there was overwhelming support for the notion that electrocution was a more humane form of punishment. As noted by the Supreme Court of New York, "It is within easy reach of electrical science at this day to so generate and apply to the person of the convict a current of electricity of such known and sufficient force as certainly to produce instantaneous, and therefore painless death." This sentiment was echoed by every court that heard Kemmler's appeal, including the Supreme Court, which held that unless a punishment involves torture or lingering death, it will not be deemed a violation of the Constitution. Electrocution as a method of execution remained unchallenged for 56 years, despite the fact that Kemmler's death was not instantaneous.

Louisiana ex rel. Francis v. Resweber
329 U.S. 459 (1947)

CAPSULE: Carrying out a second execution after a failed first attempt due to mechanical malfunction does not violate the cruel and unusual punishment clause or the double jeopardy clause of the Constitution.

FACTS: Francis was convicted of murder and in 1945 was sentenced to death. Pursuant to a proper death warrant, Francis was placed in the official electric chair of the State of Louisiana and received through his body a current of electricity intended to cause death. The execution attempt failed due to mechanical defect in the electric chair. Francis was removed from the chair and returned to prison. A new death warrant was issued.

ISSUE: Is carrying out the execution of a criminal after a failed first attempt a violation of the Eighth and Fifth Amendments to the Constitution? NO.

HOLDING: Carrying out a second execution of a convicted person after the first execution attempt failed because of a mechanical defect in the electric chair does not constitute "double jeopardy," nor does it constitute "cruel and unusual punishment" and therefore is not forbidden by the Constitution.

REASON: "Petitioner's suggestion is that because he once underwent the psychological strain of preparation for electrocution, now to require him to undergo this preparation again subjects him to lingering or cruel and unusual punishment. Even the fact that petitioner has already been subjected to a current of electricity does not make his subsequent execution any more cruel in the constitutional sense than any other execution. The cruelty against which the Constitution protects a convicted man is cruelty inherent in the method of punishment, not necessary suffering involved in any method employed to extinguish life humanely. The fact that an unforeseeable accident prevented the prompt consummation of the sentence cannot, it seems to us, add an element of cruelty to a subsequent execution.

"We cannot agree that the hardship imposed upon the petitioner rises to that level of hardship denounced as denial of due process because of cruelty."

CASE SIGNIFICANCE: In this case, the defendant was placed in the electric chair, received a current of electricity intended to cause death, but death did not occur due to a mechanical defect in the electric chair. He was returned to prison and given a new execution date. The defendant claimed that carrying out a second execution after a failed first attempt violated his constitutional protection from double jeopardy and cruel and unusual punishment.

The Court rejected both objections, holding that "when an accident, with no suggestion of malevolence, prevents the consummation of a sentence, the state's subsequent course in the administration of its criminal law is not affected on that account by any requirement of due process . . ." As for the allegation of cruel and unusual punishment, the Court did not find the second attempt at execution as constituting a violation of this constitutional protection, saying that "even the fact that the petitioner has already been subjected to a current of electricity does not make his subsequent execution any more cruel in the constitutional sense than any other execution." The Court added that "the cruelty against which the Constitution protects a convicted man is cruelty inherent in the method of punishment, not the necessary suffering involved in any method employed to extinguish life humanely." In sum, the Court said that the taking of life itself does not constitute cruel and unusual punishment; what is prohibited instead is the method of punishment, which may be cruel and unusual.

Internet Resources

History of the Death Penalty
http://deathpenaltycurriculum.org/student/c/about/history/contents.htm
http://www.deathpenaltyinfo.org/article.php?did=199&scid=15
http://www.pbs.org/wgbh/pages/frontline/shows/execution/readings/history.
  html

History of the Death Penalty and Recent Developments
http://justice.uaa.alaska.edu/death/history.html

Capital Punishment 2007
http://www.ojp.usdoj.gov/bjs/cp.htm

Notes

1. *Gregg v. Georgia*, 428 U.S. 153 (1976).

2. The Eighth Amendment was incorporated to the states in the 1962 case of *Robinson v. California*, 370 U.S. 666 (1962).

3. This was the execution of George Kendall, a European colonist who was hanged for the crime of "spying for the Spanish." In HUGO BEDAU AND PAUL CASSELL (EDS.), DEBATING THE DEATH PENALTY (Oxford: Oxford University Press, Inc., 2004).

4. Man-stealing is akin to kidnapping.

5. BRYAN VILA AND CYNTHIA MORRIS (EDS.), CAPITAL PUNISHMENT IN THE UNITED STATES (1997), pp. 8-9.

6. *Id.*

7. MARK LANIER AND STUART HENRY, ESSENTIAL CRIMINOLOGY (2d ed. 2004).

8. J.W. PELTASON AND SUE DAVIS, UNDERSTANDING THE CONSTITUTION (15th ed. 2000).

9. Beccaria did believe that the death penalty was useful in some situations, such as when there was a need to protect the security of a nation or government. In Piers Beirne, *Inventing Criminology: The "Science of Man" in Cesare Beccaria's Dei delitti e delle pene.* CRIMINOLOGY, Vol. 29(4):777–820, 1991.

10. BRYAN VILA AND CYNTHIA MORRIS (EDS.), CAPITAL PUNISHMENT IN THE UNITED STATES (1997), p. 16.

11. Thomas Jefferson, *A Bill for Proportioning Crimes and Punishments* (1779). In BRYAN VILA AND CYNTHIA MORRIS (EDS.), CAPITAL PUNISHMENT IN THE UNITED STATES (1997), pp. 16–18.

12. In HUGO BEDAU AND PAUL CASSELL (EDS.), DEBATING THE DEATH PENALTY (2004), p. 22.

13. Benjamin Rush, *An Enquiry into the Effects of Public Punishments Upon Criminals and Upon Society* (1789). In BRYAN VILA AND CYNTHIA MORRIS (EDS.), CAPITAL PUNISHMENT IN THE UNITED STATES (1997), pp. 20–23.

14. Hugo Adam Bedau, *An Abolitionist Survey of the Death Penalty in America Today.* In HUGO BEDAU AND PAUL CASSELL (EDS.), DEBATING THE DEATH PENALTY (2004), p. 16.

15. In BRYAN VILA AND CYNTHIA MORRIS (EDS.), CAPITAL PUNISHMENT IN THE UNITED STATES (1997), p. 33.

16. Deborah W. Denno, *Is Electrocution an Unconstitutional Method of Execution? The Engineering of Death Over the Century*, 35 WM. & MARY L. REV. 551, 564 (1994).

17. ROBERT M. BOHM, DEATHQUEST (3d ed. 1993).

18. Michael C. Cokley, *Whatever Happened to That Old Saying "Thou Shall Not Kill?": A Plea for the Abolition of the Death Penalty*, 2 LOYOLA J. PUB. INT. L. 67 (Spring 2001).

19. *Id.* at 83.

20. *Id.* at 86.

21. ROBERT M. BOHM, DEATHQUEST (3d ed. 1993).

22. Death Penalty Information Center, *History of the Death Penalty*, September 20, 2004, pg. 5. Available at: http://www.deathpenaltyinfo.org/article.php?scid=15&did=410#Earlyand-Mid-TwentiethCentury.

23. *Furman v. Georgia*, 408 U.S. 153 (1972).

24. *Wilkerson v. Utah*, 99 U.S. 130 (1878).

25. Michael C. Cokley, *Whatever Happened to That Old Saying "Thou Shall Not Kill?": A Plea for the Abolition of the Death Penalty*, 2 LOYOLA J. PUB. INT. L. 67 (Spring 2001).

26. Christopher Q. Cutler, *Nothing Less Than the Dignity of Man: Evolving Standards, Botched Executions and Utah's Controversial Use of the Firing Squad*, 50 CLEVE. ST. L. REV. 335, 340 (2002–2003).

27. *Wilkerson v. Utah*, 99 U.S. 130, 131 (1878).

28. *Id.*

29. *Id.*

30. *In re Kemmler*, 136 U.S. 436 (1890).

31. *Id.*

32. Deborah W. Denno, *Is Electrocution an Unconstitutional Method of Execution? The Engineering of Death Over the Century*, 35 WM. & MARY L. REV. 551, 566 (1994).

33. *Id.*

34. Deborah W. Denno, *Lethally Humane? The Evolution of Execution Methods in the United States.* In JAMES R. ACKER, ROBERT M. BOHM, AND CHARLES S. LANIER (EDS.), AMERICA'S EXPERIMENT WITH CAPITAL PUNISHMENT: REFLECTIONS OF THE PAST, PRESENT, AND FUTURE OF THE ULTIMATE PENAL SANCTION (2003), pp. 693–762.

35. Deborah W. Denno, *Is Electrocution an Unconstitutional Method of Execution? The Engineering of Death Over the Century*, 35 WM. & MARY L. REV. 551, 584 (1994).

36. *Id.* at 581

37. *Id.* at 583.

38. *Id.* at 582.

39. *Id.* at 587.

40. *Louisiana ex rel. Francis v. Resweber*, 329 U.S. 459 (1947).

41. *Id.* at 463.

42. *Id.*

43. *Id.*

44. *Id.* at 469.

45. *Id.* at 473.

46. *Powell v. Alabama*, 287 U.S. 45 (1932).

47. *Id.* at 53.

48. *Patton v. Mississippi*, 332 U.S. 463 (1947).

49. *Id..* at 469.

50. *Witherspoon v. Illinois*, 391 U.S. 510 (1968).

51. *Id.* at 521.

52. *Gregg v. Georgia*, 428 U.S. 153 (1976).

53. *McGautha v. California*, 402 U.S. 183 (1971).

54. *Crampton v. Ohio*, 402 U.S. 183 (1971).

55. *Id.* at 196.

56. *Furman v. Georgia*, 408 U.S. 153 (1972).

57. *Powell v. Alabama*, 287 U.S. 45 (1932).

58. *Louisiana ex rel. Francis v. Resweber*, 329 U.S. 459 (1947).

59. *Baze v. Rees*, ___ U.S. ___ (2008).

60. Lonny J. Hoffman, *The Madness of the Method: The Use of Electrocution and the Death Penalty*, 70 TEXAS L. REV. ASS'N 1039, 1049 (1992).

61. *Wilkerson v. Utah*, 99 U.S. 130, 131 (1878).

Chapter Outline

I. **Introduction**

II. ***Furman v. Georgia* (1972): The Death Penalty Is Unconstitutional**
   A. The Background
   B. The Facts
   C. The Majority Opinions
   D. The Dissenting Opinions

III. ***Gregg v. Georgia* (1976): The Death Penalty Is Constitutional in Some Cases**
   A. The Background
   B. The Facts
   C. The Majority Opinions
   D. The Dissenting Opinions

IV. **In Summary, What Do these Cases Say?**

V. **Conclusion**

Cases Briefed in Chapter 2

Case Briefs
   Furman v. Georgia, 408 U.S. 238 (1972)
   Gregg v. Georgia, 428 U.S. 153 (1976)

Internet Resources

Chapter 2

The Foundation Cases: *Furman v. Georgia* and *Gregg v. Georgia*

I. Introduction

Most legal scholars will agree that the two most significant and widely known cases on the death penalty are *Furman v. Georgia* (1972) and *Gregg v. Georgia* (1976). These cases have laid the foundation for most court decisions and their effects are felt to this day. Both cases made headlines when decided, but their after-effects are different. *Furman*, decided June 29, 1972, is significant because it stopped executions during the four years and three days when it was the law of the land. That came to an end on July 2, 1976, when the decision was repudiated in *Gregg v. Georgia*. *Gregg* held that the death penalty could be constitutional in some instances. *Furman* was hailed by abolitionists for bringing about the long-delayed demise of executions by the state; *Gregg* was cheered by retentionists for restoring the death penalty but also for ushering in a new era of executions that are deemed fairer and more humane. *Furman* did not spawn many decisions during the four years it was law because the decision itself was categorical—the death penalty was unconstitutional. By contrast, *Gregg* resulted in a spate of cases that have reached the Court for almost three decades now. These cases have sought to further clarify the meaning of *Gregg* and extend or contract some of its legal boundaries.

II. Furman v. Georgia (1972): The Death Penalty Is Unconstitutional

A. The Background

The Supreme Court had decided a number of cases on the death penalty prior to *Furman v. Georgia*. Prior cases, however, dealt with the procedure for execution and did not raise the issue of constitutionality of the penalty itself, the prevailing assumption being that this ultimate form of punishment was constitutional. There were good reasons to assume this—the penalty was used in England even before the Pilgrims came to America and it was used in the colonies as a form of punishment. In *Furman*, the sole issue before the Court was: "Does the imposition and carrying out of the death penalty constitute cruel and unusual punishment in violation of the Eighth and Fourteenth Amendments?" For the first time, substance and not only process was at issue. *Furman* produced an almost unprecedented flurry of opinions from the Court, each opinion with its own nuanced reasoning. Decided on a five-to-four vote, it featured a total of nine different opinions—five for the majority and four for the dissent. The opinions are summarized in this chapter because they are the same arguments used by abolitionists and retentionists on the death penalty issue today. They are as current and controversial today as they were when first written.

Furman was the lead case of the three cases appealed to the Court that raised the same issue—the constitutionality of the death penalty. The other two cases were *Jackson v. Georgia* (a black man, 21 years old, convicted of the rape of a white woman in Georgia and given the death penalty), and *Branch v. Texas* (a black man convicted of rape in Texas and also given the death penalty). *Furman* just happened to be the lead case in the group and therefore received all the publicity and attention. *Jackson v. Georgia* and *Branch v. Texas* have been virtually forgotten. All three defendants had this in common: they were poor, powerless, black, and charged with serious crimes.

B. The Facts

The facts in *Furman* are uncomplicated. Furman, a black man, tried to enter a home at night and shot the victim through a closed door. He was 26 years old and had a sixth-grade education. His court-appointed attorney entered a defense of insanity during trial. The staff in the facility where Furman was committed pending trial recommended that "this patient should retain his present diagnosis of Mental Deficiency, Mild to Moderate, with Psychotic Episodes associated with Convulsive Disorder." The superintendent agreed with his staff's finding, but concluded that Furman was "not psychotic at present, knows right from wrong and is able to cooperate with his counsel in preparing his defense." Furman was charged with, tried, and found guilty of murder. He was given the death penalty; he appealed his conviction to the United States Supreme Court.

C. The Majority Opinions

The Court voted five to four, declaring the death penalty unconstitutional, but for different reasons. In an opinion written by Justice Douglas, three of the five justices agreed that the death penalty is "unusual" if it discriminates by reason of "race, religion, wealth, social position, or class, or if it is imposed under a procedure that gives room for the play of such prejudices." Justice Douglas's opinion is interesting because it blended the two constitutional provisions asserted by the defendants, saying "there is increasing recognition of the fact that the basic theme of equal protection is implicit in 'cruel and unusual punishments'." Justice Douglas concluded by saying that "the high service rendered by the 'cruel and unusual punishment' clause of the Eighth Amendment is to require legislatures to write penal laws that are evenhanded, nonselective, and non-arbitrary, and to require judges to see to it that general laws are not applied sparsely, selectively, and spottily to unpopular groups." Thus, while the opinion is anchored on the Eighth Amendment cruel and unusual punishment clause, it substance rests on the equal protection clause of the Fourteenth Amendment, which prohibits discrimination.

Justice Brennan, siding with the majority, was more vehement in his denunciation of the death penalty. His lengthy opinion is remembered for having popularized a phrase that has since become even more contentious in death penalty cases. He said: "We know 'that the words of the [cruel and unusual punishment clause] are not precise, and that their scope is not static.' We know, therefore, that the clause 'must draw its meaning from the *evolving standards of decency that mark the progress of a maturing society*.'" (italics added). That phrase is not original; it is in fact quoted from the majority opinion in *Trop v. Dulles* (1958), but hardly anyone heard of that phrase before its use in *Furman*. It has since become the center of the debate in death penalty cases and the mantra for abolitionists.

Justice Stewart, in a majority concurring opinion, is remembered for concluding his opinion thus: "I simply conclude that the Eighth and Fourteenth Amendments cannot tolerate the infliction of a sentence of death under legal systems that permit this unique penalty to be *so wantonly and so freakishly imposed*." (italics added). He admitted that cruel and unusual punishment is implicated in the death penalty, but said that he did not want to base his opinion on the Eighth Amendment, saying that death sentences "are cruel and unusual in the same way that being struck by lightning is cruel and unusual," meaning that there is no design or malice to it, rather that its cruel and unusual nature is remote and accidental. Since *Furman*, the phrase "wanton and freakish manner" has become the catch-all phrase for abolitionists who maintain that the death penalty is inherently discriminatory.

Justice White, concurring with the majority, based his opinion primarily on the concept that "the penalty is so infrequently imposed that the threat of execution is too attenuated to be of substantial service to criminal justice." Given this, the death penalty fails to achieve the "social ends it was deemed to serve," meaning crime deterrence. Because of the infrequency of executions even for the most atrocious of crimes, Justice White concluded that "there is no meaningful basis for distinguishing the few cases in which it is imposed from the many cases in which it is not." His opinion is based on the equal protection clause (only a few of the many who are convicted are executed) of the Fourteenth Amendment, rather than on the prohibition against cruel and unusual punishment of the Eighth Amendment.

Justice Marshall, also concurring, wrote a lengthy and exhaustive opinion. He is remembered for saying that "American citizens know almost nothing about capital punishment," and that if the public knew more about the death penalty, it would consider the punishment cruel and unusual. He said: "Assuming knowledge of all the facts presently available regarding capital punishment, the average citizen would, in my opinion, find it shocking to his conscience and sense of justice." He said that six purposes are conceivably served by the death penalty: "retribution, deterrence, prevention of repetitive criminal acts, encouragement of guilty pleas and confessions, eugenics, and economy." He then proceeds to discuss each of these purposes and concluded that none of them was served by capital punishment. He ended his lengthy prohibitionist discourse with these words:

> At a time in our history when the streets of the Nation's cities inspire fear and despair, rather than pride and hope, it is difficult to maintain objectivity and concern for our fellow citizens. But, the measure of a country's greatness is its ability to retain compassion in time of crisis. No nation in the recorded history of man has a greater tradition of revering justice and fair treatment for all its citizens in times of turmoil, confusion, and tension than ours. This is a country which stands tallest in trouble times, a country that clings to fundamental principles, cherishes its constitutional heritage, and rejects simple solutions that compromise the values that lie at the roots of our democratic system.

Justice Marshall's concluding words were: "We achieve 'a major milestone in the long road up from barbarism' and join the approximately 70 other jurisdictions in the world which celebrate their regard for civilization and humanity by shunning capital punishment."

The five majority opinions had one common theme: the death penalty is unconstitutional. Each opinion was a variation of that common theme, but the basis for the opinions differed. Nonetheless, it achieved the purpose of suspending executions in the United States for four years.

D. The Dissenting Opinions

The four dissenters in *Furman* wrote four separate opinions, although not quite with the same vehemence as the majority opinions.

Justice Burger, the Chief Justice at that time, opined that the Constitution does not prohibit the imposition of the death penalty. Even the lawyers for the defendants, he said, "properly concede that capital punishment was not impermissibly cruel at the time of the adoption of the Eighth Amendment" and that "in the 181 years since the enactment of the Eighth Amendment, not a single decision of this Court has cast the slightest shadow of a doubt on the constitutionality of capital punishment." He then added that "twentieth century modes of execution surely involve no greater physical suffering than the means employed at the time of the Eighth Amendment's adoption." In the absence of proof that "the mode of punishment authorized by a domestic legislature was so cruel as to be fundamentally at odds with our basic notions of decency," he concluded that "the primacy of the legislative role narrowly confines the scope of judicial inquiry." In sum, Justice Burger opined that in the absence of proof that the death penalty is prohibited by the Constitution or is clearly cruel and unusual, respect must be given by the Court to the judgment made by state legislatures to impose death as the ultimate punishment.

Justice Blackmun started his dissent with what amounts to a personal testimony, saying "I yield to no one in the depth of my distaste, antipathy, and, indeed, abhorrence, for the death penalty, with all its aspects of physical distress and fear and of moral judgment exercised by finite minds. That distaste is buttressed by a belief that capital punishment serves no useful purpose that can be demonstrated. For me, it violates childhood's training and life experiences, and is not compatible with the philosophical convictions I have been able to develop." He then added: "Were I a legislator, I would vote against the death penalty for the policy reasons argued by counsel for the respective petitioners and expressed and adopted in the several opinions filed by the Justices who vote to reverse these judgments." Having said all that, however, he then concludes: "Although personally I may rejoice at the Court's result, I find it difficult to accept or to justify as a matter of history, of law, or of constitutional pronouncement. I fear the Court has overstepped. It has sought and has achieved an end." The words of Justice Blackmun are significant because years later, just before he retired from the Court, he announced that were he to sit in judgment on death penalty cases again, he would vote against it. He had changed his mind.

The dissenting opinion by Justice Powell is also long and exhaustive, refuting the arguments presented by the majority opinions on wide-ranging issues—from the purposes of punishment to the state of public opinion on the issue of the death penalty. His main argument, however, focuses on the relationship between the judiciary and the legislature, agreeing with then-Chief Justice Burger and Justice Blackmun that respect must be given to laws passed by state legislatures in the absence of clear evidence that the death penalty violates the Constitution. He urged judicial restraint, particularly because the issue involved punishment for crimes, an issue that is historically a legislative concern because of the legislature's duty to protect the public.

Justice Rehnquist, who also sided with the dissenters, started by saying: "The Court's judgments today strike down a penalty that our Nation's legislators have thought necessary since our country was founded. My Brothers Douglas, Brennan, and Marshall would at one fell swoop invalidate laws enacted by Congress and 40 of the 50 state legislatures . . ." He discusses the history of the relationship between the judicial and legislative branches of government from the time of the framing of the Constitution. He observed that constitutional jurisprudence proves that judicial restraint was implied, if not expressed, by the framers of the Constitution as a condition of the grant of authority for judicial review. He then concluded that the majority decision in this case completely disregarded the limits of the doctrine of judicial review.

In sum, the majority opinions in *Furman* declaring the death penalty unconstitutional were based on two grounds: Three of the justices (Douglas, Stewart, and White) said it violated the equal protection clause of the Fourteenth Amendment; two of the justices (Brennan and Marshall) said it was a violation of the Eighth Amendment prohibition against cruel and unusual punishment. The four dissenting opinions were based on one main ground: respect for laws passed by state legislatures in the absence of proof that the death penalty is clearly unconstitutional both in its history and application.

III.   Gregg v. Georgia (1976): The Death Penalty Is Constitutional in Some Cases

A.   The Background

After the decision in *Furman v. Georgia*, 35 states and the federal government revised their death penalty laws to avoid equal protection problems. Had all five of the justices in *Furman* based their decision on the prohibition against cruel and unusual punishment, the issue would have been settled in 1972. But three of the five justices who voted with the majority based their vote on the equal protection clause of the Fourteenth Amendment, thus leaving the door open for the issue to be revisited. The death penalty states knew that if their laws and systems could be made less discriminatory, their statutes would be deemed constitutional and executions could resume. After *Furman*, states revised their laws to make them acceptable to the other members of the Court.

Four years after *Furman v. Georgia* came *Gregg v. Georgia*. This time the Georgia law that was declared unconstitutional in *Furman* had been revised by the Georgia legislature and was vastly different. Would it fare better than the earlier law? Yes.

B. The Facts

Troy Gregg was charged under the new Georgia law with armed robbery and murder. He and a traveling companion were hitchhiking in Florida and were picked up by Fred Simmons and Bob Moore. While still in Florida, they picked up another hitchhiker; all of them rode together to Atlanta. The men later interrupted their trip at a rest stop along the highway. The following day, the bodies of Simmons and Moore were discovered in a ditch nearby. Both had died from bullet wounds. Gregg later admitted that he shot Simmons and Moore but claimed that he had acted in self-defense, saying they had attacked him. Gregg was charged with and convicted of two counts of armed robbery and two counts of murder. The jury imposed the death penalty.

Gregg raised two issues on appeal to the United States Supreme Court: (1) Is the death penalty constitutional as a form of punishment? and (2) If it is, does the Georgia law contain sufficient safeguards against arbitrary and capricious imposition?

Gregg was decided on a 7-to-2 vote and had a total of five opinions. In sum, it held that "the death penalty is not a form of punishment that may never be imposed, regardless of the circumstances of the offense, regardless of the character of the offender, and regardless of the procedure followed in reaching the decision to impose it." In short, it is constitutional provided states impose proper safeguards. Eight of the nine justices who decided *Furman* were still on the Court and cast votes in *Gregg*. Only Justice Douglas was gone; his place on the Court was taken by Justice Stevens. The final vote was predictable. The dissent in *Furman* would now become the majority if the objectionable provisions were removed from the various state laws. Four years later, the tide had turned and *Furman* was history.

C. The Majority Opinions

The main majority opinion in *Gregg* was written by Justice Stewart. Four years earlier he had opined in *Furman* that the death penalty was unconstitutional because it violated the equal protection clause of the Constitution. Justice Stewart addressed the two issues raised on appeal and came to a different conclusion than he had in *Furman* because the law in Georgia had changed. On the first issue, Justice Stewart concluded that the death penalty did not violate the prohibition against cruel and unusual punishment, saying that the history of the death penalty clearly indicated its use has traditionally been accepted in the United States. He looked at previous cases and said that judicial precedents supported the constitutionality of the penalty. Conceding that the meaning of cruel and unusual punishment must be drawn from the "evolving standards of decency that mark the progress of a maturing society," he nonetheless said that "the public perceptions of standards of decency with respect to criminal sanctions are not conclusive." In the absence of a clear showing that the public is against the death penalty, judges must give deference to the wishes of legislators, saying "we may not act as judges as we might as legislators."

Having concluded on the first issue that the death penalty was not in itself unconstitutional, Justice Stewart then addressed the second issue—whether the revised Georgia law was constitutional. He started by saying: "*Furman* mandates that where discretion is afforded a sentencing body on a matter so grave as the determination of whether a human life should be taken or spared, that *discretion must be suitably directed and limited so as to minimize the risk of wholly arbitrary and capricious action.*" (italics added) He concluded with these words: "The new Georgia sentencing procedures . . . focus the jury's attention on the particularized nature of the crime and the particularized characteristics of the circumstances, it must find and identify at least one statutory aggravating factor before it may impose a penalty of death. In this way the jury's discretion is channeled. No longer can a jury wantonly and freakishly impose the death sentence; it is always circumscribed by the legislative guidelines."

The above statements are key to understanding the change of vote by Justices Stewart and White, both of whom voted with the majority in *Furman*. It highlighted the overriding concern that the Court has had in all death penalty cases since *Gregg*: that discretion must be "suitably directed and limited so as to minimize the risk of wholly arbitrary and capricious action." That said, the question is: who determines that and how? The answer is the Supreme Court, on a case-by-case basis. This explains why there is a never-ending stream of cases that reach the Court each year seeking a determination of whether state laws and practices comport with or violate that standard. The guidelines given by the Court in *Gregg* have not been always clear or authoritative, as the cases in this book show. This is perhaps inevitable because the terms "arbitrary" and "capricious" are inherently subjective and elude precise definition.

The majority decision in *Gregg v. Georgia* is best understood in the context of the Georgia law under which Gregg was prosecuted. Figure 2.1 presents the important features of that law and should be read to know better what the Court looks for in state death penalty laws. These carefully crafted provisions ensured constitutionality for the Georgia statute and serve as a template for other state laws on the death penalty.

Figure 2.1
Features of the Revised Georgia Law (1976)

These were the features of the new Georgia law, revised after *Furman v. Georgia* was decided, that led the United States Supreme Court to declare the law constitutional because they removed arbitrariness and capriciousness in the imposition of the death penalty.

- It imposed the death penalty for six categories of crime: murder, kidnapping for ransom or where the victim is harmed, armed robbery, rape, treason, and aircraft hijacking.

- Guilt or innocence is determined either by a trial judge or a jury, in the first stage of a bifurcated trial.

- "If trial is by a jury, the trial judge is required to charge lesser included offenses when they are supported by any view of the evidence."

- The law lists 10 aggravating circumstances. The sentence of death may be imposed "only if the jury or judge finds one of the statutory aggravating circumstances beyond a reasonable doubt and then elects to impose that sentence."

- The law provides for an expedited direct review of all death penalty sentences by the Supreme Court of Georgia. The expedited review aims at determining the appropriateness of imposing the death sentence in a particular case. In conducting the review, the court must determine:

  "(1) Whether the sentence of death was imposed under the influence of passion, prejudice, or any other arbitrary factor, and

  "(2) Whether, in cases other than treason or aircraft hijacking, the evidence supports the jury's or judge's finding of a statutory aggravating circumstance, and

  "(3) Whether the sentence of death is excessive or disproportionate to the penalty imposed in similar cases, considering both the crime and the defendant."

- "A transcript and complete record of the trial, as well as a separate report by the trial judge, are transmitted to the court for its use in reviewing the sentence." This report is in the form of a "6½ page questionnaire, designed to elicit information about the defendant, the crime, and the circumstances of the trial. . . . Included in the report are responses to detailed questions concerning the quality of the defendant's representation, whether race played a role in the trial, and, whether, in the trial court's judgment, there is any doubt about the defendant's guilt or the appropriateness of the sentence."

Justice White also voted in *Furman* to declare the death penalty unconstitutional. He wrote a concurring opinion that called attention to the procedures under the new Georgia law and concluded that the law was constitutional because of procedural safeguards. Among the safeguards that made a difference were: (1) a listing of the 10 aggravating circumstances that could increase the penalty to death; (2) a unanimous finding by the jury beyond a reasonable doubt that at least one statutorily defined aggravating circumstance existed; (3) provision for prompt review by the Georgia Supreme Court; (4) a questionnaire provided to the Georgia Supreme Court during review, which asked six questions designed to disclose whether race played a role in the case, and (5) a set of questions the Georgia Supreme Court must answer to determine whether the sentence of death was influenced by passion or prejudice, and whether the sentence was excessive or disproportionate to the offense committed. Taken together, Justice White concluded that, unlike the statute in *Furman*, arbitrariness and capriciousness were now purged from the Georgia death penalty process.

Justice Burger, the Chief Justice at that time, wrote a one-sentence concurring opinion saying: "We [with Justice Rehnquist] concur in the judgment and join the opinion . . . agreeing with its analysis that Georgia's system of capital punishment comports with the Court's holding in *Furman v. Georgia*." He had written a lengthy dissent in *Furman*; he simply wanted to reiterate those arguments in *Gregg*, but now he was on the winning side of the issue.

D. The Dissenting Opinions

As expected, Justices Brennan and Marshall dissented. They voted for unconstitutionality in *Furman*, saying that the death penalty itself constituted cruel and unusual punishment. They held steadfast to that view, but, as discussed in *Furman*, for different reasons.

Justice Brennan reaffirmed that the cruel and unusual punishment clause "must draw its meaning from the evolving standards of decency that mark the progress of a maturing society." After quoting some of the arguments he used in *Furman*, he then said that "the punishment of death, like punishments on the rack, the screw, and the wheel, is no longer morally tolerable in our civilized society." Then, using caustic language, he said: "The fatal constitutional infirmity in the punishment of death is that it treats 'members of the human race as nonhumans, as objects to be toyed with and discarded. It is thus inconsistent with the fundamental premise of the Clause that even the vilest criminal remains a human being possessed of common human dignity."

Justice Marshall was just as vehement in his dissent in *Gregg* as he was in his majority opinion in *Furman*. Saying that he had no intention of repeating the long and tedious journey that led to his conclusion in *Furman*, he said: "In *Furman* I concluded that the death penalty is constitutionally invalid for two reasons. First, the death penalty is excessive. And second, the American people, fully informed as to the purposes of the death penalty and its liabilities, would in my view reject it as morally acceptable." He again said that "the American people are largely unaware of the information critical to a judgment on the morality of the death penalty" and that "if they were better informed they would consider it shocking, unjust, and unacceptable." He added that the death penalty is excessive and serves no penological purpose, be it deterrence or retribution.

IV. In Summary, What Do these Cases Say?

Taken together, the *Furman* and *Gregg* cases hold that the death penalty does not constitute cruel and unusual punishment and is not in itself unconstitutional. *Gregg* makes it clear that the death penalty may be imposed if state laws are carefully crafted to avoid the twin vices of arbitrariness and capriciousness. In short, the Court said: remove arbitrariness and capriciousness from your laws and you can go ahead with executions. Other constitutional issues have been raised in death penalty cases (such as the right to counsel and the right to due process), but they have not occupied as much of the Court's attention as have the Eighth Amendment and the equal protection clause of the Fourteenth Amendment. Discrimination in the enforcement of the death penalty will continue to be the main issue as long as state laws differ and differential weights are given to aggravating and mitigating circumstances that make death penalty decisions subjective and human.

V. Conclusion

The *Furman* and *Gregg* cases deserve extensive discussion because they are landmarks and are arguably the most significant and widely known cases on death penalty law. The opinions expressed by the justices of the Court in those decisions generate as much controversy today as they did when they were decided. *Furman* suspended the imposition of death for four years, but *Gregg* is doubtless the more significant case because it restored the death penalty and is the "mother" of most death penalty cases decided since 1976. Many of the cases appealed by defendants to the Court claim that a state's death penalty law is arbitrary and capricious—descriptive words that were first used in the *Furman* and given substance and meaning in *Gregg*. Since then, the effort to remove provisions that create arbitrariness and capriciousness have been a recurring theme in legislative enactments and Court decisions. The search for a wand that draws a magical bright line between what is constitutional and what is not will likely continue as long as the death penalty is imposed. The cases in the other chapters in this book show that the search for death penalty laws and practices that are totally cleansed of legal impurities in this most severe and final of punishments is indeed long, tedious, and may never end as long as the death penalty itself exists.

Cases Briefed in Chapter 2

Case	Issue	Holding
Furman v. Georgia 408 U.S. 238 (1972)	Is the death penalty constitutional?	The death penalty is unconstitutional because it violates the equal protection clause of the Fourteenth Amendment and the prohibition against cruel and unusual punishment.
Gregg v. Georgia 428 U.S. 153 (1976)	Is the death penalty constitutional? If yes, does the Georgia law contain sufficient safeguards against arbitrary and capricious imposition?	The death penalty is constitutional as a form of punishment. The Georgia law contains sufficient safeguards against arbitrary and capricious imposition.

Case Briefs

Furman v. Georgia
408 U.S. 238 (1972)

CAPSULE: The death penalty is unconstitutional because it violates the equal protection clause of the Fourteenth Amendment and the prohibition against cruel and unusual punishment.

FACTS: Furman attempted to enter a private home at night. He shot and killed the homeowner through a closed door. He was 26 years old and had a sixth-grade education. Prior to trial, Furman was committed to the Georgia Central State Hospital for a psychiatric examination on his plea of insanity. The hospital superintendent reported that the staff diagnosis concluded that "this patient should retain his present diagnosis of Mental Deficiency, Mild to Moderate, with Psychotic Episodes associated with Convulsive Disorder." The physicians added that although Furman was not psychotic at present, he was not capable of cooperating with his counsel in the preparation of his criminal defense and they believed he needed further treatment. The superintendent later amended the report by stating that Furman knew right from wrong and was capable of cooperating with counsel. Furman was tried and found guilty of the murder of the homeowner. A jury sentenced him to death.

ISSUE: Is the death penalty constitutional? NO.

HOLDING: The death penalty is unconstitutional because it violates the equal protection clause of the Fourteenth Amendment and the Eighth Amendment prohibition against cruel and unusual punishment.

REASON: "There are, then, four principles by which we may determine whether a particular punishment is 'cruel and unusual.' The primary principle, which I believe supplies the essential predicate for the application of the others, is that a punishment must not by its severity be degrading to human dignity. The paradigm violation of this principle would be the infliction of a tortuous punishment of the type that the Clause has always prohibited. Yet '[i]t is unlikely that any State at this moment in history,' *Robinson v. California*, 370 U.S., at 666, would pass a law providing for the infliction of such a punishment. Indeed, no such punishment has ever been before this Court. The same may be said of the other principles. It is unlikely that this Court will confront a severe punishment that is obviously inflicted in wholly arbitrary fashion; no State would engage in a reign of blind terror. Nor is it likely that this Court will be called upon to review a severe punishment that is clearly and totally rejected throughout society; no legislature would be able even to authorize the infliction of such a punishment. Nor, finally, is it likely that this Court will have to consider a severe punishment that is patently unnecessary; no State today would inflict a severe punishment knowing that there is no reason whatever for doing so. In short, we are unlikely to have occasion to determine that a punishment is fatally offensive under any one principle.

"In sum, the punishment of death is inconsistent with all four principles: Death is an unusually severe and degrading punishment; there is a strong probability that it is inflicted arbitrarily; its rejection by contemporary society is virtually total; and there is no reason to believe that it serves any penal purpose more effectively than the less severe punishment of imprisonment. The function of these principles is to enable a court to determine whether a punishment comports with human dignity. Death, quite simply, does not."

CASE SIGNIFICANCE: For the first time, the Supreme Court in *Furman v. Georgia* declared the death penalty unconstitutional, based on two constitutional provisions: the equal protection clause and the prohibition against cruel and unusual punishment. Had all the five justices based their decision solely on a violation of the cruel and unusual punishment clause, the death penalty could not have been imposed for a long time after 1972, unless the Court changed its mind. Only two justices, however (Brennan and Marshall), used this provision, while the three others based their decision on the manner in which death sentences were being carried out. Their objection was not to the death penalty itself, but to the way it discriminated against the poor, minorities, and the powerless, thus violating the equal protection clause.

After the *Furman* decision, 35 states and the federal government revised their capital punishment laws to eliminate equal protection problems. Every state statute that carried the death penalty had to undergo review by the United

States Supreme Court, if appealed, to determine whether the revision removed equal protection problems. The stage was therefore set for *Gregg v. Georgia*, decided in 1976, in which the Court held that the death penalty was not in itself cruel and unusual punishment and could be imposed if there were safeguards against arbitrary and capricious imposition.

Gregg v. Georgia
428 U.S. 153 (1976)

CAPSULE: Death penalty laws that have sufficient safeguards against arbitrary and capricious imposition are constitutional.

FACTS: While hitchhiking in Florida, Gregg and a companion were picked up by two motorists. The bodies of the two motorists were later found beside a road near Atlanta, Georgia. The next day Gregg and his companion were arrested. A .25 caliber pistol was found in Gregg's possession and subsequently identified as the murder weapon. Gregg confessed to the robberies and murders but claimed self-defense. He was found guilty of all four counts and was sentenced to death.

The Georgia death penalty statute had the following features: (1) a bifurcated trial; (2) instructions from the judge to the jury on what penalties they could recommend; (3) consideration of mitigating and aggravating factors, of which they must agree that at least one aggravating factor exists if they wish to recommend death; and (4) an automatic appeal to the Georgia Supreme Court. Moreover, the Georgia Supreme Court was required to review each death sentence for evidence of passion, prejudice, or any other arbitrary factor; whether the evidence supports the finding of an aggravating circumstance; and whether the death penalty "is excessive or disproportionate to the penalty imposed in similar cases, considering both the crime and the defendant."

ISSUES:
1. Is the death penalty constitutional as a form of punishment? YES.
2. If the death penalty is constitutional, does the Georgia statute have sufficient safeguards against arbitrary and capricious imposition? YES.

HOLDING:
1. The death penalty is constitutional as a form of punishment.
2. The Georgia law is constitutional because it contains sufficient safeguards against arbitrary and capricious imposition.

REASON: "Four years ago, the petitioners in *Furman* and its companion cases predicated their argument primarily upon the asserted proposition that standards of decency had evolved to the point where capital punishment no longer could be tolerated. The petitioners in those cases said, in effect, that the evolutionary process had come to an end, and that standards of decency required that the Eighth Amendment be construed finally as prohibiting capital punishment for any crime regardless of its depravity and impact on society. This view was accepted by two Justices. Three other Justices were unwilling to go so far; focusing on the procedures by which convicted defendants were selected for the death penalty rather than on the actual punishment inflicted, they joined in the conclusion that the statutes before the Court were constitutionally invalid.

"While *Furman* did not hold that the infliction of the death penalty per se violates the Constitution's ban on cruel and unusual punishments, it did recognize that the penalty of death is different in kind from any other punishment imposed under our system of criminal justice. Because of the uniqueness of the death penalty, *Furman* held that it could not be imposed under sentencing procedures that created a substantial risk that it would be inflicted in an arbitrary and capricious manner.

"The basic concerns of *Furman* centered on those defendants who were condemned to death capriciously and arbitrarily. Under the procedures before the Court in that case, sentencing authorities were not directed to give attention to the nature of the circumstances of the crime committed or the character or record of the defendant. Left unguided, juries imposed the death sentence in a way that could only be called freakish. The new Georgia sentencing procedures, by contrast, focus the jury's attention on the particularized nature of the crime and the particularized characteristics of the individual defendant. While the jury is permitted to consider any aggravating or mitigating circumstances, it must find and identify at least one statutory aggravating factor before it may impose a penalty of death. In this way the jury's discretion is channeled. No longer can a jury wantonly and freakishly impose the death sentence; it is always circumscribed by the legislative guidelines. In addition, the review function of the Supreme Court of Georgia affords additional assurance that the concerns that prompted our decision in *Furman* are not present to any significant degree in the Georgia procedure applied here."

CASE SIGNIFICANCE: *Gregg v. Georgia*, decided four years after *Furman v. Georgia*, is the most important case ever decided by the Court on the death penalty. For the first time, the Court said that the death penalty is not in itself unconstitutional and may therefore be imposed as long are there are safeguards against arbitrariness and capriciousness. *Gregg v. Georgia* overrules *Furman v. Georgia*. This did not mean, however, that the statutes in the various states were automatically declared constitutional and that executions could resume. What it meant was that the Court could now examine each state law in an appropriate case to determine whether its provisions contain guarantees against arbitrariness and capriciousness in its imposition.

In the years since *Gregg*, the Court has decided many cases upholding the constitutionality of various state statutes. As a result, executions have taken place in a number of states. But although there are many prisoners on death row in the United States (3,374 at the end of 2003), only a small number (a total of 65, and all men) were executed. The explanation may be twofold. First, there is hesitation by the public to carry out the death penalty, despite its availability. It is easy to leave that ultimate penalty in our penal codes; it is difficult to implement it. With an increasing number of prisoners on death row being found innocent primarily because of DNA test results, the public has become wary of executions for fear it might execute the innocent. Second, numerous appeals are available to capital offenders. This frustrates the public, which believes that justice is not served by repeated delays. There is no simple solution to the problem, except to realize that the wheels of justice usually turn slowly in a civilized and constitutional society, particularly when a life-and-death decision is involved.

Internet Resources

30th Anniversary of *Gregg vs. Georgia*: The beginning of the modern era of America's Death Penalty
http://www.amnestyusa.org/abolish/greggvgeorgia www.amnestyusa.org/abolish/greggvgeorgia/study_guide.pdf

The Anniversary of *Furman v. Georgia*: Three Decades Later
http://www.aclu.org/capital/general/10403pub20030627.html

The History and Structure of Capital Punishment
http://deathpenaltycurriculum.org/student/c/about/history/history-5.htm

Chapter Outline

I. **Introduction**

II. **Statistics and Bias in Death Penalty Cases and Jury Selection in Capital Proceedings**

III. **Legislative Responses to Discrimination in Capital Proceedings**
   A. Federal Response: The Proposed Racial Justice Act and Its Failure
   B. State Responses
      1. Legislation
      2. State-Level Lack of Legislation

IV. **The Legal Community: An Assessment of Prosecutors, Defense Attorneys, and Judges**
   A. District Attorneys
   B. Defense Attorneys
   C. Judges

V. **The Jury: A Biased Bunch or Victims of Misinformation?**
   A. Jury Selection
   B. Peremptory Challenges

VI. **In Summary, What Do these Cases Say?**

VII. **Conclusion**

Cases Briefed in Chapter 3

Case Briefs
   Batson v. Kentucky, 476 U.S. 79 (1986)
   McCleskey v. Kemp, 481 U.S. 279 (1987)
   Turner v. Murray, 476 U.S. 28 (1986)
   Miller-El v. Dretke, 545 U. S. 231 (2005)
   Snyder v. Louisiana, 552 U.S. ___ (2008)

Internet Resources

Notes

Chapter 3

Racial Discrimination and the Death Penalty

I. Introduction

Claims of racial discrimination are present throughout every facet of the criminal justice system. Criminal defendants sometimes charge that minorities face harsher sentences than non-minorities and that this disparity results from a corrupt and racist system of justice. Racial profiling conducted by police officers is a concern of the courts and the legislatures. If there is racial bias in the criminal justice system, this racial bias would also likely apply to death penalty cases. Are prosecutors striking minority jury members due to the color of their skin? Does the sentence differ if the races of the perpetrator and the victim are different, as opposed to crimes in which both victim and defendant are of the same race? This chapter examines the issues that are of concern when examining racial discrimination and the death penalty.

II. Statistics and Bias in Death Penalty Cases and Jury Selection in Capital Proceedings

There was no legal examination of racial bias in administration of the death penalty prior to 1972. The states were left to enact their own capital statutes and carry out the death sentences with little or no federal intervention or oversight. In 1972, the landmark case of *Furman v. Georgia*[1] halted capital punishment due to the arbitrary manner in which death sentences were being carried out in the state of Georgia. The five-to-four decision was controversial, because three of the justices who were in the majority did not oppose the death penalty as such, but were opposed to the manner in which Georgia enforced and imposed it. The statute in *Furman* was struck down because it gave judges and juries power to exercise discretion in a capricious and arbitrary manner. Two justices in the *Furman* decision believed that the Georgia death penalty statute was "pregnant with discrimination." Justice Douglas believed that "the death sentence [was] disproportionately imposed and carried out on the poor, the Negro, and the members of the unpopular groups."[2] Two dissenting justices in *Furman* also noted racial discrimination as a salient issue. The Supreme Court chose not to set standards to stop or prevent racial disparity in the death penalty, but left the states to amend their death penalty statutes.

While *Furman v. Georgia* is an important starting point in gaining insight into the race issue, *McCleskey v. Kemp*[3] is the most prominent Supreme Court decision concerning racial discrimination and the death penalty.[4] McCleskey was a young black male who was convicted of robbing a furniture store and killing a white police officer in Georgia. McCleskey was sentenced to death by a jury comprised of 11 whites and one black. On appeal, McCleskey pointed to the statistics in the studies conducted by University of Iowa professor David C. Baldus from 1973 to 1978, in which he examined the race of the defendant and the race of the victim and their effect on capital sentencing in Georgia. Baldus's research indicated that discrepancies in capital sentencing were, in part, explained by race (particularly race of the victim).[5] McCleskey argued that, in light of this evidence, his race and the race of the victim played a significant role in the decision of the jury, and his death sentence should be overturned because it was a violation of the Fourteenth Amendment's equal protection clause.

The Court did not dispute the validity of the statistical evidence presented by McCleskey regarding the impact that race of the victim had on death sentences in Georgia. But the Supreme Court, in a six-to-three decision, held that this evidence was insufficient to support a claim of discrimination under the equal protection clause of the Fourteenth Amendment. McCleskey did not prove that the Georgia legislature enacted the state's death penalty statute with the intent to discriminate. While the Baldus studies suggested that race was a factor in capital sentencing, it did not prove discriminatory intent. The Court believed that the legislature in Georgia did not enact the statute to further a racially motivated agenda. While the Court said that a risk of racial prejudice was involved in a jury's decision, it held that the level of risk was insufficient to establish a violation of a constitutional right. The Supreme Court was reluctant to limit the discretion of juries because "it is the jury's function to make the difficult and uniquely human judgments that defy codification and that build discretion, equity, and flexibility into a legal system."[6] The majority was also concerned with the possibility that a favorable ruling in *McCleskey* would cause a flood of claims of discrimination in other types of criminal proceedings. The Court claimed that if McCleskey's arguments were accepted, statistical analysis would be used to show discrepancies in gender of victim, or the race of the trial attorneys or judges.[7] The precedent in *McCleskey* still stands, but the Supreme Court has since decided other cases that relate to the racial composition of juries.

III. Legislative Responses to Discrimination in Capital Proceedings

A. Federal Response: The Proposed Racial Justice Act and Its Failure

In response to the decision in *McCleskey v. Kemp* (1987), legislation was drafted in 1988 by Senator Edward Kennedy and Representative John Conyers. The legislation, known as the Racial Justice Act, would have created a federal statutory right to be free from discrimination in capital cases. The act would have provided a way to circumvent the Supreme Court by providing a constitutional guarantee to be free from state-sponsored racial discrimination during sentencing.[8]

The Act would have allowed statistical evidence to establish discriminatory practices and patterns in applying death sentences. "The rationale behind the Racial Justice Act . . . is that since the Supreme Court has allowed the use of statistics to prove racial discrimination under Title VII [of the Civil Rights Act of 1964], statistics should also be allowed to prove racial discrimination in death penalty cases."[9] Despite repeated attempts, the Racial Justice Act has never been approved by Congress because it has generated a lot of criticism. Challengers have argued, as did the United States Supreme Court, that the human element in determining and dispensing American justice is essential and historically based. Statistics do not account for differences in offender background and demeanor, as well as the nature and quality of offenders' actions. Statistical correlations, critics say, do not necessarily lead to racial discrimination on the part of juries. While federal attempts at legislation have failed, legislation at the state level has not fared well, either.

B. State Responses

1. Legislation

In 1998 Kentucky became the first state to enact legislation similar to the Racial Justice Act. A study conducted in 1996 showed the existence of racial disparities in the administration of Kentucky's capital sentencing. Not one inmate on Kentucky's death row was convicted of murdering a black person, while 100 percent of the death row inmates were responsible for killing white victims.[10] The statistical disparity caused concern and the Kentucky Racial Justice Act became law. The passage of this Act may encourage other states to re-examine their policies and practices in administering the death penalty.

In 2007, North Carolina became the second state to propose a Racial Justice Act. This proposed legislation would give defendants the opportunity to challenge the death penalty based on studies showing racial bias. The proposed North Carolina Racial Justice Act would place the burden of proof on the defendant. The defendant could argue before trial that race was a significant factor in other prosecutorial decisions to seek the death penalty around the same time and in the same county or prosecutorial district. After defendants have been sentenced to death, they could present evidence that race influenced decisions to exercise peremptory challenges during jury selection. The legislation notes that defendants would have to "state with particularity" how race played a role in their case.[11]

2. State-Level Lack of Legislation

While New Jersey has no legislation similar to Kentucky's Racial Justice Act, it did allow researchers to examine its death-eligible cases to examine claims of racial discrimination. The study was conducted by Baldus and his colleagues, who were made famous by the use of their statistical study in the *McCleskey* case. The researchers had found that there was racial discrimination in the Georgia capital sentencing scheme. Baldus and his research team set out to answer the following questions:

1. Is racial discrimination in death sentencing inevitable, or can legal procedures be adopted by legislators, prosecutors, or courts to prevent it?

2. Can such racial discrimination be validly detected: (a) in subgroups of cases within the system; and (b) in individual cases?

3. Can racial discrimination be corrected by subgroups of cases and in individual cases without the de facto abolition of capital punishment or the use of quotas?

In the case of *State v. Marshall*,[12] New Jersey sought to find out whether the system of capital sentencing in New Jersey was unconstitutionally discriminatory. While the court did not find evidence of unconstitutional discrimination, it was willing to take corrective measures if necessary, through judicial oversight or more detailed standards to guide prosecutorial discretion.[13] New Jersey, along with other states, believes that legislation is unnecessary, even if statistical evidence suggests that sentencing is racially discriminatory. Other states with high numbers of executions such as Virginia, Texas, Florida, and Oklahoma do not acknowledge that a possibility of racial prejudice exists within their death penalty statutes and believe that a legislative response to the death penalty is unnecessary.[14] In May 2002, the governor of Maryland imposed a moratorium on executions because of racial bias in the state's death penalty system. A January 2003 study released by the University of Maryland concluded that race and geography are major factors in death penalty decisions. Specifically, prosecutors are more likely to seek a death sentence when the victim is white and are less likely to seek a death sentence when the victim is black.[15]

Generally, studies have found that race of the victim plays more of a role than race of the offender in whether to seek the death penalty, even if states contest the findings. A recent study conducted by a professor at Yale University reviewed 207 Connecticut murder cases dating back to the early 1970s that were eligible for death penalty prosecution and found the following:

- Black defendants receive death sentences at three times the rate of white defendants in cases where the victims were white.

- Killers of white victims are treated more severely than people who kill minorities, when it comes time to decide the charges.

- Minorities who kill whites receive death sentences at higher rates than minorities who kill minorities.[16]

The study, similar to the study presented in *McCleskey*, is being used in a suit brought by death row inmates in the state challenging the constitutionality of the manner in which the death penalty is being applied.[17] The American Bar Association has conducted a review of the death penalty in Pennsylvania and made multiple recommendations, including the following:

- **Pennsylvania should ensure that it provides adequate opportunities for death row inmates to prove their innocence.** The state should require the preservation of biological evidence for as long as the defendant remains incarcerated and should require crime labs and law enforcement agencies to be certified by nationally recognized certification organizations. It should also require audio- or videotaping of all interrogations in potential capital cases and implement lineup procedures that protect against incorrect eyewitness identifications.

- **Pennsylvania should ensure that all capital defendants and death row inmates who are poor receive competent lawyers.** The assessment team found that the state fails to guarantee the appointment of two attorneys at all stages of capital cases, and that attorneys often are provided insufficient access to experts and investigators or to information in discovery. The panel also noted that Pennsylvania lacks a statewide independent appointing authority responsible for training, selecting, and monitoring capital defense attorneys.

- **Pennsylvania should provide state funding for capital indigent defense services.** The group found that the state currently has no funding for indigent defense services, but instead relies on county-funded systems. As a result, the quality of Pennsylvania's capital indigent defense system varies widely among counties and fails to afford uniform, quality representation to many capital defendants.

- **Pennsylvania should eliminate racial and geographic bias from its death penalty system.** The assessment team found that Pennsylvania is "second only to Louisiana in the percentage of blacks on death row" and that black defendants in Philadelphia County were sentenced at a "significantly higher rate" than similarly situated non-black defendants. The review concluded that one-third of black death row inmates in Philadelphia County would have received sentences of life imprisonment if they had not been black.

- **Pennsylvania should collect and make available data on death-eligible cases.** Without a statewide entity that collects data on all death-eligible cases in the state, Pennsylvania cannot ensure that its system ensures proportionality in charging or sentencing, or determine the extent of racial or geographic bias in its capital system.

- **Pennsylvania should ensure that all death row inmates receive meaningful review in state post-conviction proceedings.** State law imposes several restrictions on state post-conviction proceedings that seriously impede the adequate development and judicial consideration of a death row inmate's claims, including a 60-day time limitation for filing a successive post-conviction petition.

- **Pennsylvania should ensure that capital jurors understand their roles and responsibilities.** The group revealed that the overwhelming majority of Pennsylvania capital jurors fail to understand their roles and responsibilities when deciding whether to impose a death sentence. More than 98 percent of these jurors failed to understand "at least some" portion of the jury instructions, and of those questioned, about 82 percent did not believe "that a life sentence really meant life in prison." The ABA urged the state to redraft its capital jury instructions with the objective of preventing common juror misconceptions and to provide a clearer understanding of the definition of life in prison. [18]

The American Bar Association also examined death penalty jurisprudence in Ohio and found that Ohio's capital punishment system is so flawed that it should be suspended while the state conducts a thorough review of its fairness and accuracy. The study, conducted by a 10-member panel of Ohio attorneys appointed by the ABA, found that the state's death penalty is prone to racial and geographic imbalances and that it meets only four of the 93 ABA recommendations to ensure a fair capital punishment system. [19] Among the panel's key recommendations were the following:

- **Ohio should ensure that it provides adequate opportunities for death row inmates to prove their innocence.** This includes improved preservation of biological evidence while inmates are incarcerated, creation of nationally certified crime laboratories, videotaping of all interrogations in potentially capital cases, and implementation of lineup procedures that protect against incorrect eyewitness identification. In addition, the report recommends that Ohio Governor Ted Strickland supplement the state's current clemency process by appointing a commission to conduct investigations, hold hearings, and test evidence, to review cases of factual innocence in capital cases.

- **Ohio should ensure that all capital defendants and death row inmates who are poor receive competent lawyers.** The panel noted that Ohio does not have safeguards in place to ensure competent representation in all cases. It urged compliance with the ABA Guidelines for the Appointment and Performance of Defense Counsel in Death Penalty Cases. It also urged lawmakers to better compensate defense attorneys to ensure high-quality representation, and to provide defense teams with sufficient funds for access to experts and investigators.

- **Ohio should exempt people with severe mental disabilities from the death penalty.** The panel found that while Ohio docs protect those with mental retardation from facing the death penalty, it does not extend this protection to those with other types of serious mental disorders.

- **Ohio should eliminate racial and geographic bias from its death penalty system.** As part of its assessment, the ABA conducted a racial and geographic disparity study that examined death sentences in Ohio between 1981 and 2000. The review found that those who kill white victims are 3.8 times more likely to receive a death sentence than those who kill black victims. It also found that the chances of receiving a death sentence in Hamilton County are 2.7 times higher than in the rest of the state, 3.7 times higher than in Cuyahoga County, and 6.2 times higher than in Franklin County.

- **Ohio should provide increased discovery in state post-conviction appeals.** The panel noted that Ohio denies petitioners access to discovery procedures necessary to develop post-conviction claims. The ABA criticized an existing policy that allows reporters and other members of the public to use the public records law to obtain materials in support of post-conviction claims, but prohibits a petitioner from using this law to obtain these same documents.[20]

Less than ten percent of people placed on death row are actually executed.[21] In a recent study, scholars have found that blacks convicted of killing whites are not only more likely than non-whites to receive a death sentence, but also more likely to be executed.[22] Minorities who kill other minorities are less likely to be executed. It could be argued, as presented by research, that the American criminal justice system places more value on white lives.[23] When it comes to the death penalty, one must examine what it means to be "colorblind" and whether achievement of this is possible. Figure 3.1 presents states in which racial disparities have been found (with regard to the victim and to the offender, respectively). Figure 3.2 presents the current (as of Winter 2007) breakdown of death row populations and percentages by race of inmate.

Figure 3.1
Statistical Data in Death Penalty States Showing a Risk of Racial Discrimination

State	Race of Victim Disparities	Race of Defendant Disparities	State	Race of Victim Disparities	Race of Defendant Disparities
Alabama	v	v	Nevada		
Arizona	v		New Hampshire**		
California	v		New Jersey	v	v
Colorado	v		New Mexico*		
Connecticut	v		New York**		
Delaware	v		North Carolina	v	
Florida	v	v	Ohio	v	
Georgia	v		Oklahoma	v	v
Idaho*			Oregon*		
Illinois	v		Pennsylvania	v	v
Indiana	v	v	South Carolina	v	v
Kansas**			South Dakota*		
Kentucky	v	v	Tennessee	v	v
Louisiana	v		Texas	v	v
Maryland	v	v	Utah*		
Mississippi	v	v	Virginia	v	
Missouri	v		Washington	v	v
Montana*			Wyoming		
Nebraska	v				

*States for which no death penalty race data are available.
**States in which no death sentences imposed as of January 1, 1998.

Source: Richard C. Dieter, *The Death Penalty in Black and White: Who Lives, Who Dies, Who Decides*. Death Penalty Information Center (June 1998).

Figure 3.2
Death Row Populations and Percentages by Race, Winter 2007

State	Total	Black		White		Latino		Asian		Native American	
		#	%	#	%	#	%	#	%	#	%
Alabama	195	93	48%	100	51%	2	1%	0	—	0	—
Arizona	124	13	11%	88	71%	20	16%	0	—	3	2%
Arkansas	37	23	62%	14	38%	0	—	0	—	0	—
California	660	235	36%	254	38%	136	21%	22	3%	13	2%
Colorado	2	1	50%	0	—	1	50%	0	—	0	—
Connecticut	8	3	38%	3	38%	2	25%	0	—	0	—
Delaware	18	7	39%	8	44%	3	17%	0	—	0	—
Florida	397	139	35%	221	56%	35	9%	1	0.3%	1	0.3%
Georgia	107	50	47%	53	50%	3	3%	1	0.9%	0	—
Idaho	20	0	—	20	100%	0		0	—	0	—
Illinois	11	3	27%	5	45%	3	27%	0	—	0	—
Indiana	23	7	30%	16	70%	0	—	0	—	0	—
Kansas	9	4	44%	5	56%	0	—	0	—	0	—
Kentucky	41	9	22%	31	76%	1	2%	0	—	0	—
Louisiana	88	55	63%	30	34%	2	2%	1	1%	0	—
Maryland	8	5	63%	3	38%	0	—	0	—	0	—
Mississippi	66	35	53%	30	45%	0	—	1	2%	0	—
Missouri	51	21	41%	30	59%	0	—	0	—	0	—
Montana	2	0	—	2	100%	0	—	0	—	0	—
Nebraska	9	1	11%	5	56%	3	33%	0	—	0	—
Nevada	80	29	36%	42	53%	8	10%	1	1%	0	—
New Mexico	2	0	—	2	100%	0	—	0	—	0	—
North Carolina	185	98	53%	72	39%	4	2%	1	0.5%	10	5%
Ohio	191	96	50%	88	46%	3	2%	2	1%	2	1%
Oklahoma	88	33	38%	48	55%	3	3%	0	—	4	5%
Oregon*	33	3	9%	26	79%	2	6%	0	—	1	3%

Figure 3.2, *continued*

State	Total	Black		White		Latino		Asian		Native American	
Pennsylvania	226	137	61%	68	30%	19	8%	2	0.9%	0	—
South Carolina	67	38	57%	29	43%	0	—	0	—	0	—
South Dakota	4	0	—	4	100%	0	—	0	—	0	—
Tennessee	107	43	40%	59	55%	1	0.9%	2	2%	2	2%
Texas	393	161	41%	121	31%	107	27%	4	1%	0	—
Utah	9	1	11%	6	67%	1	11%	0	—	1	11%
Virginia	20	12	60%	8	40%	0	—	0	—	0	—
Washington	9	4	44%	5	56%	0	—	0	—	0	—
Wyoming	2	0	—	2	100%	0	—	0	—	0	—
US Gov't	44	25	57%	18	41%	0	—	0	—	1	2%
US Military	9	6	67%	2	22%	0	—	1	11%	0	—
Total	**3357**	**1397**	**42%**	**1523**	**45%**	**359**	**11%**	**39**	**1.0%**	**38**	**1.0%**

Source: NAACP, *Death Row U.S.A., Winter, 2007*. Available at: http://www.naacpldf.org/content/pdf/pubs/drusa/DRUSA_Winter_2007.pdf.

IV. The Legal Community: An Assessment of Prosecutors, Defense Attorneys, and Judges

A. District Attorneys

A study in 1998 found that 98 percent of chief district attorneys in counties that gave death sentences were white.[24] Only one percent of the chief district attorneys were black. Figure 3.3 presents an overview of the racial breakdown of prosecutors in states that have the death penalty.[25] The decision to pursue or not to pursue a death sentence rests with the prosecutor. There are no standards that govern whether a death sentence should be sought. Some prosecutors may frequently seek capital convictions, while other district attorneys may choose not to seek the death penalty at all.[26] Prosecutorial discretion plays a decisive role in how, when, and why capital murder charges are brought. Some district attorney's offices virtually admitted bias in practice, as was the case in *Miller-El v. Dretke* (2005).[27] In this case, the prosecutor's office circulated a memo calling for automatic dismissal of minority jurors through peremptory strikes regardless of education or socioeconomic status. For an example of such a "memorandum," see Figure 3.4, "Prosecutor's

Manual/Jury Selection in a Criminal Case" (p. 64). It contains excerpts regarding jury selection from one such document that was leaked from the Dallas County, Texas, prosecutor's office to *The Texas Observer* in 1973.

Figure 3.3
Racial Breakdown of District Attorneys* in U.S. Death Penalty States

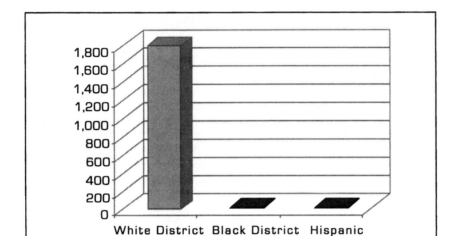

* Chief prosecuting official with discretionary power to determine charging levels.
Source: Jeffrey J. Pokorak, *Symposium: Probing the Capital Prosecutor's Perspective: Race of the Discretionary Actors*. 83 CORNELL L. REV. 1811 (September 1998). Reprinted with permission.

While many prosecutors have no "smoking gun" memorandum similar to that discussed above, they may utilize the same reservations during voir dire, believing that minority jurors are less willing to sentence someone to death, particularly if the defendant is of the same race. Another practice used by prosecutors to exclude minorities is jury shuffling. This process allows the parties to rearrange the order in which the potential jurors are questioned during voir dire. The only information available on the juror cards is juror appearance. In the *Miller-El* case,[28] the prosecutors used jury shuffling to place the blacks that were at the front of the potential jury panel, to the back of the potential jury panel, as this would lessen their chances of being selected. In the trial of Albert Jefferson in Alabama, for instance, the prosecutor exercised his discretionary challenges against 24 of the 26 blacks among the prospective jurors, resulting in an all-white jury. Long after the trial, counsel for Jefferson discovered the district attorney's juror ranking system: (a) Strong, (b) Medium, (c) Weak, and the least desirable category, (d) Black. Even in the wake of this discovery, the Alabama court did not grant Mr. Jefferson relief based on this blatant racial discrimination (although he did obtain relief on another issue).[29]

Information given to prosecutors by the police may also influence prosecutorial decisions when pursuing a death sentence. The amount of hard evidence may be different as police and sheriff's departments often pursue criminal activity in white neighborhoods more aggressively than crime in black or minority neighborhoods. Discrimination or racial bias on the part of law enforcement may have a significant and direct impact on the prosecutor's ability to pursue the death penalty. There have been few, if any, limitations on prosecutorial discretion even in light of the "death is different" position of the Supreme Court. The following examples in *The Color of Justice* (Walker et al., 2004) show some examples of prosecutorial appeals to bias:

- An Alabama prosecutor declared, "Unless you hang this Negro, our white people living out in the country won't be safe."[30]

- A prosecutor in North Carolina dismissed an implausible claim of three black men that the white women they were accused of raping had consented to sex with them. The prosecutor stated that "the average white woman abhors anything of this type in nature that had to do with a black man."[31]

- A prosecutor in a rape case involving a black man and a white woman asked the jurors, "Gentlemen, do you believe that she would have had intercourse with this black brute?"[32]

- A prosecutor in a case involving the alleged kidnapping of a white man by two black men said in his closing argument that "not one white witness has been produced" to rebut the victim's testimony."[33]

- A prosecutor stated during the penalty phase of a capital case involving Walter J. Blair, a black man charged with murdering a white woman, "Can you imagine [the victim's] state of mind when she woke up at 6 o'clock that morning staring into the muzzle of a gun held by this black man?"[34]

The judiciary rarely reviews prosecutorial decisions due to separation of powers concerns, the desire to enhance the efficiency of the criminal justice system, the potential chilling effect on law enforcement, and because the prosecutors' decisions reflect their expertise. The Supreme Court presumes that the duties of the district attorney are being carried out correctly as was evidenced by the decision in *United States v. Bass* (2002).[35] In a per curiam opinion, the Supreme Court ruled that a defendant must establish that the prosecutors were motivated by intentions to discriminate and that the actions of the prosecutor had a discriminatory impact on the defendant. Some legal scholars argue that this decision is misguided and places a different burden on defendants.[36] The Court in *Bass* relied on *United States v. Armstrong* (1993),[37] which created the general standard for selective prosecution claims in which the defendant must show evidence that individuals with similar sets of circumstances could have faced prosecution but did not. The Court did not want to intrude on the executive branch's power to enforce laws. It is not inconceivable that this decision might give prosecutors even more power to decide whom to send to a capital trial.

The case of *Snyder v. Louisiana*[38] (2006) was one in which the prosecutor's use of peremptory challenges to strike prospective black jurors has been sent to the Supreme Court. Justice Breyer commented during oral arguments that he believed if district attorneys could not learn to use peremptory challenges in a race-neutral way, then peremptory challenges should be done away with altogether. While it is unlikely that the Supreme Court would resort to such lengths in the wake of *Snyder*, the decision handed down by the Supreme Court could further restrict the ability of prosecutors to offer "racially neutral" explanations that are weak or unfeasible.

B. Defense Attorneys

Many issues surround the effectiveness of counsel for capital defendants. The American Bar Association, after an exhaustive study of the issues, found that "the inadequacy and inadequate compensation of counsel at trial" was one of the "principal failings of the capital punishment systems in the states today."[39] The *National Law Journal*, after an extensive study of death penalty cases in six Southern states, found that capital trials are "more like a random flip of the coin than a delicate balancing of the scales" because the defense lawyer is too often "ill-trained, unprepared . . . and grossly underpaid."[40] In Alabama, Georgia, Mississippi, Louisiana, Texas, and many other states that allow capital punishment, there is no similar degree of specialization or resources on the other side of capital cases. A poor person facing the death penalty may be assigned an attorney who has little or no experience in the defense of capital or even serious criminal cases, one reluctant or unwilling to defend him, one with little or no empathy or understanding of the accused or his particular plight, one with little or no knowledge of criminal or capital punishment law, or one with no understanding of the need to document and present mitigating circumstances.[41] Capital defendants are often assigned these public defenders, who have other cases and no vested interest in representing the defendant. One attorney explained his dilemma:

> I could not take days at a time out of my office to do essentially non-legal work. And investigation is necessary, certainly, to prepare a case, but it is non-legal. . . . You're actually pounding the pavement, trying to come up with the same information that a person who is paid substantially less per hour could take care of, I mean, whether it be the investigator for the Sheriff's Department or the District Attorney's office or the F.B.I., or the U.S. Attorney's office. You don't find the U.S. Attorney pounding the pavement, trying to investigate facts. . . . And it just creates a terrible situation when you have to do everything for yourself.[42]

Most counties use one of three systems to appoint counsel for indigent defendants. Some counties employ a "contract system," in which the county contracts with an attorney in private practice to handle all of the indigent cases for a specified amount. Contracts are often awarded to the lawyer or group of lawyers with the lowest bid. The lawyer is still free to generate other income through private practice. Any money spent on investigation and experts comes out of the amount the lawyer receives. These programs are well known for the inadequate representation that poor clients receive and the lack of resources for investigative and expert assistance.[43]

A third system is the employment of a group of lawyers or an organization to handle all indigent criminal cases while not engaging in any outside practice. These lawyers are usually public defenders. In some jurisdictions they lack the investigative and support staff that is believed to be part of a genuine public defender program. While some public defenders are remarkably dedicated attorneys, their jobs are made difficult by overwhelming caseloads and poor funding.[44]

It is difficult to ensure effectiveness of counsel due to lack of funding and overburdened public defenders, but it is of greater concern if the lawyer shows racial prejudice. In order for an adequate defense to be raised, lawyers must research a defendant's social history and meet with friends and family members to prepare for trial. A lawyer who has feelings of racial superiority cannot adequately fill the role of advocate for the defendant. Melvin Wade was assigned such an attorney. Wade's attorney, during the trial, used racial slurs to refer to Wade, and failed to present Wade's childhood abuse as a mitigating factor. The lawyer also told the jury during closing arguments that he believed his client should receive the death penalty.[45] In a declaration to the Ninth Circuit Court of Appeals in California, Kim Taylor summarized how counsel's racial bias influenced his trial performance: "From the evidence before me, it seems clear that race played a significant and insidious role in Mr. Wade's trial . . . he was represented by a man who viewed blacks with contempt, and this evidence is supported by the manner in which he carried himself at trial."

Another case in which the court-appointed attorney showed racial bias was the case of Wilburn Dobbs. His lawyer referred to Dobbs as "colored" and stated before the trial that he was in a better position to prosecute the case than defend it. During a federal court hearing on Dobbs' appeal, the lawyer testified that he believed blacks were uneducated and less intelligent than whites. He also admitted he used the word "nigger" in a joking context.[46]

Obviously, not all public defenders or court-assigned attorneys are so blatant about their prejudices. Would a conscientious and neutral counsel have helped Wade or Dobbs avoid a death sentence? The federal court that heard Dobbs' appeal did not believe so, ruling that neither the attitudes of the trial judge nor defense attorney, nor the racial prejudice of the jury, required that Dobbs' death sentence be set aside, because none of the jurors "viewed blacks as more prone to violence than whites or as morally inferior to whites."[47] Their logic might leave the impression that racial prejudice that is not tolerated in other facets of American society might still be tolerated in some American courts. While such blatant bias likely exists, it does not characterize the proceedings in most American courts, particularly in high-profile cases.

C. Judges

In a criminal trial the judge controls the tone and demeanor of the participants. The judge instructs the jury, allows the admission or exclusion of evidence, and admonishes attorneys when their behavior is inappropriate. Judges also appoint lawyers to defend indigent defendants. Judges have appointed lawyers who have never tried a case before to capital cases. A study of homicide cases in Philadelphia found that the quality of lawyers appointed to capital cases in Philadelphia is so poor that "even officials in charge of the system say they wouldn't want to be represented in Traffic Court by some of the people appointed to defend poor people accused of murder." The study found that many of the attorneys were appointed by judges based on political connections, not legal ability. "Philadelphia's poor defendants often find themselves being represented by ward leaders, ward committeemen, failed politicians, the sons of judges and party leaders, and contributors to the judge's election campaigns."[48]

Almost all judicial selection systems fall into one of four categories. First, judges in 11 states and the District of Columbia are never subjected to election at any time in their judicial careers. Second, the judges of three states are elected by vote of the state legislature. Third, the judges of 29 states are selected in contested elections, either partisan or nonpartisan, at some point in their careers, whether during initial selection for the bench or after appointment by the governor. The fourth category of judicial selection systems includes systems in which the judge or justice is at some time selected in a retention election but does not face an opponent.[49] Thirteen states employ such a system. There are currently 38 states with capital punishment statutes. Thirty-two states both elect their judges and sentence people to death.

In his dissent in *Harris v. Alabama* (1995),[50] Justice John Paul Stevens stated that "[t]he 'higher authority' to whom present-day capital judges may be 'too responsive' is a political climate in which judges who covet higher office —or who merely wish to remain judges—must constantly profess their fealty to the death penalty. . . . The danger that they will bend to political pressures when pronouncing sentence in highly publicized capital cases is the same danger confronted by judges beholden to King George III."[51] The single county in the United States responsible for the most death sentences and executions is Harris County, Texas, which includes Houston. Judge Norman E. Lanford, a Republican, was voted off the state district court in Houston in 1992 after he recommended in post-conviction proceedings that a death sentence be set aside due to prosecutorial misconduct, and directed an acquittal in another murder case due to constitutional violations. A prosecutor who specialized in death cases, Caprice Cosper, defeated Judge Lanford in the

Republican primary. In the November election, Cosper was elected after a campaign in which radio advertisements on her behalf attacked her Democratic opponent for having once opposed the death penalty.[52]

In Texas and Alabama, judges run under party affiliations. The success of the party in national or state elections may have a significant impact on the judiciary. Republicans won every elected position they sought on the Texas Court of Criminal Appeals and the Texas Supreme Court.[53] Republican straight-ticket voting contributed to the defeat of 19 Democratic judges and a Republican sweep of all but one of the 42 contested races for countywide judgeships in Harris County, Texas. The dean of one Texas law school observed that "[i]f Bozo the Clown had been running as a Republican against any Democrat, he would have had a chance."[54] Such straight-ticket voting, which comprised one-quarter of all votes cast in Harris County, also resulted in the removal of the only three black judges and left only one Hispanic on the bench. The lack of racial diversity now found in Houston is consistent with the exclusion of minorities from the bench throughout the country.[55] One reason for the lack of minority judges is that in many states, particularly those in the "death belt" states such as Florida and Texas, judges have long been elected from judicial districts in which the voting strength of racial minorities is diluted.[56]

Judges, however, are human and may bring to the courtroom their attitudes, morals, beliefs, and even prejudices. This was evident in the *Dobbs* case, in which the trial judge repeatedly referred to the defendant as "colored" or as the "colored boy." Clearly, the judge would not find the use of racial slurs or comments offensive courtroom behavior. In *Peek v. Florida* (1986),[57] the judge referred to the parents of the defendant as "nigger mom and dad." The judge was not penalized for his comment and the Florida Supreme Court recommended that judges avoid "appearances" of impropriety. Judges may feel pressure from constituents to be either for or against the death penalty, when as judges they should be neutral. The American Bar Association's Commission on Professionalism found that "judges are far less likely to . . . take . . . tough action if they must run for reelection or retention every few years."[58] In no other area of American law are so many tough decisions presented as in a capital case. And no other cases demonstrate so clearly the validity of the ABA Commission's finding.

A judge who faces election is more likely to sentence a defendant to death than a jury that heard the same evidence. In some instances, political considerations make it virtually impossible for judges to enforce the constitutional protections to a fair trial for the accused, such as granting a change of venue or continuance, or suppressing evidence. Judges in some cases have failed miserably to enforce the most fundamental rights of the accused in capital cases. Many judges routinely abdicate their judicial responsibility and allow the lawyers for the state to write their orders resolving disputed factual and legal issues in capital cases.[59]

V. The Jury: A Biased Bunch or Victims of Misinformation?

Juries are an American tradition and the right to a trial by jury is constitutionally guaranteed. Recently the Supreme Court decided in *Ring v. Arizona* (2002)[60] that death sentences must be determined by juries, not judges alone. In Arizona prior to the *Ring* decision, following a jury's finding of guilt in capital cases, the trial judge, sitting alone, determined the presence or absence of aggravating factors required by Arizona law for imposition of the death penalty. The *Ring* decision changed this and emphasized the importance and central fact-finding role of juries in criminal trials (and particularly in capital trials).

In the earlier case of *Walton v. Arizona* (1990),[61] the Supreme Court had upheld Arizona's law allowing judges to make the determination of aggravating factors and thus placing in their hands alone the decision of whether to sentence a defendant to death. Justice Stevens, writing for the dissent, criticized the Court's decision, arguing that the jury's critical role existed at the time the Bill of Rights was adopted. He stated that "by that time,"

> [T]he English jury's role in determining critical facts in homicide cases was entrenched. As fact-finder, the jury had the power to determine not only whether the defendant was guilty of homicide but also the degree of the offense. Moreover, the jury's role in finding facts that would determine a homicide defendant's eligibility for capital punishment was particularly well established. Throughout its history, the jury determined which homicide defendants would be subject to capital punishment by making factual determinations, many of which related to difficult assessments of the defendant's state of mind. By the time the Bill of Rights was adopted, the jury's right to make these determinations was unquestioned.[62]

Ten years later, in *Apprendi v. New Jersey* (2000),[63] the Supreme Court said that judges alone may not determine a finding of facts that increases the level of punishment for the defendant. It held that this was a violation of the right to a trial by jury. Justice Scalia, in a concurring opinion, wrote the following:

> [Such an approach might be] an admirably fair and efficient scheme of criminal justice designed for a society that is prepared to leave criminal justice to the State . . . The founders of the American Republic were not prepared to leave it to the State, which is why the jury-trial guarantee was one of the least controversial provisions of the Bill of Rights. It has never been efficient: but it has always been free.[64]

In *Ring* the Supreme Court agreed with this argument and applied it to the sentencing phase of capital cases, reemphasizing the importance of juries in the death penalty process.

A. Jury Selection

In 1880 the Supreme Court decided *Strauder v. West Virginia*[65] and stated that a West Virginia law restricting jury service to white males violated the equal protection clause of the Fourteenth Amendment. The Court concluded that it was harmful to blacks and states could no longer create laws that banned blacks from juries. Therefore, some states, particularly those in the southern United States, developed techniques to ensure that minorities were excluded from jury service. One such example existed in Delaware:

> In Delaware, for example, local jurisdictions used lists of taxpayers to select "sober and judicious" persons for jury service. Under this system, African American taxpayers were eligible for jury service, but were seldom, if ever, selected for the jury pool. The state explained this result by noting that few of the African Americans in Delaware were intelligent, experienced, or moral enough to serve as jurors. As the chief justice of the Delaware Supreme Court concluded: "That none but white men were selected is in nowise remarkable in view of the fact—too notorious to be ignored—that the great body of black men residing in this State are utterly unqualified by want of intelligence, experience, or moral integrity.[66]

Since that time the states and Supreme Court have argued about issues of racial prejudice in jury selection. While the Court has made it increasingly difficult to discriminate on the basis of race, procedures for jury selection may not always be racially neutral.

Some states use lists of potential jurors from property tax rolls, automobile registrations, and voter registration lists. While the practice seems objective on its face, in many counties or areas minorities are less likely than whites to register to vote or own a vehicle or property.[67] In his book, *No Equal Justice*, David Cole notes that many minorities are less likely to report for jury service due to a variety of reasons, including fear of alienation, loss of wages at work, and skepticism about the criminal justice system. Cole also points to the irony of American jury selection, stating, "[t]hree facts about jury discriminations are largely undisputed. First, the all-white jury has been a staple of the American criminal justice system for most of our history. Second, the Supreme Court has long condemned discrimination in jury selection. And third, race discrimination in jury selection remains a pervasive feature of our justice system to this day. The interesting question is how all of these facts can be true at the same time."[68]

Batson v. Kentucky[69] changed the precedent that required the defendant to prove that the jurisdiction had engaged in a pattern of racial discrimination that was well established.[70] During Batson's trial the prosecutor struck all four of the blacks from the jury pool. The defense attorney argued that this exclusion of minority jury members violated the Sixth and Fourteenth Amendments. The Supreme Court believed that the burden of proof should not rest with the defendant; instead, it should be the prosecution's burden to explain the exclusion of the jurors. The dissent in *Batson* was concerned that this ruling puts an additional burden on the historical tradition of peremptory challenges.

In 1995, nine years after the *Batson* decision, the Court re-interpreted *Batson v. Kentucky* in *Purkett v. Elem*[71] (1995). In *Purkett*, a prosecutor offered an explanation for striking two black men from the jury pool:

> I struck number twenty-two because of his long hair. He had long curly hair. He had the longest hair of anybody on the panel by far. He appeared not to be a good juror for that fact, the fact that he had long hair hanging down to shoulder length, curly, unkempt hair. Also, he had a moustache and goatee type beard. And juror number twenty-four also had a mustache and a goatee type beard. Those are the only two people on the jury . . . with the mustache and goatee type beard . . . And I don't like the way they looked, with the way the hair is cut, both of them. And the mustache and the beards looked suspicious to me.[72]

The Supreme Court held only that a racially neutral explanation had to be given, but did not have to be reasonable. The facial validity of the explanation offered was the key component regardless of whether it appeared to be frivolous or based on superstition. Opponents of the *Purkett* holding argue that it allows for circumvention of the requirement that a race-neutral explanation be related to the case that was being tried. In his dissent in *Purkett*, Justice Stevens cautioned as follows: "Today without argument, the Court replaces the *Batson* standard with the surprising announcement that any neutral explanation, no matter 'how implausible or fantastic,' even if it is silly or superstitious, is sufficient to rebut a prima facie case of discrimination."[73]

It has been argued that in order for people to be willing to serve on a jury, the incentive to serve must be better than a few dollars a day and a take-out lunch. Some jurisdictions offer an increase in pay, bus vouchers to and from the courthouse, and have provided money for childcare expenses.[74] Others eschew these measures, saying that jury service should not require large financial compensation. At the core of the American judicial system is the concept that citizens in the community should do their civic duty regardless of race or ethnicity.

Another, even more controversial method of selecting jurors, known as "race-conscious jury selection," has been advocated. This process could be described as affirmative action for the jury system. This is done by saving seats for minority jurors, sending disproportionate numbers of jury summonses to areas with more minority citizens, or through elimination of prospective white jurors until the jury pool matches the minority proportion in the population.[75] The arguments against race-conscious juries are similar to the arguments against affirmative action. Members who are selected because of their minority status might feel as though they are "token" jurors or may feel pressured to act as representatives of their race, rather than as neutral jurors. The Sixth Circuit Court of Appeals in *United States v. Ovalle* (1998)[76] held that subtracting whites from jury pools to reach racial proportionality violated the equal protection clause. The debate will certainly continue. Proponents believe it is a simple and effective way to create a jury that truly consists of peers in any given community.

B. Peremptory Challenges

The Supreme Court has ruled that individuals may not be excluded from jury pools based on their race, but it has not been as stringent in its requirements for jury selection. Thus, peremptory challenges, which are challenges that need no cause or explanation, can and have been used in a discriminatory way toward minorities.

Figure 3.4
Excerpt from: Prosecutor's Manual/Jury Selection in a Criminal Case (1973)

> - You are not looking for a fair juror, but rather a strong, biased and sometimes hypocritical individual who believes that defendants are different from them in kind, rather than in degree. You are not looking for any member of a minority group which may subject him to oppression— they almost always empathize with the accused. You are not looking for free thinkers or flower children.
>
> - Observation is worthwhile . . . look for physical afflictions. These people usually sympathize with the accused.
>
> - I don't like women jurors because I can't trust them. They do, however, make the best jurors in cases involving crimes against children.
>
> - Extremely overweight people, especially women and young men, indicate a lack of self-discipline and oftentimes instability. I like the lean and hungry look.
>
> - If the veniremen have not lived in the county long, ask where they were born and reared. People from small town and rural areas generally make good state's jurors. People from the east and west coasts often make bad jurors.
>
> - Intellectuals such as teachers, etc. generally are too liberal and contemplative to make good State's jurors.
>
> Ask veniremen their religious preference. Jewish veniremen generally make poor State's jurors. Jews have a history of oppression and generally empathize with the accused. Lutherans and Church of Christ veniremen usually make good State's jurors.

Source: *The Texas Observer* (May 11, 1973: p. 9).

Prosecutors might be under the impression that minorities will side with minority defendants. Conversely, defense attorneys might believe that minority jurors will be more likely to convict white defendants. In Philadelphia a district attorney advised fellow prosecutors that young black women have "resentment for law enforcement. There is resentment for authority and as a result you don't want these people on your jury."[77] The Supreme Court was recently asked to decide whether a set of different questions used for different races was unconstitutional. In *Miller-El v. Dretke* (2005),[78] Dallas County prosecutors used peremptory strikes to exclude 10 of 11 eligible blacks to serve on a capital jury. The petitioner moved that the jury be struck down on the ground that the exclusion violated the equal protection clause. Although the petitioner presented evidence supporting his motion at a pretrial hearing, he was denied relief by the trial judge. The trial judge found no evidence, under then-controlling *Swain v. Alabama* (1965),[79] that a systematic exclusion of blacks had occurred. The jury found Miller-El guilty and sentenced him to death.

Blacks were excluded from Miller-El's jury at a significantly higher ratio than whites. Twenty blacks were initially previewed by the prosecution and defense out of a possible 108. Nine of the 20 were excused by agreement or cause. All but one of the remaining black jurors were excluded by prosecution peremptory strikes (91%), while only four out of 31 (13%) of non-black jurors were stricken from the jury by the prosecution. The prosecution questioned potential jurors about their views on the death penalty and their willingness to serve on a capital jury. Responses that showed reluctance or hesitation to impose the death penalty were used as a justification for peremptory strikes (*Wainwright v. Witt*, 1985).[80] The members of the jury were given different sets of questions, by race, that attributed the varying degrees of responses. Black prospective jurors were read a description of what would happen to Miller-El in the execution chamber and then asked whether they could sentence someone to death. The majority of white jurors were asked how they felt about capital punishment and whether they could serve on a capital jury. An even greater disparity occurred in the way in which the prosecution questioned members of the venire about their willingness to impose the minimum sentence for murder. White jurors were asked if they could give a person five years if the case was justified. In *Huffman v. State*,[81] an unwillingness to do so was justified for removal from a case. All but one of the black jurors was asked what they thought a minimum sentence should be.

The prosecution in *Miller-El* also utilized jury shuffling, a Texas criminal procedure practice. Parties are permitted to rearrange the order in which the potential jurors are questioned. The only information known is juror appearance and the juror cards. The cards are shuffled into a new order. Jurors shuffled to the back of the panel are far less likely to be questioned or to serve, as jurors not questioned during voir dire are excused at the end of the week. The prosecution on at least two occasions shuffled the jury when a large number of blacks were at the beginning of the panel. The petitioner also presented evidence in which the Dallas County prosecutor's office had a formalized policy to exclude minorities from juries. A circular created by the district attorney's office in 1963 instructed prosecutors to exercise their peremptory strikes against minorities regardless of wealth or education. A manual had been distributed to prosecutors that included the reasons for minority exclusion from jury service. The manual had been available to a prosecutor in Miller-El's trial. Although the state claimed that these practices had been discontinued the state, by its own admission, it had requested a jury shuffle to reduce the number of blacks on the jury panel.

The state's defense at the trial relied on *Swain*, which did not require a judge to analyze the credibility of prosecution explanations. The *Batson* hearing was held two years after voir dire, where distortion is not uncommon due to the passage of time. The prosecution claimed that it excused black jurors in view of the fact that they showed ambivalence about the death penalty and hesitated to execute those capable of rehabilitation. White jurors who were selected for the jury also showed ambivalence and unwillingness to give a death sentence. The Court in *Batson* thought that proof of discriminatory impact "may for all practical purposes demonstrate unconstitutionality because in various circumstances the discrimination is very difficult to explain on nonracial grounds."[82] The state's use and delay of jury shuffling also shows a desire to dismiss minority jurors. The Dallas County District Attorney's office had admitted using jury shuffling to exclude minorities. Blacks had historically been excluded from jury service. In *Minnesota v. McRae* (1992),[83] the prosecutor questioned and struck down the only black member of the venire. She was struck down due to her views that the judicial system had been historically unfair to minorities. The Minnesota Supreme Court found this to be a *Batson* violation as the race of the juror was given relevant consideration. Should jurors be excluded purely on their belief that the system has been unfair to minorities? This question may soon be before the Supreme Court. Recently, in *Rico v. Leftridge-Byrd* (2003),[84] the Third Circuit Court of Appeals ruled that *Batson* applied to Italian-Americans. Jurors in the case were stricken from the jury due to their Italian surnames.[85] To extend *Batson* beyond the scope of blacks could prove to be difficult, because ethnicity can be difficult to define.[86] Although the Court decided in *United States v. Martinez-Salazar*[87] that a peremptory challenge to remove a juror solely on the basis of gender, ethnic group, or race was unconstitutional, confusion as to what is a valid race-neutral argument still exists in the courts today.[88]

The case of *Snyder v. Louisiana*[89] is the newest case that tackles the issue of peremptory challenges and striking of jurors and the offering of "racially neutral" explanations. The prosecutor in this case, whose self-proclaimed specialty was securing the death penalty for murderers, told reporters that this was, his "O.J. Simpson case."[90] Even more of an issue is that he did not limit these comments to reporters but commented on this to the all-white jury that they should not let this defendant "get away with it" like O.J. This, when coupled with the fact that the prosecutor struck all prospective black jurors, was enough to raise the question of whether the prosecutor was purposely discriminatory.

One example given by the defense attorney for Snyder during oral arguments before the Supreme Court was a black college student. The student was in the middle of student teaching and concerned that the trial would interfere with him completing his teaching duties. The court clerk contacted the dean who said that serving on the jury would not be a problem. The student said he was "OK" with the dean's comments and would be fine with serving on the jury. A white juror expressed concern that as a contractor he would not be able to finish promised work and that his wife, who had just had surgery, would need help at home with their two children. The prosecutor moved successfully to strike the black juror but raised no objections to the white contractor. The defense attorney for Snyder believed that when a black juror's circumstances are almost identical to a white juror's circumstances and only the black juror is excluded, it is difficult to rule out race as a motivation.[91] The decision by the Supreme Court in *Snyder v. Louisiana*[92] focused mainly on the prosecutor's decision to strike this particular black college student, Mr. Brooks. He was one of 50 individuals who expressed concern about missing work and then expressed willingness to serve once permission or exception was granted by a superior. The Supreme Court also examined the prosecutor's explanation that Mr. Brooks appeared "nervous." Because the trial judge did not make note of Brooks' demeanor, the Court could not assume that Mr. Brooks was any more nervous than most prospective jurors. The decision by the Supreme Court reaffirms the importance of *Batson v. Kentucky*[93] and the role that race might play in jury selection.

Peremptory challenges carry a great potential for misuse.[94] The judicial system should take every precaution to ensure that they are carried out within the boundaries set forth by the Constitution.[95] The vast corruption in the jury process makes systematic changes necessary.[96] The cliché, "if it looks like a duck, and walks like a duck and talks like a duck . . . then it must be a duck" would apply to racial discrimination in jury selection. The judicial system is so deeply saturated with procedural issues that it fails to examine unfairness that is obvious even to laypeople. The decisions by the Supreme Court have undoubtedly played a role in America's response to racial discrimination and its effect on the death penalty.

The inappropriate use of peremptory challenges was commented on in *Batson v. Kentucky* by Justice Marshall, who stated, "misuse of the peremptory challenge to exclude black jurors has become both common and flagrant."[97] *Batson v. Kentucky* (1986) provided that prosecutors must prove that their exclusions were not racially motivated, *Purkett v. Elem* allowed for a racially neutral explanation to stand regardless of its frivolity. Would changes to the use of peremptory challenges help to alleviate claims of racial prejudice? It might be possible to limit the number of strikes allowed to each side. Because the demise of the peremptory challenge is unlikely, the role of racial bias in jury selection will continue to be an issue.

VI.   In Summary, What Do these Cases Say?

The Supreme Court began examining racial bias in the death penalty with *Furman v. Georgia* (1972),[98] in which they found the Georgia statute to be biased against racial minorities, particularly blacks. In *Furman*, the Court declared the death penalty unconstitutional but believed that it could be reinstated if the statutes were changed to ensure safeguards that would protect defendants from racial prejudice. After its reinstatement in 1976, the Court once again wrestled with issues of racial discrimination in *McCleskey v. Kemp* (1987).[99] McCleskey sought to use statistics to prove that racial discrimination existed in Georgia's administration of the death penalty. The Court said that general statistics could not show discrimination in particular cases and that defendants must prove that prosecutors and jurors acted discriminatorily, specifically in their case. Just one year before *McCleskey v. Kemp* was decided, the Court decided in *Turner v. Murray* (1986)[100] that defendants had the right to tell jurors in the jury pool the race of their victims to see whether this would prejudice the veniremen against the defendant. Death penalty opponents were struck another blow when the Supreme Court decided *Purkett v. Elem* (1995).[101] In *Purkett*, the Court concluded that if prosecutors offered race-neutral explanations for minority juror exclusion, prosecutors could not be considered as acting in a racially discriminatory manner. This was problematic, because any racially neutral explanation could be offered, regardless of its credibility or truth. The most recent development in racial discrimination jurisprudence was the decision in *Miller-El v. Dretke* (2005),[102] in which the Supreme Court decided that racially disparate questioning and jury shuffling could not be used to exclude minority jurors and that a Certificate of Eligibility (COE) should have been granted. The Louisiana Supreme Court upheld the lower court's ruling that the peremptory challenges made by the prosecutor did not constitute racial discrimination. The Supreme Court reversed the state supreme court's decision finding that the prosecutor in the case did engage in purposeful discrimination. This decision could potentially re-clarify for prosecutors and defendants alike the necessary protections against racial discrimination in jury selection in light of *Batson* and *Miller-El*.

The above cases paint an erratic picture. The Supreme Court, while making decisions to disallow racial discrimination, has also seemingly made it easy for prosecutors and other players in the court process to discriminate, as long as it is explained.

VII.   Conclusion

Literature is a way in which one can express views that may not be popular at the time but become accepted as philosophies and societies evolve. In *To Kill a Mockingbird*, Harper Lee declared, "In our courts, when it's a white man's word against a black man's the white man always wins. They're ugly but those are the facts of life. The one place where a man ought to get a square deal is a courtroom, be he any color of the rainbow, but people have a way of carrying their resentments right into a jury box."[103] As noted in the court cases, racial discrimination and bias still exist in decisions about the death penalty, whether subtle or blatant. *Turner v. Murray* (1986) gave defendants the right to bring the issue of potential bias to the jury on the issue of the victim's race. One year later, death penalty opponents were dealt a major setback when the Supreme Court ruled in *McCleskey v. Kemp*[104] that general statistics do not in themselves establish unconstitutional discrimination in individual cases. There is still no definitive answer as to how racial bias can be eradicated in capital proceedings. With human beings involved in every phase of the criminal justice system, it is perhaps naive to think that discrimination can be eliminated in death penalty cases where bias-free proceedings should be the constitutional norm.

Cases Briefed in Chapter 3

Case	Issue	Holding
Batson v. Kentucky 476 US 79 (1986)	Does the equal protection clause forbid the use of peremptory challenges based solely on race?	It is unconstitutional to use peremptory challenges on the basis of race.
McClesky v. Kemp 481 U.S. 279 (1987)	Does a statistical study showing racial disparity in death penalty cases establish an individual's claim of racial bias as a violation of the Eighth and Fourteenth Amendment of the Constitution?	Statistical studies that show racial prejudice in capital proceedings do not indicate constitutional violations because they fail to prove that the decision makers in a particular case acted with racial prejudice.
Turner v. Murray 476 US 28 (1986)	Does a defendant have the right to inform the jury that he or she is accused of an inter-racial capital crime and to question jurors on their racial bias?	A defendant accused of an inter-racial capital crime is entitled to have prospective jurors informed of the victim's race and questioned on the issue of racial bias.
Miller-El v. Dretke 545 U.S. 231 (2005)	Is the use of racially disparate questioning in jury selection a violation of the Equal Protection Clause of the 14th Amendment?	It is a violation of the Constitution to use racially disparate questioning to exclude prospective jurors in a capital proceeding.
Snyder v. Louisiana 552 U.S. ___ (2008)	Did the state's exclusion of all black prospective jurors through the use of peremptory challenges, coupled with the prosecutor's reference to the O.J. Simpson case, constitute a violation of the Equal Protection Clause of the 14th Amendment?	It is a violation of the equal protection clause to strike all black jurors if no substantiated racially neutral explanations are offered.

Case Briefs

Batson v. Kentucky
476 U.S. 79 (1986)

CAPSULE: Excluding members of the defendant's race from a jury solely on racial grounds violates the equal protection rights of both the defendant and the excluded jurors.

FACTS: Batson was brought to trial on charges of second-degree burglary and receipt of stolen goods. During voir dire the prosecutor utilized peremptory strikes to exclude all four black individuals in the jury pool. The jury that was selected was comprised only of white individuals. Counsel for the defendant moved to strike the jury before it was sworn in because the removal of all of the black veniremen was a violation of the Sixth Amendment right to a jury of one's peers, and a Fourteenth Amendment violation of equal protection. The trial judge ruled that peremptory challenges could be utilized to "strike anybody they wanted to," reasoning that the cross section of the community component of the Sixth Amendment only applied to the venire and not the actual jury itself.

ISSUE: Does the equal protection clause forbid the use of peremptory challenges based solely on race? YES.

HOLDING: It is unconstitutional to use peremptory challenges to exclude potential jurors on the basis of race.

REASON: "A defendant has no right to a petit jury composed in whole or in part of persons of his own race. *Strauder v. West Virginia*, 100 U.S. 303, 305. However, the Equal Protection Clause guarantees the defendant that the State will not exclude members of his race from the jury venire on account of race, or on the false assumption that members of his race as a group are not qualified to serve as jurors. By denying a person participation in jury service on account of his race, the State also unconstitutionally discriminates against the excluded juror. Moreover, selection procedures that purposefully exclude black persons from juries undermine public confidence in the fairness of our system of justice."

"The same equal protection principles as are applied to determine whether there is discrimination in selecting the venire also govern the State's use of peremptory challenges to strike individual jurors from the petit jury. Although a prosecutor ordinarily is entitled to exercise peremptory challenges for any reason, as long as that reason is related to his view concerning the outcome of the case to be tried, the Equal Protection Clause forbids the prosecutor to challenge potential jurors solely on account of their race or on the assumption that black jurors as a group will be unable impartially to consider the State's case against a black defendant."

"A defendant may establish a prima facie case of purposeful discrimination solely on evidence concerning the prosecutor's exercise of peremptory challenges at the defendant's trial. The defendant first must show that he is a member of a cognizable racial group, and that the prosecutor has exercised peremptory challenges to remove from the venire members of the defendant's race. The defendant may also rely on the fact that peremptory challenges constitute a jury selection practice that permits those to discriminate who are of a mind to discriminate. Finally, the defendant must show that such facts and any other relevant circumstances raise an inference that the prosecutor used peremptory challenges to exclude the veniremen from the petit jury on account of their race. Once the defendant makes a prima facie showing, the burden shifts to the State to come forward with a neutral explanation for challenging black jurors. The prosecutor may not rebut a prima facie showing by stating that he challenged the jurors on the assumption that they would be partial to the defendant because of their shared race or by affirming his good faith in individual selections."

CASE SIGNIFICANCE: *Batson v. Kentucky* re-established the principle that peremptory strikes cannot be based solely upon the race or racial assumptions. The Court extended the *Swain v. Alabama* (1965)[105] decision in that once the prima facie case of racial discrimination has been made, the burden of proof is no longer on the defendant to establish that the elimination of blacks was part of an established pattern of discrimination. The Court, however, in *Purkett v. Elem* (1995)[106] noted that *Batson* required only that the prosecutor provide a race-neutral justification for the exclusion, not that the justification is plausible. In *Batson* the Court outlined three steps that courts must follow in resolving cases of peremptory jury disqualification based on race:

1. The side making the allegations must establish a prima facie (at first sight) case of discrimination based on race or other forbidden grounds.

2. If step 1 is established, then the burden shifts to the side that made the peremptory strike to come up with a race-neutral explanation for the strike.

3. The trial court is then required to decide whether the side opposing the peremptory challenges has proved purposeful discrimination.

McCleskey v. Kemp
481 U.S. 279 (1987)

CAPSULE: Statistical studies that indicate racial bias in capital sentencing do not violate the Eighth and Fourteenth Amendments. What is needed is proof of racial bias in that defendant's case.

FACTS: McCleskey, who was black, was sentenced to death for the murder of a white police officer that occurred during the commission of a robbery. McCleskey challenged the death sentence as a violation of the equal protection clause of the Fourteenth Amendment, and claimed that it was a cruel and unusual sentence under the Eighth Amendment. McCleskey used the "Baldus Study," which claimed to show that racial disparity existed in the imposition of death sentences in Georgia. The study shows that black defendants who are accused of killing white victims have the highest likelihood of receiving the death penalty.

ISSUE: Does a statistical study showing racial disparity in death penalty cases establish an individual's claim of racial bias as a violation of the Eighth and Fourteenth Amendments to the Constitution? NO.

HOLDING: Statistical studies that show racial prejudice in capital proceedings do not indicate constitutional violations because they fail to prove that the decision makers in a particular case acted with racial prejudice.

REASON: "McCleskey's first claim is that the Georgia capital punishment statute violates the Equal Protection Clause of the Fourteenth Amendment. He argues that race has infected the administration of Georgia's statute in two ways: persons who murder whites are more likely to be sentenced to death than persons who murder blacks, and black murderers are more likely to be sentenced to death than white murderers. As a black defendant who killed a white victim, McCleskey claims that the Baldus study demonstrates that he was discriminated against because of his race and because of the race of his victim. In its broadest form, McCleskey's claim of discrimination extends to every actor in the Georgia capital sentencing process, from the prosecutor who sought the death penalty and the jury that imposed the sentence, to the State itself that enacted the capital punishment statute and allows it to remain in effect despite its allegedly discriminatory application. We agree with the Court of Appeals, and every other court that has considered such a challenge, that this claim must fail."

"McCleskey also suggests that the Baldus study proves that the State as a whole has acted with a discriminatory purpose. He appears to argue that the State has violated the Equal Protection Clause by adopting the capital punishment statute and allowing it to remain in force despite its allegedly discriminatory application. But "'[d]iscriminatory purpose' . . . implies more than intent as volition or intent as awareness of consequences. It implies that the decisionmaker, in this case a state legislature, selected or reaffirmed a particular course of action at least in part 'because of,' not merely 'in spite of,' its adverse effects upon an identifiable group." To evaluate McCleskey's challenge, we must examine exactly what the Baldus study may show. Even Professor Baldus does not contend that his statistics prove that race enters into any capital sentencing decisions or that race was a factor in McCleskey's particular case. Statistics at most may show only a likelihood that a particular factor entered into some decisions. There is, of course, some risk of racial prejudice influencing a jury's decision in a criminal case. There are similar risks that other kinds of prejudice will influence other criminal trials. See *infra*, at 315–318. The question "is at what point that risk becomes constitutionally unacceptable," *Turner v. Murray*, 476 U.S. 28, 36 (1986). McCleskey asks us to accept the likelihood allegedly shown by the Baldus study as the constitutional measure of an unacceptable risk of racial prejudice influencing capital sentencing decisions. This we decline to do.

"Because of the risk that the factor of race may enter the criminal justice process, we have engaged in 'unceasing efforts' to eradicate racial prejudice from our criminal justice system. *Batson v. Kentucky*, 476 U.S. 79, 85 (1986). Our efforts have been guided by our recognition that "the inestimable privilege of trial by jury . . . is a vital principle, underlying the whole administration of criminal justice."

CASE SIGNIFICANCE: This case declares that in death penalty cases, statistical studies showing discrimination in the imposition of the penalty do not in themselves prove that the state has violated the equal protection clause of the Constitution. In order for a claim of discrimination to succeed, 'petitioner must prove that decision makers in his case acted with discriminatory purpose.' It is not enough to allege and prove through statistical study that a particular race has been discriminated against (as established by the Baldus study); the person alleging discrimination must prove that there was discrimination in his or her particular case."[107]

The Court said that discretion is essential in criminal justice and that "exceptionally clear proof is required before this Court will infer that the discretion has been abused." That was not proved in this case. All that the defendant proved was that there was discrimination against blacks in the imposition of the death penalty in Georgia, not that discretion was clearly abused. The Court added that the defendant's claim, taken to its logical conclusion, "throws into serious question the principles that underlie the entire criminal justice system." Were the defendants to prevail, his claim could be extended "to apply to other types of penalties and to claims based on unexplained discrepancies correlating to membership in other minority groups and even to gender." Absolute equality in sentences is not required by the Constitution. What the Constitution prohibits is abuse of discretion that amounts to a violation of the equal protection clause.[108]

Turner v. Murray
476 U.S. 28 (1986)

CAPSULE: A defendant accused of an interracial capital crime is entitled to have prospective jurors informed of the victim's race and questioned on the issue of racial bias.

FACTS: Turner, who was black, shot and killed a white jewelry store proprietor with a sawed-off shotgun during the robbery of the jewelry store. During voir dire of the jury, Turner's counsel requested that the prospective jurors be told that Turner was black and that his victim was white and be asked if this would prejudice them against Turner. This request was denied by the judge. The jury, which consisted of eight whites and four blacks, sentenced Turner to death.

ISSUE: Does a defendant have the right to inform the jury that he or she is accused of an interracial capital crime and to question jurors on their racial bias? YES.

HOLDING: A defendant accused of an interracial capital crime is entitled to have prospective jurors informed of the victim's race and questioned on the issue of racial bias.

REASON: "Because of the range of discretion entrusted to a jury in a capital sentencing hearing, there is a unique opportunity for racial prejudice to operate but remain undetected. On the facts of this case, a juror who believes that blacks are violence prone or morally inferior might well be influenced by that belief in deciding whether petitioner's crime involved the aggravating factors specified under Virginia law. Such a juror might also be less favorably inclined toward petitioner's evidence of mental disturbance as a mitigating circumstance. More subtle, less consciously held racial attitudes could also influence a juror's decision in this case. Fear of blacks, which could easily be stirred up by the violent facts of petitioner's crime, might incline a juror to favor the death penalty."

"The risk of racial prejudice infecting a capital sentencing proceeding is especially serious in light of the complete finality of the death sentence. "The Court, as well as the separate opinions of a majority of the individual Justices, has recognized that the qualitative difference of death from all other punishments requires a correspondingly greater degree of scrutiny of the capital sentencing determination." *California v. Ramos*, 463 U.S. 992, 998–999 (1983). We have struck down capital sentences when we found that the circumstances under which they were imposed "created an unacceptable risk that 'the death penalty [may have been] meted out arbitrarily or capriciously' or through 'whim . . . or mistake.'" *Caldwell, supra*, at 343 (O'Connor, J., concurring in part and concurring in judgment) (citation omitted). In the present case, we find the risk that racial prejudice may have infected petitioner's capital sentencing unacceptable in light of the ease with which that risk could have been minimized. By refusing to question prospective jurors on racial prejudice, the trial judge failed to adequately protect petitioner's constitutional right to an impartial jury."

"The inadequacy of voir dire in this case requires that petitioner's death sentence be vacated. It is not necessary, however, that he be retried on the issue of guilt. Our judgment in this case is that there was an unacceptable risk of racial prejudice infecting the capital sentencing proceeding. This judgment is based on a conjunction of three factors: the fact that the crime charged involved interracial violence, the broad discretion given the jury at the death-penalty hearing, and the special seriousness of the risk of improper sentencing in a capital case."

CASE SIGNIFICANCE: Race affects the thinking of nearly everyone in society. For some, this is neither conscious nor malicious. Justice White explained that three factors—the interracially violent crime, the broad discretion given the jury at the death penalty hearing, and the special seriousness of the risk of improper sentencing in a capital case—make the risk of racial prejudice unacceptable in capital sentencing proceedings. Mock jury studies examining the effects of the defendant's race on jurors' decisions, however, show that the defendant's race affects guilt determinations more often than it affects sentences; it is the subtle, unconscious alteration of judgment, not the conscious desire to injure, that most threatens the fair administration of the criminal justice system. A meta-analysis of experimental studies on racial bias in criminal sentencing found that both the race of the defendant and that of the victim influenced white mock jurors' sentencing decisions across a range of cases, resulting in a pattern that most negatively affects black defendants whose victims are white.[109]

Miller-El v. Dretke
545 U.S. 231 (2005)

CAPSULE: Prosecutors cannot use racially disparate questioning or jury shuffling to exclude minorities from jury service.

FACTS: Dallas County prosecutors used peremptory strikes to exclude 10 of 11 eligible blacks to serve on a capital jury. The petitioner moved that the jury be struck down on the ground that the exclusion violated the equal protection clause. Although the petitioner presented evidence supporting his motion at a pretrial hearing, he was denied relief by the trial judge. The trial judge found no evidence, as required by the controlling precedent in *Swain v. Alabama* (1965),[110] that a systematic exclusion of blacks had occurred. The jury found Miller-El guilty and sentenced him to death. While his appeal was pending, the Supreme Court established a three-part process for evaluating equal protection claims like that of the petitioner in *Batson v. Kentucky* (1986).[111] The Texas Court of Criminal Appeals remanded the case in light of *Batson* and the original trial court reheard the evidence. The trial court believed that the petitioner failed to meet the first step outlined in *Batson* because the evidence did not infer racial motivation by the state's peremptory challenges. The three-step process outlined in *Batson* is:

1. The side making the allegations must establish a prima facie (at first sight) case of discrimination based on race or other forbidden grounds.

2. If step 1 is established, then the burden shifts to the side that made the peremptory strike to come up with a race-neutral explanation for the strike.

3. The trial court is then required to decide whether the side opposing the peremptory challenges has proved purposeful discrimination.

The court also believed that the state did not violate steps two or three because the prosecutors had reasonable race-neutral explanations for excluding the blacks. Miller-El then filed a federal habeas petition after appeals and state habeas petitions were denied.

ISSUE: Is the use of racially disparate questioning in jury selection a violation of the equal protection clause of the Fourteenth Amendment? YES.

HOLDING: It is a violation of the Constitution to use racially disparate questioning to exclude prospective jurors from a capital proceeding.

REASON: "A comparative analysis of the venire members demonstrates that African-Americans were excluded from petitioner's jury in a ratio significantly higher than Caucasians were. Of the 108 possible jurors reviewed by the prosecution and defense, 20 were African-American. Nine of them were excused for cause or by agreement of the parties. Of the 11 African-American jurors remaining, however, all but one were excluded by peremptory strikes exercised by the prosecutors. On this basis, 91% of the eligible black jurors were removed by peremptory strikes. In contrast, the prosecutors used their peremptory strikes against just 13% (4 out of 31) of the eligible non-black prospective jurors qualified to serve on petitioner's jury. These numbers, while relevant, are not petitioner's whole case. During voir dire, the prosecution questioned venire members as to their views concerning the death penalty and their willingness to serve on a capital case. Responses that disclosed reluctance or hesitation to impose capital punishment were cited as a justification for striking a potential juror for cause or by peremptory challenge. *Wainwright v. Witt*, 469 U.S. 412 (1985). The evidence suggests, however, that the manner in which members of the venire were questioned varied by race. To the extent a divergence in responses can be attributed to the racially disparate mode of examination, it is relevant to our inquiry."

"In this case, three of the State's proffered race-neutral rationales for striking African-American jurors pertained just as well to some white jurors who were not challenged and who did serve on the jury. The prosecutors explained that their peremptory challenges against six African-American potential jurors were based on ambivalence about the death penalty; hesitancy to vote to execute defendants capable of being rehabilitated; and the jurors' own family history of criminality. In rebuttal of the prosecution's explanation, petitioner identified two empaneled white jurors who expressed ambivalence about the death penalty in a manner similar to their African-American counterparts who were the subject of prosecutorial peremptory challenges. One indicated that capital punishment was not appropriate for a first offense, and another stated that it would be "difficult" to impose a death sentence. Similarly, two white jurors expressed hesitation in sentencing to death a defendant who might be rehabilitated; and four white jurors had family members with criminal histories. As a consequence, even though the prosecution's reasons for striking African-American members of the venire appear race-neutral, the application of these rationales to the venire might have been selective and based on racial considerations. Whether a comparative juror analysis would demonstrate the prosecutors' rationales to have been pretexts for discrimination is an unnecessary determination at this stage, but the evidence does make debatable the District Court's conclusion that no purposeful discrimination occurred."

CASE SIGNIFICANCE: Race seemed to be a historical motivator in the Dallas County prosecutor's office and continued in the *Miller-El* case. In *Brown v. State* (2002),[112] a prosecutor who offered justifications for excluding a particular black individual while on its face seemed plausible, upon further inspection the Georgia Court of Appeals found that the explanations were not race-neutral and constituted a *Batson* violation. In *Batson*, the Court held that to exclude members of the defendant's race from a jury solely on racial grounds violates the equal protection rights of both the defendant and the excluded jurors. In *Hernandez* and *Purkett*, even after the prosecutor offers a race-neutral explanation, the trial court may find a *Batson* violation, if the explanation is pretextual. In *Minnesota v. McRae* (1992),[113] the prosecutor questioned and struck down the only black member of the venire. She was struck down due to her views that the judicial system had been historically unfair to minorities. The Minnesota Supreme Court found this to be a *Batson* violation because the race of the juror was given relevant consideration. Should jurors be excluded purely on their belief that the system has been unfair to minorities? This question may soon be before the Court. Recently, in *Rico v. Leftridge-Byrd* (2003),[114] the Third Circuit Court of Appeals ruled that *Batson* applies to Italian-Americans. Jurors in the case were stricken from the jury due to their Italian surnames. To extend *Batson* beyond the scope of blacks could prove to be difficult, as ethnicity is difficult to define. The Court decided in *United States v. Martinez-Salazar* (2000)[115] that a peremptory challenge to remove a juror solely on the basis of gender, ethnic group, or race was unconstitutional. The Supreme Court stated that obvious racial prejudice in jury selection through ostensibly "racially neutral" means was still in fact racial discrimination.

Snyder v. Louisiana
552 U.S. ___ (2008)

CAPSULE: It is a violation of the equal protection clause of the Fourteenth Amendment to strike black jurors without substantiated racially neutral reasons that apply equally to jurors of all races.

FACTS: In 1996, Snyder was indicted in Jefferson Parish for first-degree murder of his estraged wife's companion Howard Wilson in which he inflicted nine knife wounds. During *voir dire*, the prosecution used peremptory challenges to eliminate all five black prospective jurors. The defendant charged that the State had exercised its peremptory challenges against black jurors in a racially discriminatory manner violating *Batson v. Kentucky* (1986). In his closing argument, the prosecutor, having struck from the panel all the potential black jurors, compared the defendant, a black man charged with stabbing his wife to death, to O.J. Simpson and told the all-white jury that Mr. Simpson, acquitted of murder 10 months earlier, had "got away with it." Snyder's *Batson* claim was denied by the trial court and the defendant, who was black, was tried by an all-white jury and sentenced to death. The decision of the trial court was affirmed by the Louisiana Supreme Court, stating that the trial court had not abused its discretion or erred in denying Snyder's *Batson* claim. Snyder filed a writ of certiorari to the Supreme Court in which they vacated the judgment of the Louisiana Supreme Court and remanded the case for further consideration in light of the decision in *Miller-El v. Dretke* (2005). The Louisiana Supreme Court again upheld the conviction of Snyder, holding that the trial court did not err in denying Snyder's *Batson* claim. The Supreme Court agreed to hear the case.

ISSUE: Did the state's exclusion of all black prospective jurors through the use of peremptory challenges, coupled with the prosecutor's reference to the O.J. Simpson case, constitute a violation of the equal protection clause of the Fourteenth Amendment? YES.

HOLDING: It is a violation of the equal protection clause to strike all black jurors if no substantiated racially neutral explanations are offered.

REASON: The Supreme Court held that both of the two arguments for challenging prospective juror Brooks, a black college student, were not racially neutral when taken in light of the white jurors who were not challenged. The prosecutor contended that Mr. Brooks was "nervous," although there was no record of the trial judge believing him to be overly nervous. Because the trial judge gave no reason for upholding the prosecutor's challenge of Mr. Brooks, the Supreme Court believed they could not presume that the trial judge perceived him as more nervous or uncharacteristically nervous. The prosecutor also stated that he believed Mr. Brooks would be motivated to have a quick trial as to not miss his student teaching obligations and therefore would be easily swayed by the majority so as to obtain a quick verdict. The Supreme Court noted that the prosecutor himself believed that the trial would be brief. The Supreme Court found the prosecutor's argument to be faulty especially when considering that Mr. Brooks appeared more than willing to serve once his Dean assured him he would be able to make up his student teaching. Peremptory strikes that are shown to have been motivated by discrimination should not and must not be sustained.

CASE SIGNIFICANCE: The case reiterates the confusion over the issue of race and peremptory challenges. The Louisana Supreme Court relied heavily upon the three-part *Batson* test outlined by the Supreme Court:

> A defendant's *Batson* challenge to a peremptory strike requires a three-step inquiry. First, the trial court must determine whether the defendant has made a prima facie showing that the prosecutor exercised a peremptory challenge on the basis of race. Second, if the showing is made, the burden shifts to the prosecutor to present a race-neutral explanation for striking the juror in question. Although the prosecutor must present a comprehensible reason, the second step of this process does not demand an explanation that is persuasive, or even plausible; so long as the reason is not inherently discriminatory, it suffices. Third, the court must then determine whether the defendant has carried his burden of proving purposeful discrimination. This final step involves evaluating the persuasiveness of the justification proffered by the prosecutor, but the ultimate burden of persuasion regarding racial motivation rests with, and never shifts from, the opponent of the strike. [Internal quotations and citations omitted.]

The Supreme Court found that the trial court was in error in denying Snyder's *Batson* claim and should not have sustained the peremptory chellenges of the prosecutor.

Internet Resources

The Death Penalty in Black and White: Who Lives, Who Dies, Who Decides?
http://www.deathpenaltyinfo.org/article.php?scid=45&did=539

Challenging Racial Discrimination in Capital Cases
www.criminaljustice.org/CHAMPION/ARTICLES/97jan01.htm

United States of America: Death by Discrimination—The Continuing Role of Race in Capital Cases
http://web.amnesty.org/library/index/engamr510462003

NCADP: Racial Bias in Execution
http://www.ncadp.org/index.cfm?content=19

Explaining Death Row's Population and Racial Composition
www.prisonsucks.com/scans/aclu_dp_factsheet4.pdf

Notes

1. *Furman v. Georgia*, 408 U.S. 238 (1972).

2. 408 U.S. at 257 (Douglas, J., dissenting).

3. *McCleskey v. Kemp*, 481 U.S. 279 (1987).

4. *McCleskey v. Zant*, 580 F. Supp 338 (N.D. Ga. 1984).

5. David C. Baldus, Charles Pulaski, and George Woodworth, *Comparative Review of Death Setences:An Empirical Study of the Georgia Experience*. 74 J. Crim. L. & Criminology, 661–753 (1983).

6. *McCleskey v. Kemp* (quoting H. Kalven and H. Ziesal, The American Jury 498, 1966).

7. *Id.* at 46.

8. Monica Wiley, McCleskey v. Kemp: *Race-conscious Decision Making in Reforming Capital Decision Making*, 3 Howard Scroll: The Social Justice Review 81 (1995).

9. *Id.* at 96.

10. Richard C. Deiter, *Death Penalty in Black and White: Who Lives, Who Dies, Who Decides* (1998), available at: http://www.deathpenaltyinfo.org/racept.html (accessed August 16, 2004).

11. Death Penalty Information Center, Race News and Developments, accessed Feb 5, 2008, at http://www.deathpenaltyinfo.org/article.php?&did=2569.

12. *State v. Marshall*, 613 A.2d 1059 (N.J. 1992).

13. David Baldus, George Woodworth, and Charles Pulaski, *Reflections on the Inevitability of Racial Discrimination in Capital Sentencing and the Impossibility of its Prevention, Detection, and Correction*, 51 WASH. & LEE L. REV. 359 (1994).

14. Amnesty International, http://www.amnestyusa.org/abolish/racialprejudices.html.

15. *Id.*

16. Dave Collins, "Yale Study: Racial Bias, Randomness Mar Conn. Death Penalty Cases," Associated Press, December 12, 2007.

17. Death Penalty Information Center, "Race News and Developments," accessed Feb 5, 2008, at http://www.deathpenaltyinfo.org/article.php?&did=2569.

18. *American Bar Association Pennsylvania Death Penalty Assessment Report*, October 2007.

19. *ABA Death Penalty Moratorium Implementation Project Ohio Death Penalty Assessment Report.*

20. *Id.*

21. Liebman, James, Jeffrey Fagan, and Valerie West (2000). *A Broken System: Error Rates in Capital Cases. 1973–1995.* Columbia University Law School. Public Law Research Paper 15. www2.law.columbia.edu/instructionalservices/liebman.

22. Jacobs, David, Qian Zhenchao, Jason Carmichael, and Stephanie Kent (2007). *Who Survives on Death Row? An Individual and Contextual Analysis*, AMERICAN SOCIOLOGICAL REVIEW 72, 610–632.

23. *Id.*

24. Amnesty International, http://www.amnestyusa.org/abolish/racialprejudices.html.

25. Jeffrey J. Pokorak, *Symposiums: Probing the Prosecutor's Perspective: Race of the Discretionary Actors.* 83 CORNELL L. REV. 1811 (September 1998).

26. Stephen S. Bright, *Discrimination, Death and Denial: The Tolerance of Racial Discrimination in Infliction of the Death Penalty*, 35 SANTA CLARA L. REV. 433 (1995).

27. *Miller-El v. Dretke*, 545 U.S. 231 (2005).

28. *Id.*

29. Bryan A. Stevenson & Ruth E. Friedman, *Deliberate Indifference: Judicial Tolerance of Racial Bias in Criminal Justice*, 51 WASH. & LEE L. REV. 509, 520, 527 n.45 (1994).

30. *Moulton v. State*, 199 Ala. 411 (1917).

31. *Miller v. North Carolina*, 583 F.2d 701 (4th Cir. 1978).

32. *State v. Washington*, 67 So. 930 (La. Sup. Ct. 1915).

33. *Withers v. United States*, 602 F.2d 124 (6th Cir. 1976).

34. *Blair v. Armontrout*, 916 F.2d 1310 (8th Cir. 1990).

35. *United States v. Bass*, 536 U.S.862 (2002).

36. Jessie Larson, Unequal Justice: *The Supreme Court's Failure to Curtail Selective Prosecution for the Death Penalty*, 93 J. CRIM. L. & CRIMINOLOGY 1009 (2003).

37. 992 F.2d 171 (8th Cir. 1993).

38. *Snyder v. Louisiana*, 942 So. 2d 484 (2006)

39. American Bar Association, *Toward a More Just and Effective System of Review in State Death Penalty Cases*, 40 AM. U. L. REV. 1, 79–92 (1990).

40. Marcia Coyle et al., *Fatal Defense: Trial and Error in the Nation's Death Belt*, NAT. L.J., June 11, 1990, at 30.

41. Stephen Bright, *Counsel for the Poor: The Death Sentence Not for The Worst Crime but for The Worst Lawyer*, 103 YALE L.J. 1835 (1994).

42. *Id.*

43. Richard Klein, *The Emperor Gideon Has No Clothes: The Empty Promise of the Constitutional Right to Effective Assistance of Counsel*, 13 HASTINGS CONST. L.Q. 625, 679 (1986).

44. *Id.*

45. *Wade v. Calderon*, 29 F.3d 1342 (1994).

46. *Dobbs v. Zant*, 963 F.2d at 1407 (1991).

47. *Id.*

48. *Supra* note 28 at 1856.

49. Stephen Bright and Patrick Keenan, *Judges and the Politics of Death: Deciding Between the Bill of Rights and the Next Election in Capital Cases*, 75 B.U. L. REV. 759 (1995).

50. *Harris v. Alabama*, 513 U.S. 504 (1995).

51. *Harris v. Alabama*, 513 U.S. 504 (1995) (Stevens, J., dissenting).

52. *Supra* note 37 at 781.

53. John Williams, *Election '94: GOP Gains Majority in State Supreme Court*, HOUSTON CHRON., Nov. 10, 1994, at A29.

54. *Id.*

55. Mark Curriden, *Racism Mars Justice in U.S., Panel Reports*, ATLANTA JOURNAL & CONST., Aug. 11, 1991, at D1.

56. *Supra* note 37 at 780.

57. 488 So. 2d 52 (Fla. 1986).

58. American Bar Association, *Report of Commission on Professionalism*, 112 F.R.D. 243, 293 (1986).

59. *Supra* note 37 at 793.

60. *Ring v. Arizona*, 536 U.S. 584 (2002).

61. *Walton v. Arizona*, 497 U.S. 639 (1990).

62. *Id.* at 710–711, quoting White, *Fact-Finding and the Death Penalty: The Scope of a Capital Defendant's Right to Jury Trial*, 65 NOTRE DAME L. REV. 1, 10–11 (1989).

63. *Apprendi v. New Jersey*, 530 U. S. 466 (2000).

64. *Id.* at 498.

65. 100 U.S. 303 (1880).

66. SAMUEL WALKER, CASSIA SPOHN, AND MIRIAM DeLONE, THE COLOR OF JUSTICE (3d ed. 2004).

67. *Id.*

68. DAVID COLE, NO EQUAL JUSTICE: RACE AND CLASS IN THE AMERICAN CRIMINAL JUSTICE SYSTEM (1999) at 103.

69. 476 U.S. 79 (1986).

70. *Swain v. Alabama*, 380 U.S. 202 (1965).

71. 514 U.S. 765 (1995).

72. *Purkett v. Elem*, 514 U.S. 765 (1995).

73. *Purkett v. Elem*, 514 U.S. 765 (1995) (Stevens, J., dissenting).

74. Michael Higgins, *Few Are Chosen*, A.B.A.J. 50 (1999).

75. *Supra* note 30 at 1840.

76. 136 F.3d 1092 (1998).

77. *Former Philadelphia Prosecutor Accused of Racial Bias in Election Year*, NEW YORK TIMES (April 3, 1997:B19).

78. 545 U.S. 231 (U.S. 2005).

79. 380 U.S. 202 (1965).

80. 469 U.S. 412 (1985).

81. 450 S.W.2d 858 (Tex. Crim. App. 1970).

82. *Batson v. Kentucky*, 476 U.S. at 93.

83. 494 N.W.2d. 252 (1992).

84. 340 F.3d 178 (3d Cir. 2003).

85. Shannon Duffy, *Extension of* Batson *Valid Approach*, 229 THE LEGAL INTELLIGENCER 1 (2003).

86. *Id.* at 2.

87. 528 U.S. 304 (2000).

88. Shannon Duffy, *Extension of* Batson *to Whites is Valid*, NEW JERSEY L.J. (August 15, 2003).

89. *Snyder v. Louisiana*, 552 U.S. ___ (2008).

90. Robert Barnes, *Blacks Were Improperly Kept Off La. Jury.* THE WASHINGTON POST, Thursday, March 20, 2008:A3.

91. Lyle Denniston, *Commentary: Trial Judges on Trial?* Tuesday, December 4th, 2007, accessed Feb 4, 2008 at http://www.scotusblog.com/wp/uncategorized/commentary-trial-judges-on-trial.

92. Snyder v. Louisiana, *supra.*

93. *Batson v. Kentucky*, 476 US 79 (1986).

94. Cherie Song, *A Twist on the* 'Batson' *Jury Rule*, NAT'L L.J. Vol. 25, No. 44:7 (2003).

95. 28 U.S.C.A. § 1411.

96. *Supra* note 12.

97. *Batson v. Kentucky*, 476 U.S. 79 (1986) (Marshall, J., concurring).

98. *Furman v. Georgia*, 408 U.S. 238 (1972).

99. *McCleskey v. Kemp*, 481 U.S. 279 (1987).

100. *Turner v. Murray*, 476 U.S. 28 (1986).

101. 514 U.S. 765 (1995).

102. 545 U.S. 231 (2005),

103. HARPER LEE, TO KILL A MOCKINGBIRD (1960) at 220.

104. 481 U.S. 279 (1987).

105. *Swain v. Alabama*, 380 U.S. 202 (1965).

106. *Purkett v. Elem*, 514 U.S. 765 (1995).

107. ROLANDO DEL CARMEN ET AL., BRIEFS OF LEADING CASES IN CORRECTIONS (4th ed. 2005) p. 217.

108. *Id.*

109. Laura T. Sweeney and Craig Haney, *The Influence of Race on Sentencing: A Meta-Analytic Review of Experimental Studies*, 10 BEHAV. SCI. & L. 179 (1992).

110. *Swain v. Alabama*, 380 U.S. 202 (1965).

111. *Batson v. Kentucky*, 476 U.S. 79 (1986).

112. *Brown v. State*, 568 S.E.2d 62 (Ga. App. 2002).

113. *Minnesota v. McRae*, 494 N.W.2d 252 (1992).

114. *Rico v. Leftridge-Byrd*, 340 F.3d 178 (3d Cir. 2003).

115. *United States v. Martinez-Salazar*, 528 U.S. 304 (2000).

Chapter Outline

I. **Introduction**

II. **Supreme Court Cases: Past and Present**
   A. A Starting Point: *Penry v. Lynaugh* (1989)
   B. Executing the Mentally Retarded Is Now Unconstitutional: *Atkins v. Virginia*
   C. Cases after *Atkins*

III. **Emerging Issues**
   A. Definition of Mental Retardation
   B. The Fear of "Faking"
   C. Mental Retardation versus Mental Illness
   D. What Is to Be Done with the Mentally Retarded Now on Death Row?

IV. **Insanity and the Death Penalty**
   A. Insanity: Different From Other Mental Impairments
   B. Reasons for Not Executing the Insane
      1. Failure to Achieve Penological Goals
         a. Deterrence
         b. Retribution
      2. Theological
      3. Humanity
   C. Mental Competence and the Death Penalty.

V. **In Summary, What Do these Cases Say?**

VI. **Conclusion**

Cases Briefed in Chapter 4

Case Briefs
   Ford v. Wainwright, 477 U.S. 399 (1986)
   Penry v. Lynaugh, 492 U.S. 302 (1989)
   Atkins v. Virginia, 536 U.S. 304 (2002)
   Singleton v. Norris, 319 F.3d 1018 (2003)
   Tennard v. Dretke, 542 US 274 (2004)
   Panetti v. Quarterman, 551 U.S. ___ (2007)

Internet Resources

Notes

Chapter 4

The Mentally Impaired and the Death Penalty

I. Introduction

The Supreme Court of the United States has struggled with issues that have surrounded the death penalty since its reinstatement in 1976. Laws of various states provide that some offenders should receive special treatment due to special circumstances, including age at the time of offense and the lack of mental capacity to understand and comprehend the crime that was committed. This special treatment poses legal questions: Do certain classes or categories of persons deserve to be treated differently when considering the death penalty as punishment? Should those who suffer from mental retardation be exempted from death as punishment and, if so, what tests should be used to determine whether an individual is mentally retarded? Should those who suffer from psychiatric disorders or mental illness but who are not insane also be treated differently? This chapter examines the issues and significant cases that address mental impairment in relation to the death penalty in the United States.

II. Supreme Court Cases: Past and Present

A. *A Starting Point:* Penry v. Lynaugh *(1989)*

In *Penry v. Lynaugh* the Supreme Court was asked to decide whether the execution of the mentally retarded was a violation of the Eighth Amendment's ban on cruel and unusual punishment. The Court concluded that it was not a violation of the Eighth Amendment because at the time there was no national consensus against executing mentally retarded individuals. The majority believed that if more state legislatures banned the execution of the mentally retarded it might offend the "evolving standards of decency," making the execution of mentally retarded individuals unconstitutional. In *Penry* the Court stated that mental retardation was an issue that should be raised as a mitigating factor but should not automatically exclude someone from facing a death sentence. Mitigating factors are those presented by the defendant to show a lessened state of culpability or harmful intent. The Court noted in *Penry* that juries should consider the testimony of experts about mental retardation as a crucial component to a "reasoned moral response" about whether to impose the death penalty.[2]

At the time of the *Penry* decision, the American Association of Mental Retardation (AAMR) concluded that mentally retarded individuals have deficits in cognition and moral reasoning that prevented them from having the level of blame needed to impose capital punishment.[3] The Supreme Court has recently overturned its decision in *Penry*. It now contends that it is unconstitutional to execute the mentally retarded. What made the Court change its mind? This is explained in *Atkins v. Virginia* (2002).[4]

B. Executing the Mentally Retarded Is Now Unconstitutional: Atkins v. Virginia

More than a decade after *Penry*, the Court agreed to hear the *Atkins* case and thus re-examine the *Penry* decision. After 1989, many state legislatures debated the issue and passed statutes prohibiting the execution of mentally retarded offenders. The Court thought it was time to revisit the issue and determine whether times had indeed changed. The Court concluded that they had, and reversed the *Penry* decision. Voting five to four, the Court said: "Our independent evaluation of the issue reveals no reason to disagree with the judgment of 'the legislatures that have recently addressed the matter' and concluded that death is not a suitable punishment for a mentally retarded criminal. We are not persuaded that the execution of mentally retarded criminals will measurably advance the deterrent or the retributive purpose of the death penalty. Construing and applying the Eighth Amendment in the light of our 'evolving standards of decency,' we therefore conclude that such punishment is excessive and that the Constitution 'places a substantive restriction on the State's power to take the life' of a mentally retarded offender."[5]

Daryl Atkins was convicted of capital murder and related crimes by a Virginia jury and sentenced to death. Affirming, the Virginia Supreme Court relied on *Penry v. Lynaugh* in rejecting Atkins' contention that he could not be sentenced to death because he is mentally retarded. The Court decision in *Atkins* is not surprising when examined against the backdrop of "evolving standards of decency" first enunciated in *Trop v. Dulles* (1958).[6] The Court concluded that the national consensus against the death penalty for the mentally retarded that was absent in *Penry* in 1989 had in fact become a reality in 2002. Times had indeed changed.

Retribution is something done to an offender as punishment or vengeance for a crime or act that he or she has committed ("just deserts"). The Court concluded that retribution is not served when imposing capital punishment on the mentally retarded, adding that if the offender is not fully aware of the severity of the offense, the purposes of retribution would not be served.[7] The Court also observed that the execution of the mentally retarded did not serve as a deterrent to further offenses because the mentally retarded offender is not capable of the level of logical reasoning assumed in deterrence theory. Moreover, exempting the mentally retarded offender from capital punishment does not lessen the potential of capital punishment to deter offenders who are fully able to understand the seriousness of their criminal behavior.

The decision in *Atkins* has left many questions unanswered. Because it is now unconstitutional to execute mentally retarded offenders, what definition of mental retardation will be used? Will all offenders who suffer from mental retardation be exempted regardless of the degree or severity of the retardation? Will the capital punishment of mentally retarded inmates who are currently on death row be commuted to life? Will the courts be flooded with petitions from defendants claiming mental retardation? Will "expert" testimony on mental retardation have limitations, and what qualifications will be used to classify someone as an expert qualified to diagnose mental retardation? These questions are addressed in a later portion of this chapter.

C. *Cases after* Atkins

Three major related cases have emerged since the ruling of *Atkins* in 2002. In 2003, the Eighth Circuit ruled in *Singleton v. Norris* that it was not a violation of the Eighth Amendment to execute an individual who became incompetent while on death row and was rendered competent through forced medication. The case points to state interests and whether the state is willing to forcefully medicate solely for the purpose of rendering the offender competent to be executed. The Eighth Circuit relied on a rationale that states would have more important reasons to forcefully medicate for competency beyond that of an impending death sentence. If the state deemed the forced medication to be in the inmate's best medical interests, additonal motives, including execution, are not important. It could be maintained that ulterior motives by the state should be considered when forcing an individual to take medication that will ultimately lead to their death. Of particular interest in the *Singleton* decision is the fact that Singleton was diagnosed with schizophrenia while on death row. This distinction is important when coupled with the decision made in *Panetti v. Quarterman* in 2007 (discussed below).

In 2004, *Tennard v. Dretke*[8] was decided, in which it was concluded that jurors must be allowed to consider mental retardation as a mitigating factor, particularly when life and death are at stake. Jurors in the case were not asked to consider this at sentencing and were instead asked the two "special issue" questions that were in current use in Texas to determine whether someone was deserving of a death sentence, which were:

1. Was the conduct of the defendant that caused the death of the deceased committed deliberately and with reasonable expectation that death of the deceased or another would result? (known as the "deliberateness special issue")

2. Is there a probablility that the defendant would commit criminal acts of violence that would constitute a continuing threat to society? (known as the "future dangerousness special issue")

These two questions were both affirmed by the jury and Tennard received a death sentence. At issue in the case was Tennard's IQ of 67, which was evidence of significantly impaired functioning. The Court believed that such impaired functioning warranted consideration by a jury and might also be a basis for a sentence less than death. The Decision in *Tennard* once again points to the unwillingness of courts to instruct jurors to consider mental impairment as a mitigating factor in the sentencing phase of capital trials. The Court's decision reaffirms the importance of weighing mental and developmental disabilities in capital proceedings, upholding the tradition that "death is different."

Mental competence was again considered by the Court in *Panetti v. Quarterman*.[9] At issue in *Panetti* was the difference between an inmate being "aware" of a state's rationale for execution and "understanding" that rationale. Panetti was sentenced to death in Texas for murder. Panetti had a long documented history of mental illness. According to Panetti's lawyers, Panetti knew that Texas was seeking to execute him for the murder of his in-laws, but believed that Texas had conspired against him and sentenced him to death so that he would stop "preaching." The Court held that the Fifth Circuit's formal and narrow test of competence to be executed was "too restrictive." Not allowing for any consideration of a inmate's rational awareness and understanding of an impending execution was deemed unconsitutional; however, the Court also acknowledged that what constitutes a "rational understanding" is difficult to determine. The Court failed to set down a rule for competency hearings and remanded the case, requiring the district court to try to formulate and apply a better standard. If the Court is unwilling to define "rational awareness," it is not surprising that jurors, lawyers, judges, and circuit courts are unsure of or unwilling to establish a standard. The decision in *Panetti* points to the confusion about terms such as "competence," and "developmental disability," and how these terms should be defined for consideration in death penalty proceedings.

III. Emerging Issues

A. *Definition of Mental Retardation*

The Supreme Court in *Atkins* did not define what constitutes "mental retardation," leaving it instead to the discretion of the states. A recent article by Douglas Mossman, M.D., states that the diagnosis of mental retardation is an "entirely abstract construct" and that the line that separates persons who are given this diagnosis and those who are "just below average" is changing and arbitrary.[10] The American Association on Mental Retardation (AAMR) has updated its definition of mental retardation 10 times in the past century. Until 2007, the AAMR defined mental retardation as "a disability characterized by significant limitations both in intellectual functioning and adaptive behavior as expressed in conceptual, social, and practical adaptive skills. This disability originates before the age of 18."[11] Of great importance to the debate about "mental retardation" is even in the name itself. In February 2007, the AAMR became the American Association of Individuals with Developmental Disabilities (AAIDD). The AAIDD recently changed the term mental retardation and their organizational title by using what was perceived to be a less stigmatizing term, "intellectual disability." The change in wording also reflects the association's attempt to broaden the scope to include developmental disorders, such as autism. The definition, according to AAIDD, has not changed since its 2002 manual,[12] although clearly the change in name signifies a change in thinking about how individuals are perceived and punished. In a recent article in the *AAIDD Journal*, it was noted that the term "intellectual disability" covers the same population of individuals who were diagnosed previously with mental retardation in number, kind, level, type, and duration of the disability, and the need of people with this disability for individualized services and supports. Furthermore, every individual who is or was eligible for a diagnosis of mental retardation is eligible for a diagnosis of intellectual disability.[13]

The Diagnostic and Statistical Manual IV (DSM-IV-TR) of the American Psychiatric Association characterizes mental retardation as "significantly sub average general intellectual functioning accompanied by significant limitations in adaptive functioning in at least two of the following skill areas: communication, self-care, home living, social/interpersonal skills, use of community resources, self-direction, functional academic skills, work, leisure, health, and safety. The onset must occur before age 18 years."[14] While the AAMR and the American Psychiatric Association have similar definitions, they vary on one significant point. The DSM-IV-TR categorizes mental retardation by its severity, as mild, moderate, severe, or profound.[15] The AAMR, in contrast, examines patterns of limitations as a means of categorization and uses support needed as a means of classification, such as: intermittent, limited, extensive, pervasive, or completely necessary.[16]

Therefore, how can mental retardation be best determined for purposes of capital punishment?

Many states have currently set 70 as the minimum IQ score for death penalty consideration. States vary significantly as to the level of impairment in adaptive behavior that would qualify an individual as mentally retarded. Figure 4.1 presents an overview of states that have death penalty statutes and their current definitions of Mental Retardation. States also vary on the issue of whether the deficits in adaptive functioning must occur before a certain age. In North Carolina and Tennessee the deficit must be reached before the age of 18, while Maryland's statute says that the deficit must occur before the age of 22. Washington, New Mexico, and Nebraska have no set age limit.[17] Arizona and Arkansas have set the minimum IQ at 65, although their definitions of mental retardation differ, as well as their procedures for establishing mental retardation. Will IQ test administrators be able to remain objective when point assessments may mean the possibility of life or death? If point systems are used, a person who has an IQ of 72 could possibly be given the death penalty while a person with an IQ of 69 could not. Does this small three-point distinction mean a significant difference in culpability?

The American Psychiatric Association indicates three important Standard Error of Measurement (SEM) considerations when discussing IQ point assessments:

1. Instruments vary in SEM; example Wecshler scale of 70 represents the range of scores 65–75.

2. No MR diagnosis if individual IQ score below 70 without significant deficits in adaptive functioning.

3. Possible to diagnose MR in an individual with IQ score 70–75 who presents with significant deficits in adaptive functioning. Otherwise will receive diagnosis of Borderline Intellectual Functioning.[18]

One should also note three other important considerations in a diagnosis of a mental retardation or developmental disability:

1. IQ score considered a more stable construct, whereas adaptive functioning can improve with "support."

2. Comorbid disorders in individuals with MR estimated 3–4 times more likely than general population. Most common disorders include ADHD, mood disorders, pervasive developmental disorders (PDD), stereotypic movement disorders, and mental disorders due to a medical condition—dementia due to head trauma.

3. "MR often accompanies PDD."

Precise IQ cutoffs may create the impression that a one- or two-point difference in IQ score shows a substantial difference in criminal intent. This is why some states have taken IQ score out of their definition of mental retardation. The statutory definitions range from the general requirement of sub-average intelligence and shortfalls in adaptive functioning to the definition in Kansas, which requires an inability to appreciate the criminality of one's conduct. There is no uniform definition as to what constitutes mental retardation. As noted above, individuals in some states will be spared execution if they have an IQ of 67, but if they test four points higher they could face execution. This is particularly problematic when considering the measurement error of five points in IQ testing. The courts will have to decide what methods they believe will most accurately justify a claim of mental retardation in death penalty cases.

Scholars are debating whether states should be bound by the language and strict definition of mental retardation in considering who should face capital punishment when individuals who demonstrate the same vulnerabilities as persons who are "developmentally disabled" are not given the same considerations. Baroff (2003)[19] and Kanaya et al. (2002)[20] argue that more flexibility in defining mental retardation is necessary due to issues in evaluating IQ across tests and over time. Should IQ tests be given less consideration than adaptive functioning tests? Kanaya et al. (2002) state that:

> Some borderline death row inmates or capital murder defendants who were not classified as mentally retarded in childhood because they took an older version of an IQ test might have qualified as retarded if they had taken a more recent test . . . Our results imply that the year that a capital murder defendant was tested can determine whether she or he is sentenced to death as opposed to life imprisonment. This raises concerns regarding inmates on death row who tested above 70–75 cutoff on a test that was near the end of its normal cycling—when scores are highly inflated as well as an inmate who tested in the mental retardation range during the earliest years of a new norm—when the test is the hardest.[21]

No standard definition exists in the legal community as to what constitutes mental retardation or developmental disability and, in light of the decision in *Atkins*, it is unlikely that the Court will resolve this issue for death penalty states that are trying to comply with the ruling in *Atkins*. Cooperation between psychologists, psychiatrists, other mental health professionals, and criminal justice agents could potentially bridge the gap in understanding that surrounds defining and diagnosing "developmental disabilities."

Figure 4.1
Statutory Definitions of Mental Retardation

	Statute Citation	Definition of Mental Retardation	Qualified Examiners	Determined
Alabama				
Arizona	Ariz. Rev. Stat. Sect. 13-3982	A condition based on a mental deficit that has resulted in significantly subaverage general intellectual functioning existing concurrently with significant limitations in adaptive functioning, where the onset of the forgoing conditions occurred before the defendant reached the age of eighteen.	Requires the trial court in a capital case to appoint a licensed psychologist to conduct a prescreening evaluation to determine the defendant's IQ.	
Arkansas	Ark. Code Ann. Sect. 5-4-618 (1993)	Significantly subaverage general intellectual functioning accompanied by significant deficits or impairments in adaptive functioning, and manifested in the developmental period. The age of onset is 18. There is a rebuttable presumption of mental retardation when the defendant has an IQ of 65 or below.	There is no information on this aspect of the statute.	
California	Penal Code 1376	Significantly subaverage general intellectual functioning existing concurrently with deficits in adaptive behavior and manifested before the age of 18.	None stated. Burden of proof is on the defense.	In a Pre-Trial hearing by a Judge or Jury.
Colorado	Colo. Rev. Stat. Sect. 16-9-401-403	Any defendant with significantly subaverage general intellectual functioning existing concurrently with substantial deficits in adaptive behavior and manifested and documented during the developmental period. The requirements for documentation may be excused by the court upon a finding that extraordinary circumstances exist. The court does not define extraordinary circumstances. The law does not give a numerical IQ level.	There is no information on this aspect of the statute.	

Figure 4.1, *continued*

	Statute Citation	Definition of Mental Retardation	Qualified Examiners	Determined
Connecticut	Public Act No, 01-151	Significantly sub-average general intellectual functioning existing concurrently with deficits in adaptive behavior and manifested during the developmental period. (as defined in Conn. Gen. Stat. § 1-1g (2001))	There is no information on this aspect of the statute.	
Delaware	11-4209	"Seriously mentally retarded" or "serious mental retardation" means that an individual has significantly subaverage intellectual functioning that exists concurrently with substantial deficits in adaptive behavior and both the significantly subaverage intellectual functioning and the deficits in adaptive behavior were manifested before the individual became 18 years of age; "Significantly subaverage intellectual functioning" means an intelligent quotient of 70 or below obtained by assessment with 1 or more of the standardized, individually administered general intelligence tests developed for the purpose of assessing intellectual functioning; and "Adaptive behavior" means the effectiveness or degree to which the individual meets the standards of personal independence expected of the individual's age group, sociocultural background and community setting, as evidenced by significant limitations in not less than 2 of the following adaptive skill areas: communication, self-care, home living, social skills, use of community resources, self-direction, functional academic skills, work, leisure, health or safety.	None stated. Burden of proof is on the defense.	

Figure 4.1, *continued*

	Statute Citation	Definition of Mental Retardation	Qualified Examiners	Determined
Florida	Florida Statutes, Sect. 921.137	significantly subaverage general intellectual functioning existing concurrently with deficits in adaptive behavior and manifested during the period from conception to age 18	Court-appointed experts in the field of mental retardation shall evaluate the defendant and report their findings to the court and all interested parties prior to the final sentencing hearing.	
Georgia	Ga. Code. Ann. Sect. 17-7-131(i)	". . . Significantly subaverage intellectual functioning resulting in or associated with impairments in adaptive behavior which manifests during the developmental period."	Court-appointed licensed psychologists or psychiatrists; or physicians or licensed clinical psychologists chosen and paid for by the defendant.	
Idaho	19-2515A	"Mentally retarded" means significantly subaverage general intellectual functioning that is accompanied by significant limitations in adaptive functioning in at least two (2) of the following skill areas: communication, self-care, home living, social or interpersonal skills, use of community resources, self-direction, functional academic skills, work, leisure, health and safety. The onset of significant subaverage general intelligence functioning and significant limitations in adaptive functioning must occur before age eighteen (18) years. (b) "Significantly subaverage general intellectual functioning" means an intelligence quotient of seventy (70) or below.	No specific qualifications specified. Refers only to "expert witness" for either side.	Before the Trial by a Judge

Figure 4.1, *continued*

	Statute Citation	Definition of Mental Retardation	Qualified Examiners	Determined
Illinois	725 ILCS 5/114–15	The mental retardation must have manifested itself by the age of 18. An intelligence quotient (IQ) of 75 or below is presumptive evidence of mental retardation. IQ tests and psychometric tests administered to the defendant must be the kind and type recognized by experts in the field of mental retardation. In order for the defendant to be considered mentally retarded, a low IQ must be accompanied by significant deficits in adaptive behavior in at least 2 of the following skill areas: communication, self-care, social or interpersonal skills, home living, self-direction, academics, health and safety, use of community resources, and work.	If a motion to disqualify a case as a capital case based upon the mental retardation of the defendant is filed, the issue of the defendant's mental retardation shall be determined in a pretrial hearing. The court shall be the fact finder on the issue of the defendant's mental retardation and shall determine the issue by a preponderance of evidence in which the moving party has the burden of proof. The court may appoint an expert in the field of mental retardation. The defendant and the State may offer experts from the field of mental retardation. The court shall determine admissibility of evidence and qualification as an expert.	Before the Trial (if the proseucutor agrees) by the Judge, or during sentencing by the Jury
Indiana	Ind. Code Sect. 35-36-9-1 et. seq.	An individual before becoming 22 years of age manifests: (1) significantly subaverage intellectual functioning; and (2) substantial impairment of adaptive behavior that is documented in a court-ordered evaluative report.	State does not specify if the court can appoint psychologists or psychiatrists. Attorneys should probably obtain this information from trial court at pre-trial.	

Figure 4.1, *continued*

	Statute Citation	Definition of Mental Retardation	Qualified Examiners	Determined
Kansas	Kan. Stat. Ann. Sect. 21-4623	An individual having significantly subaverage general intellectual functioning to an extent that substantially impairs one's capacity to appreciate the criminality of one's conduct or conform one's conduct to the requirements of law. The statute does not define adaptive behavior or the age of onset. However, Kan. Stat. Ann Sect. 76-12b01 defines these terms. Adaptive behavior refers to the effectiveness of personal independence and social responsibility expected of that person's age, cultural group and community. The age of onset must be prior to 18 years old.	There is no information on this aspect of the statute.	
Kentucky	Ky. Rev. Stat. Sect. 532.130–140	A significant subaverage intellectual functioning existing concurrently with substantial deficits in adaptive behavior and manifested during the developmental period. The age of onset is 18 years old. Significantly subaverage general intellectual functioning is defined as an IQ of 70 or below.	There is no information on this aspect of the statute.	
Louisiana	2003 LA Acts 698, Code of Criminal Procedure Article 905.5.1	A disability characterized by significant limitations in both intellectual functioning and adaptive behavior as expressed in conceptual, social, and practical adaptive skills. Onset must have occurred before age 18.	When a defendant makes a claim under this article the state has the right to an independent psychological and psychiatric examination of the defendant. Must be licensed by Louisiana state board of examiners of psychologists.	Before the Trial (if the proseucutor agrees) by the Judge, or during sentencing by the Jury

Figure 4.1, *continued*

	Statute Citation	Definition of Mental Retardation	Qualified Examiners	Determined
Maryland	Md. Code. Ann. art. 27 Sect.412	An individual who has significantly subaverage intellectual functioning as evidenced by an IQ of 70 or below on an individually administered IQ test, and impairment in adaptive behavior. The age of onset is before the age of 22.	There is no information on this aspect of the statute.	
Mississippi				
Missouri	RSMo 565.030	Significantly subaverage general intellectual functioning which originates before age eighteen; and is associated with a significant impairment in adaptive behavior.	There is no information on this aspect of the statute.	
Montana				
Nebraska	R.R.S. Neb. Sect. 28-105.01 (2000)	Mental retardation means significantly subaverage general intellectual functioning existing concurrently with deficits in adaptive behavior. An IQ of 70 or below on a reliably administered IQ test shall be presumptive evidence of mental retardation.	There is no information on this aspect of the statute.	
Nevada	NRS 174	Significant subaverage general intellectual functioning which exists concurrently with deficits in adaptive behavior and manifested during the developmental period.	None stated. Only reference to examiners is that they are to be selected by the prosecution.	Before the Trial
New Hampshire				
New Jersey				

Figure 4.1, *continued*

	Statute Citation	Definition of Mental Retardation	Qualified Examiners	Determined
New Mexico	N.M. Stat. Ann. Sect. 31-20A-2.1 (1978)	Mental retardation refers to significantly subaverage general intellectual functioning existing concurrently with deficits in adaptive behavior. An IQ of 70 or below on a reliably administered IQ test shall be presumptive evidence of mental retardation.	There is no information on this aspect of the statute.	
New York (except for murder by a prisoner)	N.Y. Crim. Proc. Sect. 400.27(12)	The statute uses the most recent American Association on Mental Retardation definition (1992).** The N.Y Statute does not list specific levels of intelligence, nor does it go into detail regarding adaptive skills.	No specifics noted — "Psychiatrist, psychologist or other trained individual."	
North Carolina	2001 N.C. Sess. Laws 346	Significantly subaverage general intellectual functioning (defined as having an IQ of 70 or below), existing concurrently with significant limitations in adaptive functioning (defined as having significant limitations in two or more of the following adaptive skill areas: communication, self-care, home living, social skills, community use, self-direction, health and safety, functional academics, leisure skills and work skills) both of which were manifested before the age of 18.	A licensed psychiatrist or psychologist	
Ohio				
Oklahoma				
Oregon				
Pennsylvania				
South Carolina				

Figure 4.1, *continued*

	Statute Citation	Definition of Mental Retardation	Qualified Examiners	Determined
South Dakota	S.D. Codified Laws Sect. 23A-27A-26.1 (2000)	Mental retardation means significant subaverage general intellectual functioning existing concurrently with substantial related deficits in applicable adaptive skill areas. An IQ exceeding 70 on a reliable standardized measure of intelligence is presumptive evidence that the defendant does not have significant subaverage general intellectual functioning. Mental retardation must have been manifested and documented before the age of 18 years.	A psychiatrist, licensed psychologist, or licensed psychiatric social worker designated by the state's attorney, for the purpose of rebutting evidence offered by the defendant.	
Tennessee	Tenn. Code. Ann. tit.39. Ch. 13 pt. 2 sect. 39-13-203	(1) Significantly subaverage general intellectual functioning as evidenced by a functional IQ of 70 or below; (2) deficits in adaptive behavior; (3) the mental retardation must have been manifested during the developmental period or by age 18. The state does not define "deficits in adaptive behavior." The statute clearly provides that adaptive behavior and intellectual functioning are independent criteria.	There is no information on this aspect of the statute.	
Texas				
Utah	77-15a-101	Significant subaverage general intellectual functioning that results in and exists concurrently with significant deficiencies in adaptive functioning that exist primarily in the areas of reasoning or impulse control, or in both of these areas; and the subaverage general intellectual functioning and the significant deficiencies in adaptive functioning under Subsection (1) are both manifested prior to age 22.	The court shall order the Department of Human Services to appoint at least two mental health experts to examine the defendant and report to the court. The experts: (i) may not be involved in the current treatment of the defendant; and (ii) shall have expertise in mental retardation assessment.	Before the Trial

Figure 4.1, *continued*

	Statute Citation	Definition of Mental Retardation	Qualified Examiners	Determined
Virginia	§ 19.2-264.3	"Mentally retarded" means a disability, originating before the age of 18 years, characterized concurrently by (i) significantly subaverage intellectual functioning as demonstrated by performance on a standardized measure of intellectual functioning administered in conformity with accepted professional practice, that is at least two standard deviations below the mean and (ii) significant limitations in adaptive behavior as expressed in conceptual, social and practical adaptive skills.	A psychiatrist, a clinical psychologist or an individual with a doctorate degree in clinical psychology, (b) skilled in the administration, scoring and interpretation of intelligence tests and measures of adaptive behavior and (c) qualified by experience and by specialized training, approved by the Commissioner of Mental Health, Mental Retardation and Substance Abuse Services, to perform forensic evaluations. The defendant shall not be entitled to a mental health expert of the defendant's own choosing or to funds to employ such expert.	By the Jury (or Judge in Non-jury trials) during the Sentencing Phase
Washington	Was. Rev. Code Ann. Sect. 10.95.030 (West)	The individual has (1) significantly subaverage general intellectual functioning; (2) existing concurrently with deficits in adaptive behavior; and (3) both significantly subaverage general intellectual functioning and deficits in adaptive behavior were manifested during the developmental period. The age of onset is 18 years of age. The required IQ level is 70 or below.	A court-appointed licensed psychiatrist or psychologist experienced in the diagnosis and evaluation of metal retardation. This leaves open the issue of whether or not the defendant may hire his own expert.	
Wyoming				

Figure 4.1, *continued*

	Statute Citation	Definition of Mental Retardation	Qualified Examiners	Determined
Federal Govern-ment	18 U.S.C.A. Sect. 3596(c) (Federal Crime Bill of 1994)	In 1994, Congress adopted legislation to ban the execution of individuals with mental re-tardation. The statute states that a sentence of death shall not be carried out upon a person who has mental retardation. The statute does not define mental retardation, or discuss at what stage in the criminal proceed-ings the determination of men-tal retardation must be made. Earlier, Congress had also pro-vided a form of an exemption for this issue in the Anti-Drug Abuse Act of 1988 (pub. L. No. 100–690).		

Source: http://www.deathpenaltyinfo.org/article.php?scid=28&did=138
http://www.deathpenaltyinfo.org/article.php?scid=28&did=668
States that haven't executed an inmate since 1976: Kansas, New Hampshire, New Jersey, New York, & South Dakota

B. The Fear of "Faking"

The evidence suggests that mental retardation is difficult to effectively fake because it has its roots in childhood. Historically, the American legal system has had a fear of "feigned insanity" and is skeptical of expert testimony about mental illness and insanity.[22] The *Atkins* decision may in fact only serve to make members of the legal and criminal justice community more apprehensive. A defendant who is diagnosed as mentally retarded may never be executed regardless of the severity or nature of the crimes. In his dissenting opinion in *Atkins*, Justice Scalia expresses serious concerns about what he considers to be the new capital trial "game." He argues that many of the AAMR and DSM-IV symptoms could be feigned, with nothing to lose. Of key concern is the role that mental health professionals play in effective diagnosis of mental retardation. Malingering, or faking mental illness, is of concern to the American Psychiatric Association and it lists four conditions that in combination could show malingering. These four conditions are:

1. Medico-legal context of presentation (i.e., referral from an attorney for diagnosis);

2. Discrepancy between the person's deemed disability or stress and objective findings;

3.   Lack of cooperation during the diagnostic evaluation and in complying with treatment program; and

4.   The presence of antisocial disorder.[23]

Mental health clinicians are now able to use tests that can identify faked psychological symptoms. These tests include the Test of Memory Malingnancy (TOMM), the Structured Interview of Repeated Symptoms (SIRS), and the Minnesota Multiphasic Personality Inventory (MMPI).

Mental health professionals must remain unbiased and base their evaluations on actual behavior and assessment tools, rather than gut feelings, in death penalty cases. The American Psychological Association (APA) Ethical Principles of Psychologists and Code of Conduct provide standards of professional conduct for psychologists. While this code was written for members of the APA, it is frequently applied by state boards and courts to those practicing in the field of psychology.[24] The APA ethics code states that evaluations for courts must be based solely "on information that is sufficient to appropriate substantiation for their findings."[25] The APA has also provided a set of guidelines for psychologists who are experts in the legal system. These "specialty guidelines" require the psychologist to conduct an adequate examination utilizing the most up-to-date tests and measures and to avoid providing testimony "about the psychological characteristics of particular individuals when they have not had an opportunity to conduct an examination of the individual adequate to the scope of the statements, opinions, or conclusions."[26] Psychiatrists may have a unique dilemma, because they take the Hippocratic Oath, which requires that the physician's first consideration be the benefit of the patient and imposes a duty that the doctor do no harm and take no life.

C.   *Mental Retardation versus Mental Illness*

Mental illness is different from mental retardation in significant ways. The diagnosis of mental illness relies more heavily on subjective diagnosis, whereas mental retardation is most often found through objective (IQ) tests. The DSM-IV alludes to the fact that it may be difficult to distinguish between a strongly held idea and a delusion, and "bizarreness" of delusions may be difficult to judge, particularly across varying cultures.[27] Mental illness is typically more treatable than mental retardation, which could make the mentally ill more responsible. For example, if a mentally ill person chooses not to take medication, knowing the consequences of doing so, should that person not be held liable for his or her actions? It could also be argued that a mentally ill offender has a higher mental competence to understand the rules and laws that govern society.

Atkins focused on the issue of mental retardation, which is different from mental illness. Courts and legislatures agree that mental illness is a mitigating circumstance. Mental illness has also been used to mitigate punishments in death penalty offenses. The Court has not decided whether people with other mental impairments or mental illness will receive the protections against execution afforded to those with mental retardation. Mental illness is a broad term that has a variety of diagnoses. In light of the decision in *Atkins*, will the mentally ill be considered a death penalty-excluded class?

Many individuals with mental illnesses suffer from the same limitations that diminish blame in the case of the mentally retarded. Recent studies suggest that as many as 20 percent of death row offenders have a mental disorder that is accompanied by impaired reasoning and cognition.[28] The language in *Atkins* could also be applied to mental illness, because most mentally ill offenders have a "diminished capacity to understand and process information, to communicate, to abstract from mistakes and learn from experience, to engage in logical reasoning to control impulses, and to understand the reaction of others."[29] An individual suffering from schizophrenia could be described in a similar way.

D. What Is to Be Done with the Mentally Retarded Now on Death Row?

In his dissent in *Atkins*, Justice Scalia noted that he believed the courts would soon be overburdened by offenders claiming mental retardation.[30] Should offenders who had not previously cited mental retardation as a mitigating factor be entitled to a stay of execution to evaluate their intelligence and adaptive functioning? Offenders on death row who were deemed mentally retarded by statutory standards set by the state would have to be commuted to life, as their execution would now violate the Eighth Amendment's ban on cruel and unusual punishment. Who will administer the IQ tests and complete the extensive social history necessary to determine mental retardation? How many times could a person be tested and would the "best out of" rule apply? States may also struggle with expenditures on adequate testing as many states are cutting criminal justice spending.

IV.   Insanity and the Death Penalty

A.   Insanity: Different from Other Mental Impairments

It is important to separate insanity from mental retardation and mental illness. Sanity is a legal term, not a medical or psychiatric term. While psychiatrists and mental health clinicians examine individuals and present their findings to the court, it is ultimately judges and juries who determine whether a defendant is "sane" or "insane."

What about an offender who is sane at the time of the commission of the offense but becomes insane after being given the death penalty? Can that defendant be executed? The Court in *Ford v. Wainwright* (1986)[31] held that it is unconstitutional to execute a person who is insane at the time of the scheduled execution because it would constitute cruel and unusual punishment. Historically, the banning of the execution of the insane has its roots in the common law. Prior to the *Ford* decision the Court had not addressed the execution of the insane under the Eighth Amendment. The Supreme Court took into account in *Ford*, "objective evidence of contemporary values before determining whether a particular punishment comports with the fundamental human dignity that the Eighth Amendment protects."[32] What is a recognizable standard for determining competency? The American Bar Association states that:

> A condemned individual must have sufficient mental capacity to understand the nature of the proceedings against him, for what he was tried, the purpose of the punishment, and his impending fate. Furthermore, he must exhibit sufficient understanding to recognize and comprehend any existing fact which might render his punishment unjust or unlawful, and he must have the intelligence necessary to convey such information to his attorney or the court. The offender must comprehend the rationale behind society's moral outrage concerning his actions and must have an affective knowledge of facts regarding both his crime and his punishment. If this knowledge and understanding is not present then the offender can be characterized as insane.[33]

B. Reasons for Not Executing the Insane

The United States Supreme Court in *Ford v. Wainwright*[34] decided that it violates the Eighth Amendment to execute an insane person, basing its decision on two reasons. First, for centuries no insane person had been executed in this country. States were unwilling to do so even though the constitutional question had never been addressed. Second, the Court believed that the justifications for the death penalty were not met by executing a mentally incompetent person.

1. Failure to Achieve Penological Goals

a. Deterrence

Because an insane individual does not fully understand the consequences of his or her behavior, it is difficult to believe that the execution of an insane individual would deter other people from committing crimes, particularly because the American criminal justice system seeks not only to deter crime, but also to incapacitate and rehabilitate criminal wrongdoers. Deterrence is divided into two categories. The first is general deterrence, in which punishment is meant to discourage all people from engaging in criminal activity. Specific deterrence is meant to prevent a particular individual from engaging in future criminal behaviors. Executing the mentally insane would not deter society as a whole because the vast majority of people are not mentally incompetent and generally do not have the same patterns of thinking as insane persons. In seeking specific deterrence, the death penalty for the insane is not altogether necessary because insane offenders will be isolated from society at a mental health facility or institution and therefore the commission of further harm or violence is no longer a fear.

b.   Retribution

Retribution is a goal of punishment imposed upon a person who has violated the rights of others. It embodies the "eye for an eye and a tooth for a tooth" approach. The severity of the sanction generally fits the severity of the crime. If individuals do not have the capacity to understand that their behavior harms society, they will not understand why they need to be punished. There is no moral equivalence between the sanction and the offense. There will be no suffering or anguish because the person does not fully appreciate that he or she will be put to death due to criminal actions; therefore, retribution is not achieved.

2.   Theological

The Court in *Ford* said that it is cruel and unusual to end a person's life without first affording him the opportunity to prepare himself spiritually for the journey into the afterlife.[35] An insane person does not have the mental capacity for the type of preparation that is necessary to secure peace for themselves. While this religious argument has been supported by some groups, the approach has been understandably controversial in the legal and religious communities.

3.   Humanity

The premise that underlies the argument against the execution of the insane is that "madness itself is its own punishment."[36] Inmates who are deemed "insane" spend their lives at an institution and are not exonerated. For an inmate to have no concept of his surroundings or live freely in society is considered punishment enough.

The above discussion explains why the Supreme Court found the execution of the insane to be a violation of the Eighth Amendment.

It should be noted that, although it is unconstitutional to execute an inmate deemed mentally ill or insane at the time of execution, this does not exempt them completely from being executed. If restored to sanity or mental health, the execution may then be carried out. Psychiatric treatment, including the use of medication, may be used to restore an inmate to competency for execution.[37]

C. Mental Competence and the Death Penalty

The decision in *Ford v. Wainright* banned the execution of the insane. This applied only to those who were determined to be insane at the time of execution, or, in other words, mentally incompetent for execution. How is a defendant declared incompetent? One definition of mental incompetence is described as:

> An individual is defined as mentally incompetent if he is manifestly psychotic or otherwise of unsound mind, either consistently or sporadically, by reason of mental defect, among which are retardation, schizophrenia or other acute hallucinatory and delusory defects of mind, certain types of epilepsy and other seizure disorders which render the individual coordinated and mobile but of unsound mind, bipolar disorder which results in sporadic psychosis (but not simply mild or moderate bipolar disorder), and other disorders which consistently or sporadically render the individual starkly incapable of maintaining awareness of and responsibility for his actions.[38]

The definition clearly points to mental deficiencies that render the individual unable to understand their current surroundings or circumstances and actions occurring in the moment. *Singleton v. Norris*[39] highlighted the notion that states could execute individuals who were made competent through medication even if the competence was gained through forced medication. States only had to maintain that the medicine was not solely for the purposes of execution but also for other medical benefits. As noted earlier, ulterior motives behind the medication were irrelevant as long as the state had a legitimate claim that he medication would be medically beneficial to the inmate.

The most recent Supreme Court decision pertaining to mental competence and the death penalty is *Panetti v. Quarterman*.[40] Panetti had a long history of severe mental illness including documented chronic schizophrenia and schizoaffective disorder. At his initial trial, Panetti was taking his medication; though his attorney reported that he had not had a meaningful conversation with his client. Although his attorney attempted to challenge his competence to stand trial, he was found competent by a Texas jury. As noted previously, jurors are reluctant to declare a defendant mentally incompetent, fearing that the defendant may be "getting one over" on them. Even if Panetti was initially found competent to stand trial it is up to the court to reassess his competency based on his behavior and condition. Panetti, white at trial, was no longer taking his medication and chose to represent himself. The judge in the case ruled that Panetti was competent to represent himself, without re-evaluating his competency. According to the trial record Panetti wore cowboy garb, and attempted to call more than 200 witnesses, including John F. Kennedy and Jesus. A psychiatrist who had treated Panetti for a period of six years prior to trial noted that his courtroom behavior pointed to his severe mental illness.[41] If the judge believed that Panetti was not actually mentally ill, it is not surprising that the jury in Panetti's case found him guilty and sentenced him to death.

Panetti filed a *Ford* petition claiming he was not competent to be executed. Panetti's competence hinged on medication, or in his case, forced medication. Prior to the decision in *Panetti*, states were allowed to execute offenders who were competent when taking medication, whether it be voluntarily or involuntarily. There is much debate about whether it is ethical or moral to make an ill person well only for the purpose of carrying out an execution. The issues brought to the surface in *Panetti* embody the struggles that are present when competence of a capital defendant is in question.

Figure 4.2
ABA Standards for the Competency and the Death Penalty

> **Standard d 7-5.6. Currently incompetent condemned convicts; stay of execution**
>
> (a) Convicts who have been sentenced to death should not be executed if they are currently mentally incompetent. If it is determined that a condemned convict is currently mentally incompetent, execution should be stayed.
>
> (b) A convict is incompetent to be executed if, as a result of mental illness or mental retardation, the convict cannot understand the nature of the pending proceedings, what he or she was tried for, the reason for the punishment, or the nature of the punishment. A convict is also incompetent if, as a result of mental illness or mental retardation, the convict lacks sufficient capacity to recognize or understand any fact which might exist which would make the punishment unjust or unlawful, or lacks the ability to convey such information to counsel or the court.
>
> **Standard 7-5.7. Evaluation and adjudication of competence to be executed; stay of execution; restoration of competence**
>
> (a) Whenever a correctional official, other state official, the prosecution, or counsel for the convict have reason to believe that a convict who has been sentenced to death may be currently incompetent, such person should petition the court for an order requiring an evaluation of the convict's current mental condition. If the court concludes that the information in the petition indicates reasonable cause to believe that the convict may be incompetent, it should order an evaluation. Unless counsel for the defendant is the petitioner, counsel should be notified that such an evaluation is to be conducted. If the convict is not represented by counsel, the court should appoint counsel at the same time it orders the evaluation.
>
> (b) Any interested person who has reason to believe that the convict may be currently incompetent may petition the court for an order requiring an evaluation of the convict's current mental condition. If the court concludes that

Figure 4.2, *continued*

the information in the petition indicates reasonable cause to believe that the convict may be incompetent, it should order an evaluation, and, if the convict is not represented by counsel, appoint counsel for the convict.

(c) In the absence of a petition, if the court obtains information that indicates reasonable cause to believe that the convict may be incompetent, it should order an evaluation *sua sponte*. If the convict is not represented by counsel, the court should appoint counsel at the same time it orders the evaluation.

(d) All evaluations of a convict's current mental condition for purpose of determining the issue of competence to be executed should be conducted by mental health and/or mental retardation professionals whose qualifications meet the requirements of Standards 7-3.10 and 7-3.12(c)(ii). The convict should be entitled to an evaluation by a qualified professional or professionals who should present the results of their evaluation to the convict's counsel. If the convict is indigent, the court should appoint an appropriate professional evaluator or evaluators for the convict, and such evaluators should be compensated at public expense. The state should be permitted to have its own qualified professional or professionals conduct an evaluation as well.

(e) If, after receiving the reports of the evaluation or evaluations, counsel for the convict believes that the convict is currently incompetent, counsel should move for a hearing on the issue of competence. Upon receiving such a motion, the court should order a hearing.

(f) Following the hearing, if the court finds, by a preponderance of the evidence, that the convict is currently incompetent, it should stay the order of execution for the duration of the convict's incompetence. The court's finding on the issue of competence should be considered a final, appealable order.

(g) If evaluations or proceedings under this standard cannot be accomplished before the scheduled date of the convict's execution, the court should order a stay of execution until the proceedings on the issue of competence are completed.

(h) In the absence of good faith doubt about the convict's current competence, it is improper for an attorney to move for an evaluation pursuant to paragraph (a) or (b) of this Standard. It is improper to use proceedings on the issue of current mental condition solely for the purpose of delay.

(i) When the appropriate state official has reason to believe that a condemned convict who has been found incompetent pursuant to paragraph (f) of this Standard has been restored to competence, the official may petition the court for an order recognizing the restoration to competence and lifting the stay of execution. Upon receipt of such a petition, the court should order the convict's current mental condition reevaluated under the provisions of paragraph (d) of this Standard. Counsel for the defendant should be notified that such an evaluation is to be conducted. Following the reevaluation, the court should hold a hearing on the convict's current mental condition. The convict should be represented by counsel at the hearing. Following the hearing, the court should lift the stay of execution if it finds, by a preponderance of the evidence, that the convict is no longer incompetent. The court's finding on the issue of competence should be considered a final, appealable order.

V.   In Summary, What Do these Cases Say?

The Supreme Court established in *Ford v. Wainwright*[42] (1986) that it is unconstitutional to execute a person who is insane at the time of their execution, because doing so constitutes cruel and unusual punishment. Three years later, however, the Court concluded in *Penry v. Lynaugh* (1989)[43] that it was not a violation of the Eighth Amendment to execute the mentally retarded. Mental retardation could and should be a mitigating factor, but should not necessarily preclude someone from being executed, particularly because their was no national consensus against the death penalty for the mentally retarded. But in 2002, the Court revisited the issue of whether it was unconstitutional to execute the mentally retarded and came to a conclusion different from that in *Penry*. The reason for this change in *Atkins v. Virginia* (2002)[44] was due to the "evolving standards of decency." The Court found that most states and countries believed that it was cruel and unusual to execute people who are mentally retarded. *Tennard v. Dretke*[45] (2004) pointed to the need for jurors to consider serious mental impairment as a mitigating factor in making sentencing decisions in capital cases. The cases of *Singleton v. Norris*[46] and *Panetti v. Quarterman* highlight the confusion and challenge in applying competency standards to individuals on death row.

VI.   Conclusion

The execution of the mentally retarded is unconstitutional because it violates the Eighth Amendment ban on cruel and unusual punishment. The Supreme Court in *Atkins* only addressed individuals who are mentally retarded and did not include people who suffer from mental illnesses. Because those who are diagnosed as mentally ill may continue to exhibit symptoms similar to those who are mentally retarded, in spite of treatment, will the Supreme Court have to determine whether it is also cruel and unusual to execute the mentally ill? This is a question the Court may have to address in the future. More recent cases have highlighted the confusion that exists in defining and applying competence labels to individuals on trial or who are facing executions. The Court also allows inmates to be medicated involuntarily thus becoming competent to be executed. The Court has failed to set a standard definition of mental competency to be executed, leaving states to decide what it means to have "rational understanding" and to be "rationally aware." Is it moral to execute individuals who are forced into competency in their "best interest" only to be executed as a result of medication they neither desired nor chose to take? Is forced competency really competency at all? It is likely that the Court will continue to be faced with these and other issues involving mental competency and developmental disabilities for some time to come.

Cases Briefed in Chapter 4

Case	Issue	Holding
Ford v. Wainwright 477 US 399 (1986)	1. Does it violate the Eighth Amendment to execute a prisoner who is insane at the time of his scheduled execution? 2. Were the Florida procedures to determine sanity of a person to be executed sufficient?	1. It is a violation of the Eighth Amendment to put to death a prisoner who is insane at the time of execution. 2. An evidentiary hearing to determine competency must be granted to determine if a person who has received a death sentence is insane.
Penry v. Lynaugh 492 US 302 (1989)	1.Does the execution of a mentally retarded offender violate the Eighth Amendment prohibition against cruel and unusual punishment? 2.When requested, should a jury be instructed by the judge to consider mental retardation as a mitigating factor at the sentencing portion of a capital trial?	1. It is constitutional to impose the death penalty on a mentally retarded defendant who has the ability to reason. 2.If the defense requests jury instructions concerning mental retardation as a mitigating factor such requests must be granted.
Atkins v. Virginia 536 US 304 (2002)	Is it a violation of the Eighth Amendment to execute a mentally retarded offender?	It is a violation of the Eighth Amendment to put to death an offender who is mentally retarded.
Singleton v. Norris 319 F.3d 10184 (2003)	Is it a violation of due process and the 8th Amendment to forcefully medicate an inmate to render him competent to be executed?	It is not a violation of the constitution to execute an inmate who is being involuntarily medicated to obtain competency as long as it is not the sole purpose for the medication.
Tennard v. Dretke 524 U.S. 274 (2004)	Should mental retardation be considered as a mitigating factor even if that mental retardation is not shown to be related to the crime?	Evidence of mental retardation should be considered as possible mitigation by a capital jury even if the defendant's crime is not directly attributable to such intellectual or cognitive impairment.
Panetti v. Quarterman 551 U.S. ___ (2007)	1. Is it a violation of the Eighth Amendment to execute an inmate who, because of mental illness, lacks a rational understanding of the State's rationale for the execution but has a factual awareness that rationale?	1. The Supreme Court refused to make a determinative statement regarding standards for what constitutes a "rational understanding" of the state's rationale for execution.

Cases Briefed in Chapter 4, *continued*

Case	Issue	Holding
	2. Is it a violation of the Constitution to fail to provide adequate measures to challenge an execution based on claims of mental incompetency?	2. It is a violation of the Constitution to fail to provide adequate measures for a defendant to challenge an execution based on claims of incompetency to be executed.

Case Briefs

Ford v. Wainwright
477 U.S. 399 (1986)

CAPSULE: A prisoner who is insane may not be executed.

FACTS: In 1974, Ford was convicted of murder in Florida and sentenced to death. Ford was not considered incompetent at the time of the offense, at trial, or at sentencing. After sentencing Ford began to manifest changes in behavior, indicating a mental disorder that rendered him incapable of communication. Ford had separate examinations by two psychiatrists at his counsel's request, one of whom concluded that he was not competent to suffer execution because he had a severe mental disease that resembled paranoid schizophrenia. This diagnosis would limit Ford's ability to assist in his defense. The governor appointed three psychiatrists, to ascertain whether Ford had the mental capacity to understand his death sentence. The psychiatrists interviewed Ford together for a total of 30 minutes. Each psychiatrist filed a separate report with the governor, to whom the statute delegates the final decision. The reports all concluded that Ford had a mental disorder but all three agreed that petitioner was competent. The governor subsequently signed a death warrant without explanation or statement based solely upon the accounts of the three state-appointed psychiatrists.

ISSUES:
1. Does it violate the Eighth Amendment to execute a prisoner who is insane at the time of his scheduled execution? YES.
2. Were the Florida procedures used to determine a person's competence to be executed sufficient? NO.

HOLDING:
1. It is a violation of the Eighth Amendment to put to death a prisoner who is insane at the time of execution.
2. An evidentiary hearing to determine competency must be granted to determine whether a person who has received a death sentence is insane.

REASON: "The Eighth Amendment prohibits the State from inflicting the penalty of death upon a prisoner who is insane. Petitioner's allegation of insanity in his habeas corpus petition, if proved, therefore, would bar his execution. The question before us is whether the District Court was under an obligation to hold an evidentiary hearing on the question of Ford's sanity. In answering that question, we bear in mind that, while the underlying social values encompassed by the Eighth Amendment are rooted in historical traditions, the manner in which our judicial system protects those values is purely a matter of contemporary law. Once a substantive right or restriction is recognized in the Constitution, therefore, its enforcement is in no way confined to the rudimentary process deemed adequate in ages past."

"Having identified various failings of the Florida scheme, we must conclude that the State's procedures for determining sanity are inadequate to preclude federal redetermination of the constitutional issue. We do not here suggest that only a full trial on the issue of sanity will suffice to protect the federal interests; we leave to the State the task of developing appropriate ways to enforce the constitutional restriction upon its execution of sentences. It may be that some high threshold showing on behalf of the prisoner will be found a necessary means to control the number of nonmeritorious or repetitive claims of insanity. Other legitimate pragmatic considerations may also supply the boundaries of the procedural safeguards that feasibly can be provided."

CASE SIGNIFICANCE: The Court decided that an insane person could not be executed because such would be a violation of the Eighth Amendment ban on cruel and unusual punishment. The case was a departure from traditional insanity cases in that Ford was sane at the time of his trial and conviction but became insane while awaiting execution. If Ford had been insane at the time of his trial, he could not have been tried, because competency is required for a defendant to stand trial. The issue here, however, was different from whether a person who was insane at the time the offense was committed could be given the death penalty.

Penry v. Lynaugh
492 U.S. 302 (1989)

CAPSULE: It is constitutional to impose the death penalty on a mentally retarded defendant who has the ability to reason.

FACTS: Penry, who was 22 years old when the crime was committed, was convicted of capital murder. Penry raised the insanity defense at trial. The insanity defense failed but psychiatric testimony during the trial described him as mentally retarded with an IQ of 54 and a mental age of six years. The jury found Penry competent to stand trial and he was found guilty of capital murder. At that time, during the penalty phase of a capital trial, Texas law provided that the jury consider three "special issues":

1. Whether the conduct of the defendant that caused the death of the deceased was committed deliberately and with the reasonable expectation that death would result;

2. Whether the defendant would constitute a continuing threat to society; and

3. Was the killing an unreasonable response to provocation, if any, by the victim?

Penry requested that the jury receive specific instructions defining terms in the special issues and that mercy be considered on the basis of mitigating circumstances. The jury sentenced Penry to death.

ISSUES:
1. Does the execution of a mentally retarded offender violate the Eighth Amendment prohibition against cruel and unusual punishment? NO
2. When requested, should a jury be instructed by the judge to consider mental retardation as a mitigating factor at the sentencing portion of a capital trial? YES

HOLDING:
1. It is constitutional to impose the death penalty on a mentally retarded defendant who has the ability to reason.
2. If the defense requests jury instructions concerning mental retardation as a mitigating factor, such requests must be granted.

REASON: "Since the common law prohibited the punishment of 'idiots'—which term was generally used to describe persons totally lacking in reason, understanding, or the ability to distinguish between good and evil—it may indeed be 'cruel and unusual punishment' to execute persons who are profoundly or severely retarded and wholly lacking in the capacity to appreciate the wrongfulness of their actions. Such persons, however, are not likely to be convicted or face the prospect of punishment today, since the modern insanity defense generally includes 'mental defect' as part of the legal definition of insanity, and since *Ford v. Wainwright, supra*, prohibits the execution of persons who are unaware of their punishment and why they must suffer it. Moreover, petitioner is not such a person, since the jury (1) found him competent to stand trial and therefore to have a rational as well as factual understanding of the proceedings; and (2) rejected his insanity defense, thereby reflecting the conclusion that he knew his conduct was wrong and was capable of conforming it to the requirements of law. Nor is there sufficient objective evidence today of a national consensus against executing mentally retarded capital murderers, since petitioner has cited only one state statute that explicitly bans that practice and has offered no evidence of the general behavior of juries in this regard. Opinion surveys indicating strong public opposition to such executions do not establish a societal consensus, absent some legislative reflection of the sentiment expressed therein."

"To be sure, retardation has long been regarded as a factor that may diminish culpability, and, in its most severe form, may result in complete exculpation . . . Mentally retarded persons, however, are individuals whose abilities and behavioral deficits can vary greatly depending on the degree of their retardation, their life experience, and the ameliorative effects of education and habilitation. On the present record, it cannot be said that all mentally retarded people of petitioner's ability—by virtue of their mental retardation alone, and apart from any individualized consideration of their personal responsibility—inevitably lack the cognitive, volitional, and moral capacity to act with the degree of culpability associated with the death penalty."

CASE SIGNIFICANCE: The Court affirmed that a state could sentence a mentally retarded offender to death, stating that, "the Eighth Amendment does not categorically prohibit the execution of mentally retarded capital murderers of petitioner's reasoning ability." The decision was controversial because it gave a "go ahead" signal for the execution of mentally retarded defendants. The Court used the concept of "evolving standards of decency" to determine whether this practice is constitutional or not, adding that there was no national consensus at that time against such penalties. Thirteen years later, the Court changed its mind in *Atkins v. Virginia* (2002)[47] and overturned the *Penry* decision. In *Atkins*, the Court held that the "evolving standards of decency" had reached a point where it is now deemed unconstitutional to execute a mentally retarded offender. The decision in the case is no longer binding or significant. It is here primarily for historical purposes.

Atkins v. Virginia
536 U.S. 304 (2002)

CAPSULE: Executing a mentally retarded offender violates the Eighth Amendment prohibition against cruel and unusual punishment.

FACTS: Atkins was convicted of abduction, armed robbery, and capital murder, and sentenced to death. In the penalty phase, the defense relied on one witness, Dr. Evan Nelson, a forensic psychologist who had evaluated Atkins before trial and concluded that he was "mildly mentally retarded." His conclusion was based on interviews with people who knew Atkins, a review of school and court records, and the administration of a standard intelligence test, which indicated that Atkins had an IQ of 59. The jury sentenced Atkins to death, but the Virginia Supreme Court ordered a second sentencing hearing because the trial court had used a misleading verdict form. At the resentencing, Dr. Nelson again testified. The state presented an expert rebuttal witness, Dr. Stanton Samenow, who testified that Atkins was not mentally retarded, but rather was of "average intelligence, at least," and had antisocial personality disorder. The jury again sentenced Atkins to death. The decision was affirmed by the Virginia Supreme Court, relying on the precedent set in *Penry v. Lynaugh* (1989).[48]

ISSUES: Is it a violation of the Eighth Amendment to execute a mentally retarded offender? YES.

HOLDING: It is a violation of the Eighth Amendment to put to death an offender who is mentally retarded.

REASON: "As Chief Justice Warren explained in his opinion in *Trop v. Dulles*, 356 U.S. 86 (1958): "The basic concept underlying the Eighth Amendment is nothing less than the dignity of man . . . The Amendment must draw its meaning from the evolving standards of decency that mark the progress of a maturing society." *Id.*, at 100–101. Proportionality review under those evolving standards should be informed by 'objective factors to the maximum possible extent,' . . . This consensus unquestionably reflects widespread judgment about the relative culpability of mentally retarded offenders, and the relationship between mental retardation and the penological purposes served by the death penalty. Additionally, it suggests that some characteristics of mental retardation undermine the strength of the procedural protections that our capital jurisprudence steadfastly guards.

"In light of these deficiencies, our death penalty jurisprudence provides two reasons consistent with the legislative consensus that the mentally retarded should be categorically excluded from execution. First, there is a serious question as to whether either justification that we have recognized as a basis for the death penalty applies to mentally retarded offenders. *Gregg v. Georgia*, 428 U.S. 153, 183 (1976), identified "retribution and deterrence of capital crimes by prospective offenders" as the social purposes served by the death penalty. Unless the imposition of the death penalty on a mentally retarded person, 'measurably contributes to one or both of these goals, it is nothing more than the purposeless and needless imposition of pain and suffering,' and hence an unconstitutional punishment. The reduced capacity of mentally retarded offenders provides a second justification for a categorical rule making such offenders ineligible for the death penalty."

The risk "that the death penalty will be imposed in spite of factors which may call for a less severe penalty," *Lockett v. Ohio*, 438 U.S. 586, 605 (1978), is enhanced, not only by the possibility of false confessions, but also by the lesser ability of mentally retarded defendants to make a persuasive showing of mitigation in the face of prosecutorial evidence of one or more aggravating factors. Mentally retarded defendants may be less able to give meaningful assistance to their counsel and are typically poor witnesses, and their demeanor may create an unwarranted impression of lack of remorse for their crimes. As *Penry* demonstrated, moreover, reliance on mental retardation as a mitigating factor can be a two-edged sword that may enhance the likelihood that the aggravating factor of future dangerousness will be found by the jury. 492 U.S., at 323–325. Mentally retarded defendants in the aggregate face a special risk of wrongful execution.

CASE SIGNIFICANCE: This case is important because it puts an end to the execution of mentally retarded offenders. The Supreme Court had decided the controversial *Penry* case differently more than a decade prior to *Atkins*. This case reverses *Penry*.

The Court said that the states must create suitable methods to enforce the *Atkins* decision. The Court did not, however, provide any guidance as to what constitutes mental retardation and how to assess and diagnose mental retardation. Thus, although the *Atkins* case prohibits the execution of the mentally retarded, it has left many questions unanswered. These issues will likely be considered by the Court in future cases. For now, however, the issue of the constitutionality of executing the mentally retarded is settled. It is unconstitutional.

Singleton v. Norris
319 F.3d 1018 (8th Cir. 2003)

CAPSULE: It is not a violation of the Eighth Amendment to execute a prisoner who became mentally incompetent while on death row, but regained competency through forced medication.

FACTS: Charles Singleton murdered a woman (Mary Lou York) on June 1, 1979. York died from two stab wounds inflicted in her neck. Singleton was convicted of capital murder and sentenced to death in June of 1982. Many years of appeals followed. During Singleton's federal habeus corpus petition, Singleton conceded in his appeal that through voluntary taking of antipsychotic medication he was competent for execution. In 1997, after a period in which Singleton failed to take medication, a review panel decreed that Singleton should be give involuntary medication as he was a danger to himself and/or others. Singleton then filed another habeus corpus petition arguing that the state could not forcefully medicate him solely to make him competent to be executed because it violated his due process and Eighth Amendment rights. The district court dismissed the case stating that it believed the state was not forcefully medicating him solely for the purpose of carrying out his execution. The Eighth Circuit upheld the decision. The Supreme Court denied certiorari.

ISSUE: If there are medically necessary purposes for the medication, is it a violation of due process and the Eighth Amendment to forcefully medicate an inmate to render him competent to be executed? NO.

HOLDING: It is not a violation of the constitution to execute an inmate who is being involuntarily medicated to obtain competency as long as it is not the sole purpose for the medication.

REASON: The Eighth Circuit held that, " the mandatory medication regime, valid under the pendancy of a stay of execution, does not become unconstitutional under *Harper* when an execution date is set." The court adopted the same rule that had been applied in *United States v. Sell*, 539 U.S. 166 (2003). The Eighth Circuit noted that in order to justify the forcible medication of an inmate when the medication rendered the inmate competent for execution, three conditions must be met:

1. present an essential state interest that outweighs the individual's interest in remaining medication free.

2. prove that there is no less intrusive way to fulfill the essential interest

3. prove by clear and convincing evidence that the medication is medically appropriate[49]

Medication is appropriate and in the best medical interest of the inmate when the medication renders the inmate competent and when the severity of the side-effects of the medication does not surpass its benefits. The Eighth Circuit held that when a state executes an inmate who lost competency while on death row but regains competency due to medical care, including forced medication, it is not a violation of a prisoner's Eighth Amendment rights. If the state has an obligation to administer medication in the prisoner's best medical interest, any additional motives, if they are present, are immaterial.

CASE SIGNIFICANCE: The decision in this case allows for states to execute offenders who, without medication, would be considered to be incompetent but with medication are declared competent, regardless of Eighth Circuit also allows states to forcefully medicate an inmate if it is in their "medical best interest" even if they have an ulterior motive of carrying out a death sentence.

Tennard v. Dretke
542 U.S. 274 (2004)

CAPSULE: Mental retardation has applicable mitigating effect beyond its relationship to the crime and the defendant's ability to act deliberately.

FACTS: In 1986 the petitioner was convicted of capital murder in which Tennard and two accomplices killed two of his neighbors while robbing their home. Tennard had stabbed one of the victims. During the penalty phase of the trial defense counsel called Tennard's parole officer as the only witness who testified that Tennard's IQ was 67 when tested at age 17. The parole officer had obtained the information from Tennard's prison record. Tennard had been convicted of rape at age 16, in which his victim had escaped when she was allowed to use the bathroom on the promise that she would not run away. During deliberation, jurors were asked two "special issue" questions used at the time in Texas to determine wether a life or death sentence would be imposed:

1. Was the conduct of the defendant, which caused the death of the deceased committed deliberately and with reasonable expectation that death of the deceased or another would result? (known as the "deliberateness special issue")

2. Is there a probablility that the defendant would commit criminal acts of violence that would constitute a continuing threat to society? (known as the "future dangerousness special issue")

The jury answered "yes" to both questions and Tennard was subsequently sentenced to death. Tennard, on appeal, argued that his death sentence was in violation of *Penry* in that the jury instructions were not sufficient for the jury to consider mental retardation as a mitigating factor. The Texas Court of Criminal Appeals rejected Tennard's *Penry* claim, citing that Tennard failed to meet the standard of mental retardation in Texas. The District Court denied his habeus corpus petition and the Court of Appeals for the Fifth Circuit denied his request for a Certificate of Appealability (COA) on the grounds that even if Tennard was determined to be mentally retarded, he had failed to show that his crime was in any way attributable to such mental retardation.

ISSUE: Should mental retardation be considered as a mitigating factor even if that mental retardation is not shown to be related to the crime? YES.

HOLDING: Evidence of mental retardation should be considered as possible mitigation by a capital jury even if the defendant's crime is not directly attributable to such intellectual or cognitive impairment.

REASON: "Reasonable jurists could conclude that the low IQ evidence Tennard presented was relevant mitigating evidence. Evidence of significantly impaired intellectual functioning is obviously evidence that 'might serve as a basis for a sentence less than death.'"

"Reasonable jurists also could conclude that the Texas Court of Criminal Appeals' application of Penry to the facts of Tennard's case was unreasonable. The relationship between the special issues and Tennard's low IQ evidence has the same essential features as the relationship between the special issues and Penry's mental retardation evidence. Impaired intellectual functioning has mitigating dimension beyond the impact it has on the individual's ability to act deliberately. A reasonable jurist could conclude that the jury might well have given Tennard's low IQ evidence aggravating effect in considering his future dangerousness, not only as a matter of probable inference from the evidence but also because the prosecutor told them to do so: '[W]hether he has a low IQ or not is not really the issue. Because the legislature, in asking you to address that question, the reasons why he became a danger are not really relevant. The fact that he is a danger, that the evidence shows he's a danger, is the criteria to use in answering that question.' Indeed, the prosecutor's comments pressed exactly the most problematic interpretation of the special issues, suggesting that Tennard's low IQ was irrelevant in mitigation, but relevant to the question whether he posed a future danger."

CASE SIGNIFICANCE: The definition of mental retardation is still an issue in states that have the death penalty. The Fifth Circuit denied a COA based upon whether Tennard's mental retardation was "uniquely severe" and a "nexus" to the crime. The Supreme Court held that this was not in line with the standard set in *Penry* and that members of a jury must be able to fully consider a capital defendant's mitigating circumstances. The decision in *Tennard* reaffirms the notion that impaired intellectual functioning is a relevant mitigating factor to be considered by capital juries in sentencing decisions.

Panetti v. Quarterman
551 U.S. ___ (2007)

CAPSULE: A prisoner's awareness of a state's rationale for an execution is not the same as a rational understanding of it.

FACTS: The petitioner was convicted of capital murder in a Texas state court and sentenced to death, even in light of a well-documented history of mental illness. Panetti was denied relief on direct appeal and his habeas corpus petition was denied by the district court and Fifth Circuit. At no point in his initial appeal did the petitioner argue that he was mentally incompetent to stand trial. Once an execution date was set, the petitioner, for the first time, filed a motion that he was not competent to be executed due to his mental illness. Panetti had a well-documented history of severe mental illness including at least 12 involuntary commitments in Wisconsin and Texas. The psychiatrist who found him competent to stand trial noted his "chronic delusions and occasional hallucinations . . ." The trial judge denied the motion without a hearing and the Texas Criminal Court of Appeals dismissed the appeal for lack of jurisdiction. Panetti then filed a second habeas petition in which the District Court stayed his execution so that the state trial court could consider his current mental state. Without ruling on the outstanding motions, the judge found the petitioner competent and closed the case. Petitioner then returned to the Federal District Court, seeking a resolution of his pending habeus petition. The District Court concluded that the state-court competency proceedings failed to comply with Texas law and were constitutionally inadequate in light of the procedural requirements mandated by *Ford* v. *Wainwright*, 477 U.S. 399. Although the court therefore reviewed petitioner's incompetency claim without deferring to the state court's finding of competency, it nevertheless granted no relief, finding that petitioner had not demonstrated that he met the standard for incompetency. Under Fifth Circuit precedent, the court explained, petitioner was competent to be executed as long as he knew the fact of his impending execution and the factual predicate for it. The Fifth Circuit affirmed.

ISSUES:
1. Is it a violation of the Eighth Amendment to execute an inmate who, because of mental illness, lacks a rational understanding of the State's rationale for the execution but has a factual awareness of that rationale? UNANSWERED.
2. Is it a violation of the Constitution to fail to provide adequate measures to challenge an execution based on claims of mental incompetency? YES.

HOLDINGS:
1. The Supreme Court refused to make a determinative statement regarding standards for what constitutes a "rational understanding" of the state's rationale for execution.
2. It is a violation of the Constitution to fail to the provide adequate measures for a defendant to challenge an execution based on claims of incompetency to be executed.

REASON: "The state court failed to provide the procedures to which petitioner was entitled under the Constitution. *Ford* identifies the measures a State must provide when a prisoner alleges incompetency to be executed. As Justice Powell elaborated, once a prisoner seeking a stay of execution has made 'a substantial threshold showing of insanity,' 477 U.S., at 424, the Eighth and Fourteenth Amendments entitle him to a fair hearing including an opportunity to submit 'expert psychiatric evidence that may differ from the State's own psychiatric examination,' *id.*, at 427. The procedures the state court provided petitioner were ruled so deficient that they cannot be reconciled with any reasonable interpretation of the *Ford* rule. It is uncontested that petitioner made a substantial showing of incompetency. It is also evident from the record, however, that the state court reached its competency determination without holding a hearing or providing petitioner with an adequate opportunity to provide his own expert evidence. Moreover, there is a strong argument that the court violated state law by failing to provide a competency hearing. If so, the violation undermines any reliance the State might now place on Justice Powell's assertion that 'the States should have substantial leeway to determine what process best balances the various interests at stake.' *Id.*, at 427. Having determined that the state court unreasonably applied *Ford* when it accorded petitioner the procedures in question, the Court then considered petitioner's claim on the merits without deferring to the state court's competency finding."

"Although the Court rejects the Fifth Circuit's standard, it does not attempt to set down a rule governing all competency determinations. The record is not as informative as it might be because it was developed by the District Court under the rejected standard, and, thus, this Court finds it difficult to amplify its conclusions or to make them more precise. It is proper to allow the court charged with overseeing the development of the evidentiary record the initial opportunity to resolve petitioner's constitutional claim."

CASE SIGNIFICANCE: The case affirms the belief that "death is different" and that the protection of the severely mentally ill sentenced to death is still an issue in American death penalty jurisprudence. While the decision in *Atkins v. Virginia* instituted a ban on the execution of the mentally retarded, there is no universal ban on capital punishment for the mentally ill. The case highlights the notion that states are still struggling with the standard set out in *Ford* and how incompetence to stand trial is defined. Panetti had a history of severe mental illness and yet was still found to be competent by a Texas jury (after his first jury deadlocked and a mistrial was declared). This case also confirms the continued belief by many in the criminal justice system that mental illness is an "excuse" or a "way to get off easy." Jurors, even when faced with substantial evidence of schizophrenic delusions and acute psychiatric disorders, are skeptical at best and may be even less likely to show sympathy if they believe the defendant is "pretending." The Supreme Court in *Panetti* has reaffirmed that mentally ill defendants in capital proceedings must be afforded protection in establishing competency to be executed.

Internet Resources

Mental Retardation and the Death Penalty
www.deathpenaltyinfo.org/dpicmr.html

FAQ about The Death Penalty and People with Mental Retardation
http://www.aamr.org/Policies/faq_death_penalty.shtml

Mental Retardation and the Death Penalty: A Guide to State Legislative Issues

www.internationaljusticeproject.org/pdfs/STATE_LEGISLATIVE_GUIDE.
   pdf

Death Penalty and People with Mental Illness
http://www.mha-mi.org/policy44.html

**SSRN—"What *Atkins* Could Mean for People with Mental Illness"
   by Christopher Slobogin**
Available at: papers.ssrn.com/sol3/papers.cfm?abstract_id=407041.

Notes

1. *Penry v. Lynaugh*, 492 U.S. 302 (1989).

2. 492 U.S. at 322 (1989).

3. 492 U.S. at 336 (1989).

4. *Atkins v. Virginia*, 534 U.S. 1122 (2002).

5. *Atkins v. Virginia*, 122 S. Ct. at 2252.

6. 356 U.S. 86 (1958).

7. Christopher Slobogin, *What* Atkins *Could Mean for People with Mental Illness*, 33 N.M L. REV. 293 (2003).

8. *Tennard v. Dretke*, 542 U.S. 274 (2004).

9. *Panetti v. Quarterman*, 448 F.3d 815 (2007).

10. Douglas Mossman, M.D., Atkins v. Virginia: *A Psychiatric Can of Worms*, 33 N.M. L. REV. 255 (2003).

11. American Association of Mental Retardation, AAMR Homepage. Available at http://www. aamr.org (accessed June 6, 2004).

12. American Association of Intellectual and Developmental Disabilities, AAIDD Homepage. Available at http://www.aaidd.org (accessed February 4, 2008).

13. Robert L. Schalock, Ruth A. Luckasson, and Karrie A. Shogren, with Sharon Borthwick-Duffy, Val Bradley, Wil H. E. Buntinx, David L. Coulter, Ellis (Pat) M. Craig, Sharon C. Gomez, Yves Lachapelle, Alya Reeve, Martha E. Snell, Scott Spreat, Marc J. Tassé, James R. Thompson, Miguel A. Verdugo, Michael L. Wehmeyer, and Mark H. Yeager, *The Renaming of* Mental Retardation: *Understanding the Change to the Term* Intellectual Disability. INTELLECTUAL AND DEVELOPMENTAL DISABILITIES 45, 2: 116–124, 2007.

14. American Psychiatric Association, *Diagnostic and Statistical Manual for Mental Disorders* (4th ed. 2000).

15. *Id.*

16. *Supra* note 6.

17. Alexis Krulish Dowling, *Post-Atkins Problems with Enforcing the Supreme Court's Ban on Executing the Mentally Retarded*, 33 SETON HALL LAW REVIEW 773 (2003).

18. V62.89-This category can be used when the focus of clinical attention is associated with borderline intellectual functioning—that is, an IQ in the 71–84 range. Differential diagnosis between Borderline Intellectual Functioning and Mental Retardation (an IQ of 70 or below) is especially difficult when the coexistence of certain mental disorders (e.g., schizophrenia) is involved.

19. Baroff, G.S. (2003). *Establishing Mental Retardation in Capital Cases: An Update.* MENTAL RETARDATION, 41, 198–202.

20. Kanaya, Y., M. Scullin and S. Ceci (2002). *The Flynn Effect and U.S. Policies: The Impact of Rising IQ Scores on American Society via Mental Retardation Diagnosis.* AMERICAN PSYCHOLOGIST, 58, 778–779.

21. *Id.* at 788–789.

22. MICHAEL L. PERLIN, THE HIDDEN PREJUDICE: MENTAL DISABILITY ON TRIAL 236 (2000).

23. *Supra* note 7 at 739.

24. American Psychological Association, *Ethical Principles of Psychologists and Code of Conduct.* In DONALD BERSOFF (ED.), ETHICAL CONFLICTS IN PSYCHOLOGY 6 (1995).

25. *Id.*

26. Committee on Ethical Guidelines for Forensic Psychologists, *Specialty Guidelines for Forensic Psychologists.* In DONALD BERSOFF (ED.), ETHICAL CONFLICTS IN PSYCHOLOGY 441 (1995).

27. *Supra* note 307 at 307.

28. Mark D. Cunningham and Mark P. Vigen, *Death Row Inmate Characteristics, Adjustment and Confinement: A Critical Review of the Literature,* 20 BEHAV. SOC. LAW 191 (2002).

29. 536 U.S. at 318.

30. *Moore v. Texas,* 535 U.S. (2002) (Scalia, J., dissenting).

31. *Ford v. Wainwright,* 477 U.S. 399 (1986).

32. *Id.* at 406 (1986).

33. AMERICAN BAR ASSOCIATION, CRIMINAL JUSTICE MENTAL HEALTH STANDARDS 7-5.6 (b) (1989).

34. *Ford v. Wainwright, supra.*

35. *Id.* at 407.

36. *Id.*

37. KENT S. MILLER AND MICHAEL L. RADELET, EXECUTING THE MENTALLY ILL: THE CRIMINAL JUSTICE SYSTEM AND THE CASE OF ALVIN FORD (1993).

38. www.mega.nu/webconst/section_Definition_of_Mental_Incompetence.html. Accessed January 21, 2008. LORETTA M. KOPELMAN, AND JOHN C. MOSKOP, ETHICS AND MENTAL RETARDATION (1984) at 131.

39. *Singleton v. Norris,* 319 F.3d 10184 (2003).

40. *Panetti v. Quarterman,* 551 U.S. ___ (2007).

41. Joint Appendix, *Panetti v. Quarterman,* 127 S. Ct. 2842 at 29.

42. *Ford v. Wainwright,* 477 U.S. 399 (1986).

43. *Penry v. Lynaugh*, 492 U.S. 302 (1989).

44. *Atkins v. Virginia*, 536 U.S. 304 (2002).

45. *Tennard v. Dretke*, 542 US 274 (2004).

46. *Singleton v. Norris*, 319 F.3d 10184 (2003).

47. *Id.*

48. *Penry v. Lynaugh*, 492 U.S. 302 (1989).

49. Citing *United States v. Sell*, 282 F.3d 560, 567 (2002).

Chapter Outline

Chapter 5

Death Penalty for Juveniles

I. Introduction

    The death penalty for juveniles has undergone jurisprudential evolution with a 180-degree twist. Common law practice was to punish offenders without considering their age.[1] The first recorded execution in the United States of a juvenile happened in Plymouth Colony, Massachusetts.[2] The juvenile, Thomas Graunger, was convicted of bestiality and subsequently put to death at age 16. At that time, the death penalty could be imposed for a variety of crimes committed by children; however, records indicate that between the years of 1806 and 1882 there were only two children under the age of 14 put to death in the United States.[3] From 1973 to 2005, there were 227 death sentences imposed on juveniles; however, only 22 resulted in executions.[4]

    The Supreme Court interprets limitations on the death penalty based on "evolving standards that mark the progress of a maturing society."[5] Sharp disagreement prevails among Supreme Court Justices as to the factors that determine evolving standards of decency. Conservatives maintain that the interpretation of evolving standards should be strictly based on objective factors such as the acts of state legislatures and the sentencing practices of juries. In contrast, the liberals advocate a broader interpretation. Their view considers objective factors and the social purposes of the death penalty: these include factors such as moral proportionality, penal goals, and the views of relevant groups on the juvenile death penalty. Although the Court uses contemporary standards of decency to evaluate the death penalty for juveniles, their ongoing debate concerns the appropriate age for executing juveniles.

    This chapter reviews United States Supreme Court decisions on the juvenile death penalty. It begins with an analysis of three major U.S. Supreme Court cases: *Thompson v. Oklahoma* (1988),[6] *Stanford v. Kentucky* (1989),[7] and *Roper v. Simmons* (2005).[8] It then devotes extended coverage to the *Simmons* case because of its recency and impact on the execution of juveniles.

129

The chapter closes with an examination of the Court's interpretations of evolving standards of decency in the context of the juvenile death penalty.

II. *Thompson v. Oklahoma:* Executing Juveniles Age 15 and Younger Is Unconstitutional

A. Facts

Thompson, along with three accomplices, actively participated in the murder of his former brother-in-law during the early hours of January 23, 1983. The victim was shot two times and sustained multiple knife wounds to his throat, chest, and abdomen. Thompson and his accomplices threw the body into a river, where it was undiscovered for approximately four weeks.

Although Thompson was considered a child according to Oklahoma law, he was certified to stand trial as an adult and subsequently convicted. During the penalty phase, the prosecutor sought the death penalty. The prosecutor asked the jury to find that aggravating circumstances existed, namely: (1) that the murder was particularly heinous and cruel, and (2) that there was a reasonable probability that the defendant would present a continuing threat to society if set free. The jury found that the first aggravating circumstance existed and Thompson was given the death penalty.

The Supreme Court granted certiorari in *Thompson* to decide whether the death penalty was constitutional for juveniles who committed their crime at the age of 15. At the time *Thompson* was decided, the Supreme Court had not established a minimum age for executing juveniles. States had the power to set their own minimum age for imposing the death penalty.

B. The Court's Holding

The Court held that the execution of juveniles who committed the crime at age 15 constitutes cruel and unusual punishment. The Court said that the interpretation of evolving standards should be based on "relevant legislative enactments, jury determinations and explaining why a young person is not capable of acting with the degree of culpability that can justify the ultimate penalty."[9] Four of the Supreme Court Justices shared this view. A separate concurring opinion was written by Justice O'Connor. In her concurring opinion, Justice O'Connor agreed with the plurality's decision but claimed that when a state has not established a minimum age for execution the Court cannot assume that the state intended such executions to take place. Because the majority of state legislatures did not set a minimum age for execution, she concluded that the execution of 15-year-olds was unconstitutional.

C. Reasoning

The Court first examined the acts of state legislatures in order to determine whether a national consensus existed against the execution of juveniles who committed their crime before reaching the age of 16. In their analysis of state laws, the Court distinguished between the rights of minors and the rights of adults. Because most states, including Oklahoma, prohibited 15-year-olds from serving as jurors, voting, or using alcohol or cigarettes, the Court concluded that adult and juvenile rights were different.[10] The Court said that different rights for adults and juveniles meant that "society assumes that minors do not act as adults do, and thus [society] acts in their interest by restricting certain choices that they are not yet ready to make with the full benefit of the costs and benefits attending to such decisions."[11]

At the time *Thompson* was decided, most states did not statutorily define their minimum age for execution. In states with no minimum age for execution, judges and prosecutors were required to certify juveniles in order for them to be eligible for the death penalty. However, a total of 18 states set their legal age at 16.[12] The Court inferred that these 18 states constituted a national consensus against the death penalty for juveniles because no states set their minimum age for execution below the age of 16.

The Court then looked at the sentencing patterns of juries and concluded that society did not believe that the death penalty should be constitutional for juveniles 15 and younger because most juries did not sentence these individuals to death. As evidence of then-contemporary sentencing patterns, the Court noted that between the years of 1982 and 1986, only five of about 1,400 capital offenders were under the age of 16.[13] The Court was also influenced by the fact that only 18 to 20 juveniles age 15 and younger were put to death during the twentieth century, all of which occurred before 1948.[14] These factors, taken together, led the Court to conclude that executing juvenile offenders 15 years of age and younger was unconstitutional. But what about juveniles who were 16 or 17 years of age? It did not take long for the Court to resolve the issue left unanswered in *Thompson*. The Court addressed that issue in *Stanford v. Kentucky* the following year.

II. *Stanford v. Kentucky:* Executing Juveniles Ages 16 to 17 Is Constitutional

A. Facts

Kevin Stanford was 17 years old when he brutally murdered Barbel Poore in Jefferson County, Kentucky. On January 7, 1981, Stanford and his accomplice repeatedly raped and sodomized Poore, who worked as a gas station attendant. The perpetrators then drove their victim to a removed area, where Stanford shot her twice in the head. Stanford and his accomplice obtained 300 cartons of cigarettes, a couple of gallons of gas, and a nominal amount of cash. A corrections officer testified that Stanford explained the crime in this manner: "He said, I had to shoot her, [she] lived next door to me and she would recognize me. . . . I guess we could have tied her up or something or beat [her up] . . . and tell her if she tells, we would kill her . . . Then after he said that he started laughing."[15]

Because Stanford was charged with a Class A felony or capital crime and was over 16 years of age at the time of his crime, the juvenile court waived jurisdiction. Given Stanford's past record of juvenile delinquency, the juvenile court certified Stanford to stand trial as an adult. He was convicted of numerous crimes, including murder, and sentenced to death plus 45 years. On appeal, Stanford argued that the death penalty was cruel and unusual punishment for offenders who committed their crime at the age of 16 or 17.

B.   The Court's Holding

In *Stanford*, the Court addressed the same issue raised in a companion case, *Wilkins v. Missouri* (1989).[16] Wilkins and Stanford were 16 and 17 years old, respectively. Although the two cases are separate and involved different facts, the cases are often referred to as the *Stanford* case because they involved the same rule. The *Stanford* Court addressed the issue of whether the death penalty was cruel and unusual punishment for juveniles 16 or 17 years old at the time of the crime. As in *Thompson*, the Court used "evolving standards of decency"[17] to determine whether a national consensus against the death penalty for juveniles under the age of 18 had emerged. In a five-to-four decision, the Court held that the death penalty was not cruel and unusual punishment for juveniles aged 16 or 17 at the time the crime was committed.

C.   Reasoning

The *Stanford* Court took a narrow approach to analyzing the evolving standards doctrine. Justice Scalia, writing for the majority, said that evolving standards of decency must be evaluated according to "statutes passed by society's elected representatives"[18] and also the sentencing practices of state juries. The Court said that a categorical rule prohibiting the death penalty for juveniles ages 16 or 17 would unnecessarily restrict states from exercising their legislative authority to establish minimum ages for execution. Justice Scalia claimed that the views of professional, religious, and international groups on the execution of 16- or 17-year-olds should not be considered influential when evaluating evolving standards.

At the time *Stanford* was decided, 37 states had the death penalty.[19] After noting the number of states authorizing the death penalty, the Court focused on states allowing the death penalty for 16- and 17-year-olds. According to then-existing law, the Court found that 15 states rejected the death penalty for juveniles who committed their crime prior to reaching the age of 16. It also determined that 12 states refused to impose the death penalty on individuals who committed their crime when younger than 17.[20] The Court then concluded that the number of states permitting the death penalty for 16- or 17-year-olds was sufficient to establish a national consensus in favor of the juvenile death penalty.

The *Stanford* Court conceded that the number of state juries sentencing juveniles to death was far fewer than that for adults. The Court acknowledged that only about two percent of offenders executed during the years 1642 to 1986 were under the age of 18 at the time of their crime.[21] However, the Court considered the statistics unimportant because it was "not only possible, but overwhelmingly probable, that the very considerations which induce petitioners and prosecutors and juries to believe that death should never be imposed on offenders under 18 cause prosecutors and juries to believe that it should rarely be imposed."[22] The Court held that the death penalty was not cruel and unusual punishment for 16- or 17-year-olds.

IV. *Atkins v. Virginia:* A Case Involving the Mentally Retarded, but a Prelude to the Abolition of the Juvenile Death Penalty

A. *The Issue and Holding*

In *Atkins v. Virginia* (2002),[23] the Court addressed the question of whether the death penalty was cruel and unusual punishment for mentally retarded offenders. The *Atkins* Court held that imposing the death penalty on mentally retarded defendants violates the Eighth and Fourteenth Amendments. In *Atkins*, the Court overruled its earlier decision in *Penry v. Lynaugh* (1989),[24] in which the Court held that the execution of mentally retarded defendants was not cruel and unusual punishment. The Court returned to the evolving standards of decency test, focusing on state legislation, sentencing practices, and the diminished culpability of mentally retarded defendants.

The Court first examined the number of state laws that changed between 1989 and 2002.[25] The Court considered important the fact that 16 states legislatively banned the practice of executing mentally retarded offenders during these years, noting "the consistency and direction of change"[26] of state legislation, which was a critical component of the holding. In addition, the Court said that since *Penry*, juries were less likely to impose death as punishment for mentally retarded defendants. The Court took into account the opinions of the professional, social, religious, and international communities on the execution of mentally retarded defendants. It concluded that "although these factors are by no means dispositive, their consistency with the legislative evidence lends further support to our conclusion that there is a consensus among those who have addressed the issue."[27]

The Court assessed the policy implications served by executing the mentally retarded offenders, saying that mentally retarded offenders "have diminished capacities to understand and process information, to communicate, to abstract from mistakes and learn from experience."[28] The Court then concluded that the deterrent and retributive value of the death penalty was undermined by allowing further executions of the mentally retarded.

B.   Significance of Atkins for the Juvenile Death Penalty: The Missouri Supreme Court's Decision in Simmons v. Roper

The *Atkins* case is important because of its impact on the death penalty for juveniles. One year after *Atkins*, the Missouri Supreme Court decided *Simmons v. Roper*.[29] In that case, the Missouri Supreme Court held that the Eighth and Fourteenth Amendments prohibited the execution of juveniles who committed their crime before reaching the age of 18. Most of the state court's opinion rested on the logic used in *Atkins*. In *Atkins*, the United States Supreme Court cited changes in state legislation since *Penry* on the execution of the mentally retarded, as well as trends in sentencing practices by juries and the policy implications behind the death penalty. Holding that current standards of decency now prohibit the execution of the mentally retarded, the Missouri Supreme Court then found that a national consensus against the execution of juveniles had emerged since the Supreme Court decided *Stanford*.

The Missouri Supreme Court compared the number of states opposing the death penalty for the mentally retarded in *Penry* (2) to the number in *Atkins* (18). While only six states had raised their minimum statutory age between the time *Stanford* and *Simmons* were decided, the "consistency and direction of change"[30] of state legislation was the most critical factor.

Based on the analysis adopted in *Atkins*, the Missouri Supreme Court said that juveniles, as well as the mentally retarded, are less likely to receive death sentences by state juries. The Missouri Supreme Court noted that of the 22 states allowing the death penalty for juveniles, only six states had executed juvenile defendants since *Stanford*. It indicated that only three of these six states—Texas, Virginia, and Oklahoma—had imposed the death penalty on a juvenile since 1993.[31] The Missouri Supreme Court said that the international, professional, social, and religious communities opposed the death penalty for the mentally retarded the same way it did for juvenile defendants. It noted that while the U.S. Supreme Court had taken different approaches to interpreting evolving standards of decency in the past, "*Atkins* clearly demonstrated a shift back to reliance on such evidence."[32]

The Missouri Supreme Court declared the execution of juveniles unconstitutional, which made it difficult for the United States Supreme Court to dodge the issue. The Missouri high court said the execution of juveniles was cruel and unusual based on contemporary standards of decency: in effect, it boldly overruled what the Supreme Court held in *Stanford*.

V. *Roper v. Simmons:* The Supreme Court Declares the Execution of Juveniles Unconstitutional

A. Facts

Christopher Simmons was 17 years old when he committed a brutal murder. Before committing the crime, Simmons stated that he wanted to kill someone, and discussed his plan to commit the act with his friends. On the night of the crime Simmons and his accomplice entered the home of Shirley Crook through an open window and awakened her. Simmons later stated that he intended to kill Mrs. Crook because of their mutual involvement in a previous car accident.

Simmons and his accomplice used duct tape to cover the victim's eyes, mouth, and hands. They used the victim's van to drive her to a nearby state park. After walking to the top of the bridge, they covered her face with a towel, tied her feet and hands together with wire, and threw her into the Meramec River. The victim was later discovered by fisherman; she had drowned.

During police interrogation, Simmons confessed to the crime. He was charged with burglary, kidnapping, stealing, and murder in the first degree. Because Simmons was 17 at the time of his crime, he was not considered a juvenile under Missouri law. In seeking the death penalty, the state submitted aggravating factors to the jury. The defense also offered mitigating evidence in Simmons' behalf, including the fact that he had no prior convictions and that he cared for his family. The trial court convicted Simmons and sentenced him to death.

After the decision in *Atkins*, Simmons subsequently filed a habeas corpus claim on the grounds that the Eighth and Fourteenth Amendments prohibited the execution of a juvenile who committed the crime while under the age of 18. The Missouri Supreme Court agreed.

B. The Holding

After the Missouri Supreme Court decided *Simmons*, the defendant's death sentence was set aside and he was given life imprisonment without eligibility for probation, parole, or release except by act of the governor. The U.S. Supreme Court granted certiorari in order to determine whether the death penalty for 16- or 17-year-olds violated the Eighth and Fourteenth Amendments to the Constitution. Using the evolving standards test, the United States Supreme Court, in a five-to-four vote, held that the Eighth and

Fourteenth Amendments prohibited the imposition of the death penalty for offenders who commit their crimes prior to reaching the age of 18.33 This means that the execution of juvenile defendants 16 or 17 years old is no longer constitutional.

C. Majority Opinion

The majority opinion in *Simmons* was written by Justice Kennedy and joined by Justices Stevens, Souter, Ginsburg, and Breyer. This section analyzes the majority opinion.

The *Simmons* Court used the same approach taken in *Thompson* and *Atkins* to assess whether the death penalty for 16- or 17-year-olds violates the Eighth and Fourteenth Amendments. The Court first examined trends in state legislation and the sentencing practices of juries during the years since the decision in *Stanford*. The Court used the evolving standards test to determine whether the death penalty for juveniles was "so disproportionate as to be cruel and unusual."[34] Relying on *Atkins*, the Court compared the number of states prohibiting the execution of 16- and 17-year-olds to those that maintained it for adults. The Court indicated that 18 states prohibited the execution of the mentally retarded, but retained it for other adults. Next, it said that since *Stanford*, only six states had executed juveniles ages 16 or 17. Similarly, five states had executed mentally retarded defendants since *Penry* (when the Court held that the death penalty for the mentally retarded was not unconstitutional). The Court said, "[t]he evidence of national consensus against the death penalty for juveniles is similar, and in some respects parallel, to the evidence *Atkins* held sufficient to demonstrate a national consensus against the death penalty for the mentally retarded.[35] However, the Court noted a key difference between the decisions in *Penry* and *Atkins* on the one hand, and those of *Stanford* and *Simmons*. The Court said that the rate of change was greater in the cases dealing with the mentally retarded—16 states banned the death penalty for the mentally retarded since *Penry*, making a total of 18 states opposing executions at the time of *Atkins*. Conversely, only five states banned the death penalty for 16- or 17-year-olds between *Stanford* and *Simmons*, a much smaller number. The *Simmons* Court stressed that it was not only the number of states changing legislation, but the "consistency and the direction of change"[36] of that legislation. The *Simmons* Court stressed the idea that a national consensus against the execution of 16- or 17-year-olds gained stronger support earlier rather than later because 12 states opposed the death penalty for 16- or 17-year-olds at the time of *Stanford*.

In part two of its opinion, the Court used its own "independent judgment to demonstrate that the death penalty is a disproportionate punishment for juveniles."[37] It relied heavily on the logic developed in *Atkins*, claiming that juveniles are "categorically less culpable than the average criminal."[38]

The Court indicated that there are three significant differences between juveniles and adults that make juveniles undeserving of the death penalty:

1. Juveniles lack the maturity level of adults. The Court said that a juvenile's lack of maturity is more likely to result in unreasoned, spontaneous action. States have passed forms of legislation prohibiting juveniles from serving on juries, voting, or marrying without their parents' consent based on this premise.

2. Juveniles are more vulnerable to peer pressure. The Court cited recent studies saying that juveniles were more likely to engage in dangerous behavior and therefore have less control over their environment.

3. Juveniles have less developed personality traits. The Court indicated that the relationship between a juvenile's under-developed personality traits and his or her actions makes a juvenile more prone to act irrationally.

These general differences, the Court said, means that juveniles do not belong to the worst class of offenders; therefore, they should not be executed. Using current research on juvenile behavior, the Court reasoned that juveniles were not worthy of the death penalty because "only a relatively small proportion of adolescents who experiment with risky or illegal activities develop entrenched patterns of problem behavior that persist into adult-hood."[39]

Addressing the policy objectives behind the juvenile death penalty, the Court indicated that the social purposes of the death penalty—retribution and deterrence—could not be accomplished by allowing juveniles to be executed. Juveniles, like the mentally retarded, do not have the same culpability as a typical murderer, let alone the worst murderers. Because *Atkins* acknowledged that average murderers were not worthy of the death penalty, the *Simmons* Court similarly concluded that the death penalty for juveniles is cruel and unusual punishment.

The Court said the Eighth Amendment requires more than individualized consideration of aggravating and mitigating factors in juvenile death penalty cases. It claimed that it is too risky to allow juries and judges to decide whether the death penalty is an appropriate form of punishment for juveniles because trained psychiatrists and psychologists frequently disagree on the subject. Instead, the Court said that one's youth constitutes an automatic exception to the death penalty because "an unacceptable likelihood exists that the brutality or cold-blooded nature of any particular crime would overpower mitigating arguments based on youth as a matter of course."[40]

The Court found that most foreign nations viewed the death penalty for juveniles to be a form of disproportionate punishment; therefore, the practice must be abolished. The majority said the laws of foreign nations were "instructive for interpretation of the Eighth Amendment's prohibition of cruel and unusual punishments."[41] It indicated that Article 37 of the United Nations Convention on the Rights of the Child, a form of international legislation rejecting the death penalty for juveniles, was ratified by every country in the world except for the United States and Somalia.[42] The Court was influenced by this fact, and by the reality that almost every other country in the world opposes the juvenile death penalty. Although the Court acknowledged that the views of the international community should not control evolving standards, it concluded that it is clear for now that international laws play an important role in the understanding of what is truly cruel and unusual punishment.

D. Dissenting Opinions

Justices O'Connor and Scalia wrote separate dissenting opinions. This section discusses Justice O'Connor's opinion, followed by that of Justice Scalia.

The important points in Justice O'Connor's dissenting opinion are as follows:

1. The Court's moral proportionality analysis does not account for the fact that some juveniles, like adults, can commit crimes that are equally heinous.

She acknowledged the Court had a "constitutional obligation"[43] to determine whether a certain type of punishment was appropriate for a given group of offenders. Although the majority believed that a categorical exemption for juveniles was appropriate given their diminished culpability, Justice O'Connor said that the proportionality of punishment must be considered in terms of the amount of harm inflicted on the victim, in addition to the defendant's culpability. She recalled her earlier opinion in *Thompson*, in which she stated, "it does not necessarily follow that all 15-year-olds are incapable of the moral culpability that would justify the imposition of capital punishment."[44]

Next, Justice O'Connor differentiated between categorical rules for juveniles and the mentally retarded. She said that in *Atkins*, the Court concluded that mentally retarded defendants were so different from average adults that "these deficits called into serious doubt whether the execution of mentally retarded offenders would measurably contribute to the principal penological goals that capital punishment is intended to serve—retribution and deterrence."[45]

2. There is a lack of objective evidence establishing a national consensus against the death penalty for juveniles.

Justice O'Connor criticized the majority for affirming the decision of the Missouri Supreme Court without so much as a "slap on the hand."[46] She said that only the Supreme Court has the power to overrule one of its own precedents; furthermore, the Missouri Supreme Court abused its authority when it, in effect, overruled the *Stanford* decision. She concluded that the majority's affirmation of the lower court's decision "threatens to invite frequent and disruptive reassessments of our Eighth Amendment precedents."[47]

After pointing out the majority's failure to address this error, Justice O'Connor explained why a national consensus against the death penalty for juveniles had not been established. She said that although the number of states opposing the death penalty for juveniles and the mentally retarded were identical (18), the consensus was stronger in *Atkins*. She concluded that because eight states still permitted the death penalty for juveniles, there was no consensus among legislatures on the death penalty for 16- and 17-year-olds.

Justice O'Connor criticized the majority's determination of a national consensus against the death penalty for juveniles on other grounds. She said that the Court did not present clear evidence demonstrating that juveniles, unlike adults, are incapable of committing crimes that are just as bad. Justice O'Connor said that the majority was wrong for not considering cases on a factual basis. The majority was wrong, she said, because it did not show that juries were incapable of determining when the death penalty is appropriate, it simply concluded this without a valid explanation.

Justice Scalia wrote a separate dissenting opinion in *Simmons*. He was joined by the Chief Justice and Justice Thomas. His dissenting opinion consisted of four main arguments, which are:

1. The fact that less than 50 percent of states oppose the juvenile death penalty does not establish a national consensus.

Justice Scalia said "words have no meaning if the views of less than 50 percent of the death penalty States can constitute a national consensus."[48] There must be significant opposition to a given punishment in order for there to be a national consensus. Justice Scalia cited *Coker v. Georgia* (1977),[49] in which the Court held that the Eighth Amendment prohibited a state from imposing the death penalty on an offender who committed rape when only one state allowed rape offenders to be executed. Justice Scalia said *Simmons* was drastically different from *Coker* due to the fact that "twelve States favoring no executions says something about consensus against the death penalty, but nothing—absolutely nothing—about consensus that offenders under 18 deserve special immunity from such a penalty."[50]

2. The real factor driving the majority opinion in this case is not the actions of state legislators but their own subjective judgment that juveniles can never be deserving of the death penalty, regardless of the circumstances.

Justice Scalia said that the majority was wrong for returning to the approach used in *Thompson*, when the Court acknowledged that its own subjective opinion about the morality of executing juveniles should be the decisive factor when determining the propriety of a particular punishment. He claimed that the Court should only interpret evidence of evolving standards, rather than form its own opinion about what society believes is truly moral.

3. The views of the international community should not be considered when determining the constitutionality of the juvenile death penalty.

Justice Scalia claimed that the majority was mistaken when it concluded that the laws of the international community should influence the Court's decision. He said that the United States' reluctance to ratify the International Covenant on Civil and Political Rights was not evidence of a national ban against the execution of juveniles, but legislative evidence that the practice is acceptable in this country. He indicated that the majority failed to consider the fact that the laws of the United States and many foreign nations differ in many respects. For example, he cited laws regarding religion in other countries, where foreign governments do not require the laws separating church and state. In Justice Scalia's opinion, these laws conflict with the provision of the First Amendment that "Congress shall make no law respecting an establishment of religion."[51]

4. The Missouri Supreme Court does not have the authority to overrule *Stanford*, which it obviously did when it decided *Roper v. Simmons* and disregarded United States Supreme Court precedent.

Justice Scalia chastised the majority for not reprimanding the Missouri Supreme Court when it disregarded the Supreme Court's decision in *Stanford* (which held the execution of 16- and 17-year-olds constitutional). He noted that the majority "silently approved"[52] the Missouri Supreme Court's decision by choosing not to address the issue. In Justice Scalia's view, this is "no way to run a legal system."[53]

VI. Evaluating Evolving Standards: *Thompson, Stanford,* and *Simmons*

The Court has weighed factors affecting evolving standards differently in each of the three cases dealing with the juvenile death penalty. In addition, the Court has relied heavily on case law dealing with the execution of the mentally retarded when evaluating the constitutionality of the juvenile death penalty. This final section assesses the Court's interpretation of evolving standards with relevant case law.

The United States Supreme Court has always interpreted the Eighth Amendment's cruel and unusual punishment clause according to "evolving standards of decency that mark the progress of a maturing society."[54] It has acknowledged that what constitutes cruel and unusual punishment is not static and must be reevaluated according to society's changing views. In *Thompson*, the Court first interpreted evolving standards in the context of the juvenile death penalty. The Court said that executing juveniles who commit their crime before reaching the age of 16 violates the Eighth and Fourteenth Amendments. One year later, the *Stanford* Court revisited the issue of whether the death penalty was cruel and unusual punishment for defendants who commit their crime when they are 16 or 17 years old. After the Court held that the imposition of the death penalty for 16- and 17-year-olds was constitutional, the states had a national standard to follow. For the next 14 years the law as interpreted by the Supreme Court did not change. States had the authority to set their minimum age for execution. In *Simmons*, the Court reevaluated the same issue that was raised in *Stanford*. The *Simmons* Court said that the evolving standards of decency prohibited the execution of juveniles who commit their crimes before reaching the age of 18.

Supreme Court Justices have disagreed on the appropriate test for interpreting evolving standards. Justices Rehnquist, Scalia, and Thomas (the conservatives) firmly believe that the death penalty for juveniles should be interpreted according to objective factors, such as trends in state legislation and jury practices. Justices Ginsburg, Souter, Stevens, and Breyer (the liberals) contend that the interpretation of evolving standards should also include an analysis of penal goals and proportionality. Each of the three cases dealing with the juvenile death penalty has been decided by a five-to-four decision.

In *Thompson*, the Court used a two-part test to evaluate the death penalty for juveniles. Justice Stevens delivered the opinion of the Court. He said that state statutes and the sentencing practices of juries were important factors to consider when interpreting evolving standards. In addition, Justice Stevens claimed that the extreme nature of the death penalty had a disproportionate relationship to a defendant who was less than 16 years old at the time of his or her crime.[55] The two penal goals of the death penalty—retribution and deterrence—were not served, he asserted, because juveniles have a diminished level of culpability compared to adults.

The *Stanford* Court said that the acts of state legislatures and the sentencing practices of juries should be the only factors to be considered when analyzing evolving standards of decency. Justice Scalia wrote the majority opinion in *Stanford*, a case in which the conflict of ideologies among Supreme Court justices became more apparent. Because Justice Scalia did not consider penal goals and measures of proportionality to be compelling factors when interpreting evolving standards, there was no established Eighth Amendment test for the juvenile death penalty. Since then, the Court has disagreed on the correct approach for evaluating evolving standards under the Eighth Amendment.

Chief Justice Rehnquist wrote the dissenting opinion in *Atkins*. According to him, "two sources—the work product of legislatures and sentencing jury determinations—ought to be the sole indicators by which courts ascertain the contemporary American conceptions of decency for the purposes of the Eighth Amendment."[56]

In *Simmons*, the Court's debate about the evolving standards test continued. The majority opinion was written by Justice Kennedy, who was a member of the majority in *Stanford*. In *Stanford*, Justice Kennedy said that measures of proportionality should not be considered sufficient to demonstrate a national consensus. Moreover, he claimed that previous decisions "have never invalidated a punishment on that basis alone, but have done so only when there was also objective evidence of state laws or jury determinations establishing a societal consensus against the penalty."[57] Justice Kennedy believes that a two-part test is more effective than the alternative when interpreting evolving standards, but only when there is compelling objective evidence to go along with it.

In summary, the Court's conservative Justices—Chief Justice Rehnquist, Scalia, and Thomas—believe that evolving standards should be strictly based on state legislation and the sentencing practices of juries. It is clear to them that there must be compelling evidence of a consensus in order for there to be a national consensus. On the other hand, the Court's moderate-to-liberal justices—Kennedy, O'Connor, Souter, Stevens, and Ginsburg—have taken a different approach. Their view uses state legislation and jury behavior along with contemporary arguments about penal goals and proportionality. After *Simmons*, it is apparent that five Justices believe the latter approach is more effective at gauging evolving standards.

VII. A Comparison of *Thompson, Stanford,* and *Simmons*

Figure 5.1

A Comparison of *Thompson, Stanford,* and *Simmons*

Issue	Thompson v. Oklahoma	Stanford v. Kentucky	Roper v. Simmons
Is the death penalty cruel and unusual punishment for juveniles who commit their crime while 16–17 years old?	Not answered because it was not an issue	No	Yes
Majority Justices	Justices Stevens, Brennan, Marshall, Blackmun, O' Connor	Justices Scalia, Kennedy, O'Connor, White, Chief Justice Rehnquist	Justices Kennedy, Souter, Stevens, Ginsburg, Breyer

Figure 5.1, *continued*

Issue	Thompson v. Oklahoma	Stanford v. Kentucky	Roper v. Simmons
Dissenting Justices	Justices Scalia, Rehnquist, White	Justices Brennan, Stevens, Blackmun, Marshall	Justices Scalia, Thomas, Chief Justice Rehnquist, O'Connor
Court used objective factors (trends in State legislatures and sentencing practices of juries)	Yes	Yes	Yes
Number of States authorizing the death penalty in general but prohibiting it for Juveniles	32 States with no minimum age, 18 States set the minimum age at 16	15 States set the minimum age at 17 and 12 States set it at age 18	18 States set the minimum age at 18
Court used subjective factors (penal goals analysis and measures of proportionality)	Yes	No	Yes
Should the views of the international community be considered when interpreting 'evolving standards'?	Yes	No	Yes
Has the concept of 'stare decisis' (let the decision stand) been undermined by *Simmons*?	Not a factor	Not a factor	Majority did not address this— Dissent said yes
Are defendants who commit their crimes between the ages of 15 and 18 as equally deserving of the death penalty?	No	Yes	No

VIII.   In Summary, What Do these Cases Say?

The legal perspective on the juvenile death penalty has evolved a great deal over time. The *Thompson* Court first declared the juvenile death penalty unconstitutional for offenders who committed their crime before the age of 15. The *Thompson* Court did not, however, say whether the execution of juveniles ages 16 or 17 at the time of the crime was constitutional. One year later, the Court decided *Stanford*, which held that the death penalty was constitutional for juveniles who commit their crime at the ages of 16 or 17. Thus, within a two-year period the Court gave the states a definitive age cutoff for imposing the death penalty. The Court's debate about what constitutes evolving standards can generally be discussed based on a two-part analysis. The framework for this analysis consists of: (1) trends in state legislation and the sentencing practices of juries, and (2) measures of proportionality, which include the views of the professional, social, and international communities.

In *Atkins*, the Supreme Court held that the execution of mentally retarded offenders is cruel and unusual punishment. *Atkins* is significant because it reaffirmed the analysis used to evaluate evolving standards by the *Thompson* Court. *Atkins* said that measures of proportionality and penal goals should be included when interpreting evolving standards. This set the stage in *Roper v. Simmons* to strike down the juvenile death penalty.

At the state level, The Missouri Supreme Court held in *Simmons* that the juvenile death penalty violates evolving standards of decency because such standards have evolved since *Stanford*. Although controlling precedent was established by the Supreme Court, the Missouri Supreme Court disregarded *Stanford* and ruled the practice of executing juveniles to be unconstitutional. It virtually urged the nation's highest court to change its mind about juvenile executions.

On appeal, the U.S. Supreme Court affirmed the decision of the Missouri Supreme Court and indeed changed its mind. *Roper v. Simmons* has become the most important case thus far in juvenile death penalty jurisprudence because of its reach. The Court in *Simmons* held that the Eighth and Fourteenth Amendments prohibit the death penalty for offenders who committed their crimes when they were under the age of 18. *Simmons* said the evolving standards of decency prohibited the execution of juveniles for two reasons:

1. The number of states (18) prohibiting the death penalty for juveniles is the same as the number of states deemed sufficient to establish the objective standard held in *Atkins*.

2. Juveniles are categorically less culpable than average criminals. Therefore, the social goals of the death penalty—retribution and deterrence—are not served.

IX. Conclusion

After *Stanford*, the debate about the juvenile death penalty accelerated. The "evolving standards of decency that mark the progress of a maturing society"[58] has been the test for determining whether a particular type of punishment is cruel and unusual. Traditionally, states have been given the legislative power to decide what age is appropriate for executing juveniles as long as they do not set the age below 16. At the time the Court decided *Simmons*, 30 states and the federal government banned the juvenile death penalty for offenders who were less than 18 years old at the time of their crime. Twelve of these states, however, do not allow the death penalty at all.

The *Simmons* case is significant because it revived the two-part analysis originally used in *Thompson*. This analysis includes: (1) a consideration of penal goals and measures of proportionality, and (2) the sentencing behavior of juries and trends in state legislation. The *Simmons* Court rejected the *Stanford* approach because it does not account for subjective factors that must be considered when analyzing the Eighth Amendment. The *Simmons* Court instead returned to the approach used in *Thompson* and affirmed that the evolving standards of decency should be based solely on the sentencing practices of juries and patterns in state legislation.

Simmons is also significant because in that decision the majority declared that the views of foreign nations may be taken into account when determining "evolving standards of decency," a view rejected by the dissenting justices. *Simmons* reaffirms that evolving standards of decency are not only shaped by legislative action and the sentencing patterns of juries, but also by such other factors as the subjective views of the Supreme Court justices on measures of proportionality and penal goals, as well as by the views and practices of foreign countries. It is clear that evolving standards of decency, now given broader dimension by the majority in *Simmons*, remains a major factor when determining the constitutionality of all death penalty cases in general and juvenile death penalty cases in particular.

Cases Briefed in Chapter 5

Case	Issue	Holding
Thompson v. Oklahoma 487 U.S. 815 (1988)	Is the death penalty cruel and unusual punishment for a crime committed by an offender under the age of 16?	The Execution of a person under the age of 16 at the time of offense is prohibited by the Eighth and Fourteenth Amendments.
Stanford v. Kentucky 492 U.S. 361 (1989)	Does the imposition of the death penalty for a crime committed at the age of 16 or 17 constitute cruel and unusual punishment?	The death penalty for juveniles who are older than 15 at the time of the crime does not violate the Eighth Amendment's prohibition of cruel and unusual punishment.
Roper v. Simmons 543 U.S. 551 (2005)	Does the imposition of the death penalty for offenders under the age of 18 violate the Eighth Amendment's ban on cruel and unusual punishment?	The Eighth Amendment prohibits the death penalty for individuals who are under the age of 18 at the time of the offense.

Case Briefs

Thompson v. Oklahoma
487 U.S. 815 (1988)

CAPSULE: It is cruel and unusual punishment to impose the death penalty on an individual who commits their crime at the age of 15 or younger.

FACTS: Thompson, along with three accomplices, actively participated in the murder of his former brother-in-law during the early hours of January 23, 1983. The victim had been shot two times and his throat, chest, and his abdomen had been sliced. Once these injuries were inflicted on the victim, Thompson and his accomplices threw the body into a river, where it rested for approximately four weeks.

Although Thompson was considered a child according to Oklahoma law, he was certified to stand trial as an adult. He subsequently was convicted. During the penalty phase, the prosecutor sought the death penalty. The prosecutor asked the jury to find that aggravating circumstances existed, namely: (1) that the murder was particularly heinous and cruel, and (2) that there was a reasonable probability that the defendant would present a continuing threat to society if set free. The jury found that the first aggravating circumstance was present, but rejected the second. Thompson was given the death penalty.

ISSUE: Is the death penalty cruel and unusual punishment for a crime committed by a 15-year-old? YES.

HOLDING: The Eighth and Fourteenth Amendments prohibit the imposition of the death penalty for offenders 16 or 17 years old at the time of their crime.

REASON: "In determining whether the categorical Eighth Amendment prohibition applies, this Court must be guided by the 'evolving standards of decency that mark the progress of a maturing society,' *Trop v. Dulles*, 356 U.S. 86, 101, and in doing so must review relevant legislative enactments and jury determinations and consider the reasons why a civilized society may accept or reject the death penalty for a person less than 16 years old at the time of the crime.

Relevant state statutes—particularly those of the 18 states that have expressly considered the question of a minimum age for imposition of the death penalty, and have uniformly required that the defendant have attained at least the age of 16 at the time of the capital offense—support the conclusion that it would offend civilized standards of decency to execute a person who was less than 16 years old at the time his or her offense was committed.

The juvenile's reduced culpability, and the fact that the application of the death penalty to this class of offenders does not measurably contribute to the essential purposes underlying the penalty, also support the conclusion that the imposition of the death penalty on persons under the age of 16 constitutes unconstitutional punishment."

CASE SIGNIFICANCE: In this case, the Court said that juveniles under the age of 16 at the time of their crime could not be given the death penalty. Interpreting the Eighth Amendment, the Court claimed "it would offend civilized standards of decency to execute a person who was less than 16 years old at the time of his or her offense." This case marked the first time the Court established a bright-line rule for states to follow when imposing the death penalty for juveniles. At the time *Thompson* was decided, there were 18 states with legislation prohibiting the execution of individuals who committed their crime prior to reaching the age of 16. According to the Court, 18 states was sufficient evidence that legislatures opposed the death penalty for individuals less than 16 at the time of their offense. The Court also said that the sentencing practices of juries were important when considering whether the death penalty violates evolving standards. The Court indicated that juries rarely imposed death as punishment for individuals under the age of 16.

The *Thompson* Court said the death penalty for juveniles was unconstitutional because "adolescents as a class are less mature and responsible than adults." The Court reasoned that the death penalty would be cruel and unusual punishment for juveniles because they inherently fail to evaluate the costs and benefits of their actions. Because juveniles have diminished culpability, the Court said the death penalty would not serve the social purposes of the death penalty—retribution and deterrence.

What this decision did not say was whether juveniles could be executed at all. Is 15 the minimum age, or would juvenile status be a better determinant of whether the offender should be executed? Opponents of the Oklahoma law wanted the Court to declare any execution of a juvenile to be unconstitutional. The Court did not go that far; however, one year later the Court said it was not cruel and unusual punishment to execute 16- or 17-year-olds in *Stanford v. Kentucky*, 492 U.S. 361 (1989).

Stanford v. Kentucky
492 U.S. 361 (1989)

CAPSULE: The cruel and unusual punishment clause of the Eighth Amendment does not prohibit the death penalty for juveniles who commit their crime at the age of 16 or 17.

FACTS: Kevin Stanford was 17 years old when he brutally murdered Barbel Poore in Jefferson County, Kentucky. On January 7, 1981, Stanford and his accomplice repeatedly raped and sodomized Poore, who worked as a gas station attendant. The perpetrators then drove their victim to a removed area, where Stanford shot the victim twice in the head. Stanford and his accomplice obtained 300 cartons of cigarettes, a couple of gallons of gas, and a nominal amount of cash. A corrections officer later testified that Stanford explained the crime in this manner: "He said, I had to shoot her, [she] lived next door to me and she would recognize me. . . . I guess we could have tied her up or something or beat [her up] . . . and tell her if she tells, we would kill her . . . Then after he said that he started laughing."

Because Stanford had been charged with a Class A felony, or capital crime, and was over 16 years of age at the time of his crime, the juvenile court waived jurisdiction. Given Stanford's past record of juvenile delinquency, the juvenile court certified Stanford to stand trial as an adult. He was convicted of numerous crimes, including murder, and sentenced to death plus 45 years.

ISSUE: Does sentencing an offender to the death penalty for a crime they committed at the age of 16 or 17 constitute cruel and unusual punishment? NO.

HOLDING: The Eighth and Fourteenth Amendments do not prohibit the death penalty for juveniles who were 16 or 17 years old at the time of their crime.

REASONING: "Whether a particular punishment violates the Eighth Amendment depends on whether it constitutes one of 'those modes or acts of punishment . . . considered cruel and unusual at the time that the Bill of Rights was adopted,' *Ford v. Wainwright*, 477 U.S. 399, 405, or is contrary to the 'evolving standards of decency that mark the progress of a maturing society,' *Trop v. Dulles*, 356 U.S. 86, 101. Petitioners have not alleged that their sentences would have been considered cruel and unusual in the eighteenth century, and could not support such a contention, since, at that time, the common law set the rebuttable presumption of incapacity to commit felonies (which were punishable by death) at the age of 14.

"In determining whether a punishment violates evolving standards of decency, this Court looks not to its own subjective conceptions, but, rather, to the conceptions of modern American society as reflected by objective evidence. E.g., *Coker v. Georgia*, 433 U.S. 584, 592. The primary and most reliable evidence of national consensus—the pattern of federal and state laws —fails to meet petitioners' heavy burden of proving a settled consensus against the execution of 16- and 17-year-old offenders."

CASE SIGNIFICANCE: This case is a sequel to *Thompson v. Oklahoma*, 487 U.S. 815 (1988), in which the Court held that the death penalty was unconstitutional for juveniles who commit their crime prior to reaching the age of 16. The Court stated "the imposition of capital punishment on an individual for a crime committed at 16 or 17 years of age does not constitute cruel and unusual punishment under the Eighth Amendment." The *Stanford* Court answered the question left open in *Thompson*, which was whether juveniles over the age of 15 at the time of their crime could be given the death penalty.

The *Stanford* Court based its interpretation of the Eighth Amendment solely on the acts of state legislatures and the sentencing practices of juries. The Court rejected the penal goals and proportionality arguments used by the *Thompson* Court. Justice Scalia, writing for the majority, said "it is not only possible, but overwhelmingly probable, that the very considerations which induce petitioners and their supporters to believe that death should never be imposed on offenders under the age of eighteen cause prosecutors and juries to believe that it should rarely be imposed."

The *Stanford* Court said that history as well as then-contemporary standards of decency did not prohibit the death penalty for individuals who commit their crime before reaching the age of 18. By establishing the minimum age at 16, the Court gave states the power to set their minimum age for execution by statute at 16, 17, or 18 years of age.

Roper v. Simmons
543 U.S. 551 (2005)

CAPSULE: The Eighth and Fourteenth Amendments prohibit the death penalty for juveniles who commit their crime before the age of 18.

FACTS: When Christopher Simmons was 17 years old he committed a brutal murder. Before committing the crime, Simmons stated that he wanted to kill someone, even going to the extent of discussing his plan to commit the act with his friends. On the night of the crime at about 2:00 A.M., Simmons and his accomplice entered the home of Shirley Crook through an open window and awakened the victim. Simmons later stated that he intended to kill Mrs. Crook because of their mutual involvement in a previous car accident.

Simmons and his accomplice used duct tape to cover the victim's eyes, mouth, and hands. They then used the victim's van to drive her to a nearby state park. After walking to the top of the bridge, they covered her face with a towel, tied her feet and hands together with wire, and threw her into the Meramec River. The victim drowned and was later discovered by fishermen.

During police interrogation, Simmons confessed to the brutal crime. Simmons was then charged with burglary, kidnapping, stealing, and murder in the first degree. Because Simmons was 17 at the time of his crime, he was not considered a juvenile by the state of Missouri. In seeking the death penalty, the state submitted aggravating factors to the jury. The defense also offered mitigating evidence in Simmons' behalf, including the fact that he had no prior convictions and that he cared for his family. After weighing the evidence, the trial court convicted Simmons and sentenced him to death.

ISSUE: Is it cruel and unusual punishment to impose the death penalty on offenders who commit crimes before reaching the age of 18? YES.

HOLDING: The Eighth and Fourteenth Amendments prohibit the imposition of the death penalty on offenders who commit their crimes before reaching the age of 18.

REASONING: "Both objective indicia of consensus, as expressed in particular by the enactments of legislatures that have addressed the question, and the Court's own determination in the exercise of its independent judgment, demonstrate that the death penalty is a disproportionate punishment for juveniles."

"As in *Atkins*, the objective indicia of national consensus here—the rejection of the juvenile death penalty in the majority of States; the infrequency of its use even where it remains on the books; and the consistency in the trend toward abolition of the practice—provide sufficient evidence that today society views juveniles, in the words *Atkins* used respecting the mentally retarded, as "categorically less culpable than the average criminal."

"Rejection of the imposition of the death penalty on juvenile offenders under 18 is required by the Eighth Amendment. Capital punishment must be limited to those offenders who commit 'a narrow category of the most serious crimes' and whose extreme culpability makes them 'the most deserving of execution.' Three general differences between juveniles under 18 and adults demonstrate that juvenile offenders cannot with reliability be classified among the worst offenders. Juveniles' susceptibility to immature and irresponsible behavior means their irresponsible conduct is not as morally reprehensible as that of an adult. Their own vulnerability and comparative lack of control over their immediate surroundings mean juveniles have a greater claim than adults to be forgiven for failing to escape negative influences in their whole environment. The reality that juveniles still struggle to define their identity means it is less supportable to conclude that even a heinous crime committed by a juvenile is evidence of irretrievably depraved character. The *Thompson* plurality recognized the import of these characteristics with respect to juveniles under 16. The same reasoning applies to all juvenile offenders under 18. Once juveniles' diminished culpability is recognized, it is evident that neither of the two penological justifications for the death penalty—retribution and deterrence of capital crimes by prospective offenders—provides adequate justification for imposing that penalty on juveniles."

CASE SIGNIFICANCE: This case is arguably the most important case decided thus far on the issue of the constitutionality of the death penalty for juveniles. It holds that the death penalty constitutes cruel and unusual punishment for offenders who commit their crime before reaching the age of 18. The Court, in *Thompson v. Oklahoma* (1988) held that executing offenders who were 15 years old or younger at the time of the commission of the offense is unconstitutional. *Simmons* extends that rule to include 16- and 17-year-olds, and therefore overturns its earlier decision in *Stanford v. Kentucky.*

This case puts an end to the execution of juveniles in the United States—for now. The Court can always change its mind, reverse this decision, and declare the execution of juveniles constitutional again. This case was decided on a five-to-four vote. A change in the composition of the United States Supreme Court can lead to a change of vote in a proper case. For now, however, juveniles in the United States cannot be executed, regardless of the seriousness of their crime. This decision renders unconstitutional all laws (state and federal) that allow juveniles to be executed. Legislatures can repeal those laws or allow them to stay on the books, but they cannot now be enforced.

Internet Resources

American Bar Association: Juvenile Death Penalty
http://www.abanet.org/crimjust/juvjus/jdppolicy.html

Amnesty International: The Death Penalty Gives Up on Juvenile Offenders
http://www.amnestyusa.org/abolish/juveniles.html

Death Penalty Information Center: Juveniles and the Death Penalty
http://www.deathpenaltyinfo.org/article.php?did=205&scid=27

Human Rights Watch
http://hrw.org/english/docs/1999/02/04/usint813.htm

Physicians For Human Rights
http://physiciansforhumanrights.org/library/news-2005-03-01-juvenile.html

Notes

1. *Dendy v. Wilson*, 142 Tex. 460, 464 (1944).

2. Victor L. Streib, *Moratorium on the Death Penalty For Juveniles*, 61 Law & Contemp. Probs. 55, n.1 (1998).

3. Anthony Platt and Bernard Diamond, *The Origins of the "Right and Wrong" Test of Criminal Responsibility and Its Subsequent Development in the United States: An Historical Survey*, 54 Cal. L. Rev. 1227, 1233–34 (1966).

4. Carrie Martin, Spare *The Death Penalty, Spoil The Child: How the Execution of Juveniles Violates the Eighth Amendment's Ban on Cruel and Unusual Punishment in 2005*, 46 S. Tex L. Rev. 695 (2005).

5. *Trop v. Dulles*, 356 U.S. 86 (1958).

6. *Thompson v. Oklahoma*, 487 U.S. 815 (1988).

7. *Stanford v. Kentucky*, 492 U.S. 361 (1989).

8. *Roper v. Simmons*, 543 U.S. 551 (2005).

9. *Thompson*, 487 U.S. at 821–823.

10. *Id.*

11. *Id.* at 825.

12. *Id.* at 826–829.

13. *Id.* at 832–833.

14. *Id.*

15. 734 S.W.2d 781, 788 (Ky. 1987).

16. 492 U.S. 361 (1989).

17. *Id.* at 369.

18. *Id.* at 370–374.

19. *Id.* at 370.

20. *Id.*

21. *Id.* at 373–374.

22. *Id.* at 374.

23. 536 U.S. 304 (2002).

24. 492 U.S. 302 (1989).

25. *Id.* at 314–315.

26. *Id.*

27. *Id.* at 316.

28. *Id.* at 318.

29. *Simmons v. Roper*, 112 S.W.3d 397 (Mo. 2003).

30. *Id.* at 408.

31. *Id.* at 409.

32. *Id.* at 411.

33. *Roper v. Simmons*, 543 U.S. 551 (2005).

34. *Id.* at 11.

35. *Id.*

36. *Atkins*, 536 U.S. 315–316.

37. *Id.* at 13.

38. *Id.*

39. *Id.* at 15.

40. *Id.* at 16.

41. *Id.* at 18.

42. *Id.*

43. *Id.* at 68.

44. *Thompson*, at 853.

45. *Atkins*, at 319–321.

46. *Simmons*, at 71.

47. *Id.*

48. *Id.* at 81.

49. *Coker v. Georgia*, 433 U.S. 584, 595–596 (1977).

50. *Simmons*, at 82.

51. *Id.* at 90.

52. *Id.* at 92.

53. *Id.* at 93.

54. *Trop*, 356 U.S. 86, 100–101 (1958).

55. *Thompson*, at 834–835.

56. *Id.* at 324.

57. *Stanford*, at 493.

58. *Trop*, 356 U.S. 86, 101 (1958).

Chapter Outline

I. **Introduction**

II. **The Ultimate Responsibility: Bifurcated Trials and the Role of Capital Juries**
   A. Jury Override: Judges Trumping Juries
   B. *Ring v. Arizona*: The End of Judicial Sentencing in Capital Cases?

III. **Jury Instructions: Guided Discretion in Capital Cases**
   A. Guilt Phase: Lesser Included Offenses
   B. Penalty Phase: Future Dangerousness and Parole Eligibility

IV. **Jury Selection in Capital Cases: Death Qualification**

V. **In Summary, What Do these Cases Say?**

VI. **Conclusion**

Cases Briefed in Chapter 6

Case Briefs
   Witherspoon v. Illinois, 391 U.S. 510 (1968)
   Beck v. Alabama, 447 U.S. 625 (1980)
   Lockhart v. McCree, 476 U.S. 162 (1986)
   Mills v. Maryland, 483 U.S. 367 (1988)
   Morgan v. Illinois, 504 U.S. 719 (1992)
   Simmons v. South Carolina, 512 U.S. 154 (1994)
   Weeks v. Angelone, 528 U.S. 225 (2000)
   Ring v. Arizona, 536 U.S. 584 (2002)
   Uttecht v. Brown, 551 U.S. ___ (2007)

Internet Resources

Notes

Chapter 6

Juries, Jurors, and the Death Penalty

I. Introduction

The United States Constitution gives U.S. citizens the right to a trial by jury. The Sixth Amendment further states that citizens have the right to "a speedy and public trial, by an impartial jury . . ." Moreover, all states have incorporated this right in their constitutions upon entering the union.[1] This is perhaps the most sacred of all rights pertaining to the judicial process and one that places the greatest duty on citizens. The Supreme Court recently reinforced and strengthened this right in the case of *Apprendi v. New Jersey* (2000),[2] in which the Court said that "the jury tradition . . . is an indispensable part of our criminal justice system."[3]

By granting citizens the right to a jury trial, the criminal justice system also requires a great deal from citizens who serve on juries. This burden is particularly demanding on juries in capital cases. Since the *Furman* and *Gregg* decisions in the 1970s, juries have played multiple and increasingly crucial roles in capital cases. In *Gregg*, several procedural safeguards were required by the Court in order to ensure fair and consistent application of the death penalty. Among them was the bifurcated trial (a trial that is split into separate guilt and penalty phases) and the requirement of "guided discretion," which includes adequate consideration of aggravating and mitigating circumstances in determining the appropriate sentence. In the 2002 case of *Ring v. Arizona*,[4] the Supreme Court, citing *Apprendi*, held that juries, not judges, must make any determination of fact that determines an elevated or more severe punishment. Although in most states the same jury determines both guilt and sentence, there are several states whose statutes allow for judges to play a more decisive role. How these states must change their statutes to conform with the decision in *Ring* is still being worked out.[5]

The Supreme Court has consistently reinforced the centrality and importance of jury discretion in capital cases. As sacred as the jury is to a capital trial, however, this institution has not been without controversy. Jury discretion and decision making in capital cases are scrutinized more carefully by the Supreme Court. Thus, much of the Supreme Court's time and energy in the last few decades have been spent considering the appropriate role, makeup, and guidance of capital juries. In this chapter, each of these issues and what the Supreme Court has had to say about them will be discussed. Three primary areas of Supreme Court decisions will be examined: (1) the role of capital juries in sentencing, (2) jury selection and "death qualified" juries, and (3) jury instructions. Key Supreme Court cases will be considered in each area and current issues will be discussed.

II. The Ultimate Responsibility: Bifurcated Trials and the Role of Capital Juries

In *Gregg v. Georgia* (1976), when the Supreme Court reinstated the death penalty, state death penalty statutes under consideration were deemed constitutional contingent upon the presence of certain procedural safeguards. Primary among these safeguards was the bifurcated trial. A bifurcated trial is a trial separated into two phases: a guilt phase and a sentencing phase. In most cases the same jury sits for both phases and determines both guilt and the appropriate sentence. Upon finding a defendant guilty, a separate hearing is held to decide the punishment. Usually the options are limited to life in prison (in some cases without the possibility of parole) or death. During this phase, the jury hears both aggravating and mitigating circumstances (discussed in greater detail in Chapter 9) and decides whether these circumstances warrant the death penalty (based on aggravating factors) or mercy via a life sentence (based on mitigating factors). In some states judges have traditionally had either the sole authority to impose the sentence or the authority to override the sentence imposed by the jury. Nevertheless, the Supreme Court has consistently reiterated the importance and centrality of juries in capital trials and most recently made its strongest statement in *Ring v. Arizona* (2002),[6] holding that the factual determination of aggravating factors that elevates a punishment to death must be made by a jury and not a judge. This case has severely called into question the role of judges in capital sentencing and several states have already revised their statutes to conform to the Court's decision. However, the full effects on some states' capital sentencing statutes are yet to be fully realized.[7] But what is certain is that states allowing judges to override a jury and impose a harsher punishment (i.e., death over a life sentence) will violate the Court's decision in *Ring*.

A. Jury Override: Judges Trumping Juries

In most states, both phases of capital trials rely on juries for the final decisions. Juries decide both a defendant's guilt and punishment. However, in several states, death penalty statutes have granted judges a substantial role in the sentencing of capital defendants. Some state statutes (Arizona, Colorado, Idaho, Montana, and Nebraska) have historically placed sole discretion for capital sentencing in the trial judge's hands. Others (Alabama, Delaware, Indiana, and Florida) enacted hybrid sentencing schemes in which the jury makes a sentencing recommendation but the trial judge is responsible for making the final determination and imposition of sentence—in effect, the trial judge has the authority to override the conclusion of the jury.[8] Table 6.1 indicates the states that historically fell under each of the different sentencing schemes.

Table 6.1
States' Pre-*Ring* Capital Sentencing Schemes

Jury Sentencing States		Judicial Sentencing States	Hybrid States
Arkansas	New York	Arizona	Alabama
California	North Carolina	Colorado	Delaware
Connecticut	Ohio	Idaho	Florida
Georgia	Oklahoma	Montana	Indiana
Illinois	Oregon	Nebraska	
Kansas	Pennsylvania		
Kentucky	South Carolina		
Louisiana	South Dakota		
Maryland	Tennessee		
Mississippi	Texas		
Missouri	Utah		
Nevada	Virginia		
New Hampshire	Washington		
New Jersey	Wyoming		
New Mexico			

In *Spaziano v. Florida* (1984),[9] the Supreme Court first addressed the constitutionality of statutes allowing judges to override a jury's recommendation in a capital case. Although a majority of jurors recommended a life sentence for Spaziano, the trial judge, upon his own assessment of aggravating and mitigating circumstances, sentenced him to death. Florida's hybrid sentencing scheme was challenged on appeal as being in violation of the Eighth Amendment's prohibition of cruel and unusual punishment. Although accepting that "the jury is in the best position to decide whether a particular crime is so heinous that the community's response must be death,"[10] the Court upheld Florida's statute and thus the trial judge's authority to override sentencing recommendations of capital juries.

In *Walton v. Arizona* (1990),[11] the Supreme Court further strengthened the trial judge's authority to determine the sentence in capital cases by upholding

Arizona's statute in which judges have full authority over the sentencing of capital defendants. In Arizona and other states with judicial sentencing schemes, judges are solely responsible for determining the presence of aggravating and mitigating circumstances based on testimony and evidence presented during the sentencing phase of trial. Based on their discretion in weighing these factors, they decide whether a death sentence is appropriate. Under those death penalty statutes, the jury's role in capital trials is restricted to the guilt phase.

Although the Supreme Court has historically allowed states to make their own determination as to whether a judge or jury imposes the sentence in capital trials, it has consistently emphasized the importance and value of the jury in criminal cases.[12] In *Duncan v. Louisiana* (1968),[13] the Supreme Court held that the right to a jury trial in serious criminal cases applies to the states as a fundamental protection against unfettered judicial and prosecutorial discretion. The Court stated that "[t]he guarantees of jury trial in the Federal and State Constitutions reflect a profound judgment about the way in which law should be enforced and justice administered."[14] More than 30 years later, in *Apprendi v. New Jersey* (2000),[15] the Court struck down a hate-crime statute that allowed a judge to make a determination of facts that led to an increase in a defendant's sentence. The Court held that only a jury can make an "assessment of facts that increase the prescribed range of penalties to which a criminal defendant is exposed" and that "[o]ther than the fact of a prior conviction, any fact that increases the penalty for a crime beyond the prescribed statutory maximum must be submitted to a jury, and proved beyond a reasonable doubt."[16] The Court's message was clear: The ultimate fate of criminal defendants is best left in the hands of a jury, not a judge.

B. Ring v. Arizona: *The End of Judicial Sentencing in Capital Cases?*

Following *Apprendi*, the Supreme Court in *Ring v. Arizona* (2002)[17] placed strict limitations on the capacity for judges to override a jury's decision or determine the sentence in capital cases. The Court held that, based on the decision in *Apprendi v. New Jersey* (2000),[18] it was unconstitutional for judges to make determinations of aggravating factors that effectively elevate the crime to one warranting an increase in punishment—in capital cases, from life in prison to death. Because the jury failed to conclude that the death penalty was warranted in Ring's case, the judge, as authorized by statute, weighed the aggravating and mitigating circumstances and overrode the jury's conclusion and sentenced Ring to death. The Supreme Court held that this violated Ring's Sixth Amendment right to a jury trial in that the judge's finding regarding aggravating circumstances was "the functional equivalent of an element of a greater offense than the one covered by the jury's guilty verdict."[19] Importantly, the Court, in *Schriro v. Summerlin* (2004),[20] declared the holding in *Ring* not to be retroactive. Citing *Teague v. Lane* (1989),[21] the Court noted that *Ring* did not create a "watershed rule of criminal procedure" and thus did not warrant a retroactive application to previously concluded cases.[22] Thus, death row inmates who, prior to *Ring*, had been sentenced under schemes in which the judge made the ultimate sentencing decision were not spared by the Court's decision.

As for future cases, the question remains open as to whether the the judicial override function will remain intact in any form in the wake of *Ring*. Statutes giving judges sole discretion in elevating the level of punishment in a sentence are invalidated by *Ring*. Arizona, Colorado, Idaho, and Montana have already revised their death penalty sentencing schemes to comport with the *Ring* decision. Montana has adopted a hybrid sentencing scheme and Arizona, Colorado, and Idaho have revised their statutes to remove the judge's discretion in sentencing and place the capital sentencing decision in the hands of the jury.[23] The Supreme Courts of Idaho and Colorado have both begun to reconsider death sentences imposed under the old sentencing schemes.[24] The fate of hybrid sentencing schemes is less clear. At this point only Indiana has revised its statute to allow only juries to make sentencing determinations in capital cases.[25] Delaware, Nebraska, and Montana, taking a more narrow interpretation of the *Ring* holding, now require the jury to make a determination on the presence of at least one aggravating circumstance beyond a reasonable doubt, but leave the sentencing decision in the judge's hands.[26] Alabama and Florida have maintained their capital sentencing schemes, arguing that the *Ring* decision did not apply to their statutes in spite of the characterization of jury recommendations as advisory and non-binding.[27] It remains to be seen whether their statutes will hold up in the wake of *Ring*.

III. Jury Instructions: Guided Discretion in Capital Cases

When the Supreme Court, in 1976, reinstated the death penalty in *Gregg v. Georgia*[28] (along with *Proffitt v. Florida*[29] and *Jurek v. Texas*[30]), it approved only statutes that provided "guided discretion" for juries. In an effort to alleviate the "arbitrary," "capricious," and "wanton" nature of capital sentencing cited in *Furman*, the Court required in *Gregg* that juries' decisions be guided by judges. This guidance would consist of instructions about appropriate sentencing options and factors to be considered in weighing those options. As part of their role in the penalty phase, juries are called upon to consider extralegal factors submitted as aggravating (factors that make the crime especially heinous or worthy of the sentence of death) and mitigating (factors that mitigate either the defendant's culpability or the necessity of the penalty of death) circumstances (see Chapter 9 for further discussion of these issues).

When it approved the Georgia death penalty statute in *Gregg*, the Court also issued separate decisions striking down statutes providing for mandatory death sentences (*Woodson v. North Carolina*, 1976[31]; *Roberts v. Louisiana*, 1976[32]). Although mandatory death sentences for particular crimes resolved the problems associated with discriminatory and "arbitrary and capricious" results of unfettered jury discretion, it did not allow for the individualized case considerations necessary to ensure appropriate and proportional application of this most severe of penalties. The Court opted for "guided discretion" death penalty statutes and thus placed in the hands of juries the life and death fate of capital offenders. The Court spent much time and effort in the following decades determining the appropriate guidance that juries needed in the way of instructions in capital cases.

This guidance comes in both phases of the trial and also in the appropriate composition and limitations regarding jury instructions. Both concerns have been dealt with repeatedly by the Supreme Court since *Gregg*. In the guilt phase the Court has primarily considered instructions guiding the jury's consideration of lesser included (non-capital) offenses. The sentencing phase requires more guidance where much attention has revolved around the critical issue of future dangerousness. The major cases addressing the issues surrounding jury instructions at both these stages of trial are discussed in this section.

A. Guilt Phase: Lesser Included Offenses

The primary issue the Supreme Court has addressed regarding jury instructions during the guilt phase of capital trials is whether juries should be given special instructions about lesser (non-capital) included offenses. Lesser included offenses are those that the jury can, as an alternative to that asserted by the prosecution, consider in their determination of guilt. The Supreme Court first confronted this issue in *Beck v. Alabama* (1980).[33] Alabama's death penalty statute at the time restricted a jury's decision to either conviction of a capital crime, and thus imposition of the death penalty, or outright acquittal. The Court, acknowledging the risks inherent in such a forced decision between two extremes, held that the statute violated due process and said that capital juries must be allowed to consider lesser (non-capital) offenses in the guilt phase of the trial and must be instructed regarding these options. In effect, the Court required that capital juries have the "third option" of convicting defendants without imposing the death penalty by default.

The Court has further clarified the *Beck* decision. In *Hopper v. Evans* (1982),[34] the Court held that *Beck* only applies when evidence supports a lesser included offense. Evans had appealed his capital conviction and death sentence in light of the *Beck* decision, claiming that the jury was not instructed as to lesser included offenses and thus his due process rights had been violated. The Supreme Court determined that because the defendant's own testimony made it clear (the defendant testified during trial that he had killed the victim and "had 'no intention whatsoever of ever reforming in any way' and would return to a life of crime if released"[35]) and that he committed the capital offense with which he was charged, the jury need not be instructed about lesser included offenses. In 1998, the Supreme Court, in *Hopkins v. Reeves* (1998),[36] revisited *Beck*. The Court held that juries need not be instructed to consider options that are not provided by state law (in this case, Nebraska) as possible lesser included offenses for the crime charged. The issue was whether the jury should be instructed to consider second-degree murder and manslaughter in lieu of felony-murder—an option not legally allowed under Nebraska law. The Court noted that the jury should be instructed regarding the lesser included offenses that were allowed by law and that this case differed from *Beck* in that "the trial court did not create an 'artificial barrier' for the jury; nor did it treat capital cases differently from noncapital cases."[37]

B. Penalty Phase: Future Dangerousness and Parole Eligibility

The fact that juries not only decide guilt, but also decide the sentence in capital cases, is unique in criminal trials. Leaving this decision, which has historically been reserved for judges with the education, experience, and training for making such decisions, in the hands of a jury requires that special attention be given to ensuring the jury's adequate understanding of the factors that determine whether a defendant should live or die. These are issues that have stirred much academic debate and have repeatedly reached the docket of the Supreme Court. The issues have mainly revolved around the appropriate consideration of aggravating and mitigating circumstances and a more complete discussion of Supreme Court cases related to them will be reserved for Chapter 9. However, one of the most prominent aggravating factors presented in capital cases—future dangerousness—has given rise to some issues about jury instructions that are worthy of consideration here. The Court recently decided a series of cases pertaining to jury instructions regarding the likelihood that the defendant is a potential danger to the public—an issue that weighs heavily on the minds of jurors.

There are two aspects to the issue of future dangerousness in capital trials: (1) the defendant's predisposition toward violence or likelihood of continuing to be a violent or dangerous person, and (2) the likelihood that the defendant will be a physical threat (i.e., will be free to potentially engage in future violent acts against other people). The first aspect is often determined by forensic psychologists or other mental health professionals who provide their expert testimony during the sentencing phase of capital trials. This aspect will be discussed further in Chapter 9. It is the second aspect that is of interest here.

One of the questions that weighs most heavily on the minds of jurors is whether the defendant, if not executed, will ever be released and thus have the potential to commit murder again.[38] In *California v. Ramos* (1983),[39] the Supreme Court upheld a California law requiring that capital juries be instructed that a sentence of life without parole may be commuted to a sentence with the possibility of parole. The Court, citing *Jurek v. Texas* (1976), concluded that "[w]hat is essential is that the jury have before it all possible relevant information about the individual defendant whose fate it must determine."[40] In this case, the Court determined that the possibility of eventual release from prison was important in a jury's consideration of the future danger to society that the defendant may present. More than a decade later, a string of cases revolving around South Carolina's capital trial procedure would bring this issue to greater light.

In South Carolina, trial courts had a history of, in one legal scholar's words, "determined and malign efforts to deprive juries in capital cases of information relevant to their decisions on whether to sentence defendants to life imprisonment or to impose the death penalty."[41] Although these words may be a bit strong, South Carolina had consistently refused to allow capital juries to be instructed about parole ineligibility when prosecutors argued that the defendant would be a future danger if sentenced to life in prison. It should be added that, in South Carolina, upon a finding of any aggravating factor, a life sentence does not carry the possibility of parole. However, absent an instruction to this effect, capital jurors may not be aware of this. In fact, research shows that jurors have a very poor understanding of the meaning and concept of life imprisonment and often misperceive that defendants will be released on parole even if the only option available is life without parole.[42] In *Simmons v. South Carolina* (1994),[43] the Supreme Court held that, as a matter of due process, the defense must be allowed to have the jury instructed about parole ineligibility when the prosecution has argued future dangerousness and the only sentencing options are death and life without parole.

More recently, the Court has again been confronted with South Carolina's refusal to instruct capital juries about parole eligibility in response to claims of future dangerousness. The first case to test the *Simmons* holding was *Shafer v. South Carolina* (2001).[44] The South Carolina Supreme Court upheld a death sentence in which the trial court refused to instruct the jury about parole eligibility, arguing that life with parole was an available sentence. The United States Supreme Court overruled, pointing out that, in fact, upon the jury's finding of aggravating factors, any sentence other than life without parole or death was removed, leaving just the two options. Although the Court reaffirmed its holding in *Simmons*, the question of what constitutes argument of future dangerousness, as required under *Simmons* in order to justify a jury instruction about parole eligibility, was left open. The Court maintained that such determinations should be "left open for the state court's attention and disposition."[45]

A year later, the Supreme Court was forced to address this question and clarify the vague statement in *Simmons* that future dangerousness must be "at issue" in order to justify a jury instruction about parole eligibility. In *Kelly v.*

South Carolina (2002),[46] the Court said that in order for future dangerousness to be "at issue," it does not necessarily have to be explicitly argued by the prosecution. Rather, "evidence of future dangerousness under *Simmons* is evidence with a tendency to prove dangerousness in the future."[47] Evidence presented by the prosecution implying future dangerousness suffices to warrant a jury instruction about parole eligibility in capital cases. Some judges and scholars have suggested that this standard broadens the application of *Simmons* to virtually all capital cases.[48] This may be true. The Supreme Court, in *Kelly*, has reaffirmed its commitment to heightened due process, guided discretion, and fully informed juries in capital cases, a posture that goes back to the Court's reinstatement of the death penalty in *Gregg v. Georgia* (1976), *Jurek v. Texas* (1976), and its earliest decision regarding jury instructions in *California v. Ramos* (1983).

IV. Jury Selection in Capital Cases: Death Qualification

Having placed the sentencing decision in the hands of the jury, the jury selection process became more complex; it now requires that jurors be screened in regard to both their ability to dispassionately and objectively determine guilt and appropriate sentence. Courts use a process of voir dire to select jurors for criminal trials from a venire. The venire is a pool of potential jurors from which actual jurors will be selected upon determining that they are qualified to serve on the jury in an unbiased and objective manner. Voir dire is the process of screening jurors to ensure these qualifications. Prospective jurors during voir dire may be excluded from the venire as a result of one of two challenges: (1) A judge may remove a prospective juror from the venire "for cause," or based on statutorily defined criteria; or (2) attorneys in the case may exclude prospective jurors via peremptory challenges, in which case they need not give any explanation or specific reason for their challenge. In capital cases, voir dire must take into account potential jurors' ability to appropriately determine both guilt and the sentence. Although the voir dire process in the guilt phase of capital trials is generally the same as in other criminal trials, the sentencing phase demands something different. Specifically, prospective jurors are questioned about their views on the death penalty and whether they have moral or religious scruples that may prevent them from imposing the death penalty. Historically, those expressing any opposition to the death penalty were excluded from capital juries "for cause." This process has come to be known as "death qualification."

Prior to 1968, prospective jurors who expressed any opposition to the death penalty were generally excluded from capital juries for cause. The exclusion of such prospective jurors was based on the idea that those expressing opposition to the death penalty would not be able to make a fair determination of sentence in capital trials—meaning they would not be able to sentence the defendant to death. In 1968, this process was challenged in *Witherspoon v. Illinois* (1968)[49] and would undergo several transformations through Supreme Court decisions in the following decades.

In *Witherspoon*, the death qualification process was challenged as a violation of the Sixth Amendment right to an impartial jury. It was specifically challenged on two grounds: (1) it biased the jury toward a guilty verdict, and (2) it biased the jury toward a death sentence. The Supreme Court agreed with the second claim and held that excusing jurors simply because they opposed the death penalty was unconstitutional. However, the Court noted that its decision did "not involve the right of the prosecution to challenge for cause those prospective jurors who state that their reservations about capital punishment would prevent them from making an impartial decision as to the defendant's guilt. Nor does it involve the State's assertion of a right to exclude from the jury in a capital case those who say that they could never vote to impose the death penalty or that they would refuse even to consider its imposition in the case before them."[50] So, although it placed restrictions on the blanket exclusions common to death qualification prior to 1968, the Court did not eliminate the death qualification process itself.

The Supreme Court revisited *Witherspoon* and the death qualification issue three times in the 1980s. In *Adams v. Texas* (1980),[51] the Court qualified the ruling in *Witherspoon*, holding that jurors can be removed for cause if their views on the death penalty would preclude them from obeying their oath or conforming their decision to the law. The Court reaffirmed *Adams* in *Wainwright v. Witt* (1985),[52] adding that exclusion of a juror should occur in the same manner as in any other case. It was determined that if a juror's views would bias his or her ability to impose the death penalty, then that juror should be excluded. The Supreme Court's final word on death qualification came the following year, in *Lockhart v. McCree* (1986).[53] The Court held that, in spite of research suggesting that death-qualified juries are "conviction-prone" in comparison to non-capital juries, death qualification does not violate the Sixth Amendment right to a fair and impartial jury. The justices concluded that prospective jurors whose attitudes about capital punishment would preclude them from sentencing a defendant to death in any case or set of circumstances can be excluded. An interesting twist on the death qualification process arose in the 1992 case of *Morgan v. Illinois* (1992)[54]—a case that would come to be known as the "reverse-*Witherspoon*" case. In *Morgan* the Court held that prospective jurors who would automatically vote for the death penalty upon conviction of the defendant regardless of the specific circumstances of the case can be excluded from the jury for cause.

The process of death qualification again took center stage in 2007 in the case of *Uttecht v. Brown*.[55] This case involved the exclusion of a juror who had expressed, and presented a general demeanor suggesting, reluctance to impose the death penalty. Although unable to imagine a situation in which he would impose the death penalty as opposed to a true life sentence, the juror assured the trial judge that he could consider the sentence of death in compliance with state law. The juror was excluded by the trial judge and the defendant (Brown) was ultimately sentenced to death. The Supreme Court upheld the sentence, stating that: (1) the trial transcript indicated that the juror seemed confused about whether and in what instances he would be able to impose the death penalty and (2) the trial court is in the best position to judge the demeanor of prospective jurors and thus is entitled to deference.[56] The Court noted that the trial court found that the juror was "substantially impaired in his ability to impose the death penalty" and thus exercised its due discretion in determining the juror to be excludable under *Witherspoon* and *Lockhart* standards.[57] Some argue that this case broadens the process of death qualification by reverting back to pre-*Witherspoon* standards, making even those who simply have qualms about imposing the death penalty excludable.[58] Critics further assert that this fact removes the death-qualified jury further from any semblance of a representative cross-section of the American population.[59] Whether *Uttecht v. Brown* predicates these shifts is debatable, but what is certain is that the process of death qualification is once again raising constitutional questions and concerns.

Death qualification remains a controversial issue and the potential biasing effects of the process are much researched and discussed in academic and legal circles. Research has shown that the death qualification process leads to a conviction-prone and death sentence-prone jury. Both the composition of a death-qualified jury (meaning only those who do not oppose the death penalty) and the questioning process by which jurors are selected (in which guilt is presumed) have been cited as factors biasing the capital jury toward guilt.[60] This research supported the claims of the dissenting justices in *Lockhart* who argued that not only does death qualification produce juries that are conviction-prone, but also creates an unfair imbalance in favor of the prosecution and thus violates the defendant's Sixth and Fourteenth Amendment rights. Justice Blackmun, writing for the dissent, went so far as to proclaim: "[t]he true impact of death qualification on the fairness of a trial is likely even more devastating than the studies show."[61] Nevertheless, the death qualification process continues to be used in capital cases in virtually all jurisdictions in the United States.

V. In Summary, What Do these Cases Say?

In the wake of *Gregg v. Georgia* (1976),[62] the capital jury has been a focus of the Supreme Court's death penalty jurisprudence. Three primary issues about capital juries have caught the Court's attention: (1) The role juries play in capital trials, (2) the instructions given to juries in capital trials, and (3) the jury selection process in capital trials. In each area, the Court has upheld the importance and autonomy of juries in death penalty cases.

The crucial and central role of the jury in capital trials has most recently been re-emphasized in *Ring v. Arizona* (2002),[63] in which the Court held that juries, not judges, must make the ultimate determination of whether a defendant receives the death sentence. In *Gregg*, the Court granted capital juries the unique responsibility of making both the guilt and sentencing decisions, separated into two distinct stages of the trial—the guilt stage and the penalty stage. This bifurcated trial structure, while allowing for heightened scrutiny of the circumstances to ensure that the death penalty is only imposed in the most severe cases, also places an additional burden on the jury. Nevertheless, the Supreme Court for years allowed the practice of judicial override, in which judges had the authority to override the jury's sentencing decision, thus nullifying the jury's otherwise authoritative role. Although the extent is not yet fully clear, it appears that the Court's decision in *Ring* will bring this practice to an end, more solidly placing the sentencing decision in the hands of the capital jury.

The Supreme Court has held that the jury must be instructed about lesser included offenses for which they can convict a defendant. However, these lesser included offenses must be provided for in the state's statute and supported by evidence to warrant an instruction to the jury. The Court has also said that juries must be instructed about parole eligibility or ineligibility and the real meaning of life without parole when evidence of future dangerousness is used by the prosecution.

Issues surrounding the instructions that juries receive have occupied a significant amount of the Court's time over the past few decades as well. Of particular current interest are jury instructions surrounding the parole eligibility of the defendant. The Supreme Court has recently determined that when the prosecution argues (or even suggests) that the defendant poses a future danger, the defense, if it so requests, is entitled to jury instructions regarding the defendant's parole eligibility or ineligibility. This is based on the due process right to attempt to refute evidence with counter evidence (future dangerousness with the reality that the defendant will receive life without parole if not sentenced to death).

Jury composition and selection attracted much early attention, ultimately leading to the concept now known as "death qualification" of juries. This refers to the practice that no one unequivocally opposed to the death penalty can be included on the jury. Many, including both scholars and legal professionals, suggest that such a practice unduly biases the jury in both the guilt phase as well as the sentencing phase. However, the Court has determined that in order for a juror to fulfill her duties, she must be free of a bias that comes with strict opposition to the death penalty. These issues have recently re-emerged in the 2007 case of *Uttecht v. Brown*, in which the Court seems to be slightly loosening the restrictions on what makes a juror excludable in the death qualification process.

VI. Conclusion

The jury is one of the most sacred institutions in the American criminal justice system. The very idea of a trial by jury—that one has the right to be judged by his or her fellow citizens and not simply by an official agent of the government—is at the heart of the judicial process and the notions of due process and fundamental fairness. So it is not a surprise that capital juries, to whom we entrust decisions of the greatest gravity—those involving life and death—have occupied much of the Supreme Court's attention since the reinstatement of the death penalty in 1976.

The Supreme Court, since reinstating the death penalty in *Gregg*, has mandated "guided discretion" as the cornerstone of death penalty law and procedure. Having rejected mandatory death penalty statutes, the Court opted for guided discretion statutes in which the jury is required to consider the many facts and circumstances of the individual case and use its discretion in sentencing the defendant to either death or life in prison based on those facts and circumstances. In line with the principle of guided discretion, the Court has generally held that the jury should be given sufficiently clear and thorough instructions from the judge as a form of guidance.

The Supreme Court's 2002 decision in *Ring v. Arizona* makes probably the strongest statement regarding the critical role of juries in capital trials. The Court held in *Ring v. Arizona* that only juries, and not judges, should be given the authority to determine when a sentence as severe as death is warranted. Capital juries are granted the power to determine whether a defendant will live or die. With this power comes a great burden but also a heightened scrutiny of juries and the criminal justice processes surrounding them. The Supreme Court has consistently reinforced the importance of capital juries and held them up as a cornerstone of the American justice system. Since the reinstatement of the death penalty in *Gregg v. Georgia*, the Supreme Court has repeatedly been called upon to consider the appropriate role, guidance, and composition of capital juries. Although these issues are constantly fine-tuned and the message often changes, the centrality and importance of juries to death penalty jurisprudence never wanes.

Cases Briefed in Chapter 6

Case	Issue	Holding
Witherspoon v. Illinois 391 U.S. 510 (1968)	Is it constitutional to remove prospective jurors for cause merely because they generally oppose capital punishment?	The removal of prospective jurors for cause based only on the fact that they express conscientious scruples against the death penalty violates the rights to due process and an impartial jury.
Beck v. Alabama 447 U.S. 625 (1980)	Does the Constitution allow the death penalty to be imposed when the jury was not allowed to consider a lesser included non-capital offense?	Alabama's prohibition of the consideration of lesser included non-capital offenses, where evidence would support the lesser included offense, violates due process rights.
Lockhart v. McCree 476 U.S. 162 (1986)	Is it constitutional to remove prospective jurors whose opposition to the death penalty would impair their ability to perform their duties in the sentencing phase of a capital trial?	A prospective juror, whose opposition to the death penalty is so strong as to impair their ability to perform their duties at the sentencing phase of trial (i.e. would preclude them from *ever* imposing a death sentence), may be removed for cause.
Mills v. Maryland 486 U.S. 367 (1988)	Must a jury unanimously agree that a mitigating factor exists for that mitigating factor to be considered by any juror in their sentencing decision?	Capital jurors may not be prohibited from considering mitigating factors simply because the jury does not unanimously agree on their presence. Sentencing instructions giving the impression that unanimity is required violate a defendant's due process rights.
Morgan v. Illinois 504 U.S. 719 (1992)	Does a trial court's refusal to ask prospective jurors whether they would automatically impose the death penalty upon defendant's conviction violate due process?	The due process clause of the Fourteenth Amendment requires that, if requested by the defendant, prospective jurors must be questioned regarding whether they would automatically impose the death penalty if they find the defendant guilty.
Simmons v. South Carolina 512 U.S. 154 (1994)	Does the refusal to instruct a capital jury about parole ineligibility when the prosecution has argued future dangerousness violate due process?	In a case in which a defendant's future dangerousness is argued by the prosecution and in which state law prohibits parole, the defendant has a right to have the jury instructed about defendant's parole ineligibility.

Cases Briefed in Chapter 6, *continued*

Case	Issue	Holding
Weeks v. Angelone 528 U.S. 225 (2000)	Is it a violation of due process for a trial judge to refuse to clarify sentencing requirements beyond what is indicated in the original jury instructions?	A trial judge is not required, even if requested by the jury, to clarify the sentencing requirements in a capital case beyond the words provided in the original jury instructions.
Ring v. Arizona 536 U.S. 584 (2002)	Does the Sixth Amendment require that a jury, not a judge, must make the determination of the presence of an aggravating circumstance that elevates a punishment to death?	A judge may not alone make a determination of aggravating circumstances that elevate a punishment to death. Such aggravating circumstances are "the functional equivalent of an element of a greater offense" and therefore must be determined by a jury as required by the Sixth Amendment.
Uttecht v. Brown 551 U.S. ___ (2007)	Is a trial court judge's determination that a juror is substantially impaired in his or her ability to consider the sentence of death sufficient to remove that juror?	Trial courts should be given deference in their ability to ascertain whether a prospective juror is substantially impaired in his or her ability to follow the law and consider the death penalty in the sentencing phase of capital trials.

Case Briefs

Witherspoon v. Illinois
391 U.S. 510 (1968)

CAPSULE: Prospective jurors may not be excluded from capital juries merely because they have general scruples against the death penalty.

FACTS: At the trial of Witherspoon, charged with capital murder, the prosecution eliminated all prospective jurors who expressed general scruples against or objections to the death penalty. Illinois law allowed for challenges of any member of the venire who had reservations about the use of capital punishment. Under the authority of this law, the prosecution had nearly half of the venire removed, most of whom were never questioned to find out whether their scruples would preclude them from imposing a death sentence regardless of the specific circumstances of the case and responsibilities as a capital juror. Witherspoon was convicted and sentenced to death.

ISSUE: Is it constitutional to remove prospective jurors for cause merely because they generally oppose capital punishment? NO.

HOLDING: The removal of prospective jurors for cause based only on the fact that they express conscientious scruples against the death penalty and without questioning them about whether these scruples would cause them to automatically vote against the imposition of the death penalty regardless of the specific facts of the case violates the rights to due process and an impartial jury.

REASON: "A man who opposes the death penalty, no less than one who favors it, can make the discretionary choice of punishment entrusted to him by the State and can thus obey the oath he takes as a juror; but in a nation where so many have come to oppose capital punishment, a jury from which all such people have been excluded cannot perform the task demanded of it—that of expressing the conscience of the community on the ultimate question of life or death.

"Just as a State may not entrust the determination of whether a man is innocent or guilty to a tribunal organized to convict, so it may not entrust the determination of whether a man should live or die to a tribunal organized to return a verdict of death; and no sentence of death can be carried out, regardless of when it was imposed, if the voir dire testimony indicates that the jury that imposed or recommended that sentence was chosen by excluding veniremen for cause simply because they voiced general objections to capital punishment or expressed conscientious or religious scruples against its infliction."

CASE SIGNIFICANCE: *Witherspoon v. Illinois* was the first case to consider the process of "death qualification" or the elimination of jurors based on their opposition to the death penalty. The Supreme Court's decision substantially limited the practice of death qualification by declaring it unconstitutional to exclude jurors simply because they have scruples or views in opposition to the death penalty. The Court ruled that prospective capital jurors may only be removed for cause if their opposition meant that they would automatically refuse to sentence a defendant to death if he or she were convicted. Importantly, the Court only applied this to exclusion from the sentencing phase of trial. This restrictive standard for excusing such jurors remained intact for only a short time and was eventually replaced by the standard set in *Lockhart v. McCree* (1986).[64] This case, however, represented the Supreme Court's first pronouncement on death qualification.

Beck v. Alabama
447 U.S. 625 (1980)

CAPSULE: Capital juries must be allowed to consider a guilty verdict on lesser included offenses.

FACTS: Alabama law provides for felony murder as a lesser included offense of robbery-intentional killing, a capital crime. In contrast, Alabama capital punishment law prohibits the trial judge from granting this option to the jury. Rather, the jury must decide whether to convict on the capital charge and sentence the defendant to death or acquit him altogether. At trial, Beck admitted participating in the robbery but denied any role in the killing of the victim. He was convicted of robbery-intentional killing and sentenced to death. The state appellate courts rejected Beck's claim that the conviction and death sentence were unconstitutional due to the statutory preclusion on lesser included offense instructions. The conviction and death sentence were upheld.

ISSUE: Does the Constitution allow the death penalty to be imposed when the jury was not allowed to consider a guilty verdict on a lesser included non-capital offense that was supported by evidence? NO.

HOLDING: Alabama's prohibition of the consideration of lesser included non-capital offenses at the guilt phase of trial, where evidence would support the lesser included offense, violates due process rights.

REASON: "Providing the jury with the 'third option' of convicting on a lesser included offense ensures that the jury will accord the defendant the full benefit of the reasonable-doubt standard. This procedural safeguard is especially important in cases such as this one. For when the evidence establishes that the defendant is guilty of a serious, violent offense but leaves some doubt as to an element justifying conviction of a capital offense, the failure to give the jury such a 'third option' inevitably enhances the risk of an unwarranted conviction. Such a risk cannot be tolerated in a case in which the defendant's life is at stake.

"The jury's 'option' of refusing to return any verdict at all, thus causing a mistrial, is not an adequate substitute for proper instructions on lesser included offenses. Nor does the fact that the trial judge has the ultimate sentencing power compensate for the risk that the jury may return an improper verdict because of the unavailability of the 'third option.' If the jury finds the defendant guilty only of a lesser included offense, the judge would not have the opportunity to impose the death sentence. Moreover, the jury's verdict must have a tendency to motivate the judge to impose the same sentence that the jury did. Under these circumstances, it cannot be presumed that a post-trial hearing will always correct whatever mistakes occurred in the performance of the jury's factfinding function."

CASE SIGNIFICANCE: This was the first case following the reinstatement of the death penalty to test the requirements of "heightened standards of reliability," set forth in *Gregg*, as they apply to capital juries. This case set a standard that juries should be given all opportunities to consider options other than the death penalty. The issue here was whether the jury must be given the option of considering conviction on lesser included offenses as provided by state statute. The state law allowing a jury to consider the lesser included offense of felony murder (which did not carry a death sentence) in lieu of robbery-intentional killing (which carried a death sentence) was in conflict with Alabama's death penalty law, which only allowed the jury the option of either convicting on the capital offense of robbery-intentional killing or acquitting the defendant. The Court concluded that this was not a realistic option for the jury if it determined that the defendant's role in the crime did not warrant the death penalty. Being faced with the only other option of acquittal and release, the jury may be compelled to convict on the capital charge and send the defendant to his death even if the jury does not think the penalty is warranted. Noting the gravity of capital cases, the Court held that the jury must be allowed to consider the lesser included offenses, thus supporting the notion that a capital jury's hands should not be tied when making decisions that could cost the defendant his or her life.

Lockhart v. McCree
476 U.S. 162 (1986)

CAPSULE: Prospective jurors may be removed for cause if they oppose the death penalty.

FACTS: McCree was charged with capital felony murder after being pursued while driving a car that matched an eyewitness's description of the getaway vehicle seen leaving a gas station where the owner was robbed and murdered. McCree admitted to being at the store at the time of the robbery and murder, but claimed that "a tall black stranger wearing an overcoat" had taken McCree's gun from his car and killed the store owner. McCree further stated that the stranger rode in his car with him, eventually getting out and walking away with the gun. Two eyewitnesses, who saw McCree in his car during the time between the murder and the time McCree reported the stranger exiting his car, contradicted his story by reporting that only one person, McCree, was in the car.

During voir dire, the judge removed, for cause, all prospective jurors who stated that they could not vote for the death penalty under any circumstances. McCree was convicted of capital felony murder, but was sentenced by the jury to life imprisonment without parole. McCree filed a federal habeas corpus petition challenging the conviction and claiming that the process of "death qualification" violated his Sixth Amendment right to an impartial jury representing a cross section of the community.

ISSUE: Is it constitutional to remove prospective jurors whose opposition to the death penalty would substantially impair their ability to perform their duties in the sentencing phase of a capital trial? YES.

HOLDING: A prospective juror whose opposition to the death penalty is so strong as to impair his or her ability to perform his or her duties at the sentencing phase of trial (i.e., would preclude them from ever imposing a death sentence) may be removed for cause.

REASON: "'Death qualification' of a jury does not violate the fair-cross-section requirement of the Sixth Amendment, which applies to jury panels or venires but does not require that petit juries actually chosen reflect the composition of the community at large. Even if the requirement were extended to petit juries, the essence of a fair-cross-section claim is the systematic exclusion of a 'distinctive group' in the community—such as blacks, women, and Mexican-Americans—for reasons completely unrelated to the ability of members of the group to serve as jurors in a particular case. Groups defined solely in terms of shared attitudes that would prevent or substantially impair members of the group from performing one of their duties as jurors, such as the '*Witherspoon*-excludables' at issue here, are not 'distinctive groups' for fair-cross-section purposes. 'Death qualification' is carefully designed to serve the State's legitimate interest in obtaining a single jury that can properly and impartially apply the law to the facts of the case at both the guilt and sentencing phases of a capital trial."

CASE SIGNIFICANCE: States that impose the death penalty usually use a two-step procedure: a guilt stage and a sentencing stage. In an earlier case, *Witherspoon v. Illinois* (1968),[65] the Supreme Court said that in choosing juries for sentencing defendants (as opposed to determining guilt) in capital cases, prosecutors may exclude for cause potential jurors who say they are unwilling to vote for a death sentence under any circumstance. This means that a juror who says he or she is unwilling to vote for the death sentence could not be excluded from the guilt stage, but could be excluded from the sentencing stage. This case goes further by saying that prospective jurors whose opposition to capital punishment is so strong as to lead them to say that they would never vote for imposing the death penalty may now be excluded from the guilt stage as well as from the sentencing stage. Note, however, that prospective jurors cannot be rejected from either stage merely because they are opposed to the death penalty. To be disqualified, these jurors must indicate that they would automatically vote against the death penalty irrespective of the facts of the case.[66]

Mills v. Maryland
486 U.S. 367 (1988)

CAPSULE: Jury instructions that suggest that unanimity is required for a jury to find mitigating circumstances are unconstitutional.

FACTS: Mills was tried and convicted for the murder of his cellmate while serving time in a Maryland prison. The jury, during the sentencing phase, agreed that the murder was aggravated because it was committed while the defendant was confined to a correctional institution. Further, they answered "no" in regard to whether they had reached a unanimous decision on the presence of each mitigating circumstance indicated on the verdict form. The death penalty was imposed. Mills challenged the sentence, claiming that it was unconstitutionally mandated by the manner in which the jury was instructed and the implementation of the verdict form. He argued that, in effect, the instructions and verdict form indicated that the death penalty was mandatory if the jury unanimously agreed to the presence of the aggravating factor and failed to unanimously agree to the presence of any mitigating factor.

ISSUE: Must a jury unanimously agree that a mitigating factor exists in order for that mitigating factor to be considered by any juror in their sentencing decision? NO.

HOLDING: Capital jurors may not be prohibited from considering mitigating factors simply because the jury is not unanimous in its determination of the presence of those mitigating factors. Maryland's sentencing instructions gave the impression that unanimity was required and thus violated the defendant's due process rights.

REASON: "With respect to findings of guilt, a jury's verdict must be set aside if it can be supported on one ground but not on another, and the reviewing court is uncertain which of the two grounds was relied upon by the jury in reaching the verdict. Review of death sentences demands even greater certainty that the jury's conclusions rested on proper grounds.

"While the Court of Appeals' construction of the jury instructions and verdict form is plausible, it cannot be concluded, with any degree of certainty, that the jury did not adopt petitioner's interpretation instead. Nothing in the verdict form or the judge's instructions even arguably is construable as suggesting that the jury could leave an answer blank and proceed to the next step in its deliberations. A jury following the instructions set out in the verdict form could be precluded from considering mitigating evidence if only a single juror adhered to the view that such evidence should not be so considered.

"There is no extrinsic evidence of what the jury in this case actually thought, but the portions of the record relating to the verdict form and the judge's instructions indicate that there is at least a substantial risk that the jury was misinformed. Moreover, since the time when this case was decided below, the Court of Appeals has promulgated a new verdict form expressly covering the situation where there is a lack of unanimity as to the existence or nonexistence of a particular mitigating factor, and providing for the consideration of all mitigating evidence in determining the sentence. This shows at least some concern on that court's part that juries could misunderstand the previous instructions as to unanimity and the consideration of mitigating evidence by individual jurors."

CASE SIGNIFICANCE: This was the first case to address requirements surrounding jurors' consideration of mitigating circumstances in the sentencing phase of a capital trial. The issue here revolved around sentencing instructions given to the jury that could easily be perceived as requiring that the jury be unanimous in finding mitigating circumstances in order for those circumstances to be factors in the sentencing decision. Believing that unanimity was required, according to the jury instructions and the instructions on the verdict form, the jury (which could not unanimously agree on the presence of mitigating factors) sentenced the defendant to death. The Court ruled that the instructions gave the impression that unanimity was required and were thus unconstitutional. More important, the Court said that unanimity in findings of mitigating circumstances is not required in order for such factors to weigh in the sentencing decision. In the years to come the Court continued to emphasize that jurors must individually be allowed to consider whatever mitigating factors they believe are relevant to their decision whether to impose the death penalty.

Morgan v. Illinois
504 U.S. 719 (1992)

CAPSULE: Refusal by the court, upon defendant's request, to inquire whether prospective jurors would automatically impose the death sentence upon conviction of the defendant is a violation of due process.

FACTS: Morgan was hired to kill a narcotics dealer for $4,000. He lured the victim, a friend, into an empty apartment and shot him in the head six times. Morgan was convicted of first-degree murder and sentenced to death. Voir dire was conducted, in accordance with state law, by the trial court. The state pursued the death penalty and accordingly requested that prospective jurors, per *Witherspoon*, be questioned about whether they opposed the death penalty and would thus refuse to impose it upon conviction under any circumstances. The court allowed such inquiry and 17 potential jurors were removed. In response, the defendant requested that prospective jurors also be asked the following question: "If you found Derrick Morgan guilty, would you automatically vote to impose the death penalty no matter what the facts are?" The court refused to present the question. The Illinois Supreme Court affirmed the lower court's decision.

ISSUE: Does a trial court's refusal, upon defendant's request, to ask prospective jurors whether they would automatically impose the death penalty upon defendant's conviction violate due process? YES.

HOLDING: The due process clause of the Fourteenth Amendment requires that, if requested by the defendant, prospective jurors be questioned in voir dire regarding whether they would automatically impose the sentence of death if they find the defendant guilty.

REASON: "On voir dire a trial court must, at a defendant's request, inquire into the prospective jurors' views on capital punishment. Part of the guarantee of a defendant's right to an impartial jury is an adequate voir dire to identify unqualified jurors. Morgan could not exercise intelligently his challenge for cause against prospective jurors who would unwaveringly impose death after a finding of guilt unless he was given the opportunity to identify such persons by questioning them at voir dire about their views on the death penalty. Absent that opportunity, his right not to be tried by those who would always impose death would be rendered as nugatory and meaningless as the State's right, in the absence of questioning, to strike those who never do so.

"A juror to whom mitigating evidence is irrelevant is plainly saying that such evidence is not worth consideration, a view which has long been rejected by this Court and which finds no basis in Illinois statutory or decisional law. Here, the instruction accords with the State's death penalty statute, which requires that the jury be instructed to consider any relevant aggravating and mitigating factors, lists certain relevant mitigating factors, and directs the jury to consider whether the mitigating factors are "sufficient to preclude" the death penalty's imposition. Since the statute plainly indicates that a lesser sentence is available in every case where mitigating evidence exists, a juror who would invariably impose the death penalty would not give the mitigating evidence the consideration the statute contemplates."

CASE SIGNIFICANCE: In *Witherspoon v. Illinois* (1968),[67] and *Lockhart v. McCree* (1986),[68] the Supreme Court held that jurors may be removed for cause from serving on capital juries if their views about the death penalty would prohibit them from ever imposing a death sentence regardless of circumstances. In this case, often referred to as the "reverse-Witherspoon" case, the converse was addressed: Whether jurors may be removed if their views meant that they would automatically vote for a death sentence upon conviction of the defendant. The Court held that the defense should have the opportunity to question prospective jurors on this point and that those who, like the *Witherspoon* excludables, would never be able to consider both options of life sentence and death sentence may be excluded from capital juries. This levels the playing field for the defense and the prosecution in the selection of jurors based on their views about the death penalty.

Simmons v. South Carolina
512 U.S. 154 (1994)

CAPSULE: When future dangerousness is at issue in a capital trial and parole is prohibited if a life sentence is imposed, the jury must be informed about the defendant's parole ineligibility.

FACTS: In 1990, Simmons beat and killed an elderly woman in her home. Before the capital trial for this murder began, Simmons also pled guilty to two counts of sexual assault on two other elderly women and to first-degree burglary. His guilty pleas and convictions on the violent offenses rendered Simmons ineligible for parole if convicted on the capital murder charge.

Prior to jury selection, the prosecution requested that any mention of parole be barred throughout the trial. Despite the objection of the defense, this request was granted by the trial court. The defense was barred from mentioning parole or even questioning jurors regarding their understanding of the meaning of a "life" sentence.

In the closing arguments, the prosecution argued that Simmons was a future danger to society, adding that "[y]our verdict will be an act of self-defense." The defense, in an attempt to rebut this argument, requested that the jury be instructed about the true meaning of "life imprisonment" in this case, which would include the fact that Simmons would never be eligible for parole. The trial court refused. During deliberations, the jury sent a note asking the judge this question: "Does the imposition of a life sentence carry with it the possibility of parole?" The judge responded that the jury was not to consider parole or parole eligibility in reaching their verdict and that the terms life imprisonment and death sentence were to be understood in their plain and ordinary meaning. Simmons' appeal that the judge's refusal to instruct the jury about his parole eligibility violated the Eighth Amendment and his due process rights under the Fourteenth Amendment. The South Carolina Supreme Court rejected his appeal.

ISSUE: Does the refusal to instruct a capital jury about parole ineligibility when the prosecution has argued future dangerousness violate due process? YES.

HOLDING: Due process requires that a defendant have the right to rebut evidence presented against him. In a case in which a defendant's future dangerousness is argued by the prosecution and in which state law prohibits parole, the defendant has a right to have the jury instructed about the defendant's parole ineligibility.

REASON: "In assessing future dangerousness, the actual duration of the defendant's prison sentence is indisputably relevant. Holding all other factors constant, it is entirely reasonable for a sentencing jury to view a defendant who is eligible for parole as a greater threat to society than a defendant who is not. Indeed, there may be no greater assurance of a defendant's future nondangerousness to the public than the fact that he never will be released on parole. The trial court's refusal to apprise the jury of information so crucial to its sentencing determination, particularly when the prosecution alluded to the defendant's future dangerousness in its argument to the jury, cannot be reconciled with our well-established precedents interpreting the Due Process Clause."

"The Due Process Clause does not allow the execution of a person 'on the basis of information which he had no opportunity to deny or explain.' *Gardner v. Florida*, 430 U.S. 349, 362 (1977). In this case, the jury reasonably may have believed that petitioner could be released on parole if he were not executed. To the extent this misunderstanding pervaded the jury's deliberations, it had the effect of creating a false choice between sentencing petitioner to death and sentencing him to a limited period of incarceration. This grievous misperception was encouraged by the trial court's refusal to provide the jury with accurate information regarding petitioner's parole ineligibility, and by the State's repeated suggestion that petitioner would pose a future danger to society if he were not executed. Three times petitioner asked to inform the jury that in fact he was ineligible for parole under state law; three times his request was denied. The State thus succeeded in securing a death sentence on the ground, at least in part, of petitioner's future dangerousness, while at the same time concealing from the sentencing jury the true meaning of its noncapital sentencing alternative, namely, that life imprisonment meant life without parole. We think it is clear that the State denied petitioner due process."

CASE SIGNIFICANCE: This case deals with an issue raised by an increasing number of state laws that prohibit release on parole for certain heinous offenses. South Carolina law provided that for the type of offense committed by the defendant in this case, imprisonment for life meant that the defendant could not be released on parole. This is important because jurors might not impose the death penalty and opt for life imprisonment if they are informed that life imprisonment for some defendants means that these defendants will never be released from prison. The assumption is that if life imprisonment can mean parole, jurors would rather impose the death penalty so that society may be protected from dangerous parolees. However, if jurors know that life imprisonment means that the defendant will never be released, then future danger to society does not become a consideration in imposing the penalty. The Court said that due process requires that the information on "life without parole" as an alternative to the death penalty in certain states be made known to the jury when determining the sentence to be imposed. It could make a difference in the punishment the jury ultimately imposes.[69]

Weeks v. Angelone
528 U.S. 225 (2000)

CAPSULE: Even if a jury requests clarification, judges in capital cases are not required to further clarify sentencing requirements beyond reference to the actual words of the jury instructions.

FACTS: Lonnie Weeks Jr. was a passenger in a car he had stolen but that his uncle, Lewis Dukes, was driving. They were pursued by a state trooper and eventually stopped near an exit ramp. Upon the trooper's request, Dukes exited and stood near the rear of the car. The trooper then asked that Weeks do the same. As Weeks exited the car, he brandished a handgun loaded with hollow-point bullets and fired six shots at the trooper, killing him.

Weeks was arrested the next day and confessed to the murder of the police officer. A jury found him guilty of capital murder. During the sentencing phase of the trial, the prosecution presented evidence and testimony that he "would constitute a continuing threat to society" and that his crime was "outrageously or wantonly vile, horrible or inhuman, in that it involved depravity of mind."

During deliberations, the jurors asked the judge a series of questions. First, they asked about whether a life sentence would carry the possibility of parole, to which the judge responded that they were to make their decision within the instructions given and not concern themselves with what may happen after their decision. The jury then asked the following:

> If we believe that Lonnie Weeks, Jr. is guilty of at least 1 of the alternatives, then is it our duty as a jury to issue the death penalty? Or must we decide (even though he is guilty of one of the alternatives) whether or not to issue the death penalty, or one of the life sentences? What is the Rule? Please clarify?

The judge responded by simply referring the jury to the original instructions. The defense requested that the judge instruct the jury that even if they find the presence of aggravating factors, they may still choose to impose a life sentence. The judge refused and Weeks was sentenced to death.

ISSUE: Is it a violation of due process for a trial judge to refuse to clarify sentencing requirements beyond what is indicated in the original jury instructions? NO.

HOLDING: A trial judge is not required, even if requested by the jury, to clarify the sentencing requirements in a capital case beyond the words provided in the original jury instructions.

REASON: "A jury is presumed to follow its instructions. *Richardson v. Marsh*, 481 U.S. 200, (1987). Similarly, a jury is presumed to understand a judge's answer to its question. Weeks' jury did not inform the court that after reading the relevant paragraph of the instruction, it still did not understand its role. ('Had the jury desired further information, they might, and probably would, have signified their desire to the court. The utmost willingness was manifested to gratify them, and it may fairly be presumed that they had nothing further to ask'). To presume otherwise would require reversal every time a jury inquires about a matter of constitutional significance, regardless of the judge's answer."

"Given that petitioner's jury was adequately instructed, and given that the trial judge responded to the jury's question by directing its attention to the precise paragraph of the constitutionally adequate instruction that answers its inquiry, the question becomes whether the Constitution requires anything more. We hold that it does not."

CASE SIGNIFICANCE: This case is significant in that it marks a turning point in the degree of guidance a jury is afforded in capital cases. The jurors clearly indicated that they were confused about the meaning of the instructions they were given. They did not know: (1) the meaning of life imprisonment, (2) whether upon finding an aggravating factor, they were required to impose the death penalty, or (3) whether they were allowed to consider mitigating circumstances and potentially sentence the defendant to life as opposed to death. In response to their inquiries, the only guidance they received was the judge directing them to the written instructions they had been provided and that had confused them in the first place. Until this case, the Supreme Court had generally maintained that jurors should be given all possible guidance when considering aggravating and mitigating factors and how those factors are to weigh in their sentencing decision. In spite of the obvious confusion on the part of the jury, the Court in *Weeks* held that the written instructions were sufficient guidance and that no further instructions from the judge were needed.

Ring v. Arizona
536 U.S. 584 (2002)

CAPSULE: A judge may not alone make a determination of aggravating circumstances and then elevate the punishment to death.

FACTS: Ring and two accomplices stole an armored bank truck from in front of a mall in Glendale, Arizona, killing the driver and stealing $562,000 in cash and $271,000 in checks. Acting on the tip of an informant, Glendale police began investigating Ring and one of his accomplices, James Greenham, for their role in the robbery and murder. Their investigation revealed that each had made expensive purchases shortly after the robbery. They subsequently placed wiretaps on the telephones of Ring and Greenham and another suspected accomplice, William Ferguson. Recorded conversations implicated each of the men in the robbery and murder. A search of Ring's house revealed a duffel bag containing more than $271,000 in cash and notes indicating planned "splits" among the three suspects.

At trial, the jury failed to find Ring guilty of premeditated murder, but convicted him of felony murder in the course of armed robbery. Arizona law required further findings of aggravation in order for him to be eligible for the death penalty. Arizona law requires that a sentencing hearing be conducted in which aggravating and mitigating circumstances are considered and that the judge determine whether such circumstances are present and thus whether the defendant should receive the death penalty. The judge, having heard further testimony from Ring's accomplice Greenham that Ring had premeditated and been the one to actually kill the driver, and having found the presence of aggravating circumstances, entered a "Special Verdict" sentencing Ring to death.

ISSUE: Does the Sixth Amendment require that a jury, not a judge, make the determination of the presence of an aggravating circumstance that elevates a punishment to death? YES.

HOLDING: The decision of whether to execute a defendant must be made by a jury. A judge may not alone make a determination of aggravating circumstances that elevate a punishment to death. Such aggravating circumstances are "the functional equivalent of an element of a greater offense" and therefore must be determined by a jury as required by the Sixth Amendment.

REASON: "In various settings, the Court has interpreted the Constitution to require the addition of an element or elements to the definition of a crime in order to narrow its scope. If a legislature responded to such a decision by adding the element the Court held constitutionally required, surely the Sixth Amendment guarantee would apply to that element. There is no reason to differentiate capital crimes from all others in this regard. Arizona's suggestion that judicial authority over the finding of aggravating factors may be a better way to guarantee against the arbitrary imposition of the death penalty is unpersuasive. The Sixth Amendment jury trial right does not turn on the relative rationality, fairness, or efficiency of potential factfinders. In any event, the superiority of judicial factfinding in capital cases is far from evident, given that the great majority of states responded to this Court's Eighth Amendment decisions requiring the presence of aggravating circumstances in capital cases by entrusting those determinations to the jury. Although stare decisis is of fundamental importance to the rule of law, this Court has overruled prior decisions where, as here, the necessity and propriety of doing so has been established."

"If a State makes an increase in a defendant's authorized punishment contingent on the finding of a fact, that fact—no matter how the State labels it

—must be found by a jury beyond a reasonable doubt. A defendant may not be exposed to a penalty exceeding the maximum he would receive if punished according to the facts reflected in the jury verdict alone. . . . Based solely on the jury's verdict finding Ring guilty of first-degree felony murder, the maximum punishment he could have received was life imprisonment."

CASE SIGNIFICANCE: This is one of the most significant recent Supreme Court cases on the death penalty. It has the potential to be of great impact on states where judges are given the responsibility for making the final sentencing decision. Several state death penalty statutes give judges the authority to override the jury's sentencing "recommendation." In *Ring*, the Court held that, in accordance with *Apprendi v. New Jersey* (2000),[70] a jury must be the authority that makes the determination of the presence of aggravating factors that would elevate the sentence to death. For a judge to do so, as in Ring's case, violates due process and the Sixth Amendment right to a jury trial. In effect, the judge made an independent finding that raised the level of the offense to one in which the death penalty was appropriate.

This decision invalidated all statutes giving judges sole discretion in the sentencing of convicted capital defendants. But the full impact of this decision on states in which judges play a partial role is not yet known. Nor is it known whether the decision will be retroactive, resulting in the invalidation of existing death sentences across the United States. Several states with sentencing schemes allowing judges a role in sentencing decisions have already begun to revise their statutes to comport with the *Ring* decision.

Uttecht v. Brown
551 U.S. ___ (2007)

CAPSULE: A trial court judge's determination that a juror's views on the death penalty would substantially impair his or her ability to consider a death sentence is sufficient to exclude the juror.

FACTS: Brown robbed, raped, and stabbed to death a Washington woman then, two days later, robbed, raped, and attempted to murder a second woman in California. When apprehended, Brown confessed to these crimes and pleaded guilty to the crimes in California, for which he received a life sentence. He was subsequently tried for capital murder in Washington for the rape, robbery, and murder of the first victim. Brown was sentenced to death in the state of Washington.

The capital jury was selected over a period of several weeks during which much time was devoted to the process of "death qualification." One juror (referred to as "Juror Z") was questioned extensively about his views on the death penalty and his perceived ability to fairly apply the law in deciding whether to impose the death penalty. Juror Z was excused for cause based on his general reluctance to consider the death penalty except for in cases in which the defendant would likely re-offend if released from prison. Although Juror Z had answered that he could follow the law and impose the death penalty if warranted, the trial court judge determined that Juror Z was confused about the law and that his views and demeanor indicated that he was "substantially impaired" in his ability to do so. His conviction and sentence were upheld by the Washington State Supreme Court. Brown filed a habeas corpus petition, which was denied by the U.S. District Court. The U.S. Court of Appeals for the Ninth Circuit rejected the federal district court's denial and reversed the lower court's sentence of death, holding that the exclusion of Juror Z was a violation of Brown's Sixth and Fourteenth Amendment rights.

ISSUE: Is a trial court judge's determination that a juror is substantially impaired in his or her ability to consider the sentence of death sufficient to remove that juror? YES.

HOLDING: Trial courts should be given deference in their ability to ascertain whether a prospective juror is substantially impaired in his or her ability to follow the law and consider the death penalty in the sentencing phase of capital trials.

REASON: "Juror Z's answers on their face, could have led the trial court to believe that Juror Z would be substantially impaired in his ability to impose the death penalty in the absence of the possibility that Brown would be released and would reoffend. And the trial court, furthermore, is entitled to deference because it had an opportunity to observe the demeanor of Juror Z. We do not know anything about his demeanor, in part because a transcript cannot fully reflect that information but also because the defense did not object to Juror Z's removal. Nevertheless, the State's challenge, Brown's waiver of an objection, and the trial court's excusal of Juror Z support the conclusion that the interested parties present in the courtroom all felt that removing Juror Z was appropriate under the *Witherspoon-Witt* rule."

"Juror Z's assurances that he would consider imposing the death penalty and would follow the law do not overcome the reasonable inference from his other statements that in fact he would be substantially impaired in this case because there was no possibility of release. His assurances did not require the trial court to deny the State's motion to excuse Juror Z. The defense itself had told the trial court that any juror would make similar guarantees and that they were worth little; instead, defense counsel explained, the court should listen to arguments concerning the substance of the juror's answers. The trial court in part relied, as diligent judges often must, upon both parties' counsel to explain why a challenged juror's problematic beliefs about the death penalty would not rise to the level of substantial impairment. Brown's counsel offered no defense of Juror Z. In light of the deference owed to the trial court the position Brown now maintains does not convince us the decision to excuse Juror Z was unreasonable."

"Deference to the trial court is appropriate because it is in a position to assess the demeanor of the venire, and of the individuals who compose it, a factor of the critical importance in assessing the attitude and qualifications of potential jurors."

CASE SIGNIFICANCE: This case is significant in that it grants increased discretion to trial court judges in making the decision to exclude a juror for cause in the process of death qualification. It also relaxes the criteria for death qualification by setting the standard that a prospective juror's views about the death penalty may simply be perceived to "substantially limit" his or her ability to impose the death penalty if warranted. The Court notes that deference should be given to the trial court judge in that he or she is in the best position to gauge the attitude and demeanor of the prospective juror. The Court's decision represents a possible return to pre-*Witherspoon* standards in which prospective capital jurors could be excluded for expressing general qualms about or scruples against the death penalty. Dissenting justices and critics alike argue that this decision opens the door for arbitrariness and increases potential bias in capital juries.

Internet Resources

Capital Jury Project
http://www.albany.edu/scj/CJPhome.htm

Death Qualification and Jury Bias
http://www.encyclopedia.com/doc/1G1-72272563.html

Capital Defense Network: Jury Selection Litigation Guide
http://capdefnet.org/fdprc/contents/litigation_guides/jury_selection/f_jury_se-
    lection.htm

Capital Jury Bibliography
http://www.ajs.org/jc/bibliography/jc_bibl_capital.pdf

**Capital Punishment in Context. Jury Instructions: Jurors' Understand-
ings and Misunderstandings**
http://www.capitalpunishmentincontext.org/issues/juryinstruct

Jury Selection
http://deathpenaltycurriculum.org/student/c/courtroom/jury/question.htm

Notes

1. *Duncan v. Louisiana*, 391 U.S. 145, 153 (1968).

2. *Apprendi v. New Jersey*, 530 U.S. 466, 490 (2000).

3. *Id.* at 497.

4. *Ring v. Arizona*, 536 U.S. 584 (2002).

5. Darian B. Taylor, *Capital Sentencing in Arizona: A "Weighing State" in Name Only*, 42 AZ ATTORNEY 20 (2006).

6. *Ring v. Arizona, supra.*

7. *Taylor, supra.*

8. Marc R. Shapiro, *Re-evaluating the Role of the Jury in Capital Cases after* Ring v. Arizona, 59 N.Y.U. ANN. SURV. AM. L. 633, 633 (2004).

9. *Spaziano v. Florida*, 468 U.S. 447 (1984).

10. *Id.* at 461.

11. *Walton v. Arizona*, 497 U.S. 639 (1990).

12. *Shapiro, supra.*

13. *Duncan v. Louisiana*, 391 U.S. 145 (1968).

14. Cited in *Shapiro, supra* at 643.

15. *Apprendi v. New Jersey*, 530 U.S. 466 (2000).

16. *Id.* at 490.

17. *Ring v. Arizona, supra.*

18. *Apprendi v. New Jersey, supra.*

19. *Id.* at 605.

20. *Schriro v. Summerlin*, 542 U.S. 348 (2004).

21. *Teague v. Lane*, 489 U.S. 288 (1989).

22. *Ring v. Arizona, supra.*

23. *Shapiro, supra.*

24. *Id.*

25. *Id.*

26. *Id.*

27. *Id.*

28. *Gregg v. Georgia*, 428 U.S. 153 (1976).

29. *Proffitt v. Florida*, 428 U.S. 242 (1976).

30. *Jurek v. Texas*, 428 U.S. 262 (1976).

31. *Woodson v. North Carolina*, 428 U.S. 280 (1976).

32. *Roberts v. Louisiana*, 428 U.S. 325 (1976).

33. *Beck v. Alabama*, 447 U.S. 625 (1980).

34. *Hopper v. Evans*, 456 U.S. 605 (1982).

35. *Id.* at 607.

36. *Hopkins v. Reeves*, 524 U.S. 88 (1998).

37. *Id.* at 96.

38. J.H. Blume, S.P. Garvey, and S.L. Johnson, *Future Dangerousness in Capital Cases: Always "At Issue,"* 86 CORNELL L. REV. 397 (2001).

39. *California v. Ramos*, 463 U.S. 992 (1983).

40. *Id.* at 1003 (citing *Jurek v. Texas, supra* at 276).

41. Craig M. Bradley, *South Carolina's Death Penalty Odyssey Continues*, TRIAL, Apr. 2002, at 68.

42. See, for example, William J. Bowers and Benjamin D. Steiner, *Death by Default: An Empirical Demonstration of False and Forced Choices in Capital Sentencing*, 77 TEX. L. REV. 605 (1998) and Benjamin D. Steiner, *Folk Knowledge as Legal Action: Death Penalty Judgments and the Tenet of Early Release in a Culture of Mistrust and Punitiveness*, 33 L. & SOC. REV. 461 (1999).

43. *Simmons v. South Carolina*, 512 U.S. 154 (1994).

44. *Shafer v. South Carolina*, 532 U.S. 36 (2001).

45. *Id.* at 55.

46. *Kelly v. South Carolina*, 534 U.S. 246 (2002).

47. *Id.* at 254.

48. Scott Vollum, Rolando V. del Carmen, and Dennis R. Longmire, *Should Jurors Be Informed about Parole Eligibility in Death Penalty Cases? An Analysis of* Kelly v. South Carolina, 84 THE PRISON JOURNAL 395 (2004).

49. *Witherspoon v. Illinois*, 391 U.S. 510 (1968).

50. *Id.* at 513–514.

51. *Adams v. Texas*, 448 U.S. 38 (1980).

52. *Wainwright v. Witt*, 469 U.S. 412 (1985).

53. *Lockhart v. McCree*, 476 U.S. 162 (1986).

54. *Morgan v. Illinois*, 504 U.S. 719 (1992).

55. *Uttecht v. Brown*, 551 U.S. ___ (2007).

56. *Id.*

57. *Id.* at 3.

58. Death Penalty Information Center, "Supreme Court Decision Allows Broader Exclusion of Jurors, But May Further Isolate the Death Penalty." Accessed March 5, 2008 at http://www.deathpenaltyinfo.org/article.php?did=2367&scid=64.

59. *Id.*

60. See, for example, William J. Bowers, Marla Sandys, and Benjamin D. Steiner, *Foreclosed Impartiality in Capital Sentencing: Jurors' Predispositions, Guilt-Trial Experience, and*

Premature Decision Making, 83 CORNELL L. REV. 1476 (1998) and Craig Haney, Lorelei Sontag, and Sally Costanzo, *Deciding to Take a Life: Capital Juries, Sentencing Instructions, and the Jurisprudence of Death*, 50 J. SOC. ISSUES 149 (1994). For thorough reviews and analyses of the extant research on death qualification, see the following meta-analyses: M. Allen, E. Mabry, and D. McKelton, *Impact of Juror Attitudes about the Death Penalty on Juror Evaluations of Guilt and Punishment: A Meta-Analysis*, 22 L. & HUM. BEHAV. 715 (1998); J.W. Filkins, C.M. Smith, and R.S. Tindale, *An Evaluation of the Biasing Effects of Death Qualification: A Meta-Analytic/Computer Simulation Approach*, in R.S. TINDALE, L. HEATH, J. EDWARDS, E.J. POSAVAC, F.B. BRYANT, Y. SUAREZ-BALCAZAR, E. HENDERSON-KING, AND J. MYERS (EDS.), THEORY AND RESEARCH ON SMALL GROUPS, 153–175 (1998); M.T. Nietzel, D.M. McCarthy, and M.J. Kern, *Juries: The Current State of the Empirical Literature*, in R. ROESCH, S.D. HART, AND J.R.P. OGLOFF, (EDS.), PSYCHOLOGY AND LAW: THE STATE OF THE DISCIPLINE, 23–50 (1999).

61. *Lockhart v. McCree, supra* at 190.

62. *Gregg v. Georgia, supra.*

63. *Ring v. Arizona, supra.*

64. *Lockhart v. McCree, supra.*

65. *Witherspoon v. Illinois, supra.*

66. Adapted from ROLANDO V. DEL CARMEN, SUSAN E. RITTER, AND BETSY A. WITT, BRIEFS OF LEADING CASES IN CORRECTIONS (5th ed. 2008).

67. *Witherspoon v. Illinois, supra.*

68. *Lockhart v. McCree, supra.*

69. This case significance is taken from ROLANDO V. DEL CARMEN, SUSAN E. RITTER, AND BETSY A. WITT, BRIEFS OF LEADING CASES IN CORRECTIONS (5th ed. 2008).

70. *Apprendi v. New Jersey, supra.*

Chapter Outline

I. **Introduction**

II. ***Strickland*: A Two-Part Test for Deciding Ineffective Assistance Claims**

III. **Application of *Strickland* in Subsequent Cases**

IV. **Applying AEDPA Restrictions to Sixth Amendment Challenges in Death Penalty Cases**

V. **Evaluating Ineffective Assistance in the Twenty-First Century: Objective Standards for Disadvantaged Defendants**

VI. **State and Local Indigent Defense Systems and Funding**

VII. **Recent Claims of Ineffective Assistance of Counsel**
   A. *Mickens v. Taylor*: Successive Representation Permitted Unless Adverse Consequences Exist
   B. *Wiggins v. Smith*: Counsel's Duty to Discover a "Dysfunctional Background"
   C. *Florida v. Nixon*: The Supreme Court Closes the Door on Silence
   D. *Rompilla v. Beard*: Right to Investigate Gains Momentum
   E. *Schriro v. Landrigan*: Interference Is not Incompetence
   F. *Arave v. Hoffman*: Plea Bargaining and the Right to Counsel

VIII. **In Summary, What Do these Cases Say?**

IX. **Conclusion**

Cases Briefed in Chapter 7

Case Briefs

Internet Resources

Notes

Chapter 7

The Right to Effective Assistance of Counsel and the Death Penalty

I. Introduction

The Sixth Amendment to the United States Constitution states that "in all criminal prosecutions, the accused shall enjoy the right to have the assistance of counsel for his defense."[1] The Supreme Court has said that "of all the rights that an accused person has, the right to be represented by counsel is by far the most pervasive, for it affects his ability to assert any other rights he may have," *United States v. Cronic* (1984).[2] However, the right did not originally apply to all criminal defendants. Initially the Bill of Rights, which included the first 10 amendments, only applied to the actions of the federal government. However, in 1932, the Supreme Court decided in *Powell v. Alabama* (1932)[3] that the right to effective assistance of counsel existed for indigent, capital defendants. It was not until about 30 years later, when the Court decided in *Gideon v. Wainright* (1963),[4] that this right automatically applied to all state defendants through the due process clause.

After *Gideon*, lower courts were only required to meet the minimum expectation that a criminal defendant be represented by counsel. The assumption, however, was that counsel was competent in every case. This fundamental protection was challenged in *McMann v. Richardson* (1970).[5] In *McMann*, the Court resolved the issue of whether the guilty pleas that had been made by three defendants were valid. The Court, in *McMann*, took its first step toward acknowledging the difference between mere representation and effective assistance of counsel. The Court said that "if the right to counsel guaranteed by the Constitution is to serve its purpose, defendants cannot be left to the mercies of incompetent counsel."[6] The Court concluded that the claims made by the defendants were without merit because the attorneys had given them advice that was reasonably competent. The Court, however, did little to clarify this legal standard for the benefit of the lower courts. Throughout the 1970s and early 1980s, state courts were faced with making their own interpretations of "effective assistance" in light of *McMann*. This caused widespread disagreement among courts as to its meaning.

The Court has since made great strides toward clarifying the meaning of "effective counsel" under the Sixth Amendment. This chapter will discuss the decisions of the Court dealing with a capital defendant's right to effective assistance of counsel. The landmark decision that clarified what is now known as "effective assistance of counsel" came in *Strickland v. Washington* (1984).[7] Developing a two-part test for making a determination of whether a capital defendant was provided ineffective assistance of counsel, the Court in *Strickland* said that such a claim was valid only if: (1) the counsel's performance was objectively unreasonable, and (2) there was a reasonable likelihood that the trial would have had a different outcome because of such performance. Using this approach, the Court has maintained that defendants bear a significant burden in proving that their counsel was in fact ineffective. Much of the Court's attention has recently focused on claims involving defense counsel's failure to adequately investigate and present mitigating evidence during sentencing proceedings. Collectively, recent decisions in *Rompilla v. Beard* (2005) and *Schriro v. Landrigan* (2007) suggest that the Court has become concerned about defense counsel's strategy during sentencing, particularly when it involves the presentation of mitigating evidence. And although the Court ultimately dismissed the petition in *Arave v. Hoffman* (2007), it has signaled its willingness to consider counsel's duty concerning plea negotiations during sentencing. This chapter discusses important cases involving ineffective assistance of counsel and focuses on the rights of capital defendants.

II. *Strickland:* A Two-Part Test for Deciding Ineffective Assistance Claims

Prior to 1984, the Court did not have a definitive test for assessing ineffective assistance of counsel claims. Instead, the Court deferred authority to state and lower federal courts to decide matters arising from ineffectiveness of counsel. *Strickland* (1984) established a clear test for analyzing a defendant's Sixth Amendment claim of ineffective assistance of counsel. In *Strickland*, the defendant committed a series of stabbing murders. He was convicted and given the death penalty. Strickland's habeas corpus claim alleged that his counsel failed to present character witnesses or psychiatric testimony as mitigating evidence for him during his sentencing. Instead, his counsel chose not to present such evidence "in order to prevent the state from cross-examining Washington about his background or putting forth psychiatric testimony."[8] Defense counsel also feared that any character testimony given during sentencing could have harsh consequences for his client, a judgment call by the attorney.

On appeal, the Court held that a claim for ineffective assistance of counsel must demonstrate the following: (1) counsel's performance was deficient and (2) such deficiency prejudiced the defendant's case. This means that there must be a reasonable probability that the attorney's errors caused the wrong decision. The Court said that there is a presumption in the practice of law that an attorney's performance, knowledge, and decisions are to be considered reasonable. Recognizing the fact that an attorney's legal tactics may vary depending on the circumstances, the Court refused to adopt a more rigid standard for determining what constitutes "unreasonable" representation.

Instead of developing concrete guidelines for lower courts to follow, the *Strickland* Court gave the states the authority to define the meaning of "unreasonable" representation. The Court, however, went no further than to say that the failure to present character witnesses or psychiatric testimony as mitigating factors during sentencing did not, in itself, constitute ineffective assistance of counsel in violation of the Sixth Amendment.

III. Application of *Strickland* in Subsequent Cases

The issue of the right to a fair trial for indigent capital defendants has been raised for several reasons. Some legal commentators argue that ineffective assistance of counsel is primarily a "poverty problem"[9] that has become pervasive in the modern judicial system. Disadvantaged by popular elections of prosecutors and judges, poorer defendants who have been charged with capital crimes have less of a chance of overcoming the political power associated with these individuals. Undoubtedly, the connection between race and class in the United States has led to more executions for black defendants. These social factors cast a shadow over the doctrine of fundamental fairness. The Court has struggled to balance the rights of capital defendants prejudiced by ineffective counsel during the two decades since the decision in *Strickland*. In *Lockhart v. Fretwell* (1993),[10] the Court sought to clarify its standard of prejudice that was established in *Strickland* by making it increasingly difficult for indigent capital defendants to prevail in an ineffective assistance of counsel case.

In 1985, Fretwell was convicted of capital murder. The jury found that he committed the robbery for pecuniary gain, and this affected Fretwell in two ways: (1) it was a necessary element for the offense of robbery, and (2) it could also be used as an aggravating factor in the sentencing phase. Unaware that the prosecutor's "double-counting" technique was unconstitutional in light of *Collins v. Lockhart* (1985),[11] the defense counsel failed to object to the violation. Fretwell was sentenced to death. He then filed a habeas petition claiming ineffective assistance of counsel. However, before his case was retried, the Court decided *Perry v. Lockhart* (1989),[12] which overruled *Collins*. The Court then said that Fretwell's capital sentencing proceeding was not unconstitutional because the decision that his claim relied on had since been overruled; therefore, he was not deprived of any legal right. Under the standard set in *Strickland*, Chief Justice Rehnquist, writing for the majority of the Court, said that Fretwell was not entitled to the benefits of outdated law, despite the legal rule set in *Teague v. Lane* (1989).[13] In effect, the Chief Justice added a new rule to the *Strickland* test: Ineffective assistance claims must be determined according to the overall fairness of the proceeding, rather than simply examining the effect of the verdict by the trial court.

IV. Applying AEDPA Restrictions to Sixth Amendment Challenges in Death Penalty Cases

Thus far, this chapter has discussed case law dealing with ineffective assistance of counsel claims. Capital defendants making this claim were dramatically affected by the enactment of the Antiterrorism and Effective Death Penalty Act (AEDPA) of 1996. This law significantly affects death penalty defendants because it restricts their ability to file habeas corpus claims in federal courts.

Traditionally, habeas corpus is a way in which state and federal prisoners challenge their conviction by demanding new trials, even while they are incarcerated. Having its heritage in English common law, the writ evolved to become one of America's most sacred legal avenues for criminal defendants, and particularly capital defendants.[14] Originally, the writ applied only to federal prisoners. However, in 1867, Congress passed the Habeas Corpus Act,[15] which extended the authority of habeas corpus petitions to state prisoners. Specifically, the Act held that any federal court could issue the writ in "cases where any person may be restrained of his or her liberty in violation of the Constitution."[16]

Today, federal courts draw their authority to issue habeas writs from the Constitution. Federal habeas procedure is codified at 28 U.S.C. §§ 2241–2255.[17] Section 2254 of that title specifically deals with the authority of the federal courts to hear federal challenges by state inmates. As the federal courts became inundated with cases arising from state challenges, the federal government decided that habeas corpus writs needed to be streamlined so that only the meritorious cases reached the federal bench. In 1996, President Clinton signed the AEDPA, which has since served this purpose. The passage of the AEDPA and the amendment of § 2254(d) had the most substantial impact on death penalty defendants. The law mandates that federal judges consider state rulings regarding death penalty cases to be correct; however, there are instances in which capital defendants can succeed in a legitimate claim.

The AEDPA prohibits a capital defendant from making a successful claim unless the state proceeding "resulted in a decision that was contrary to, or involved an unreasonable application of, clearly established federal law, as determined by the Supreme Court of the United States."[18] Section 2254 (d)(1) reads:

> (d)   A determination . . . made by a State court . . . of competent jurisdiction . . . shall be presumed to be correct, unless the applicant shall establish or it shall otherwise appear . . .
>
> (1)   that the merits of the factual dispute were not resolved in the State court hearing.

One important case that involved the right to counsel and this specific provision of the AEDPA came before the Court in *Williams v. Taylor* (2000).[19] Williams had been convicted of capital murder and filed a habeas corpus petition alleging that he had been held unconstitutionally. Williams asserted that his attorney had failed to make an adequate investigation and thus was unable to present important mitigating evidence on his behalf during sentencing.

In deciding *Williams*, the Court noted a previous habeas corpus case—*Teague v. Lane* (1989). In *Teague*, the Court restricted habeas relief for capital defendants by ruling that an individual using a collateral attack may not rely on a federal law that was not in existence at the time of initial conviction. For capital defendants, this meant that any court ruling or federal law established after the conviction could not be the basis of a successful habeas claim. The *Williams* Court, in relying on *Teague*, claimed that state courts do not violate the "unreasonable application" phrase codified in § 2254 of the AEDPA when they choose the correct rule of law, but apply it incorrectly. Because the Supreme Court was only permitted to settle issues of law rather than fact, the Court said that "federal courts were not permitted to disturb the judgment of state courts for merely applying the law incorrectly."[20] Although Williams' claim prevailed in the Supreme Court, the decision effectively promoted the goal of the AEDPA by significantly limiting a capital defendant's chances of sustaining a habeas corpus claim.

The Court established that fundamental fairness was the test for the prejudice requirement mandated by the *Strickland* Court. Moreover, defendants were not entitled to rules of law that had since been overturned if their case was pending on habeas review to the Supreme Court. But the *Williams* Court also did one other important thing—it said that states were fundamentally unfair to defendants only when their substantive or procedural rights had been violated. In contrast to Fretwell, Williams was denied such rights because he was unable to "provide the jury with the mitigating evidence that his trial counsel either failed to discover or failed to offer."[21] Williams was prejudiced and his habeas corpus claim prevailed.

V. Evaluating Ineffective Assistance in the Twenty-First Century: Objective Standards for Disadvantaged Defendants

It has been argued that appellate courts have routinely failed to give much consideration to the fact that a good defense lawyer would not have exhausted every possibility to present potentially mitigating evidence to the jury.[22] While some indigent capital defendants are given competent counsel, others are not. This problem is attributed to the social link between indigent capital offenders and court-appointed counsel.[23] One source indicates that as many as 90 percent of capital defendants are indigent.[24] The competency level of public defense counsel has started to attract more attention in the legal community. The U.S. Department of Justice has established the Compendium of Standards for Indigent Defense Systems, which compiles standards from a range of sources and indicates the different rules affecting areas of criminal defense, such as capital case representation, appellate services, juvenile justice defense, attorney performance, and the administration of defense systems.[25]

VI. State and Local Indigent Defense Systems and Funding

Beginning with the *Gideon* decision, states have implemented different approaches to satisfying the Court's requirement to provide appointed counsel for indigent defendants. However, the Supreme Court has never held that states must institute indigent defense systems that provide financial assistance to capital defendants. States and counties have, nonetheless, devised their own public defender systems in response to growing concerns surrounding the competency of defense attorneys. Forty-two states have some type of statewide body or commission providing indigent defense services.[26] The various types of indigent defense systems include state public defender agencies with commissions (11); state public defender agencies without commissions (9); state public defender commissions with a director (5); states with a public defender commission with partial authority (10); state appellate commissions or agencies (7); and states without commissions (7).[27]

Table 1 presents a summary of states with indigent defense systems as well as the method and amount of funding available. The inclination among states has been to provide full state funding or expand the state's funding capacity for indigent defense services. As of July 2006, 28 states fund indigent defense systems entirely with statewide resources. Three states provide funds for at least 50 percent of indigent defense system operations. There are also 17 states that subsidize 50 percent of their indigent defense system's financial assistance through county resources. Two states depend strictly on county resources for funding purposes.

Table 7.1
State and Local Funding for Indigent Defense Systems

Full State Funding		More than 50% State Funding	Full County Funding	More than 50% County Funding
Alaska	Montana	Alabama	Pennsylvania	Arizona
Arkansas	New Hampshire	Kansas	Utah	California
Colorado	New Jersey	Oklahoma		Georgia
Connecticut	New Mexico			Idaho
Delaware	North Carolina			Illinois
Florida	North Dakota			Indiana
Hawaii	Oregon			Louisiana
Iowa	Rhode Island			Michigan
Kentucky	Tennessee			Mississippi
Maine	Vermont			Nebraska
Maryland	Virginia			Nevada
Massachusetts	West Virginia			New York
Minnesota	Wisconsin			Ohio
Missouri	Wyoming			South Carolina
				South Dakota
				Texas
				Washington

Source: *State Indigent Defense Systems* (December, 2006, p. 5).

The American Bar Association suggests that states providing full funding and oversight maintain more effective indigent defense systems than those funded entirely by counties. This is because state-funded systems have the training and resources to ensure that high-quality defense work is maintained. It is important to note that quality of indigent defense depends not only on the state's funding capacity but also individual differences among commissions and public defender systems.

VII. Recent Claims of Ineffective Assistance of Counsel

Since 1986, the Court has made significant changes to the *Strickland* rule that have clarified the meaning of "ineffective assistance" in terms of the Sixth Amendment. These changes have ultimately made the habeas appeal process much more difficult for capital defendants. The remainder of this chapter will focus on recent case decisions that have refined the concept of ineffective assistance of counsel based on the Court's decided cases.

In *Bell v. Cone* (2002),[28] the Court reconciled two competing tests that the Court used to assess ineffective assistance claims. In *United States v. Cronic* (1984),[29] the Court held that a defense counsel's performance was deficient only when the entire proceeding failed to subject the prosecution to meaningful adversarial testing. In *Cronic*, the Court considered five factors that would constitute a presumption of prejudice among defense counsel and therefore eliminate the need for the *Strickland* test. Those factors included: (1) the amount of time defense counsel had to prepare for trial, (2) the experience level of the attorney, (3) the gravity of the charge, (4) the complexity of the case, and (5) the accessibility of witnesses. In *Bell*, the Court considered the attorney's lack of time to prepare for trial, but found that counsel was given adequate time considering the type of question at issue— rebuttal of evidence showing intent to defraud. The Court concluded that because defense counsel had a reasonable amount of time to prepare— approximately three weeks—and found the other factors to be unpersuasive, there was no ineffective assistance of counsel. This test was challenged in *Bell v. Cone* when the petitioner alleged that the entire proceeding at his trial was prejudiced because his counsel's performance was deficient.

In this case, Cone had exhausted the appeals process in state and federal court. He then filed a writ of habeas corpus challenging the constitutionality of his incarceration based on an unreasonable application of clearly established law. Cone alleged that because his counsel did not present mitigating evidence or make a final argument at the sentencing stage of his trial, his legal representation was ineffective. The Supreme Court relied on the interpretation of *Cronic*, in which the Court ruled that defendants were entitled to a presumption of prejudice in certain circumstances, such as the requirement that defense counsel engage in "meaningful adversarial testing."[30] The Court had to clarify the competing standards developed in *Strickland* and *Cronic*. The Court focused on the decisions of defense counsel using the objectivity test and found that an attorney was entitled to considerable leeway in making such decisions.

The Court further stated that Cone's attorney had reasons for not introducing evidence that Cone believed to be compelling. It examined the credibility of Cone's mother as a witness and concluded that the attorney's failure to allow her testimony was simply a strategic decision to prevent the prosecution from cross-examining her. Because Cone's mother was not believed to be a good witness, his lawyer did not put her on the stand. Also, Cone claimed that his defense counsel was ineffective because he did not make a final argument on his behalf or plead for his life. The Court analyzed the consequences of not making a final argument, and found that the attorney could have reasonably believed that to do so would have put his client at a higher risk for receiving the death penalty. Because the prosecutor did not reiterate the horrific nature of Cone's crimes, the defense counsel simply elected to avoid the prosecutor's opportunity for rebuttal.

The Court held that the *Cronic* standard did not apply to situations in which a defense counsel's performance was deficient at certain points. Instead, the Court said that in order for an ineffective assistance claim to succeed, the "entire proceeding" must be prejudiced. Justice Rehnquist, writing for the majority, claimed that prejudicial errors must be evaluated in terms of degree, which means that even though Cone's attorney chose not to present certain witnesses or make a final argument on his behalf during sentencing, Cone was effectively represented.

In summary, the Supreme Court's decision in *Bell v. Cone* means that future defendants claiming ineffective assistance of counsel must show that their attorney's performance was objectively unreasonable. This, according to the Court, was the correct interpretation of the prejudice requirement in *Strickland*. If defendants do not make this showing in state court, their claims are unlikely to succeed on habeas review. For now, the Supreme Court has maintained that the *Cronic* decision applies to situations in which the defense counsel's performance was a "complete failure."[31] Because the *Cronic* Court held that a defendant does not have to satisfy the prejudice prong of *Strickland* when an attorney completely fails to subject the prosecution's case to "meaningful adversarial testing," there is some hope for future challengers alleging ineffective assistance. However, unless his or her representation is systematically deficient, success in federal court on habeas review is unlikely.

A.   Mickens v. Taylor: *Successive Representation Permitted Unless Adverse Consequences Exist*

At about the same time the Court decided *Bell v. Cone*, the Court also ruled in another important case that a trial court's failure to investigate an uncontested conflict of interest between defense counsel and her client, even though such conflict was made known to the trial judge, did not constitute a valid ineffective assistance of counsel claim. In *Mickens v. Taylor* (2002),[32] the Court said that such conflicts of interest did not constitute prejudice unless the defendant demonstrated that she was adversely affected by the existing conflict. As in *Cone*, the *Mickens* Court sent a message to state prisoners who challenged their incarceration based on a claim of ineffective assistance of counsel. The Court's ruling "lessened the day-to-day workload of a trial judges by removing any duty to inquire into counsel's conflicts of interest that may potentially adversely affect a criminal defendant . . ."[33] The Court refrained from passing on the burden of logistical problems to state judges because to fashion such a rule for trial judges would require them to investigate possible conflicts of interest in every criminal case. To illustrate this dilemma more completely, a discussion of the *Mickens* case follows.

Walter Mickens was indicted for the sodomy and murder of Timothy Hall. After he was found guilty of capital murder in state court, he filed a writ of habeas corpus in the Eastern District of Virginia, declaring ineffective assistance of counsel at his trial. At his habeas corpus proceeding, the attorney discovered that Bryan Saunders, his former counsel, had previously represented Hall in an unrelated case. The attorney discovered that the presiding judge in that case and the case involving Hall and Mickens were the same; however, Mickens was never informed by Saunders or the presiding judge about the pre-existing conflict.

Justice Scalia, writing for the majority, held that "in order to demonstrate a Sixth Amendment violation where the trial court failed to inquire into a potential conflict of interest about which it knew or should have reasonably known, the defendant must establish that the conflict of interest adversely affected counsel's performance."[34] The Court first applied one of its pre-*Strickland* rulings, *Wood v. Georgia* (1981),[35] to the facts. Justice Scalia claimed that actual conflicts and possible conflicts of interest are not governed by the same rule of law. Furthermore, because *Wood* required a reviewing court to automatically reverse a conviction where an actual conflict occurred, the same rule did not apply to Mickens. This was because Mickens did not demonstrate the occurrence of an actual conflict. Justice Scalia stated that to require an appellate court to automatically reverse a conviction without first making an inquiry as to whether a conflict in fact occurred would not "make good policy sense."[36] This meant that defendants claiming ineffective assistance of counsel based on an alleged conflict of interest between their attorney and a third party, such as a witness or victim, must demonstrate that this conflict adversely affected their case. In most cases, therefore, capital defendants face a substantial burden when seeking a reversal of their conviction on habeas corpus review.

Although no other case dealt specifically with an ineffective assistance claim based on successive prosecutions, lower courts have generally held that trial courts do not have a duty to conduct inquiries into a possible conflict of interest unless they know that there is an obvious conflict among two or more parties. In the interest of maintaining legal ethics, however, at least one legal scholar has suggested that lawyers should "avoid conflicting representations and to advise the court promptly when a conflict of interest arises during the course of trial."[37]

B. Wiggins v. Smith: *Counsel's Duty to Discover a Dysfunctional Background*

Since the decision in *Strickland*, the Court has not granted many writs of habeas corpus for claims of ineffective assistance of counsel. In fact, the Court has only recently granted claims in *Williams* and again in *Wiggins v. Smith* (2003).[38] Prior to *Williams*, the conservative Court "routinely rejected claims of ineffective assistance of counsel."[39] With the *Wiggins* decision, the Court has given new substance to protections under the Sixth Amendment. A brief examination of that case will reveal its impact and potential effect on future ineffective assistance cases.

In 1989, Kevin Wiggins was convicted of first-degree murder, robbery, and two counts of larceny. He was subsequently sentenced to death for committing a capital offense. Wiggins filed a habeas corpus case based on ineffective assistance of counsel. At his original trial, Wiggins was represented by two public defenders who allegedly performed an inadequate investigation by failing to uncover his "dysfunctional background."[40]

His new counsel later found that Wiggins had been the victim of physical and sexual abuse as a child and a young adolescent. This, however, was never raised as a mitigating factor during his original sentencing. At his habeas proceeding, the original public defenders testified that they chose not to investigate the dysfunctional background of Wiggins because their focus was to dispute his actual culpability for the murder. Furthermore, the attorneys claimed that this was simply a tactical decision, and not an act of negligence.

On appeal, the Supreme Court held that the Maryland Supreme Court unreasonably applied the two-pronged test set forth in *Strickland*. The Court said that the performance of the attorneys "fell short of professional norms"[41] because they failed to adequately investigate the mitigating evidence that existed, which prejudiced Wiggins' defense. The Court claimed that it was routine practice in Maryland at that time to conduct a background investigation of a capital defendant's history prior to sentencing. The Supreme Court also referred to standards developed by the American Bar Association, which call for an adequate investigation into potential mitigating evidence that could be presented at a defendant's sentencing hearing. Because the public defenders had only acquired "rudimentary knowledge"[42] of Wiggins' social history, the Court viewed their performance to be constitutionally deficient. The Supreme Court differentiated *Wiggins* from previous cases in which defense counsel failed to present mitigating evidence for the defendant. The Supreme Court cited *Burger v. Kemp* (1987),[43] in which the court found that a limited investigation was reasonable because the majority of the evidence that could potentially have been presented would have had a harmful outcome on the defendant's case; and *Darden v. Wainwright* (1986),[44] in which the Court said that the defense counsel's decision not to present mitigating evidence was reasonable because it would have revealed damaging testimony that would have harmed the defendant's case.

C.   Florida v. Nixon: *The Supreme Court Closes the Door on Silence*

During the last 20 years, the Supreme Court has seldom deviated from the *Strickland* standard when deciding cases regarding ineffective assistance of counsel. In *Nixon*, the Court struck down a decision by the Florida Supreme Court by relying on this legal rule, which has guided state and federal courts for some time. The *Nixon* Court ruled that death penalty defendants do not have to give their attorney express consent to waive arguments at the trial stage, when such a strategic decision is made to preserve the credibility of the defense's arguments at sentencing. This case clarified two important concepts dealing with ineffective assistance of counsel cases. First, it affirmed the fact that the Court is focused on minimizing legal loopholes that can easily be taken advantage of by death penalty defendants in state and federal courts. Second, it explained the extent to which the *Cronic* rule applies, while the majority of cases can likely be resolved by the two-part rule adopted in Strickland.

The *Nixon* Court unanimously agreed that the Florida Supreme Court had erred in its decision. The Court first differentiated the facts in *Nixon* from the facts in *Brookhart v. Janis*.[45] In *Brookhart*, the defense had agreed to a "prima facie" trial, which meant the prosecution did not have to show evidence of guilt beyond a reasonable doubt. The *Nixon* Court, however, differentiated the facts in this case from those in *Brookhart* by explaining that "while the 'prima facie' case in *Brookhart* was fairly characterized as the equivalent of a guilty plea, the full presentation to the jury in Nixon's case does not resemble that severely abbreviated proceeding."[46] Further, the Court emphasized that Nixon retained all of his constitutional rights in this case, unlike the defendant in *Brookhart*. By focusing on these issues, the Court clearly rejected the idea of adopting an automatic rule requiring the defendant's express consent to a strategy of conceding guilt, particularly when the possibility of a death sentence is imminent.

The Supreme Court also differentiated the applicability of the *Cronic* rule to ineffective assistance of counsel claims. The Court has previously reserved that rule for the most extreme circumstances, such as when the defense fails to test the merits of the adversarial process as a whole. In *Nixon*, the Court concluded that the Florida Supreme Court used the *Cronic* rule, which was incorrect given the factual circumstances. Because the Florida Supreme Court first presumed that the performance of defense counsel was deficient, it was led to apply the wrong legal test. The Court said that the *Strickland* rule was the correct legal principle because defense counsel's performance was objectively reasonable; thus, if it used *Strickland* rather than *Cronic*, it would have reached the opposite result. The Court distinguished *Cronic* from *Nixon* by stating that defense counsel's "concession of guilt does not rank as a failure to function in any meaningful sense as the government's adversary."[47] The Court emphasized the fact that defense counsel had conducted two evidentiary hearings on behalf of his client, which clearly demonstrated that he had fully informed his client of his proposed trial strategy and its costs and benefits. The justices also emphasized that the gravity of the sentencing stage in death penalty cases is much higher than in "run-of-the-mine"[48] cases; therefore, the Court concluded that the attorney's strategic decision was realistic and may have been the best tactical choice given the facts.

D. Rompilla v. Beard: *Right to Investigate Gains Momentum*

In *Rompilla v. Beard* (2005), the Court revisited the importance of counsel's responsibility to develop and present adequate mitigating evidence for capital defendants during sentencing. The Supreme Court held that defense counsel's failure to investigate Rompilla's prior charge for rape and assault constituted ineffective assistance of counsel in violation of the Sixth Amendment. Applying *Strickland's* two-part test, the Court ruled that counsel's duty was more than common sense, but that, at minimum, the American Bar Association required defense attorneys to examine the prosecutor's case file for possible mitigating leads. Finding that counsel's performance was constitutionally deficient, the Court then had to decide whether counsel's errors biased the defendant's case. The Court cited numerous factors supporting the argument that trial counsel failed to build an adequate mitigating case, such as the omission of school, medical, and imprisonment records indicating a long history of antisocial and mentally unstable behavior. The Court noted post-conviction counsel's link between this evidence and Rompilla's abusive childhood, which bore "no relation to the few naked pleas for mercy actually put before the jury."[49] However, trial counsel never explored these issues in depth. Taking these issues into consideration, the Court decided that the evidence "might well have influenced the jury's appraisal of culpability."[50]

The Court has traditionally granted defense attorneys considerable latitude in preparing the best legal strategy for their clients. Reiterating this, Justice Kennedy, arguing for the dissent, claimed the Court was wrong to conclude that defense counsel's investigation of mitigating evidence was incompetent. Relying on *Strickland*, Justice Kennedy cited the need to avoid "the temptations of analysis through hindsight."[51] Justice Kennedy opined that trial counsel's strategy was reasonable because evidence of Rompilla's upbringing and mental condition was best substantiated through testimony from the three mental health professionals, Rompilla himself, and his family. Since all of these sources were tapped during his original trial, counsel had no duty to review the prosecutor's conviction file and therefore counsel's performance was adequate. The dissent went on to say that even assuming trial counsel's performance was deficient, Rompilla was not entitled to habeas relief because the conviction record was found in an initial transfer petition, which was an obscure document located in the prosecutor's file. As a result,

Justice Kennedy concluded that the majority imposed an inflexible standard on defense attorneys defying wisdom and existing case law.

E. Schriro v. Landrigan: *Interference Is not Incompetence*

Capital defendants are not always remorseful or supportive, even during sentencing proceedings indicative of their punishment. Occasionally capital defendants refuse to assist their attorneys with the investigation of mitigating evidence, or directly impede efforts during the sentencing phase. Recently the Supreme Court addressed this particular issue in *Schriro v. Landrigan* (2007). In a 5-4 decision written by Justice Thomas, the Court held that a defendant's repeated demands that his attorney not introduce mitigating evidence during the punishment phase provided sufficient cause to deny his habeas petition. Applying the *Strickland* rule for ineffective assistance of counsel claims, the Court ruled defense counsel's performance did not bias the defendant's case. At sentencing, Landrigan instructed his ex-wife and mother not to testify on his behalf, which would have likely revealed evidence of mental health problems, such as possible brain disorder, exposure to drugs and alcohol, and an abusive family history. Instead, at his sentencing proceeding he told the judge to "bring [the death penalty] right on. I'm ready for it."[52] During habeas proceedings, Landrigan claimed that his objections were directed specifically toward the presentation of witness testimony from his ex-wife and mother, not *all* relevant mitigating evidence. The Ninth Circuit agreed, concluding that counsel's "last-minute decision regarding presentation could not excuse his [counsel's] failure to conduct an adequate investigation prior to sentencing."[53] However, the Supreme Court reversed, finding that counsel's performance was reasonable given Landrigan's repeated objections. The Court further ruled that the Anti-Effective Death Penalty Act of 1996 did not require federal courts to grant evidentiary hearings unless Landrigan could demonstrate a colorable Sixth Amendment claim on the basis of the facts. Finding that the evidence did not support the need for an evidentiary hearing, the Supreme Court reversed and remanded.

In his dissenting opinion, Justice Stevens argued that the Ninth Circuit's opinion should have been affirmed. He indicated that all reviewing courts had acknowledged that counsel's performance was ineffective, given that counsel failed to seek advice from mental health experts or investigate Landrigan's history of substance abuse. The dissent further opined that *Wiggins v. Smith* (2003)[54] required an adequate investigation of the defendant's background, which trial counsel neglected to do. Because Landrigan had no knowledge of important neurological evidence discovered later by post-conviction counsel, the dissent argued that "he could not have made a knowing, intelligent, and voluntary waiver of the right to adduce mitigating evidence."[55] Therefore, the dissent concluded that trial counsel's performance was deficient and that counsel's errors established prejudice under *Strickland*.

The *Landrigan* case is important for several reasons. First, it highlights the assumption that capital defendants are capable of aiding in their own defense, despite the inherent connection between mental illness and violent behavior. Capital defendants, and violent offenders in general, routinely flaunt the callous nature of their crimes, their lack of guilt, while portraying the image they are not afraid to be put to death.[56] Nevertheless, courts must be alert to the fact that this conduct may be associated with psychological illness, family violence, or substance abuse, which necessitates a thorough investigation of mitigating evidence. Second, this decision raises the question as to the appropriate standard for deciding a valid, intelligent, and knowing waiver of the right to counsel and presentation of mitigating evidence. Long-standing Supreme Court precedent suggests that a rigid standard for waiver determinations is required, especially in capital cases.[57] Landrigan expressly objected to the presentation of witness testimony from his ex-wife and mother, but the Court interpreted this action as an intent to waive the presentation of *all* relevant mitigating evidence. *Landrigan* highlights the importance of the need for juries to give an individualized consideration of all mitigating factors before sentencing. This is particularly important given that research shows the significant influence of mitigating evidence on jury decisions about life or death.[58] However, the Court's opinion in this case and its decision in *Abdul-Kabir v. Quarterman* (2007) that "sentencing juries must be able to give meaningful consideration and effect to all mitigating evidence"[59] appear somewhat contradictory. For now, the Court has said that a defendant has no viable Sixth Amendment claim of ineffective assistance of counsel when incompetence is due to interference.

F. Arave v. Hoffman: *The Right to Effective Plea Bargaining*

In November 2007, the Supreme Court granted certiorari to decide the question: "What, if any, remedy should be provided for ineffective assistance of counsel during plea bargain negotiations if the defendant was later convicted and sentenced pursuant to a fair trial?"[60] In 2006, a three-judge panel of the Ninth Circuit invalidated Hoffman's death sentence, holding that his attorney "failed to conduct reasonable research into the legal landscape."[61] In August 1988, Hoffman was arrested for first-degree murder. The court appointed public defender William Wellman as counsel. Although Wellman had experience performing criminal defense work, he had no formal training in death penalty cases. Shortly before Hoffman's trial the state agreed not to pursue the death penalty if Hoffman accepted a plea deal. Believing that it was only a matter of time before the Supreme Court overturned Idaho's death penalty scheme, Wellman advised Hoffman to reject the state's offer. Wellman based his advice on the Ninth Circuit's holding in *Adamson v. Ricketts* (1988),[62] which held that aggravating factors were impermissibly allowed to be decided by a judge, not a jury. Hoffman accepted Wellman's advice and rejected the plea deal. After finding Hoffman guilty of first-degree murder, the jury sentenced him to death.

During post-conviction proceedings, the Ninth Circuit found that Wellman's advice was flawed for two reasons. First, Wellman based his advice solely on Ninth Circuit's decision in *Adamson*, but failed to realize that the Arizona Supreme Court had recently affirmed the constitutionality of Arizona's death penalty statute in *State v. Walton* (1989).[63] Thus, at the time Hoffman was allowed to let the state's plea deal lapse there was an obvious conflict between the Arizona Supreme Court's decision in *Walton* and the Ninth Circuit's decision in *Adamson*. Therefore, the court found that a reasonable attorney would have known the inherent risk associated with advising a defendant to risk a potential death sentence. Because Wellman led Hoffman to believe that he would not be put to death, the court concluded that counsel's performance was deficient. Second, the court found that because Hoffman had a compliant personality there was a reasonable probability that he would have taken the prosecutor's offer had Wellman recommended it. Wellman testified that Hoffman repeatedly stated "Well, Bill, you are the lawyer, you know, you know more about it than I do."[64] The court concluded that Hoffman would have accepted the plea deal had Wellman told Hoffman that he was risking very little in exchange for not facing the death penalty. Based on these factors, the court found that Hoffman suffered prejudice from Wellman's advice. The court granted the habeas petition and ordered the district court to direct the state to release Hoffman unless it offered him a plea agreement with the same material terms present in the initial plea offer. In January 2008 the Supreme Court dismissed the petition as moot and remanded the case to the state of Idaho because it was in agreement with the Ninth Circuit's decision.

As one of the few cases challenging the effectiveness of counsel during plea negotiations, this decision has important implications for future ineffective assistance of counsel claims in capital cases. Writing for the dissent, Judge Bea criticized the panel's decision, claiming that it was "opening the court to a calvacade of challenges."[65] Based on the panel's holding, the dissent opined that every defendant whose lawyer rationally predicted a sentence that proved to be incorrect, or ultimately miscalculated the court's constitutional rulings, now has an allegation of deficient performance. If other circuit courts adopt similar policies, even in cases in which defendants receive a fair trial, this will likely cause confusion in the lower courts. Accordingly, the Court will be forced to establish consistent policies for circuit courts to follow so that judges and defense lawyers understand their constitutional obligations.

VIII.   In Summary, What Do these Cases Say?

The *Strickland* test remains authoritative in assessing ineffective assistance claims. Since the *Strickland* decision, the Supreme Court has consistently applied its two-pronged approach to virtually every capital case dealing with a Sixth Amendment violation based on ineffective assistance of counsel. *Strickland* held that in order for a defendant's claim to prevail in state court, the defendant must show that: (1) the defense counsel's performance was "objectively unreasonable" and (2) the performance led to a reasonable probability that the outcome of the trial would have been different. The decision is important because it defines the standard for future capital cases involving ineffective assistance of counsel.

In most cases that have reached the Court since that time, the defendants have not succeeded in having their death sentences overturned. In *Fretwell*, the Court said that the "double-counting" effect was not unconstitutional because the decision that his claim relied on had since been overruled; therefore, he was not deprived of any legal right. Under the standard set forth in *Strickland*, Chief Justice Rehnquist, writing for the majority of the Court, said that Fretwell should not be entitled to the benefits of outdated law, despite the legal rule established in *Teague*.

Since 1996, the Court has based its decisions on ineffective assistance claims in accordance with the restrictions set by the AEDPA. In order for a defendant to prevail under these guidelines, he or she must show that: (1) the state court unreasonably applied the law to the set of facts or (2) the decision was contrary to clearly established law as determined by the Supreme Court. What this means is that capital defendants alleging ineffective assistance of counsel claims must prove that the state court's decision was "objectively unreasonable" and that the decision prejudiced the defense.

In 2000, the Court broke new ground in *Williams*, in which Justice O'Connor held that state courts do not violate the "unreasonable application" phrase of the AEDPA when they choose the correct rule of law, but apply it incorrectly. The Court said that a defendant's "failure to develop a claim's factual basis in state court proceedings is not established unless there is lack of diligence, or some greater fault, attributable to the prisoner or his counsel."[66] The Court ruled that "the statute does not bar the evidentiary hearing petitioner seeks on his juror bias and prosecutorial misconduct claims, but bars a hearing on his *Brady* claim because he "failed to develop" that claim's factual basis in state court and concedes his inability to satisfy the statute's further stringent conditions for excusing the deficiency."[67] In this case, the Court found for the first time since *Strickland* that a defendant had a bona fide claim for ineffective assistance of counsel that could withstand the AEDPA's stringent requirements.

The *Mickens* and *Bell* Courts were reluctant to grant writs of habeas corpus to the defendants. The *Mickens* Court said that a reviewing court could not automatically reverse a conviction merely because a potential conflict existed. To do so, according to Justice Scalia, would not be in the interest of good policy. Similarly, the *Bell* Court refused to grant the defendant his Sixth Amendment claim because his counsel had made the strategic decision to prevent testimony from witnesses that could plausibly weaken the defendant's case further.

It is clear on the basis of the *Wiggins* decision that the Court will consider the reasonableness of the defendant's trial tactics as a means for determining whether the decision to present mitigating evidence in a capital defendant's trial was appropriate. This is not to say that the Court will scrutinize every judgment made by defense counsel in the form of trial tactics. The Court has, in the past, given great deference to a defense lawyer in deciding how best to represent a client's case. It is likely that the Court will continue the trend to ensure that so-called "trial tactics" do not come at a heavy price to defendants at sentencing.

The *Nixon* case clarified two important concepts that the Court has dealt with over the years when deciding ineffective assistance of counsel cases. First, it is unlikely that the Court will form blanket rules that are unrealistic and do not consider the interests of judicial expediency in terms of the trial process, even in death penalty cases. Second, the Court has explained its stance on the scope of the *Cronic* and *Strickland* tests. The Court reaffirmed the fact that the holding in *Cronic* will not easily apply to a variety of factual circumstances.

A host of recent decisions regarding ineffective assistance of counsel claims have landed in the courts. Most of the Court's decisions have revolved around counsel's duty to present mitigating evidence during the sentencing phase. For instance, the *Rompilla* decision was important because it explained counsel's obligation to investigate documented evidence available to defense counsel and that the prosecutor would likely use to support the death penalty. The *Landrigan* Court held, however, that defense counsel owes no duty to present mitigating evidence when the defendant objects to counsel's strategy in presenting that evidence. Collectively, the *Wiggins, Rompilla, and Landrigan* cases show the Court's regard for exploring and considering the mitigation evidence to its fullest potential. Although the Court ultimately dismissed the petition in *Hoffman*, the legal issue in that case has important policy implications for defense attorneys during plea negotiations. Because the Court showed its desire to settle the issue for lower courts, it is unlikely that much time will pass before the issue is resolved once and for all.

In future cases, the Court will likely continue to provide defense attorneys with a great deal of tactical discretion in determining the best legal strategy for their client. Defense attorneys will continue to use such strategies in order to preserve the defendant's credibility during sentencing, as long as counsel does not discount available mitigating evidence that may warrant a punishment less than death.

IX.   Conclusion

It is arguable that the Supreme Court has maintained a consistent perspective toward ineffective assistance of counsel claims since the decision in *Strickland*. The Court has made it clear that when a defense attorney makes "strategic decisions" regarding the presentation of mitigating evidence, that decision must be based on careful considerations about benefits and consequences. Whereas in the past the Court refused to grant writs based on ineffective assistance, saying that lawyers should be entitled to exercise discretion, that principle is now being scrutinized more carefully.

In light of *Wiggins*, defendants have to show that, because their attorney failed to present mitigating evidence on their behalf, the attorney's decision was objectively unreasonable and that the decision prejudiced the defendant. Because the Court has increasingly focused on the issue of mitigating evidence, it is likely that this will compel defense attorneys to continue to place great value on the use of mitigation experts during sentencing. The ABA *Guidelines for Death Penalty Defense* advocate the use of multiple experts who can collectively assess a defendant's social history and aid a defendant at his sentencing by presenting the maximum potential of all mitigating evidence.[68]

Although the Court has curtailed the ability of a defendant to succeed under the limiting provisions of the AEDPA, the federal courts will likely continue in the near future to hear and decide cases involving ineffective assistance of counsel claims. The door to that claim has been narrowed; however, it will likely not be closed.

Cases Briefed in Chapter 7

Case	Issue	Holding
Strickland v. Washington 466 U.S. 688 (1984)	Do defendants claiming ineffective assistance of counsel have to show that, were it not for counsel's errors, there was a reasonable probability that the result of the sentencing decision would have been different?	To demonstrate ineffective assistance of counsel, the following conditions must be met: (1) there must be objectively unreasonable deficiency in counsel's performance and (2) this deficiency must have led to a reasonable probability that the result would have been different.
Lockhart v. Fretwell 506 U.S. 364 (1993)	Does the failure to object to "double counting" constitute ineffective assistance of counsel when the precedent in question was subsequently overruled prior to habeas review?	"Double counting" is not a violation of the Strickland rule, thus no ineffective assistance of counsel is present.
Mickens v. Taylor 535 U.S. 162 (2002)	Does a trial court's failure to inquire into an alleged attorney conflict of interest require an automatic reversal of conviction?	An alleged conflict of interest involving a defense attorney must adversely impact the defendant in order to be considered ineffective assistance of counsel.

Cases Briefed in Chapter 7, *continued*

Case	Issue	Holding
Bell v. Cone 535 U.S. 685 (2002)	Do strategic decisions not to present closing arguments or witness statements in mitigation entitle a capital defendant to a presumption of prejudice? Did the state court reasonably apply the *Strickland* rule to this case?	Failure to present mitigating evidence such as testimony from select witnesses or make final arguments does not constitute ineffective assistance if viewed as strategic decisions.
Wiggins v. Smith 539 U.S. 510 (2003)	Does the failure by a defense lawyer to investigate a capital defendant's childhood history and discover evidence of a "dysfunctional background" violate the Sixth Amendment?	Failure to conduct a reasonable investigation into a defendant's childhood history and "dysfunctional background" constitutes ineffective counsel.
Florida v. Nixon 543 U.S. 175 (2004)	Does a trial strategy of conceding guilt without express consent from a capital defendant constitute ineffective assistance of counsel according to the *Strickland* rule?	No ineffective assistance of counsel exists when defense lawyers do not obtain express consent from their clients as to a trial strategy of conceding guilt.
Rompilla v. Beard 545 U.S. 374 (2005)	Does counsel's failure to make a reasonable effort to review and obtain documented evidence that counsel knows the prosecution will use to support a death sentence constitute ineffective assistance of counsel?	A defense attorney must make a reasonable effort to review and obtain documented evidence retained by the prosecutor, such as a prior conviction, that counsel knows the prosecution will likely rely on during sentencing to support a death sentence.
Schriro v. Landrigan 550 U.S. ___ (2007)	(1) Does a district court's failure to grant an evidentiary hearing when a defendant cannot demonstrate a colorable ineffective--assistance-of-counsel claim violate the Sixth Amendment? (2) Does a defense attorney's failure to present mitigating evidence such as testimony of a disadvantaged background at sentencing constitute ineffective assistance of counsel when the defendant objects to counsel's strategy?	The AEDPA does not require courts to grant evidentiary hearings when defendants cannot make colorable ineffective-assistance-of-counsel claims. Further, a defense attorney's failure to present mitigating evidence when a defendant interferes with his counsel's strategy does not constitute ineffective assistance of counsel.

Case Briefs

Strickland v. Washington
466 U.S. 688 (1984)

CAPSULE: In order for an ineffective assistance of counsel claim to succeed, the defendant must prove that the defense counsel's errors were objectively unreasonable and that this deficiency led to a reasonable probability that the sentencing outcome would have been different.

FACTS: The defendant, David Leroy Washington, was convicted in state trial court of committing three stabbing murders in 1976. Washington's attorney did not present any character witnesses or request a psychiatric evaluation of his client prior to sentencing. According to defense counsel, these were "strategic decisions" aimed at preventing the prosecution from rebuttal during cross-examination. The defense counsel claimed that Washington had no criminal history and that something had "gone badly wrong during extremely stressful circumstances." Washington was convicted. He later filed a habeas corpus petition in state trial court alleging ineffective assistance of counsel in violation of the Sixth Amendment.

ISSUE: Do defendants claiming ineffective assistance of counsel have to show that, but for defense counsel's errors, there was a reasonable probability that the result of the sentencing decision would have been different? YES.

HOLDING: Two criteria must be met in order to succeed on an ineffective assistance of counsel claim: (1) the petitioner must prove that defense counsel's performance was objectively unreasonable and (2) this deficiency led to a reasonable probability that the sentencing decision would have been different.

REASON: "The proper standard for judging attorney performance is that of reasonably effective assistance, considering all the circumstances. When a convicted defendant complains of the ineffectiveness of counsel's assistance, the defendant must show that counsel's representation fell below an objective standard of reasonableness. Judicial scrutiny of counsel's performance must be highly deferential, and a fair assessment of attorney performance requires that every effort be made to eliminate the distorting effects of hindsight, to reconstruct the circumstances of counsel's challenged conduct, and to evaluate the conduct from counsel's perspective at the time. A court must indulge a strong presumption that counsel's conduct falls within the wide range of reasonable professional assistance. These standards require no special amplification in order to define counsel's duty to investigate, the duty at issue in this case."

"With regard to the required showing of prejudice, the proper standard requires the defendant to show that there is a reasonable probability that, but for counsel's unprofessional errors, the result of the proceeding would have been different. A reasonable probability is a probability sufficient to undermine confidence in the outcome. A court hearing an ineffectiveness claim must consider the totality of the evidence before the judge or jury."

CASE SIGNIFICANCE: The *Strickland* decision established a definitive test for analyzing ineffective assistance of counsel claims raised by capital defendants. Prior to this ruling, the Supreme Court had not answered the question as to what standard a defense attorney's performance should be judged against when a claim of ineffective assistance of counsel is made. Lower courts were left to interpret the broad language of *McMann*, which left most of the discretion to state trial courts. However, trial courts had no guidance from appellate courts for judging ineffective assistance of counsel claims. The *Strickland* Court required lower courts to analyze ineffective assistance of counsel according to a two-part legal standard. The rule states that an ineffective assistance of counsel claim can succeed if the petitioner proves that: (1) his defense counsel's performance was objectively unreasonable and (2) there is a reasonable probability that the deficiency would have led to a different sentencing decision.

Lockhart v. Fretwell
506 U.S. 364 (1993)

CAPSULE: No ineffective assistance of counsel claim existed when a defense attorney failed to object to a "double-counting" technique that was based on then-existing Eighth Circuit law and subsequently overruled prior to habeas review.

FACTS: Fretwell was convicted of the capital murder of Sherman Sullins. During the sentencing phase of his trial, the jury weighed aggravating and mitigating factors. One of the aggravating factors considered by the trial court was that Fretwell had committed the crime for pecuniary gain, which also happened to be an element of the crime—capital murder. After considering the evidence, the jury sentenced Fretwell to death. According to Eighth Circuit law at the time, this so-called "double-counting" technique was unconstitutional in light of *Collins v. Lockhart*.

ISSUE: Does the failure to object to "double-counting" constitute ineffective assistance of counsel when the precedent case in question was subsequently overruled prior to habeas review? NO.

HOLDING: Defense attorneys who fail to object to an unconstitutional sentencing practice, such as "double-counting," do not give rise to an ineffective assistance claim when the law on which the claim was based had since been overruled.

REASON: "Counsel's failure to make the *Collins* objection during the sentencing proceeding did not constitute prejudice within the meaning of *Strickland*. To show prejudice under *Strickland*, a defendant must demonstrate that counsel's errors are so serious as to deprive him of a trial whose result is unfair or unreliable, not merely that the outcome would have been different. Unfairness or unreliability does not result unless counsel's ineffectiveness deprives the defendant of a substantive or procedural right to which the law entitles him. The sentencing proceeding's result in the present case was neither unfair nor unreliable, because the Court of Appeals, which had decided *Collins* in 1985, overruled it in *Perry v. Lockhart*, 871 F.2d 1384 (1989), four years later. Thus, respondent suffered no prejudice from his counsel's deficient performance. Contrary to Fretwell's argument, prejudice is not determined under the laws existing at the time of trial. Although contemporary assessment of counsel's conduct is used when determining the deficient performance component of the *Strickland* test, the prejudice component, with its focus on fairness and reliability, does not implicate the same concerns that motivated the former component's adoption: that a more rigid requirement could dampen the ardor and impair the independence of defense counsel, discourage the acceptance of assigned cases, and undermine the trust between attorney and client. The instant holding is not inconsistent with the retroactivity rule announced in *Teague v. Lane*. The circumstances that gave rise to that rule do not apply to claims raised by a federal habeas petitioner, who has no interest in the finality of the state-court judgment under which he was incarcerated and, unlike the States, ordinarily has no claim of reliance on past judicial precedent as a basis for his actions."

CASE SIGNIFICANCE: This case exemplifies the Court's unwillingness to consider serious, although individual, misjudgments by defense attorneys. The Court held that a Sixth Amendment violation would only occur when the overall fundamental fairness and reliability of the proceeding had been compromised. This means that future defendants alleging ineffective assistance of counsel cannot rely on an individual misjudgment by defense counsel as a basis for their habeas petition, even when that error would have led to a reasonable probability that a life sentence would have been imposed. By the time this case was decided, the Court had held in *Teague v. Lane* (1989) that a defendant could not prevail on habeas corpus review by relying on new rules of constitutional law because the "principle of finality in criminal convictions otherwise would be seriously undermined." This case said that the *Teague* rule could not benefit a capital defendant alleging ineffective assistance of counsel because that rule was intended to promote the interests of the state, not the defendant.

Mickens v. Taylor
535 U.S. 162 (2002)

CAPSULE: Defendant must establish that a conflict of interest adversely impacted his attorney's performance; furthermore, simply demonstrating that an inquiry into such a conflict of interest was due is insufficient to sustain a claim based on ineffective assistance of counsel.

FACTS: Mickens was convicted of the premeditated murder and sodomy of Timothy Hall. He was subsequently sentenced to death after a jury found that aggravating circumstances existed. Prior to his trial, Mickens was not aware that his attorney, Brian Saunders, had represented Hall in an unrelated case. In addition, the same judge who had presided over Hall's case in juvenile court appointed Saunders to represent Mickens in this case. At no time did Saunders disclose to the court or his client the fact that he had previously represented Hall. Mickens filed a writ of habeas corpus in district court alleging ineffective assistance of counsel based on the conflict of interest, but was denied relief. He then filed a writ of habeas corpus in federal district court, where he was again denied relief.

ISSUE: Does a trial court's failure to inquire into an alleged conflict of interest require an automatic reversal of the conviction? NO.

HOLDING: Ineffective assistance claims based on an alleged conflict of interest do not rise to the level of a Sixth Amendment claim. A conflict must adversely affect the defense's performance in order for a violation to be established.

REASON: "A defendant alleging ineffective assistance generally must demonstrate a reasonable probability that, but for counsel's unprofessional errors, the result of the proceeding would have been different. *Strickland v. Washington*, 466 U.S. 668, 694, (1986). An exception to this general rule presumes a probable effect upon the outcome where assistance of counsel has been denied entirely or during a critical stage of the proceeding. The Court has held in several cases that "circumstances of that magnitude," *United States v. Cronic*, 466 U.S. 648, 659, (1984) may also arise when the defendant's attorney actively represented conflicting interests."

"This Court rejects petitioner's argument that the remand instruction in *Wood*, directing the trial court to grant a new hearing if it determined that "an actual conflict of interest existed," established that where the trial judge neglects a duty to inquire into a potential conflict the defendant, to obtain reversal, need only show that his lawyer was subject to a conflict of interest, not that the conflict adversely affected counsel's performance."

CASE SIGNIFICANCE: In this case, the Court answered the following question: Does a trial court's failure to inquire into a conflict of interest require an automatic reversal of a conviction? The Court said no. The Court was careful to avoid making a new rule of law that required trial courts to inquire into any possible conflict between parties in a case. The Court recognized the logistical problems that would ensue if trial courts were required to make such inquiries. Instead, the Court relied on *Wood* and *Sullivan* to explain that defendants alleging ineffective assistance of counsel must demonstrate some connection between their counsel's performance and the actual conflict. Absent that, the conviction stands.

This case is also significant because it was one of the few cases in which the Court did not use the *Strickland* case as the basis for its ruling. Because the Court was dealing with circumstances that could not be adequately tested by the *Strickland* standard, the Court used previous case law instead to determine whether prejudice was shown.

Bell v. Cone
535 U.S. 685 (2002)

CAPSULE: Strategic decisions, such as the choice not to present mitigating evidence, which could be considered harmful if subjected to cross-examination, do not establish a valid claim of ineffective assistance of counsel.

FACTS: In August of 1980, Cone robbed a jewelry store and then led police on a high-speed pursuit through the city of Memphis, Tennessee. He subsequently killed two elderly individuals after breaking into their residence. Cone was convicted of first-degree murder and intent to commit robbery by use of deadly force and was given the death penalty. Although Cone appealed his case on numerous procedural grounds to the Tennessee Supreme Court, his sentence was affirmed.

ISSUES:
1. Do strategic decisions to not present closing arguments or witness statements in mitigation entitle a capital defendant to a presumption of prejudice? NO.
2. Did the state court reasonably apply the *Strickland* standard to the facts in this case? YES.

HOLDING: Defense counsel's failure to present mitigating evidence, such as witness testimony or making final arguments at sentencing do not, in themselves, constitute a valid ineffective assistance claim.

REASONING: "Section 2254(d)(1)'s "contrary to" and "unreasonable application" clauses have independent meaning. A federal habeas court may grant relief under the former clause if the state court applies a rule different from the governing law set forth in this Court's cases, or if it decides a case differently than this Court has done on a set of materially indistinguishable facts. *Williams v. Taylor*, 529 U.S. 362, 405–406, (2000). The federal court may grant relief under the latter clause if the state court correctly identifies the governing legal principle from this Court's decisions but unreasonably applies it in the particular case. Such application must be objectively unreasonable, which is different from incorrect. To satisfy *Strickland*'s two-part test for evaluating claims that counsel performed so incompetently that a defendant's sentence or conviction should be reversed, the defendant must prove that counsel's representation fell below an objective reasonableness standard and that there is a reasonable probability that, but for counsel's unprofessional error, the proceeding's result would have been different."

"The challenged aspects of counsel's performance—failing to adduce mitigating evidence and waiving closing argument—are plainly of the same ilk as other specific attorney errors subject to *Strickland*'s performance and prejudice components. See, e.g., *Darden v. Wainwright*, 477 U.S. 168, 184 (1986). Because the state court correctly identified *Strickland*'s principles as those governing the analysis of respondent's claim, there is no merit in his contention that the state court's adjudication was contrary to this Court's clearly established law."

CASE SIGNIFICANCE: This case demonstrates the difficulty capital defendants face when making an ineffective assistance of counsel claim. For capital defendants it is the prejudice prong of Strickland that causes the most difficulty on habeas review. In order for a defendant's ineffective assistance of counsel claim to be valid according to *Strickland*, the defendant must show that: (1) the defense attorney's performance was objectively unreasonable and (2) that such deficiency led to a reasonable probability that the sentencing decision would have been different. During the years since *Strickland*, the Court has increasingly limited the ability of defendants to obtain a writ of habeas corpus based on an ineffective assistance claim. This strict standard is largely the result of the respect given by the Supreme Court to tactical or strategic decisions made by trial attorneys in court.

Potential harm to capital defendants is heightened in cases in which defense attorneys make strategic decisions that are detrimental. However, the Court is reluctant to set specific guidelines or rules that define the meaning of a "reasonable probability" leading to a particular sentencing decision. On this prong, the Court has not given much guidance as to what factors will lead to an ineffective assistance of counsel claim.

Wiggins v. Smith
539 U.S. 510 (2003)

CAPSULE: Failure to conduct a reasonable investigation into a defendant's "dysfunctional background" for use as mitigating evidence for a capital defendant constitutes ineffective assistance of counsel.

FACTS: Kevin Wiggins was indicted in October 1988 for the first-degree murder of Florence Lacs. Wiggins was represented by two public defenders. After conviction, the defense attorneys chose to bifurcate the sentencing proceedings. Throughout Wiggins' trial, the attorneys maintained that their client was innocent of the crimes; therefore, the sentencing proceeding was separated in order to make final arguments contesting his innocence and to present mitigating evidence on his behalf. However, the trial judge denied the motion for bifurcation and Wiggins was sentenced to death. Wiggins filed a writ of habeas corpus, arguing that he had ineffective assistance of counsel because his attorneys failed to present evidence of his "dysfunctional background." Wiggins alleged that his attorneys should have investigated his background more thoroughly. The attorneys said that they had chosen to contest Wiggins' actual responsibility for the crime rather than to pursue a case of mitigation by investigating his childhood history. The trial judge held that the decision by the public defenders not to investigate his childhood history was simply a matter of trial tactics, which did not rise to the level of a constitutional violation.

ISSUE: Does the failure to investigate a capital defendant's childhood history and discover evidence of a "dysfunctional background" violate the Sixth Amendment? YES.

HOLDING: Ineffective assistance of counsel claims based on the defense attorney's failure to conduct a reasonable investigation into a defendant's "dysfunctional background" and childhood history constitutes ineffective assistance of counsel.

REASONING: "Here, as in *Strickland*, counsel claim that their limited investigation into petitioner's background reflected a tactical judgment not to present mitigating evidence and to pursue an alternative strategy instead. In evaluating petitioner's claim, this Court's principal concern is not whether counsel should have presented a mitigation case, but whether the investigation supporting their decision not to introduce mitigating evidence of Wiggins' background was itself reasonable. The Court thus conducts an objective review of their performance, measured for reasonableness under prevailing professional norms, including a context-dependent consideration of the challenged conduct as seen from counsel's perspective at the time of that conduct."

"Counsel's failures prejudiced Wiggins' defense. To establish prejudice, a defendant must show that there is a reasonable probability that, but for counsel's unprofessional errors, the proceeding's result would have been different. This Court assesses prejudice by reweighing the aggravating evidence against the totality of the mitigating evidence adduced both at trial and in the habeas proceedings. The mitigating evidence counsel failed to discover and present here is powerful."

CASE SIGNIFICANCE: This case is important because it is one of only two cases since the decision in *Strickland* in which the Court has ruled in favor of a capital defendant when alleging a claim based upon ineffective assistance of counsel. However, this decision is also important for two other reasons. First, the Court has made it clear that the restrictions imposed by the Antiterrorism and Effective Death Penalty Act of 1996 on capital defendants do not result in a process whereby federal courts automatically uphold state court decisions. The Court has also signaled that attorney competence in capital cases should be more closely examined by reviewing courts, particularly if it is associated with finding mitigating evidence for use during the sentencing phase of a capital trial.

Florida v. Nixon
543 U.S. 175 (2004)

CAPSULE: A defense attorney's failure to obtain consent from a death penalty defendant as to a strategy of conceding guilt does not automatically result in a Sixth Amendment violation of ineffective assistance of counsel.

FACTS: After overwhelming evidence of his guilt was gathered by the state, Nixon was indicted on charges of first-degree murder. The public defender representing Nixon, Mr. Corin, initially filed a plea of not guilty in the case but later changed that plea to guilty after reviewing all of the evidence pointing to his client's guilt. Prosecutors refused plea negotiations, intent on seeking the death penalty for Nixon. Corin decided to launch a trial strategy of conceding guilt, which was an effort to establish credibility during the sentencing phase of the trial when he would argue that his client was unsuitable for the death penalty. Nixon, nevertheless, was unresponsive to Corin's trial strategy and did not approve or disapprove of it. Corin proceeded to deliver to the court the mitigating evidence he had compiled in his client's favor, including witness testimony indicating his client's history of emotional instability and psychiatric care, low IQ, his youth, and his erratic behavior prior to committing the murder. The trial court, however, convicted Nixon and sentenced him to death. The Florida Supreme Court eventually reversed that decision, concluding that Corin's failure to obtain express consent from his client amounted to ineffective assistance of counsel under the test established in *United States v. Cronic*, 466 U.S. 648.

ISSUE: Does the failure to obtain a defendant's consent to a trial strategy of conceding guilt constitute ineffective assistance of counsel? NO.

HOLDING: A defense attorney's failure to obtain consent from a defendant as to a strategy of conceding guilt does not fall below an objective standard of reasonableness, thus it does not automatically result in ineffective assistance of counsel.

REASONING: "The Florida Supreme Court erred in requiring Nixon's affirmative, explicit acceptance of Corin's strategy because it mistakenly deemed Corin's statements to the jury the functional equivalent of a guilty plea. Despite Corin's concession of Nixon's guilt, Nixon retained the rights accorded a defendant in a criminal trial. The State was obliged to present during the guilt phase competent, admissible evidence establishing the essential elements of the crimes with which Nixon was charged. That aggressive evidence would thus be separated from the penalty phase, enabling the defense to concentrate that portion of the trial on mitigating factors."

"Counsel's effectiveness should not be evaluated under the *Cronic* standard, but under the standard prescribed in *Strickland*: Did counsel's representation "fall below an objective standard of reasonableness?" The Florida Supreme Court's erroneous equation of Corin's concession strategy to a guilty plea led it to apply the wrong standard. The court first presumed deficient performance, then applied the presumption of prejudice that *Cronic* reserved for situations in which counsel has entirely failed to function as the client's advocate. Corin's concession of Nixon's guilt does not rank as such a failure. Although a concession of guilt in a run-of-the-mine trial might present a closer question, the gravity of the potential sentence in a capital trial and the proceeding's two-phase structure vitally affect counsel's strategic calculus. Attorneys representing capital defendants face daunting challenges in developing trial strategies: Prosecutors are more likely to seek the death penalty, and to refuse to accept a plea to a life sentence, when the evidence is overwhelming and the crime heinous. Counsel therefore may reasonably decide to focus on the trial's penalty phase, at which time counsel's mission is to persuade the trier that his client's life should be spared."

CASE SIGNIFICANCE: This case has had a substantial effect on the way defense lawyers develop trial strategies, particularly in cases in which their client's guilt is obvious. In *Nixon*, the Court held that a trial lawyer may concede the guilt of his or her client when that person has neither agreed nor disagreed to such a strategy. In this case, the Court emphasized the fact that the defense attorney's statements to the jury were not the same as a guilty plea. This was because Nixon still maintained all the constitutional rights available to him in a criminal trial. The Court found that the defense attorney's strategic decision to avoid arguing for his client's innocence was reasonable given the gravity associated with the possibility of his client facing the death penalty during the sentencing phase.

The Court found that the Florida Supreme Court had mistakenly used the wrong legal test to determine whether the defense attorney's performance was unreasonable. The Court concluded that the test established in *United States v. Cronic* was inappropriate because that test was reserved for "circumstances that are so likely to prejudice the accused that the cost of litigating their effect in a particular case is unjustified."[51] Justice Ginsburg, writing for the majority, found that the defense attorney's concession did not fail to subject the government's case to meaningful adversary testing. Therefore, the *Cronic* test was improperly used by the Florida Supreme Court. The Court determined that the *Strickland* test was the appropriate rule to use given the circumstances; and furthermore, the defense attorney's performance did not violate that standard because it was not objectively unreasonable.

The Court has settled another important Sixth Amendment issue in *Nixon* regarding ineffective assistance of counsel. Allowing defendants to challenge the constitutionality of their death sentence simply because they did not approve or disapprove of their attorney's strategy of conceding guilt would lead to an endless number of cases flooding the federal court dockets. The Court has justifiably limited the ability of defendants to raise ineffective assistance claims and ensured that they will remain accountable for their actions once they have been convicted in state court.

Rompilla v. Beard
545 U.S. 374 (2005)

CAPSULE: A defense counsel's failure to make a reasonable effort to investigate documented mitigating evidence such as a prior conviction, which is likely to be disclosed by the prosecution at sentencing, constitutes ineffective assistance of counsel.

FACTS: Rompilla was convicted of first-degree murder for the brutal killing of James Scanlon. The only mitigating evidence presented by defense counsel at sentencing was the testimony of Rompilla's family members, who pled with the jury to spare his life. After finding that aggravating factors outweighed the evidence in mitigation, the Pennsylvania jury sentenced Rompilla to death. The Pennsylvania Supreme Court affirmed. In state habeas corpus proceedings, Rompilla argued that his right to effective assistance of counsel had been violated because the trial attorney failed to present documented mitigating evidence, such as a prior conviction for rape and assault. Although the prosecutor alerted defense counsel of the prior conviction, defense counsel failed to investigate the prosecutor's file. Contained in the file was significant mitigating evidence about Rompilla's troubled childhood, mental illness, and alcohol use. However, the state courts found that trial counsel had built a significant mitigation case and denied Rompilla habeas relief. On federal habeas appeal, the District Court held that trial counsel's performance was deficient because they failed to investigate documented evidence of the defendant's troubled upbringing, mental illness, and criminal history. The Third Circuit reversed, finding that trial counsel's performance was reasonable given their efforts to investigate mitigating evidence from Rompilla himself, his family members, and mental health professionals. The court held that although trial counsel's investigation was limited, there was no reason for the attorneys to believe that further investigation would reveal useful information. The Supreme Court of the United States granted certiorari to determine whether trial counsel's performance was constitutionally deficient according to the standard enunciated in *Strickland v. Washington* (1984).

ISSUE: Does counsel's failure to make a reasonable effort to review and obtain documented evidence that counsel knows the prosecution will use to support a death sentence constitute ineffective assistance of counsel? YES.

HOLDING: A defense attorney must make a reasonable effort to review and obtain documented evidence retained by the prosecutor, such as a prior conviction, that counsel knows the prosecution will likely rely on during sentencing to support a death sentence.

REASON: "Here, the lawyers were deficient in failing to examine the court file on Rompilla's prior rape and assault conviction. They knew that the Commonwealth intended to seek the death penalty by proving that Rompilla had a significant history of felony convictions indicating the use or threat of violence, that it would attempt to establish this history by proving the prior conviction, and that it would emphasize his violent character by introducing a transcript of the rape victim's trial testimony. Although the prior conviction file was a public record, readily available at the courthouse where Rompilla was to be tried, counsel looked at no part of it until warned by the prosecution a second time, and even then did not examine the entire file. With every effort to view the facts as a defense lawyer would have at the time, it is difficult to see how counsel could have failed to realize that not examining the file would seriously compromise their opportunity to respond to an aggravation case. Their duty to make all reasonable efforts to learn what they could about the offense the prosecution was going to use certainly included obtaining the Commonwealth's own readily available file to learn what it knew about the crime, to discover any mitigating evidence it would downplay, and to anticipate the details it would emphasize. The obligation to examine the file was particularly pressing here because the violent prior offense was similar to the crime charged and because Rompilla's sentencing strategy stressed residual doubt. This obligation is not just common sense, but is also described in the American Bar Association Standards for Criminal Justice, which are 'guides to determining what is reasonable.' The state court's conclusion that defense counsel's efforts to find mitigating evidence by other means were enough to free them from further enquiry fails to answer the considerations set out here, to the point of being objectively unreasonable. No reasonable lawyer would forgo examination of the file thinking he could do as well by asking the defendant or family relations what they recalled. Nor would a reasonable lawyer compare possible searches for school reports, juvenile records, and evidence of drinking habits to the opportunity to take a look at a file disclosing what the prosecutor knows and plans to read from in his case."

CASE SIGNIFICANCE: This case is significant because it clarifies the scope and importance of building an adequate mitigation case for capital defendants. In *Rompilla*, the Supreme Court faced the issue of whether defense counsel's failure to examine the prosecutor's file, which contained important mitigating evidence, constituted a Sixth Amendment violation. In delivering the opinion of the Court, Justice Souter claimed that "it flouts prudence to deny that a defense lawyer should try to look at a file he knows the prosecution will cull for aggravating evidence, let alone when the file is sitting in the trial courthouse, open for the asking." After applying the two-part test established in *Strickland*, the majority held that defense counsel's performance was deficient and that this deficiency led to a reasonable probability that the result of the trial would have been different.

Relying on the American Bar Association Standards of Criminal Justice for guidance, the Court found that trial counsel had committed a constitutional error because the prosecution's conviction file also contained a number of other untapped leads. In the file included evidence of schizophrenia, mental retardation, the fact that Rompilla had dropped out of school at the age of 16 and had been in and out of jail as a youth. Although the majority conceded that defense counsel was not constitutionally obligated to pursue every lead of mitigating possibilities, there were a number of avenues left unexplored by defense counsel.

The presumption in the practice of law is that an attorney's performance is reasonable, that hindsight should be discounted, and that deference should be given to counsel's judgments. In judging ineffective assistance of counsel claims, the Court has historically taken a case-by-case approach. The *Strickland* test has proven to be a workable framework for assessing the reasonableness of counsel's actions and omissions given the infinite number of scenarios that may render counsel's performance constitutionally deficient. Although some degree of precision and standardization may be sacrificed, intuition is sometimes more realistic where questions of fundamental fairness are at issue.

Schriro v. Landrigan
550 U.S. ___ (2007)

CAPSULE: A defense attorney's failure to present mitigating evidence such as testimony of a disadvantaged background at sentencing when the defendant objects to counsel's strategy does not constitute ineffective assistance of counsel.

FACTS: Landrigan was convicted of first-degree murder. At sentencing, Landrigan's lawyer attempted to present mitigating evidence on his behalf, including witnesses that could testify to his disadvantaged childhood and good character. He also objected when his lawyer tried to present additional mitigating evidence and told the Arizona trial judge to "bring on" the death penalty. Subsequently, the state court sentenced him to death and the sentence was affirmed. The state post-conviction court concluded that Landrigan had no colorable claim of ineffective assistance of counsel, holding that he had directed his lawyer not to present any mitigating evidence on his behalf. In response to Landrigan's federal habeas petition the District Court denied his motion for an evidentiary hearing, finding that his claim was without merit. The Ninth Circuit reversed, holding that defense counsel's performance was deficient according to *Strickland v. Washington* (1984). Landrigan argued that his counsel was ineffective because he failed to present mitigating evidence during sentencing and that he should be entitled to an evidentiary hearing of the facts.

ISSUES:
1. Does a district court's failure to grant an evidentiary hearing when a defendant cannot demonstrate a colorable ineffective assistance of counsel claim violate the Sixth Amendment? NO.
2. Does a defense attorney's failure to present mitigating evidence such as testimony of a disadvantaged background at sentencing constitute ineffective assistance of counsel when the defendant objects to counsel's strategy? NO.

HOLDING: The AEDPA does not require courts to grant evidentiary hearings when defendants cannot make colorable ineffective assistance of counsel claims. Further, a defense attorney's failure to present mitigating evidence when a defendant interferes with his counsel's strategy does not constitute ineffective assistance of counsel.

REASONING: "The Antiterrorism and Effective Death Penalty Act of 1996 (AEDPA) has not changed the basic rule that the decision to grant an evidentiary hearing is left to the district court's sound discretion, but it has changed the standards for granting federal habeas relief by prohibiting such relief unless a state court's adjudication 'resulted in a decision that was contrary to, or involved an unreasonable application of, clearly established Federal law, as determined by [this Court],' § 2254(d)(1), or 'was based on an unreasonable determination of the facts in light of the evidence presented in the State court proceeding,' § 2254(d)(2). Because § 2254's deferential standards control whether to grant habeas relief, a federal court must take into account those standards in deciding whether an evidentiary hearing is appropriate. In deciding whether to grant an evidentiary hearing, a federal court must consider whether the hearing could enable an applicant to prove the petition's factual allegations, which, if true, would entitle the applicant to federal habeas relief. It follows that if the record refutes the applicant's factual allegations or otherwise precludes habeas relief, a district court is not required to hold an evidentiary hearing.

"The Ninth Circuit also erred in rejecting the District Court's finding that the poor quality of Landrigan's alleged mitigating evidence prevented him from making a colorable prejudice claim. Because most of the evidence that Landrigan now wishes to offer would have been offered by this birth mother and ex-wife had he allowed them to testify, and because the sentencing court had much of the evidence before it by way of counsel's proffer, the District Court could reasonably conclude that any additional evidence would have made no difference in the sentencing. Even assuming the truth of all the facts Landrigan sought to prove at an evidentiary hearing, he still could not be granted federal habeas relief because the state courts' factual determination that he would not have allowed counsel to present any mitigating evidence at sentencing is not an unreasonable determination of the facts under § 2254(d)(2) and the mitigating evidence he seeks to introduce would not have changed the result."

CASE SIGNIFICANCE: This case has had a significant effect in terms of defense counsel's capacity to submit mitigating evidence on behalf of capital defendants, particularly in cases where their client's mental competency is in question. In *Landrigan*, the Court held that federal district courts retain sound discretion on the issue of granting evidentiary hearings under the guidelines established in the Antiterrorism and Effective Death Penalty Act of 1996 (AEDPA). The Court also found that the Sixth Amendment is not violated when defense counsel fails to present mitigating evidence because the defendant interferes with his lawyer's legal strategy. In this case, the Court emphasized the fact that even if an evidentiary hearing had been granted, Landrigan would have been unable to demonstrate a colorable ineffective assistance of counsel claim because he advised his lawyer not to present *any* mitigating evidence on his behalf. For this reason, the District Court was within its discretion to deny habeas relief according to AEDPA guidelines.

The Court also determined that the Ninth Circuit erred when it found that the defendant's "last-minute decision" to block testimony did not obviate defense counsel's duty to perform an adequate investigation of the mitigating evidence, as required in *Wiggins v. Smith* (2003). The Court stressed the fact that it had never decided a case where a capital defendant objected to the introduction of mitigating evidence at sentencing. Therefore, it was not objectively unreasonable for the Arizona post-conviction court to hold that counsel's performance was constitutionally deficient according to the guidelines established in *Strickland v. Washington* (1984). The Court also rejected the Ninth Circuit's requirement that a defendant's decision to block the introduction of mitigating evidence must be "informed and knowing." Opining that Landrigan had received adequate notice from his attorney as to the importance of mitigating evidence in death penalty cases, the Court held that Landrigan had been fully informed of the potential consequences of his actions.

The Court also disagreed with the Ninth Circuit when it determined that Landrigan would have been able to demonstrate a colorable ineffective assistance of counsel claim had the District Court granted the evidentiary hearing. Rejecting this argument, the Court averred that most of Landrigan's new evidence would have been proffered by his ex-wife and birth mother had he allowed them to testify at sentencing. Moreover, the District Court could have reasonably concluded that all of the available mitigating evidence was available at Landrigan's sentencing, and that the introduction of additional evidence would not have changed the outcome of the case.

An important issue in this case is the assumption that potentially incompetent capital defendants can assist their attorneys in the development of an effective defense strategy. In his dissenting opinion, Justice Stevens criticized the majority's view that Landrigan's evidence was weak and insubstantial, opining that he may suffer from an undiagnosed brain disorder —fetal alcohol syndrome. Justice Stevens further maintained that if a brain disorder were diagnosed, this would result in powerful mitigating evidence that would likely render him ineligible for the death penalty. The argument here is that there is a logical connection between mental deficiency and belligerent behavior in the courtroom and that adequate psychological testing should be conducted to determine whether a mental disorder exists prior to sentencing.

Internet Resources

American Bar Association Standing Committee on Legal Aid and
Indigent Defendants, State Indigent Defense Systems
http://www.abanet.org/legalservices/sclaid/defender/downloads/state_indigen-tdefense_feb07.pdf

American Bar Association, Guidelines for the Performance and
Appointment of Counsel in Death Penalty Cases
http://www.internationaljusticeproject.org/pdfs/guidelines-ABA.pdf

Federal Capital Defense Counsel—Habeas Assistance Project, Summaries of all Published Successful Ineffective Assistance of Counsel Claims
http://www.capdefnet.org/hat/contents/constitutional_issues/ineffective_assist/ineffective_assistance_of_counsel.htm

Notes

1. U.S. CONST., AMEND. VI.

2. *United States v. Cronic*, 466 U.S. 654 (1984).

3. *Powell v. Alabama*, 287 U.S. 45 (1932).

4. *Gideon v. Wainright*, 372 U.S. 335 (1963).

5. *McMann v. Richardson*, 397 U.S. 759 (1970).

6. *Id.* at 771.

7. *Strickland*, 466 U.S. 668 (1984).

8. David Gross, *Supreme Court Review: Sixth Amendment—Defendant's Dual Burden in Claims of Ineffective Assistance of Counsel:* Strickland v. Washington, 75 CRIM. L. & CRIMINOLOGY 755 (1984).

9. Jeffrey Levinson, *Don't Let Sleeping Lawyers Lie: Raising the Standard for Effective Assistance of Counsel*, 38 AM. CRIM. L. REV. 147 (2001).

10. *Lockhart v. Fretwell*, 506 U.S. 364 (1993).

11. *Collins v. Lockhart*, 754 F.2d 258 (8th Cir. 1985).

12. *Perry v. Lockhart*, 871 F.2d 1384 (8th Cir. 1989).

13. *Teague v. Lane*, 489 U.S. 288 (1989).

14. Stuart Walker, *"What We Meant Was . . ." The Supreme Court Clarifies Two Ineffective Assistance Cases in* Bell v. Cone, 54 MERCER L. REV. 1271 (2003).

15. 14 STAT. at 385 (1867).

16. *Id.*

17. Walker, *supra* note 9, at 3.

18. 28 U.S.C. § 2254 (d)(1).

19. *Williams v. Taylor*, 529 U.S. 362 (2000).

20. Walker, *supra* note 9, at 4.

21. *Id.* at 374.

22. Samy Khalil, *Doing the Impossible: Appellate Reweighing of Harm and Mitigation in Capital Cases after* Williams v. Taylor, 80 TEX. L. REV. 193 (2001).

23. Levinson, *supra* note 10, at 2.

24. Douglas Vick, *Poorhouse Justice: Underfunded Indigent Defense Services and Arbitrary Death Sentences*, 43 BUFF. L. REV. 329, 334 (1995).

25. *Compendium Guide for Indigent Defense Systems, A Resource Guide for Practitioners and Policymakers*, available at: http://www.ojp.usdoj.gov/indigentdefense/compendium/pdftxt/vol3.pdf.

26. Indigent Defense Advisory Group of the American Bar Association Standing Committee on Legal Aid and Indigent Defendants, *State Indigent Defense Systems* (2006), available at: http://www.abanet.org/deathpenalty/resources/home.html.

27. *Supra* note 3.

28. *Bell v. Cone*, 535 U.S. 685 (2002).

29. *United States v. Cronic*, 466 U.S. 654 (1984).

30. *Cronic*, 466 U.S. at 659.

31. *Bell v. Cone*, 535 U.S. 685 (2002).

32. *Mickens v. Taylor*, 535 U.S. 162 (2002).

33. Jeffrey Glassman, Mickens v. Taylor: *The Court's New Don't Ask, Don't Tell Policy for Attorneys Faced With a Conflict of Interest*, 18 ST. JOHN'S J.L. COMM. 919 (2004).

34. John Capone, *Supreme Court Review: Facilitating Fairness: The Judge's Role in the Sixth Amendment Right to Counsel*, 93 J. CRIM. L. & CRIMINOLOGY 881 (2003).

35. *Wood v. Georgia*, 450 U.S. 261 (1981).

36. *Mickens*, 535 U.S. at 172.

37. Glassman, *supra* note 29, at 6.

38. *Wiggins v. Smith*, 539 U.S. 510 (2003).

39. Lyn Entzeroth, *Federal Habeas Review of Death Sentences, Where Are We Now? A Review of* Wiggins v. Smith *and* Miller-El v. Cockrell, 39 TULSA L. REV. 49 (2003).

40. *Wiggins*, 123 S. Ct. at 2532.

41. *Id.* at 2542–44.

42. *Id.* at 2537.

43. *Burger v. Kemp*, 483 U.S. 776 (1987).

44. *Darden v. Wainright*, 477 U.S. 168 (1986).

45. *Brookhart v. Janis*, 384 U.S. 1 (1966).

46. *Florida v. Nixon*, 543 U.S. 175 (2004).

47. *Id.*

48. *Id.*

49. *Rompilla v. Beard*, 125 S. Ct. 2456 (2005).

50. *Id.* at 2469.

51. *Id.* at 2478.

52. *Schriro v. Landrigan*, 127 S. Ct. 1938 (2007).

53. *Landrigan*, 441 F.3d at 647 (9th Cir. 2006).

54. *Wiggins*, 593 U.S. 510 (2003).

55. *Schriro v. Landrigan*, 127 S. Ct. 1947 (2007).

56. Harvard Law Review Association, *The Supreme Court, 2006 Term: Leading Case-Ineffective Assistance of Counsel*, 121 HARV. L. REV. 255 (2007).

57. See *Rees v. Peyton*, 384 U.S. 312, 314 (1966); *Johnston v. Zerbst*, 304 U.S. 458, 464 (1938); *Schneckloth v. Bustamonte*, 412 U.S. 218, 237–38 (1973).

58. Michelle E. Barnett et al., *When Mitigation Evidence Makes a Difference: Effects of Psychological Mitigating Evidence on Sentencing Decisions in Capital Trials*, 22 BEHAV. SCI. & L. 751, 764–66. (2004).

59. *Abdul-Kabir v. Quarterman*, 127 S. Ct. 1654, 1664 (2007).

60. *Arave v. Hoffman*, 128 S. Ct. 532 (2007).

61. *Hoffman v. Arave*, 455 F.3d 926 (2006).

62. *Adamson v. Ricketts*, 865 F.2d 1011 (1988).

63. *State v. Walton*, 769 P.2d 1017 (Ariz. 1989).

64. *Hoffman*, 455 F.3d 932 (2006).

65. *Hoffman v. Arave*, 481 F.3d 686 (2007).

66. *Williams*, 529 U.S. 362 (2000).

67. *Id.*

68. American Bar Association, "Guidelines for the Performance and Appointment of Counsel in Death Penalty Cases," available at http://internationaljusticeproject.org/pdfs/guidelines-ABA.pdf.

Chapter Outline

I. **Introduction**

II. **Tracing the Origin of Due Process in Death Penalty Cases**
   A. Taking a Two-Part Approach: Due Process versus Cruel and Unusual Punishment
      1. The Concept of Guided Discretion
         a. *Woodson v. North Carolina*
         b. *Lockett v. Ohio*
         c. *Eddings v. Oklahoma*
         d. *Gardner v. Florida*
      2. The Evolution of the "Guided Discretion" Standard

III. **Recent Death Penalty Cases Dealing with Due Process**
   A. Admissibility of Psychiatric Examinations
   B. Future Dangerousness and Capital Sentencing
   C. The Importance of the "Jury" Verdict
   D. Shackling and the Defendant's Entitlement to the Presumption of Innocence
   E. Third-Party Guilt Evidence and Admissibility Standards

IV. **In Summary, What Do these Cases Say?**

V. **Conclusion**

Cases Briefed in Chapter 8

Case Briefs
   Gardner v. Florida, 430 U.S. 349 (1977)
   Estelle v. Smith, 451 U.S. 454 (1981)
   Eddings v. Oklahoma, 455 U.S. 104 (1982)
   Gray v. Netherland, 518 U.S. 152 (1996)
   Sattazahn v. Pennsylvania, 537 U.S. 101 (2003)
   Deck v. Missouri, 544 U.S. 622 (2005)
   Holmes v. South Carolina, 547 U.S. 319 (2006)

Internet Resources

Notes

Chapter 8

Due Process and the Death Penalty

I. Introduction

The death penalty requires that particular attention be given to the legal rights of capital defendants. Whether in criminal prosecutions or on habeas corpus review, courts must give maximum attention to Eighth and Fourteenth Amendment principles in death penalty cases. The United States Supreme Court mandates that courts make decisions that adhere to societal standards of decency in capital cases. Capital cases have repeatedly raised questions about procedural fairness for death penalty defendants.

In general, the Supreme Court has interpreted the due process clause as that which "guarantees more than fairness . . . [it] provides heightened protection against government interference with certain fundamental rights and liberty interests."[1] In death penalty cases, the due process clause grants capital defendants fundamental fairness on the basis of rights that are not clearly stated in the Constitution. Traditionally, the Court has used "the evolving standards of decency" test to determine the constitutionality of state procedures and practices. Recently, the Court has moved away from this legal standard and instead used the due process clause as a means to resolve procedural issues in capital cases.

This chapter presents an analysis of some of the Supreme Court's cases regarding the death penalty and how due process has affected its decisions during the last 30 years. It begins by reviewing the Court's early cases on due process and the death penalty, focusing on seminal decisions since *Gregg v. Georgia* (1976).[2] The chapter concludes with a focus on current due process issues and trends as they relate to the trial process, the admissibility of evidence, and juror decisionmaking.

II. Tracing the Origin of Due Process in Death Penalty Cases

Following the Court's seminal decision in *Gregg*, state legislatures began to develop capital sentencing laws that followed the guidelines set by the Supreme Court in that case. In *Gregg*, the Court declared the death penalty constitutional as long as the trial process was not arbitrary or capricious. The Court's mandate to the jury regarding the consideration of aggravating and mitigating circumstances led to a new legal philosophy based on fairness and equity for capital defendants. The same day as the *Gregg* decision, the Court also decided *Woodson v. North Carolina* (1976).[3] Instead of basing its decision on the Eighth Amendment's prohibition against cruel and unusual punishment, the Court used the due process clause of the Fourteenth Amendment for its ruling.

A. *Taking a Two-Part Approach: Due Process versus Cruel and Unusual Punishment*

Historically, the United States Supreme Court has used two different approaches for analyzing death penalty cases.[4] Under the original approach, the Court relied heavily on the Eighth Amendment's prohibition of cruel and unusual punishment to invalidate state laws that do not permit individualized sentencing in capital cases—in particular, the consideration of possible mitigating evidence. More recently, the Court has been more inclined to use the due process clause of the Fourteenth Amendment to strike down state laws that are fundamentally unfair to capital defendants. The following cases illustrate the Court's legal perspectives in capital sentencing procedures. Some of the cases are based on the Eighth Amendment, while others are based on the due process clause. The following section explores seminal cases that used the Eighth Amendment and Fourteenth Amendment to strike down state laws that were deemed unconstutional. Through an exploration of case law the latter sections illustrate the meaning of due process and its role in the implementation of capital punishment in our current system of justice.

1. The Concept of Guided Discretion

Using its landmark decision in *Gregg*, the Supreme Court sought to prevent juries and judges from making decisions that were arbitrary or capricious. The *Gregg* Court forced states to enact statutory guidelines for sentencing bodies to follow when deciding whether to impose life imprisonment or death on a capital defendant. The concept of "guided discretion" has remained seminal in the Court's decisions since *Gregg*. However, the Court has also implemented due process protections for capital defendants. Recently, the Court has relied on due process in cases involving:

(1) the right to deny or explain incriminating evidence, (2) the right to representation of counsel, (3) the privilege against self-incrimination, and (4) issues of future dangerousness and jury verdicts.

a.   Woodson v. North Carolina

In *Woodson*, the Court examined a North Carolina statute that mandated the death penalty for defendants convicted of first-degree murder despite the presence of mitigating circumstances. Because the Court in *Furman v. Georgia* (1972)[5] ruled that unguided discretion on the part of the jury was unconstitutional, the legislature responded by enacting laws that were more restrictive, and therefore less discriminatory. The *Woodson* Court concluded that the North Carolina statute violated the "evolving standards of decency" test that was established in *Trop v. Dulles* (1958),[6] and reiterated in *Gregg*. The Court used the Eighth Amendment's cruel and unusual punishment prohibition to strike down the statute because the Court did not consider mitigating evidence for the defendant. Specifically, the Court stated that factors concerning his character, criminal background, or any circumstances surrounding the offense that could potentially lead to a sentence less severe than death should have been taken into account during sentencing. Citing the need to ensure individualized sentencing in capital trials, the Court claimed that the finality associated with the death sentence required heightened reliability to ensure that the penalty is applied fairly. The Court ruled that individualized sentencing is needed to ensure that state courts are sufficiently guided when deciding the appropriate punishment for a capital defendant. While the Court held in *Woodson* that sentencing bodies should consider certain types of mitigating evidence before issuing a sentence, it also maintained that discretion must be limited

b.   Lockett v. Ohio

In *Lockett v. Ohio* (1978),[7] the Court expanded the application of the Eighth and Fourteenth Amendments by invalidating an Ohio capital sentencing statute. The law under review by the Court did not mandate that the state trial judge consider individual mitigating factors, such as criminal history, offense characteristics, or age of the defendant when deciding the appropriate sentence. In this case, the trial judge interpreted the defendant's age as the only relevant mitigating factor, but the Supreme Court disagreed, holding that the statute was unconstitutional because the Eighth and Fourteenth Amendments required consideration of any mitigating evidence offered by the defendant that supported a sentence less than death.

Prior to this case, the Court had not decided the issue as to the type of evidence to be considered in mitigating a death sentence. Citing the need for courts to make individualized determinations regarding each mitigating factor, the Court reinforced its command in *Lockett* by holding that all mitigating evidence must be weighed before a death sentence can be imposed.

c.   Eddings v. Oklahoma

In a later case, *Eddings v. Oklahoma* (1982),[8] the Supreme Court held that a sentencing body may not refuse to consider a pertinent mitigating fact even when that fact has been deemed insignificant. In *Eddings*, the trial judge instructed the jury to disregard certain mitigating evidence presented by the defense. On appeal, the Court rejected the lower court's decision to exclude mitigating evidence altogether by ruling that the due process clause required that evidence be weighed independently in the context of all other aggravating and mitigating factors. The Court held that the Oklahoma trial and appellate courts should have allowed certain mitigating evidence to be introduced to the jury "that might indicate a sentence lesser than death."[9] Therefore, while the *Lockett* Court required that all mitigating evidence be introduced during sentencing, the *Eddings* Court gave sentencing juries more discretionary power by allowing them to make individual determinations as to whether a particular fact should be considered as mitigating evidence. In an effort to achieve the goals sought in *Gregg*, while also being cognizant of the fears raised after *Woodson* and *Lockett*, the *Eddings* Court struck a middle ground by acknowledging the importance of individual differences among capital defendants.

d.   Gardner v. Florida

While the initial cases involving individual sentencing guidelines dealt with both the Eighth and Fourteenth Amendments, the Court deviated from this approach in *Gardner v. Florida* (1977).[10] In this case, the Court invalidated a trial court's decision by exclusively relying on the concept of due process as basis for its holding. Whereas the *Eddings* and *Lockett* Courts held that juries must be able to consider any type of mitigating factor during sentencing, the *Gardner* Court found that the due process clause precluded a court from sentencing a defendant to death when he "had no opportunity to deny or explain the evidence against him."[11] In this case, the Court held that the due process clause prohibited a trial court from sentencing a defendant to death on the basis of confidential information found in a presentence report that was not initially available for consideration by the jury during sentencing.

The facts in *Gardner* presented a different problem for the Court compared to previous cases. The trial court originally imposed a life sentence after convicting the defendant of first-degree murder. After reviewing the separate confidential presentence report, however, the trial judge found that the aggravating factors outweighed the mitigating circumstances presented by the defense and changed the sentence from life imprisonment to death. On appeal, the Supreme Court of Florida affirmed the trial court's decision. The U.S. Supreme Court reversed, finding that the defendant's right to due process was violated when the trial judge withheld confidential information from the jury during sentencing.

The Court acknowledged the significance of giving the defense the chance to rebut evidence held in a confidential presentence report, especially in death penalty cases. The Court explained that sentencing Gardner to death on the basis of confidential information that had never been made available to him at his trial, which led to his death sentence, was unconstitutional. This case is important because it recognizes that the due process clause protects a defendant from arbitrary sentencing procedures that can potentially take place in death penalty cases.

The Court addressed this issue again in *Netherland v. Gray* (1996).[12] In that case, the Court held that Gray's due process rights were not violated when the prosecutor announced, one day before sentencing, that he planned to use evidence from an unrelated murder case during the penalty phase of the trial. Chief Justice Rehnquist, writing for the majority, said that Gray's claim was different because he "had the opportunity to hear the testimony of the witnesses and to cross-examine them."[13] Because Gray had the opportunity to request a continuance, he was not deprived of adequate notice; thus, there was no due process violation.

2.   The Evolution of the "Guided Discretion" Standard

In the Supreme Court's previous rulings on the due process rights of capital defendants, it tried to balance individuality with consistency and predictability in sentencing practices. While the decisions in *Furman* and *Gregg* required that juries be guided by law so that arbitrariness may be eliminated, the Court's holdings in *Woodson, Lockett,* and *Eddings* indicated that capital defendants are entitled to stricter standards of fairness that can only be achieved through individualized consideration of mitigating circumstances on a case-by-case basis. These holdings demonstrate that while aggravating factors such as future dangerousness can be set by statute, a jury must be able to openly consider particular mitigating factors when deciding on the appropriate punishment. Likewise, the Court has said that the due process clause requires a capital jury to be given the opportunity to weigh all of the evidence presented by both parties to the case and that a defendant must be able to deny or explain confidential evidence considered by a sentencing body. Some critics have argued that the Court's decisions on capital sentencing practices contradict the goals of deterrence and retribution, therefore making the doctrine of guided discretion self-defeating.[14] Conversely, proponents maintain that goals such as deterrence and retribution sought to be accomplished in the *Gregg* and *Furman* decisions are based solely on Eighth Amendment principles; therefore, they are different from the constitutional principles guiding cases such as Eddings, which use the Fourteenth Amendment to ensure that due process is given to capital defendants.

Justices have argued that the decisions in *Gregg* and *Furman* were based on Eighth Amendment principles, whereas *Lockett* and *Eddings* established due process protections for capital defendants. On the other hand, other justices claim that all of these cases are grounded on the same constitutional protections. For example, Justice White claimed that Eighth Amendment objectives such as deterrence and retribution have the same practical effect as that of due process. In *Woodson*, Justice White wrote a separate opinion rejecting the application of the due process clause to capital sentencing procedures because it was "unnecessary other than as a vehicle by which the strictures of the Eighth Amendment are triggered."[15] Justice Scalia, on the other hand, has argued that giving a jury unlimited discretion increases the potential for arbitrariness, which was a fundamental problem cited by the Court in *Furman*. Justice Scalia maintains that *Lockett* and *Eddings* ran afoul of Eighth Amendment principles because their law produced "a system in conflict with itself."[16]

Since the early 1980s, the Court has acknowledged that the "evolving standards of decency" must first account for individual treatment of capital defendants within the bounds of statutory restrictions. The Court's shift in legal philosophy regarding the concept of guided discretion has led to a proliferation of cases in which the Court has invoked the due process clause as a means to ensure fairness in capital sentencing procedures.

III. Recent Death Penalty Cases Dealing with Due Process

A. Admissibility of Psychiatric Examinations

The Court began to extend the application of due process to other legal areas following the *Gardner* and *Eddings* decisions. In *Estelle v. Smith* (1981),[17] the Court held that testimony from a psychiatrist based on a court-ordered psychiatric examination violated the Fifth, Sixth, and Fourteenth Amendments when the defendant was not advised of his constitutional rights. By using the Fourteenth Amendment, which was made applicable to the states through the due process clause, the Court claimed that Smith's Fifth and Sixth Amendment rights were violated because due process ensures that these protections apply to the sentencing as well as the guilt determination stage of a capital trial.

Prior to Smith's trial, the judge ordered that he undergo a psychiatric examination by the state's psychiatrist. The competency examination was performed, and the psychiatrist concluded that Smith was competent to stand trial. After the defendant was found guilty of capital murder, the psychiatrist testified at the sentencing stage that Smith represented a future danger to society because he was a severe sociopath. Finding that the privilege against self-incrimination applied equally to the guilt as well as the sentencing stage of a capital trial, the Supreme Court stated that the introduction of such evidence was prohibited "unless the defendant was warned prior to questioning that his statements could be introduced against him at the sentencing stage."[18] However, the Court cautioned that such a defense might not succeed in some cases, such as when the state's psychiatrist was testifying to rebut evidence proffered by a defense psychiatrist.

The *Smith* Court also found that the government had violated the defendant's right to counsel when he was denied the opportunity to consult with his lawyer concerning the psychiatrist's testimony. When the state failed to notify Smith's attorney that such testimony would address their client's future dangerousness to society, the state also violated his Sixth Amendment right to counsel. The Court stated that in order for the psychiatrist's testimony to be admissible, Smith would have to have been told that he had a right to remain silent prior to the psychiatrist's examination.

Since the decision in *Smith*, the Court has not directly addressed the issue of pretrial examinations and the capital defendant's rights in these situations. However, the Supreme Court clarified the Smith ruling in *Buchanan v. Kentucky* (1987).[19] In this case, the Court held that government psychiatric testimony could be used to rebut capital defense testimony by a psychiatrist concerning the emotional background of the defendant. Speaking for the Court, Justice Blackmun claimed that when a capital defendant presents evidence of "extreme emotional disturbance,"[20] the government could, in turn, impugn the defense psychiatrist's testimony on the grounds that it was unreliable. This issue of emotional stability raises several implications for the prosecution as well as the defense during the rebuttal process.

Since 1987, the Court has not considered individual factors beyond "extreme emotional stability" that can determine when a prosecutor's right to rebuttal is invoked. One scholar has claimed that a plausible solution to this problem would be to allow a defense psychiatrist to testify regarding the defendant's emotional stability at the time of the crime without accounting for prior criminal history.[21] One benefit to this defense is that the prosecution would be precluded from introducing evidence regarding the defendant's uncharged conduct. By the same token, if testimony by a defense psychiatrist is perceived to be biased, the prosecutor can argue that his or her evaluation is unreliable. Whether a court considers a particular psychological evaluation to be valid or invalid, the defendant is protected by two legal interests: (1) the right to limit the range of the state psychiatrist's examination, and (2) an interest in not being compelled to reveal information about his or her prior criminal history. A frequent response by the government is to provide use immunity for capital defendants in these situations. This legal tactic prohibits the state's psychiatrist from using prior criminal history as a determinative factor of emotional stability, which can be used as a mitigating factor during the sentencing stage.

B. Future Dangerousness and Capital Sentencing

Capital juries often must decide whether a defendant's conduct represents a future danger to society before imposing this form of punishment. The Supreme Court has increasingly relied on the due process clause to decide issues about the types of evidence that can be used to demonstrate future dangerousness. These issues will be introduced in this section in order to show how the Court has applied the due process clause to various facets of capital sentencing law.

The Court first used the due process clause to decide issues on future dangerousness in *Skipper v. South Carolina* (1986).[22] In *Skipper*, the Court decided that the defendant's Eighth and Fourteenth Amendment rights were violated when the trial court denied the defendant the opportunity to introduce evidence of his good behavior in jail as a mitigating factor at his sentencing. Therefore, the Court found that his constitutional rights had been violated because the *Lockett* decision mandated that a sentencing body make an individualized determination of aggravating and mitigating factors when the prosecutor alleges future dangerousness. In addition, the petitioner's right to due process was violated because he was unable to deny or explain the evidence used against him as specified by the *Gardner* Court.

In *California v. Ramos* (1983),[23] the Court held that a jury instruction regarding the possibility of a commuted life sentence did not violate the Eighth Amendment or due process clause of the Fourteenth Amendment. In this case, the Court considered whether such an instruction interfered with the jury's ability to make a reliable determination regarding individual mitigating elements. The Court held that the instruction was not unconstitutional because it merely afforded the jury an opportunity to consider each of the defendant's characteristics individually. Since *Ramos*, the Court began to examine future dangerousness and sentencing standards predominantly in the context of the due process clause.

C. The Importance of the "Jury" Verdict

Until recently, there has been no answer as to whether a life sentence imposed by a court constitutes an acquittal and bars a retrial for a harsher sentence. In *Sattazahn v. Pennsylvania* (2003),[24] the Court resolved this issue by relying on the concept of due process and the Fifth Amendment's double jeopardy clause. The *Sattazahn* case raised questions regarding the consequences associated with the appeals process, especially in capital punishment cases. In this case, the Court held that, because the jury made no findings with respect to the alleged aggravating circumstance, Sattazahn was not acquitted of death in the first trial. Therefore, he was not legally entitled to his life sentence and could be retried without being put twice in jeopardy. Although the Pennsylvania statute obligated the trial judge to impose a life sentence when the jury failed to unanimously agree on the sentence, Justice

Scalia, writing for the majority, disagreed with the dissent's position that the ruling by the trial judge "had the hallmarks of guilt or innocence."[25] The Court claimed that when Sattazahn opted for a retrial he invoked a separate "process," therefore the Fourteenth Amendment did not render immutable any "life" or liberty" interest given by Pennsylvania law. Likewise, no due process violation occurred.

After *Sattazahn*, criminal defendants who have not technically been acquitted will be confronted with a momentous choice: they must accept the original verdict as final in an effort to avoid the death penalty or take the chance of obtaining an acquittal from the jury on retrial. Although placing criminal defendants in this position was not found by the Court to be unconstitutional, future cases will likely cause some individuals to be fearful of the notion that they may receive a more severe punishment after a second trial. Overall, the Court has carved an exception to previous case law on the double jeopardy clause as it applies to capital murder cases.

D.   Shackling and the Defendant's Entitlement to the Presumption of Innocence

Courts have traditionally recognized, as a product of state or constitutional law, a defendant's right to appear in court free of obvious restraints.[26] The basis for this reasoning lies in the defendant's right to due process and the presumption of innocence until proven guilty beyond a reasonable doubt. However, the Supreme Court had never addressed this issue until recently in *Deck v. Missouri* (2005).[27] In a 7-2 vote written by Justice Breyer, the majority held that, absent an overwhelming state interest such as courtroom security, the practice of shackling capital defendants is inherently biasing and fundamentally unfair, therefore violating a defendant's right to due process of law.

The Court began its opinion addressing the practice of shackling in the context of its prior holdings in *Estelle v. Williams* (1976),[28] *Illinois v. Allen* (1970),[29] and *Holbrook v. Flynn* (1986).[30] In each of these cases the Court noted that the practice of shackling was always used as a last resort. In *Flynn*, for example, the Court distinguished the presence of additional security personnel in the courtroom from the practice of shackling, calling the latter inherently prejudicial. In general, the Court's ruling was based on three central criticisms: (1) that shackling may lead to biased juror perceptions undermining the presumption of innocence; (2) that shackling is likely to interfere with a defendant's capacity to assist in his own defense; and (3) that shackling may undercut key principles characterizing this nation's courtrooms—dignity, fairness, and justice.

Using this framework of analysis, the Court opined that the concerns about guilt-phase shackling also apply to the sentencing phase of capital trials. The Court reasoned that, although the issue of guilt or innocence is moot during the penalty phase, the jury is still deliberating between life or death, a decision of equal significance for capital defendants. The issue of juror bias was of particular concern to the Court because shackling implies that the defendant represents a future danger to society, which many states consider to be an aggravating factor supporting a death sentence. Shackling, according to the majority's view, undermines the presumption of innocence and insinuates that a defendant needs to be separated from the rest of society. The Court next explained that the practice of shackling generally interferes with a defendant's right to counsel and to communicate or participate normally with defense counsel. As an example, the Court pointed to a 1696 King's Bench case illustrating a criminal defendant's decision to avoid taking the witness stand because he was in shackles and could not move about freely.[31] The Court's third justification for supporting a general prohibition on the practice of shackling focused on the maintenance of dignity, equality, and justice, principles essential to the courtroom. The Court proffered that the atmosphere of the Nation's courts "reflect a seriousness of purpose that helps to explain the judicial system's power to inspire the confidence and to affect the behavior of a general public whose demands for justice our courts seek to serve."[32]

In his dissenting opinion, Justice Thomas argued that the majority's conception of the history of shackling was misplaced. He opined that common law restrictions on shackling were traditionally applied for the welfare of defendants, not the principles outlined by the majority. Justice Thomas distinguished modern restraints from the types of shackles used at common law, noting that irons of that period were heavy and extremely painful. To counter the majority's opinion, Justice Thomas noted that most states had not addressed the issue of shackling, at least as defined by modern practice, until the end of the twentieth century. To further his argument, Justice Thomas reasoned that state opinions on the issue were contradictory, with many opinions resting heavily on the discretion of trial judges. In response to the three fundamental legal tenets that the majority outlined, the dissent claimed that Deck had never asserted that his right to counsel had been impaired, thus he had no legitimate claim. Second, Justice Thomas stated that the right to dignity and decorum in the courtroom was not an essential part of due process, and that the practice only minimally affected courtroom security. He conceded that shackling raised concerns during the guilt phase, but reasoned that the same concerns did not exist during the penalty phase. Justice Thomas opined that the presumption of innocence was negated at this stage and therefore no constitutional violation existed.

E. Third-Party Guilt Evidence and Admissibility Standards

In *Holmes v. South Carolina* (2006),[33] the overarching issue before the Court was federalism—specifically, the power of states to enact their own rules of evidence for criminal proceedings.[34] The South Carolina law the Court addressed in *Holmes* posited that if the state has strong forensic evidence, then a defendant cannot raise an "alternative perpetrator defense."[35] States have devised these rules to prevent juror confusion and to prevent the introduction of misleading stories by additional parties.[36] Writing for a unanimous majority opinion, Justice Alito held that the South Carolina law violated the Sixth and Fourteenth Amendments. The case is significant because the Court's reasoning can be similarly applied to all criminal cases, not just capital cases. However, given the variety of evidentiary standards that exist among the states, it is possible that the Court's holding may have caused more confusion in the lower courts than what was intended.

The Court stated that South Carolina's evidence rule was unconstitutional for three main reasons. First, in *State v. Gay* (2001),[37] the South Carolina Supreme Court barred defendants from invoking the "alternative perpetrator" defense in some instances, which prevented the defendant from successfully challenging the state's case. If the judge, not the jury, determined that the prosecutor's evidence was "strong," then the defendant could not proffer evidence suggestive of third-party guilt. The state's law precluded Holmes from suggesting the that the state's evidence was flawed, staged, or tainted. Further, Justice Alito claimed that the South Carolina procedure was arbitrary, meaning that it did not further the interests of typical third-party guilt rules. Next, the Court stated that the standard set in *Gay* was deficient because it did not allow juries to determine the credibility of witnesses and thus whether this evidence was considered "strong." To emphasize the prejudicial effect of state's rule, the Court suggested that it is as irrational as its opposite: "a rule barring the prosecution from introducing evidence of a defendant's guilt if the defendant is able to proffer, at a pretrial hearing, evidence that, if believed, strongly supports a verdict of not guilty."[38] The Court concluded that without requiring jury consideration of the evidence the law was illogical. And last, the Court reasoned that a defendant must be given a meaningful opportunity to present a thorough defense. Without allowing a defendant to advance an alternative theory for the crime solely on the thrust of the prosecution's evidence, the rule fails to serve a legitimate purpose that related rules are intended to promote.

At present, state and federal courts use a mixture of standards to evaluate the admissibiltity of evidence.[39] Generally speaking, there are two main types. Under the first scheme, 17 states, including South Carolina, require defendants to present evidence indicating a "direct link" between a particular third party and the offense. Although this the most common approach, other states use variations of this model. A second category of states rely on Federal Rule of Evidence 401 to determine evidence admissibility. Regardless of whether a state adopts either approach, courts frequently use characteristics of both when relating the law to a given set of facts.[40] Given the many variations of these rules within the states, it is likely that the U.S. Supreme Court and lower appellate courts will confront similar challenges to state evidentiary standards in capital cases in the future.

IV.   In Summary, What Do these Cases Say?

Since the decision in *Gregg*, the Supreme Court has used the "evolving standards of decency" test as a means for determining whether state sentencing laws comport with constitutional standards. This standard is what has guided the Court in cases that have been decided since 1976; however, it has increasingly relied on the Fourteenth Amendment's due process clause to decide capital sentencing cases. The decisions in *Woodson, Lockett*, and *Eddings* were three of the Court's earliest cases expressing a need for juries to be able to consider mitigating evidence proffered by the defendant that could potentially lead to a sentence less than death. The need to ensure individualized sentencing and heightened reliability in future capital cases was primarily based on the Eighth Amendment's cruel and unusual punishment clause during this era.

As additional cases were decided, the Court began to use the right to due process of law instead of the Eighth Amendment as a basis for invalidating state capital sentencing procedures. In *Gardner v. Florida* (1977), the Court found that a capital defendant's right to due process precluded a trial court from sentencing a defendant to death when he or she "had no opportunity to deny or explain the evidence against him." Recognizing that a defendant must have a constitutional right to rebut evidence used during the trial stage, the Court has observed that more cases on state capital sentencing law are based on due process protections rather than individualization in sentencing standards.

The Court's decisions on the concept of future dangerousness indicated a similar trend. Since the decision in *Simmons*, the Court has addressed procedural protections such as the need to inform a jury of a capital defendant's parole ineligibility by relying exclusively on the Fourteenth Amendment. For example, the *Kelly* Court reinforced its stance on the connection between a capital defendant's due process rights to rebut a prosecutor's argument regarding a defendant's future dangerousness if such an argument is put forth by the state. Arguably, the Court could resolve cases such as *Kelly* by relying on Eighth Amendment precedent; however, it has chosen to avoid this more subjective standard for evaluating state sentencing laws and replaced it with a due process framework that is somewhat more predictable.

In *Sattazahn*, the Court recently invalidated another state law that mandated a life sentence on retrial when the defendant was given the death penalty in the first trial. Choosing the due process rationale as a basis for its holding, the Court asserted that Sattazahn's rights had not been violated when he invoked a separate process at his own discretion; therefore, he had forfeited his claim to a punishment of life imprisonment after he was sentenced to death on retrial.

The Court's recent decisions in *Deck* and *Holmes* suggest that due process is a key safeguard that transcends many aspects of death penalty law. The

Deck Court settled the issue on the practice of shackling in both the guilt and penalty phases, declaring it unconstitutional. The *Holmes* Court addressed an area of death penalty law that typically does not receive much attention—the viability of state evidentiary rules. *Holmes* declared the South Carolina evidentiary rule as violative of the Sixth and Fourteenth Amendments. It is clear that the right to due process can be found in most challenges on capital punishment, whether they involve the trial process, evidentiary standards, or jury deliberations.

V. Conclusion

It has been the aim of this chapter to present a cross section of Supreme Court cases that have dealt with a capital defendant's right to due process as it relates to capital sentencing procedures. As mentioned in the above sections, the right to due process is often combined by the Court with other fundamental rights, such as those included in the Fifth, Sixth, and Eighth Amendments. Specifically, this chapter has concentrated on specific protections for death penalty defendants provided by the Court by way of the due process clause, such as: (1) the right to deny or explain incriminating evidence, (2) the right to representation of counsel, (3) the privilege against self-incrimination, and (4) issues involving future dangerousness and jury verdicts.

The trend of the Supreme Court has recently been to use the due process clause as a justification for granting or limiting rights for death penalty defendants. The Court has been less inclined to use the cruel and unusual punishment clause to explain why particular aspects of a capital trial do not conform to constitutional standards. Whether the Court continues to use the due process clause or the Eighth Amendment's cruel and unusual punishment clause as a basis for deciding cases, it is clear that the Court has become more aware of procedural misfires in trial courts and has taken significant measures to balance state and individual interests accordingly.

Cases Briefed in Chapter 8

Case	Issue	Holding
Gardner v. Florida 430 U.S. 349 (1977)	Is a capital defendant deprived of the right to refute or explain testimony or evidence such as a confidential presentence report at sentencing if such information was not made available to him?	The right to deny or explain evidence used for prosecution must be given to capital defendants at sentencing.
Estelle v. Smith 451 U.S. 454 (1981)	Does the failure to advise a capital defendant of his Fifth and Sixth Amendment rights during a pretrial psychiatric examination constitute constitutional error, thus barring statements made regarding his future dangerousness to society?	Fifth, Sixth, and Fourteenth Amendment rights apply to capital defendants during pretrial psychiatric examinations.
Eddings v. Oklahoma 455 U.S. 104 (1982)	Must a trial court consider individualized mitigating factors, such as evidence of a difficult family history and emotional disturbance, when deciding death penalty cases?	Trial courts must consider character evidence such as that which indicates a difficult family history or emotional disturbance.
Gray v. Netherland 518 U.S. 152 (1996)	Does the failure to provide defendants with adequate notice of incriminating evidence at sentencing constitute a violation of due process?	Due process is not violated when the state fails to give adequate notice regarding evidence used at the sentencing to show future dangerousness.
Sattazahn v. Pennsylvania 537 U.S. 101 (2003)	Does the due process clause prohibit a state from seeking the death penalty upon retrial if the state mandates a life sentence when the jury is unable to reach a verdict?	No due process violation occurs if states seek the death penalty upon retrial after the imposition of a life sentence based on state statute.
Deck v. Missouri 544 U.S. 622 (2005)	Does shackling a death penalty defendant during the sentencing stage of a capital case violate the due process clauses of the 5th and 14th Amendments?	The shackling of a capital defendant during the penalty phase violates the 5th and 14th Amendments to the Constitution, unless it is justified by an overwhelming, essential state interest such as courtroom security.
Holmes v. South Carolina 547 U.S. 319 (2006)	Does an evidence rule restricting the introduction of third-party guilt evidence violate a capital defendant's right to due process, compulsory process, or confrontation of witnesses?	An evidence rule that bars the introduction of third-party guilt evidence if a prosecutor produces strong forensic evidence of guilt violates a capital defendant's constitutional right to due process, compulsory process, and confrontation of witnesses.

Case Briefs

Gardner v. Florida
430 U.S. 349 (1977)

CAPSULE: A capital defendant must be given the opportunity to deny or explain testimony or evidence used by the state during sentencing. The prosecutor's reliance on a confidential presentence report, which was not made available to defense counsel, violates the defendant's Eighth and Fourteenth Amendment rights.

FACTS: Gardner was found guilty by a jury of first-degree murder in the Circuit Court of Citrus County, Florida. At sentencing, the jury recommended a sentence of life in prison because the relative mitigating circumstances outweighed the aggravating factors. Based on his reliance on a confidential presentence report that was not made available to the jury, the trial judge replaced the jury's verdict and entered a death sentence for Gardner. Furthermore, the trial judge differed with the jury on the weight of aggravating factors associated with the case, calling the crime "heinous, atrocious and cruel." Although the judge claimed that a copy of the confidential report was given to the defendant's counsel, he did not comment on the contents of the confidential portion as it related to Gardner's crime.

ISSUE: Is a capital defendant deprived of the right to refute or explain testimony or evidence, such as a confidential presentence report, at sentencing if such information was not made available to him? NO.

HOLDING: The prosecutor's reliance on a confidential presentence report, which was not made available to defense counsel, violates the defendant's Eighth and Fourteenth Amendment rights.

REASON: "Even if it were permissible upon finding good cause to withhold a portion of a presentence report from the defendant, and even from defense counsel, nevertheless the full report must be made a part of the record to be reviewed on appeal. Since the State must administer its capital-sentencing procedures with an even hand, that record must disclose to the reviewing court the considerations motivating the death sentence in every case in which it is imposed, since otherwise the capital-sentencing procedure would be subject to the defects that resulted in the holding of unconstitutionality in *Furman v. Georgia*, 408 U.S. 238 (1972)."

"Here defense counsel's failure to request access to the full presentence report cannot justify the submission of a less complete record to the reviewing court than the record on which the trial judge based his decision to sentence petitioner to death, nor does such omission by counsel constitute an effective waiver of the constitutional error.

CASE SIGNIFICANCE: Before *Gardner*, the Supreme Court had not specifically relied on the due process clause as the sole basis for declaring unconstitutional state capital sentencing practices. Because Gardner had no opportunity to deny or explain the evidence that was used against him, which was contained in the presentence report, his constitutional right to due process was violated. The Court claimed that the defense had no opportunity to defend itself from the adverse impact of the confidential presentence document.

By relying on the due process clause, the Court generated controversy from legal critics regarding the impact of the Eighth and Fourteenth Amendments. Some have argued that the sentencing procedures at issue did not allow the sentencing body to make a reliable sentencing determination; therefore, the Eighth Amendment was a more effective means for banning such practices. Since *Gardner*, however, the Court has increasingly used the due process clause of the Fourteenth Amendment, rather than the Eighth Amendment's cruel and unusual punishment clause, as a reason for striking down capital sentencing procedures.

Estelle v. Smith
451 U.S. 454 (1981)

CAPSULE: Testimony of a psychiatrist based on court-ordered psychiatric evaluation, if the defendant was not advised of his constitutional rights, violates the Fifth, Sixth, and Fourteenth Amendments; therefore, testimony from the evaluation is not admissible during sentencing.

FACTS: After being indicted for murder in Texas, Smith was evaluated for competency to stand trial by a state psychiatrist as prescribed by the trial court. Without being advised of his Fifth Amendment right to be protected from self-incrimination, the psychiatrist obtained information that would later be used to demonstrate Smith's future dangerousness. Smith was subsequently convicted of capital murder. At the sentencing stage, the psychiatrist testified that Smith would pose a continuing threat to society; therefore, he was sentenced to death.

ISSUE: Does the failure to advise a capital defendant of his Fifth and Sixth Amendment rights during a pretrial psychiatric examination result in constitutional error, which bars the resulting testimony from being introduced at sentencing to establish future dangerousness? YES.

HOLDING: Testimony of a psychiatrist based on a court-ordered psychiatric evaluation when the defendant was not advised of his constitutional rights violates the Fifth, Sixth, and Fourteenth Amendments; therefore, evidence presented during the sentencing phase is rendered inadmissible.

REASON: "The admission of the doctor's testimony at the penalty phase violated respondent's Fifth Amendment privilege against compelled self-incrimination, because he was not advised before the pretrial psychiatric examination that he had a right to remain silent and that any statement he made could be used against him at a capital sentencing proceeding."

"Respondent's Sixth Amendment right to the assistance of counsel also was violated by the State's introduction of the doctor's testimony at the penalty phase. Such right already had attached when the doctor examined respondent in jail, and that interview proved to be a 'critical stage' of the aggregate proceedings against respondent. Defense counsel was not notified in advance that the psychiatric examination would encompass the issue of their client's future dangerousness, and respondent was denied the assistance of his counsel in making the significant decision of whether to submit to the examination and to what end the psychiatrist's findings could be employed."

CASE SIGNIFICANCE: In this case, the Supreme Court used the due process clause as a means of extending Fifth and Sixth Amendment rights to capital defendants during the penalty phase of a capital trial. It was one of the Court's original cases using the due process clause as a way to apply other constitutional rights to capital defendants. In this case, the Court held that the state psychiatrist's evaluation of a capital defendant prior to trial may be protected by the Fifth Amendment's self-incrimination clause in some cases. The Court said that because the defendant never raised the insanity defense, the government could not impugn the testimony of the defense psychiatrist by providing testimony from its own psychiatric expert. However, Buchanan acknowledged that when a capital defendant presents evidence of "extreme emotional disturbance," the defendant waives her Fifth Amendment protection against self-incrimination. Therefore, the evidence obtained during the evaluation can be used. Since Smith was decided, lower courts interpret the Court's holding to mean that any type of mental defense raised by the defendant opens the door for state prosecutors to rebut evidence by using a government psychiatrist's testimony.

Another significant issue that was raised in the *Smith* case was the defendant's right to be notified that a state psychiatrist's testimony would be used against him as proof of his future dangerousness to society. Because Smith was interviewed by the government psychiatrist in the absence of his lawyer, the state violated his right to counsel. In this case, the Court said that there was no difference between the type of protections provided by the Fifth Amendment during the guilt or sentencing stages of a capital trial. Because a defendant's exposure to punishment is the same, a person cannot be denied Fifth or Sixth Amendment rights in either stage of the trial.

Eddings v. Oklahoma
455 U.S. 104 (1982)

CAPSULE: Mitigating circumstances, including age and relevant social history, must be considered in juvenile capital cases.

FACTS: Eddings was a 16-year-old offender who was tried and convicted as an adult of the capital murder of a police officer. At the time of the trial, the state of Oklahoma had a statute prescribing that "any mitigating circumstances," as well as any of the designated aggravating factors, could be considered by a sentencing body. The state presented certain aggravating factors to the jury for consideration; however, Eddings proffered extensive evidence describing his exposure to a traumatic family history, including child abuse and emotional distress. The trial judge found that each of the three alleged aggravating factors had been proven by the state. However, the judge did not consider the evidence presented in mitigation to be persuasive, such as the offender's youth and traumatic background, and therefore he was sentenced to death.

ISSUE: Must mitigating circumstances, such as social history, be considered in the sentencing phase of a juvenile capital case? YES.

HOLDING: The court must consider any and all mitigating factors in determining the sentence in a juvenile capital case. The weight and relevance of such factors are discretionary, but total exclusion of a mitigating factor is improper.

REASON: "The Eighth and Fourteenth Amendments require that the sentencer . . . not be precluded from considering, as a mitigating factor, any aspect of a defendant's character or record and any of the circumstances of the offense that the defendant proffers as a basis for a sentence less than death. This rule follows from the requirement that capital punishment be imposed fairly and with reasonable consistency or not at all, and recognizes that a consistency produced by ignoring individual differences is a false consistency."

"The limitation placed by the courts below upon the mitigating evidence they would consider violated the above rule. Just as the State may not by statute preclude the sentencer from considering any mitigating factor, neither may the sentencer refuse to consider, as a matter of law, any relevant mitigating evidence. The sentencer and the reviewing court may determine the weight to be given relevant mitigating evidence but cannot totally exclude it from their consideration. Here, the evidence of a difficult family history and of emotional disturbance petitioner offered at the sentencing hearing should have been duly considered in sentencing."

CASE SIGNIFICANCE: In this case, the Supreme Court held that all reasonably relevant mitigating factors must be considered in a juvenile capital offense sentencing determination. This includes social history factors that may or may not have an impact on the behavior that resulted in the current charge of murder in the first degree. The Court did not say what weight should be given to specific evidence, choosing instead to leave such decisions up to the judge in whose court the case is tried. It required, however, that there be proof in the record of the case that all relevant mitigating evidence was considered by the court prior to sentencing.

The Court ruled that "age" is a relevant mitigating factor to consider. It also held that, in cases involving juveniles, all social history mitigating factors must be seriously considered by the court prior to sentencing. While a judge usually enjoys discretion in determining which mitigating factors are to be considered during sentencing, that discretion is narrowed in capital cases involving juveniles.

Gray v. Netherland
518 U.S. 152 (1996)

CAPSULE: Due process is not violated when the state fails to give notice regarding evidence used at the sentencing stage to show future dangerousness.

FACTS: At the beginning of petitioner's trial, the prosecutor announced that, if the trial should reach the sentencing stage, the state would submit evidence to the jury indicating that Gray admitted to inmates that he had murdered Lisa Sorrell and her daughter. Once convicted of capital murder, Gray's case was submitted to the jury for sentencing. The prosecutor proceeded to introduce evidence, which included testimony from the investigating officer assigned to the Sorrell case, as well as crime scene photographs, all of which incriminated Gray in the Sorrell murders. Defense counsel objected to the prosecutor's introduction of evidence for an unrelated crime because he did not have adequate notice to rebut the state's case. The motion to exclude was denied by the trial judge and Gray was sentenced to death. Gray filed a habeas corpus petition in federal district court alleging that his due process rights had been violated when the state sought to introduce evidence at sentencing without giving him adequate notice of it, and that the prosecutor failed to produce exculpatory evidence in his favor, which tended to misrepresent his case.

ISSUE: At a capital murder trial, does the failure to provide a defendant with adequate notice of incriminating evidence at sentencing constitute a violation of the due process clause? NO.

HOLDING: On habeas corpus review, a capital defendant's right to due process is not violated when the state fails to give adequate notice regarding evidence used at the sentencing stage to show future dangerousness.

REASON: "A petitioner does not satisfy the exhaustion requirement by presenting the state courts only with the facts necessary to state a claim for relief. Nor is it enough to make a general appeal to a constitutional guarantee as broad as due process to present the "substance" of such a claim to a state court."

"Petitioner contends that he was deprived of adequate notice when he received only one day's notice of the additional evidence, but, rather than seeking a continuance, he sought to have all such evidence excluded. For him to prevail, he must establish that due process requires that he receive more than a day's notice of the Commonwealth's evidence. He must also show that due process required a continuance whether or not he sought one, or that, if he chose not to seek a continuance, exclusion was the only appropriate remedy. Only the adoption of a new constitutional rule could establish these propositions. A defendant has the right to notice of the charges against which he must defend. However, he does not have a constitutional right to notice of the evidence which the state plans to use to prove the charges, and *Brady*, which addressed only exculpatory evidence, did not create one. Even if notice were required, exclusion of evidence is not the sole remedy for a violation of such a right, since a continuance could minimize prejudice. Petitioner made no such request here, and in view of his insistence on exclusion, the trial court might well have felt that it would have been interfering with counsel's tactical decision to order a continuance on its own motion."

CASE SIGNIFICANCE: In this case, the Supreme Court said that there was a difference between being provided the opportunity to refute or deny evidence used by the prosecution and being denied that opportunity. In *Gardner*, the Court held that the defendant's right to due process was violated because confidential information included in a presentence report was not made available to the defense, but was relied on by the court during sentencing. The Court said that the factual circumstances in this case were different. Because Gray had the opportunity to request a continuance but failed to do so, his due process right was not violated. The Court claimed that, in order for Gray to show that such a right had been violated, he would have to establish that due process required a continuance even though he did not request one, or that it required more than one day's notice for preparation. The court found that due process did not entitle the petitioner to an exclusion of the evidence in this case. In the Court's opinion, the petitioner could not be granted habeas relief because it would give him the benefit of a new rule of federal constitutional law, in violation of *Teague v. Lane*, 489 U.S. 288 (1989).

Sattazahn v. Pennsylvania
537 U.S. 101 (2003)

CAPSULE: A life sentence imposed by state law when a jury is unable to reach a unanimous verdict at the penalty stage does not constitute an "acquittal" and therefore does not bar the imposition of the death penalty upon retrial following a reversal of the defendant's conviction on appeal.

FACTS: At Sattazahn's original death penalty trial, the jury reported to the trial judge that it was hopelessly deadlocked nine-to-three for life imprisonment. The jury was unable to reach a unanimous decision regarding the presence of certain aggravating or mitigating factors, which determine whether life in prison or the death penalty should be imposed. In this case, the trial judge was required to enter, as a matter of Pennsylvania law, a default judgment of life imprisonment for Sattazahn. On appeal, Sattazahn alleged that the trial court erred in its instructions given to the jury, and the Pennsylvania Supreme Court reversed the lower court's decision in favor of the petitioner and remanded the case. At retrial, the state of Pennsylvania announced that it would be seeking the death penalty once again; however, this time, the jury imposed the death penalty. The second time around, the Supreme Court of Pennsylvania affirmed the decision of the trial court, holding that neither the Fifth Amendment's double jeopardy clause nor the Fourteenth Amendment's due process clause precluded the state of Pennsylvania from seeking the death penalty on retrial.

ISSUE: Does the Fifth Amendment's double jeopardy clause or the Fourteenth Amendment's due process clause preclude a state from seeking the death penalty upon retrial if state law mandates a life sentence in cases in which the jury is unable to reach a unanimous decision? NO.

HOLDING: No due process violation occurs if states seek the death penalty on retrial after the imposition of the death penalty based on statutory law; furthermore, the failure to reach a unanimous verdict at the penalty stage does not constitute an "acquittal" or trigger double jeopardy protections.

REASON: "Double-jeopardy protections were not triggered when the jury deadlocked at petitioner's first sentencing proceeding and the court prescribed a life sentence pursuant to Pennsylvania law. The jury in that first proceeding was deadlocked and made no findings with respect to the alleged aggravating circumstance. That result, or nonresult, cannot fairly be called an acquittal, based on findings sufficient to establish legal entitlement to a life sentence. Neither was the entry of a life sentence by the judge an "acquittal." Under Pennsylvania's scheme, a judge has no discretion to fashion a sentence once he finds the jury is deadlocked, and he makes no findings and resolves no factual matters. The Pennsylvania Supreme Court also made no finding that the Pennsylvania Legislature intended the statutorily required entry of a life sentence to create an "entitlement" even without an "acquittal."

"The Due Process Clause also did not bar Pennsylvania from seeking the death penalty at the retrial. Nothing in § 1 of the Fourteenth Amendment indicates that any 'life' or 'liberty' interest that Pennsylvania law may have given petitioner in the first proceeding's life sentence was somehow immutable, and he was "deprived" of any such interest only by operation of the "process" he invoked to invalidate the underlying first-degree murder conviction. This Court declines to hold that the Due Process Clause provides greater double-jeopardy protection than does the Double Jeopardy Clause."

CASE SIGNIFICANCE: In this case, the Court had not addressed the issue as to whether a life sentence imposed by a court constitutes an acquittal and bars a retrial for a harsher sentence. Sattazahn resolved this issue but raised questions regarding the consequences associated with the appeals process. When Sattazahn was given life imprisonment, Pennsylvania law provided that the judge had to impose the penalty of life imprisonment rather than death if the jury could not unanimously agree that an aggravating circumstance existed. Sattazahn received a life sentence during the first trial not because he was acquitted of the death penalty charge, but because of the automatic operation of state law. His new trial constituted a new proceeding in which he could be given the death penalty. The problem with this case is that this precedent may discourage a defendant who has escaped the death penalty during the first trial from appealing a conviction for fear that a second trial will result in a death sentence.

Deck v. Missouri
544 U.S. 622 (2005)

CAPSULE: The Fifth and Fourteenth Amendments forbid the use of visible shackles during a capital trial's penalty phase, as it does during the guilt phase, unless that use is justified by an overwhelming state interest, such as courtroom security.

FACTS: In July 1996, petitioner Deck robbed and murdered an elderly couple. The state required Deck to wear leg braces that were allegedly invisible to the jury. Deck was convicted of the crimes, but an en banc panel of the state supreme court set aside the sentence. The state then conducted a new sentencing proceeding. In the new proceeding, Deck was shackled with leg irons, handcuffs, and a belly chain. Although Deck's counsel repeatedly objected to the use of shackles, the judge overruled counsel's objections. At sentencing, Deck was again required to be placed in shackles. He was sentenced to death. Deck appealed the state's decisions, claiming that his shackling violated both Missouri law and the Federal Constitution. However, the Missouri Supreme Court disagreed, stating that: (1) the jury was not aware of the restraints; (2) there was no proof that the restraints prevented Deck from participating in his trial; and (3) there was evidence to support the claim that Deck may have been a flight risk because he was a repeat offender. Further, the State Supreme Court held that Deck had not established that the use of shackles had prejudiced the outcome of his trial at any stage of his trial. The Court reaffirmed his death sentence.

ISSUE: Does shackling a death penalty defendant during the sentencing stage of a capital case violate the due process clauses of the Fifth and Fourteenth Amendments? YES.

HOLDING: The shackling of a capital defendant during the penalty phase violates the Fifth and Fourteenth Amendments to the Constitution, unless it is justified by an overwhelming, essential state interest such as courtroom security.

REASON: "The law has long forbidden routine use of visible shackles during a capital trial's guilt phase, permitting shackling only in the presence of a special need. In light of *Holbrook*, early English cases, and lower court shackling doctrine dating back to the nineteenth century, it is now clear that this is a basic element of due process protected by the Federal Constitution. Thus, the Fifth and Fourteenth Amendments prohibit using physical restraints visible to the jury absent a trial court determination, in the exercise of its discretion, that restraints are justified by a state interest specific to the particular defendant on trial.

If the reasons motivating the guilt phase constitutional rule—the presumption of innocence, securing a meaningful defense, and maintaining dignified proceedings—apply with like force at the penalty phase, the same rule will apply there. The latter two considerations obviously apply. As for the first, while the defendant's conviction means that the presumption of innocence no longer applies, shackles at the penalty phase threaten related concerns. The jury, though no longer deciding between guilt and innocence, is deciding between life and death, which, given the sanction's severity and finality, is no less important. Nor is accuracy in making that decision any less critical. Yet the offender's appearance in shackles almost inevitably implies to a jury that court authorities consider him a danger to the community (which is often a statutory aggravator and always a relevant factor); almost inevitably affects adversely the jury's perception of the defendant's character; and thereby inevitably undermines the jury's ability to weigh accurately all relevant considerations when determining whether the defendant deserves death. The constitutional rule that courts cannot routinely place defendants in shackles or other restraints visible to the jury during the penalty phase is not absolute. In the judge's discretion, account may be taken of special circumstances in the case at hand, including security concerns, that may call for shackling in order to accommodate the important need to protect the courtroom and its occupants."

CASE SIGNIFICANCE: In *Deck*, the United States Supreme Court decided that the due process clause prohibits capital defendants from appearing before juries in shackles in either the guilt or penalty phase of a capital proceeding unless a state interest specific to the defendant, such as courtroom safety, exists. The Court began its examination of the constitutionality of visible shackling by noting that most states prohibited the practice at the guilt stage. The Court relied on three of its previous holdings—*Illinois v. Allen*, *Holbrook v. Flynn*, and *Estelle v. Williams*—all of which established the constitutional rule reflecting an early common law ban against the use of visible restraints at trial. The Court's opinion hinged on three main tenets supporting the sentencing phase shackling rule: the presumption of innocence, the right to counsel, and the maintenance of the order and stateliness of the Nation's courtrooms. In applying this approach, the Court ruled that the use of visible restraints during the sentencing stage of a capital trial violates due process and is therefore unconstitutional. However, the Court acknowledged that judges are authorized to make exceptions to this rule, such as in cases where courtroom security is at issue.

Holmes v. South Carolina
547 U.S. 319 (2006)

CAPSULE: A capital defendant's constitutional rights are violated by an evidence rule prohibiting the introduction of third-party guilt evidence when the prosecutor has produced forensic evidence strongly supporting a guilty verdict.

FACTS: Eighty-six-year-old Mary Stewart was beaten, raped, and murdered in her home on the morning of December 31, 1989. At Holmes' trial, the prosecutor relied heavily on forensic evidence linking him to the crimes. As a counter-strategy, Holmes sought the introduction of expert witness testimony indicating that the forensic evidence was tainted and that the police had intended to frame him. Additionally, Holmes alleged that another suspect, White, was in the neighborhood at the time the crimes occurred and had ostensibly incriminated himself in regard to the crimes. However, White later denied making the alleged statements and produced an alibi. Petititioner Holmes was convicted and sentenced to death. Relying on the *Gregory* rule that third-party guilt evidence must be more than bare suspicion but raise a reasonable inference of innocence, the trial court excluded petitioner's evidence. The state supreme court affirmed, citing its earlier decisions in *Gregory* and *Gay* regarding restrictions on the introduction of third-party guilt evidence. The state supreme court held that when the prosecutor produces strong forensic evidence of the defendant's guilt a defendant cannot raise a reasonable inference as to actual innocence. Therefore, the court held that Holmes could not rebut the forensic evidence against him.

ISSUE: Does an evidence rule restricting the introduction of third-party guilt evidence violate a capital defendant's right to due process, compulsory process, or confrontation of witnesses? YES.

HOLDING: An evidence rule that bars the introduction of third-party guilt evidence if a prosecutor produces strong forensic evidence of guilt violates a capital defendant's constitutional right to due process, compulsory process, and confrontation of witnesses.

REASON: "State and federal rulemakers have broad latitude under the Constitution to establish rules excluding evidence from criminal trials. This latitude, however, has limits. Whether rooted directly in the Due Process Clause of the Fourteenth Amendment or in the Compulsory Process or Confrontation clauses of the Sixth Amendment, the Constitution guarantees criminal defendants 'a meaningful opportunity to present a complete defense.' This right is abridged by evidence rules that 'infringe upon a weighty interest of the accused' and are 'arbitrary' or 'disproportionate to the purposes they are designed to serve.'"

"Interpreted in this way, the rule applied by the State Supreme Court does not rationally serve the end that the *Gregory* rule and its analogues in other jurisdictions were designed to promote, i.e., to focus the trial on the central issues by excluding evidence that has only a very weak logical connection to the central issues. The rule applied in this case appears to be based on the following logic: Where (1) it is clear that only one person was involved in the commission of a particular crime and (2) there is strong evidence that the defendant was the perpetrator, it follows that evidence of third-party guilt must be weak. But this logic depends on an accurate evaluation of the prosecution's proof, and the true strength of the prosecution's proof cannot be assessed without considering challenges to the reliability of the prosecution's evidence. Just because the prosecution's evidence, if credited, would provide strong support for a guilty verdict, it does not follow that evidence of third-party guilt has only a weak logical connection to the central issues in the case. And where the credibility of the prosecution's witnesses or the reliability of its evidence is not conceded, the strength of the prosecution's case cannot be assessed without making the sort of factual findings that have traditionally been reserved for the trier of fact and that the South Carolina courts did not purport to make in this case."

CASE SIGNIFICANCE: In Judge Alito's first Supreme Court opinion, a unanimous Court invalidated South Carolina's rule prohibiting the introduction of third-party guilt evidence as a means to rebut strong forensic evidence, as a means of suggesting the defendant's actual innocence. States have formed these doctrines to limit prejudice, potential confusion, and probativeness. Most states have similar restrictions regarding the admissibility of evidence, but South Carolina defense attorneys had long claimed that their rules were far more rigid than schemes used in other states. The Supreme Court found that South Carolina's rule was unconstitutional for several reasons. First, the state's rule in *Gay* prevented the defense, to some degree, from successfully challenging the state's case. Second, the Court determined that determinations regarding the credibility of witnesses should be left to the jury, particularly the witnesses who claimed White was the person who committed the murder. And third, the Court said that the constitution requires that a defendant be given the chance to present an adequate defense.

The significance of this case goes well beyond South Carolina's "third-party perpetrator" evidence rule. The fact that this was a capital case may have prompted Supreme Court review; however, the decision has implications for all state rules restricting the admissibility of evidence in certain instances. The Court has signaled that it is willing to consider the constitutionality of these rules in the context of due process, confrontation, and compulsory process. Further, the Court's opinion is particularly important because its reasoning is equally applicable to all criminal cases.

Internet Resources

Cornell Law School, *Chronicle Online*: "Supreme Court Unanimously Backs Cornell Law Professor John Blume's Argument in Death Penalty Case."
http://www.news.cornell.edu/stories/May06/Blume.Supreme.win.lbm.html

Death Penalty Information Center, The Federal Death Penalty
http://deathpenaltyinfo.org/article.php?scid=29&did=147

Findlaw, "A Trial Court Ruling That the Federal Death Penalty is Unconstitutional Leaves a Key Question Unanswered."
http://writ.corporate.findlaw.com/dorf/20020710.html

ACLU: Fairness and the Death Penalty
http://www.aclu.org/capital/general/10441pub19971231.html#unfair

PBS: The Death Penalty, Pro and Con
http://www.pbs.org/wgbh/pages/frontline/angel/procon/deathissue.html

Notes

1. Daniel Bird, *Life on the Line: Pondering the Fate of a Due Process Challenge to the Death Penalty*, 40 AM. CRIM. L. REV. 1329.

2. *Gregg v. Georgia*, 428 U.S. 153 (1976).

3. *Woodson v. North Carolina*, 428 U.S. 280 (1976).

4. Paul M. Dillbeck, Kelly v. South Carolina: *Extending Due Process Creates an Untenable Standard for Determining When Capital Sentencing Juries Should Be Informed of Parole Ineligibility*, 62 MD. L. REV. 143 (2003).

5. *Furman v. Georgia*, 408 U.S. 238 (1972).

6. *Trop v. Dulles*, 356 U.S. 86 (1958).

7. *Lockett v. Ohio*, 438 U.S. 586 (1978).

8. *Eddings v. Oklahoma*, 455 U.S. 104 (1982)

9. Eric W. Richardson, *Due Process Requirements of Jury Charges in Capital Cases*, 64 U. CIN. L. REV. 755 (1996).

10. *Gardner v. Florida*, 430 U.S. 349 (1977).

11. *Id.*

12. *Netherland v. Gray*, 519 U.S. 1301 (1996).

13. *Id.* at 1307.

14. Mary Sigler, *Contradiction, Coherence, and Guided Discretion in the Supreme Court's Capital Sentencing Jurisprudence*, 40 AM. CRIM. L. REV. 1151 (2003).

15. Dillbeck, *supra* note 4 at 4.

16. *Supra* note 4 at 6.

17. *Estelle v. Smith*, 451 U.S. 454 (1981).

18. Welsh White, *Government, Psychiatric Examinations and the Death Penalty*, 37 ARIZ. L. REV. 869 (1995).

19. *Buchanan v. Kentucky*, 483 U.S. 402 (1987).

20. White, *supra* note 16 at 4.

21. White, *supra* note 16 at 5.

22. *Skipper v. South Carolina*, 476 U.S. 1 (1986).

23. *California v. Ramos*, 463 U.S. 992 (1983).

24. *Sattazahn v. Pennsylvania*, 537 U.S. 101 (2003).

25. *Id.*

26. Brandon Dickerson, *Bidding Farewell ot the Ball and Chain: The United States Supreme Court Unconvincingly Prohibits Shackling in the Penalty Phase in Deck v. Missouri*, 39 CREIGHTON L. REV. 741 (2006).

27. 544 U.S. 622 (2005).

28. 425 U.S. 560 (1986).

29. 397 U.S. 337 (1970).

30. 475 U.S. 560 (1986).

31. Cranburne's Case, 13 How. St. Tr. 222, indicating that the practice of shackling "could interfere with a defendant's right to participate in his own defense."

32. *Deck*, 544 U.S. 626.

33. *Holmes*, 547 U.S. 319 (2006).

34. Klein, *Richard, Eighteenth Annual Supreme Court Review: Death Penalty and Right to Counsel Decisions in the October 2005 Term*, 22 TOURO L. REV. 1003 (2007).

35. *Supra* note 5.

36. Andrew Seigel, *A Tale of 2 Terms: A Transitional Year for the United States Supreme Court*, 18 S. CAROLINA LAWYER 30 (2006).

37. 541 S.E.2d 541 (S.C. 2001).

38. 547 U.S. 327.

39. J.H. Blume, S.L. Johnson, and E.C. Paavola, *Every Juror Wants a Story: Narrative Relevance, Third Party Guilt and the Right to Present a Defense*, 44 AM. CRIM. L. REV. 1069 (2007).

40. *Supra* note 8.

Chapter Outline

I. **Introduction**

II. ***Gregg v. Georgia* and the Emerging Importance of Aggravating and Mitigating Factors**

III. **Aggravating Factors**
   - A. General Procedural Requirements
   - B. Vagueness and Guided (or Unguided) Discretion
   - C. The Special Case of Victim Impact Statements
   - D. The Special Case of Future Dangerousness

IV. **Mitigating Factors**
   - A. General Procedural Requirements
   - B. Evidence Allowed
   - C. Jury Instructions

V. **In Summary, What Do these Cases Say?**

VI. **Conclusion**

Cases Briefed in Chapter 9

Case Briefs

Internet Resources

Notes

Chapter 9

Aggravating and Mitigating Factors in Death Penalty Cases

I. Introduction

In *Gregg v. Georgia* (1976),[1] the Supreme Court noted that "death is different." The Court approved death penalty statutes with adequate procedural safeguards to ensure that only the most serious cases receive the ultimate punishment. A major requirement of statutes in the wake of *Gregg* is that they narrow the range of cases for which the death penalty could be an option. The death penalty is to be reserved for only the most extreme acts of violence. Moreover, the Court requires individualized consideration in the application of the death penalty—each case and defendant are to be considered separately in deciding whether death is an appropriate punishment. The Court therefore struck down mandatory death penalty statutes in Louisiana (*Roberts v. Louisiana*, 1976)[2] and North Carolina (*Woodson v. North Carolina*, 1976)[3] which, although potentially narrowing the death-eligible crimes, did not allow individual consideration in the penalty decision. The central features of both the narrowing and individualization features of death penalty statutes consist of aggravating and mitigating factors.[4]

This chapter focuses on procedural issues inherent in the consideration of aggravating and mitigating factors required in capital cases. The Supreme Court has had much to say about these special factors since it approved them in *Gregg v. Georgia* in 1976. The nature of capital trials (particularly the penalty phase) is to a great degree shaped by aggravating and mitigating factors and the Supreme Court's many decisions surrounding them. In the sections that follow, the Supreme Court's decisions will be analyzed to determine how they have shaped death penalty law and capital trial procedure. Further, the many constitutional issues that have arisen in the context of "special" factors and what the Supreme Court has said about them will be considered. But first, death penalty statutes and the role of aggravating and mitigating factors in capital punishment schemes are addressed.

II. *Gregg v. Georgia* and the Emerging Importance of Aggravating and Mitigating Factors

Prior to the abolition of the death penalty in *Furman v. Georgia* (1972),[5] death penalty statutes varied widely by state in regard to the consideration of "special" factors or circumstances calling for death or mercy. Juries were given very little, if any, guidance when considering such factors, if presented. Rather, the decision of whether to sentence a defendant to death was left to the "judgment, conscience, and absolute discretion of the jury."[6] The lack of consistent and formal standards in the structure of death penalty statutes and the "unfettered discretion" that resulted were, in part, the bases for the Supreme Court's decision in *Furman* declaring the death penalty, as administered at the time, unconstitutional. When the death penalty was reinstated in *Gregg v. Georgia* (1976), a new approach to capital cases emerged—one that requires the consideration of special factors in determining whether a defendant should be sentenced to death or life in prison. These factors are referred to as aggravating and mitigating factors.

Aggravating factors are those that make the offense or the offender particularly "worthy" of a penalty as extreme as death. This narrowed the range of murders for which the penalty of death is appropriate. These aggravating factors may come into play at multiple points in the capital trial process and generally revolve around three factors: (1) characteristics of the offense, (2) characteristics of the offender, and (3) characteristics of the victim.[7] The two primary functions of aggravating factors are: (1) restricting eligibility for the death penalty (the eligibility function); and (2) guiding the selection of those for whom the death penalty is appropriate (the individualization function). The eligibility function primarily exists prior to the sentencing phase of capital trials and acts as a filter ensuring that the death penalty is available in only the most extreme cases. Virginia's death penalty statute, for example, lists 15 "aggravated" offenses that constitute capital murder.[8] Some examples that are typical of death penalty statutes are murder during a kidnapping, murder during the commission of felony, murder of a police officer, and multiple murders. Aggravating factors also play a significant role in the sentencing phase of capital trials and thus perform that second function of guiding the selection of defendants for the death penalty. Aggravating factors may be explicitly listed in the statute for the jury to consider, or they may be non-statutory factors presented by the prosecution for the jury's consideration in determining the appropriate punishment. Some examples of aggravating factors serving this individual selection function are whether the murder was particularly brutal or "heinous," whether the offender has a history of violence, and whether the offender is likely to be a danger to society in the future.

Mitigating circumstances are those that provide some level of explanation or justification (but not excuse or defense of the act) for the murder and are reserved for the sentencing phase of capital trials. Common mitigating circumstances are cognitive deficits or a history of the defendant's own violent victimization. As with aggravating factors, mitigating factors can be statutory (meaning they are specifically listed in a state's death penalty statute) or non-statutory. Mitigating factors may also come in the form of refutations to common aggravating factors. For example, factors such as a lack of criminal or violent history or good adjustment to institutional life in jail or prison may be presented to indicate a lack of what would otherwise be potentially aggravating factors in the minds of capital jurors.

Consideration of both aggravating and mitigating circumstances was approved as a necessary procedural safeguard when the Court upheld the "guided discretion" statutes of Florida, Georgia, and Texas in 1976 (See Figure 9.1 for excerpts of each of these states' current statutes). Each of these statutes, however, provided a different framework for the consideration of these factors in the sentencing phase of capital trials. As a result, there are various ways in which states institute aggravating and mitigating circumstances into their death penalty law and capital trial procedure. The Supreme Court, although strictly requiring the inclusion of aggravating and mitigating factors, left up to the states the specific structure and framework within which such considerations would occur. Bohm, using the Florida, Georgia, and Texas statutes (the three statutes the Supreme Court originally approved in *Gregg v. Georgia*) as examples, identifies three types of guided discretion statutes pertaining to their treatment of aggravating and mitigating circumstances: (1) aggravating versus mitigating, (2) aggravating only, and (3) structured discretion.[9]

Aggravating versus mitigating death penalty statutes are those that require the jury to first consider whether any aggravating factors exist. Upon finding the presence of at least one aggravating factor, the jury then considers both statutory and non-statutory mitigating factors and weighs the aggravating factors against the mitigating factors. If, in the minds of the jurors, mitigating factors do not outweigh aggravating factors, then the appropriate sentence is death. It is important to note that this is not simply a call to enumerate the aggravating and mitigating factors and base the sentence on which set of factors is greatest. Rather, it is up to the jurors to apply what they believe to be appropriate weights to each particular factor. Florida's death penalty statute is an example of the aggravating versus mitigating scheme (See Figure 9.1).

Aggravating only statutes require a jury to consider statutory aggravating factors and then decide whether those factors warrant the death penalty. In contrast to the aggravating versus mitigating form of statute, the jury is not required to consider mitigating factors and may decide to impose either a death sentence or life imprisonment based solely on their consideration of aggravating factors. Mitigating factors are generally not listed in the statute but may be considered by the jury prior to sentencing. Georgia's death penalty statute is an example of the aggravating only form of statute (See Figure 9.1).

Structured discretion statutes, the rarest form of death penalty statute, call upon a jury to answer specific questions after hearing all relevant evidence presented as either aggravating factors or mitigating factors during the sentencing phase of the trial. The answers to these questions determine the sentence. In Texas, for example (See Figure 9.1), the jury is asked to answer "yes" or "no" to two questions: one pertaining to the likelihood of the defendant presenting a future danger to society and the other pertaining to whether the defendant directly committed the murder in question. If the jury unanimously answers "yes" to both questions, it is then asked a third question regarding whether there are sufficient mitigating factors to warrant mercy in the case and thus a lesser sentence of life in prison. If all 12 jurors answer "no" to this question, a death sentence is imposed.[10] The Texas statute has recently drawn attention by the United States Supreme Court that, in the cases of *Brewer v. Quarterman* and *Abdul-Kabir v. Quarterman* (2007)[11], held that capital sentencing statutes cannot restrict a jury from giving, and being instructed to give, full consideration to all relevant mitigating evidence. Juries must be instructed, beyond a simple verbatim reading of the statutory special issues, to consider all mitigating evidence presented during the sentencing hearing.

The United States Supreme Court has generally deferred to states in how they set up their capital sentencing schemes as long as the state statute allows for due consideration of both aggravating and mitigating factors. This fact is illuminated in the recent case of *Kansas v. Marsh* (2006).[12] In *Kansas v. Marsh*, the Court considered whether the Kansas capital sentencing statute, which requires the imposition of the death penalty when a unanimous jury finds that aggravating and mitigating factors are in equipoise (i.e., are, in the minds of the jurors, equal in weight). This was the first time the Court was faced with this issue as the weighing function has generally been concerned with whether there are more or fewer aggravating factors in comparison to mitigating factors. The Supreme Court decided that Kansas' statute is constitutional. In spite of arguments that such a sentencing scheme creates a presumption in the favor of death, the Court held that it is constitutional to impose the death penalty as long as mitigating factors do not outweigh aggravating factors even if that means that they are at equivalent levels.[13]

Figure 9.1
Texas, Georgia, and Florida Death Penalty Statutes

Texas

Texas Code of Criminal Procedure

Art 37.071. Procedure in capital case.

Sec. 2. (a) If a defendant is tried for a capital offense in which the state seeks the death penalty, on a finding that the defendant is guilty of a capital offense, the court shall conduct a separate sentencing proceeding to determine whether the defendant shall be sentenced to death or life imprisonment. The proceeding shall be conducted in the trial court and, except as provided by Article 44.29(c) of this code, before the trial jury as soon as practicable. In the proceeding, evidence may be presented by the state and the defendant or the defendant's counsel as to any matter that the court deems relevant to sentence, including evidence of the defendant's background or character or the circumstances of the offense that mitigates against the imposition of the death penalty. This subsection shall not be construed to authorize the introduction of any evidence secured in violation of the Constitution of the United States or of the State of Texas. The state and the defendant or the defendant's counsel shall be permitted to present argument for or against sentence of death. The court, the attorney representing the state, the defendant, or the defendant's counsel may not inform a juror or a prospective juror of the effect of a failure of a jury to agree on issues submitted under Subsection (c) or (e) of this article.

(b) On conclusion of the presentation of the evidence, the court shall submit the following issues to the jury:

(1) whether there is a probability that the defendant would commit criminal acts of violence that would constitute a continuing threat to society; and

(2) in cases in which the jury charge at the guilt or innocence stage permitted the jury to find the defendant guilty as a party under Sections 7.01 and 7.02, Penal Code, whether the defendant actually caused the death of the deceased or did not actually cause the death of the deceased but intended to kill the deceased or another or anticipated that a human life would be taken.

(c) The state must prove each issue submitted under Subsection (b) of this article beyond a reasonable doubt, and the jury shall return a special verdict of "yes" or "no" on each issue submitted under Subsection (b) of this Article.

(d) The court shall charge the jury that:

(1) in deliberating on the issues submitted under Subsection (b) of this article, it shall consider all evidence admitted at the guilt or innocence stage and the punishment stage, including evidence of the defendant's background or character or the circumstances of the offense that militates for or mitigates against the imposition of the death penalty;

(2) it may not answer any issue submitted under Subsection (b) of this article "yes" unless it agrees unanimously and it may not answer any issue "no" unless 10 or more jurors agree; and

(3) members of the jury need not agree on what particular evidence supports a negative answer to any issue submitted under Subsection (b) of this article.

Figure 9.1, *continued*

(e)(1) The court shall instruct the jury that if the jury returns an affirmative finding to each issue submitted under Subsection (b) of this article, it shall answer the following issue:

Whether, taking into consideration all of the evidence, including the circumstances of the offense, the defendant's character and background, and the personal moral culpability of the defendant, there is a sufficient mitigating circumstance or circumstances to warrant that a sentence of life imprisonment rather than a death sentence be imposed.

(2) The court, on the written request of the attorney representing the defendant, shall:

    (A) instruct the jury that if the jury answers that a circumstance or circumstances warrant that a sentence of life imprisonment rather than a death sentence be imposed, the court will sentence the defendant to imprisonment in the institutional division of the Texas Department of Criminal Justice for life; and

  (B) charge the jury in writing as follows:

    "Under the law applicable in this case, if the defendant is sentenced to imprisonment in the institutional division of the Texas Department of Criminal Justice for life, the defendant will become eligible for release on parole, but not until the actual time served by the defendant equals 40 years, without consideration of any good conduct time. It cannot accurately be predicted how the parole laws might be applied to this defendant if the defendant is sentenced to a term of imprisonment for life because the application of those laws will depend on decisions made by prison and parole authorities, but eligibility for parole does not guarantee that parole will be granted."

(f) The court shall charge the jury that in answering the issue submitted under Subsection (e) of this article, the jury:

(1) shall answer the issue "yes" or "no";

(2) may not answer the issue "no" unless it agrees unanimously and may not answer the issue "yes" unless 10 or more jurors agree;

(3) need not agree on what particular evidence supports an affirmative finding on the issue; and

(4) shall consider mitigating evidence to be evidence that a juror might regard as reducing the defendant's moral blameworthiness.

(g) If the jury returns an affirmative finding on each issue submitted under Subsection (b) of this article and a negative finding on an issue submitted under Subsection (e) of this article, the court shall sentence the defendant to death. If the jury returns a negative finding on any issue submitted under Subsection (b) of this article or an affirmative finding on an issue submitted under Subsection (e) of this article or is unable to answer any issue submitted under Subsection

Figure 9.1, *continued*

(b) or (e) of this article, the court shall sentence the defendant to confinement in the institutional division of the Texas Department of Criminal Justice for life.

(h) The judgment of conviction and sentence of death shall be subject to automatic review by the Court of Criminal Appeals.

(i) This article applies to the sentencing procedure in a capital case for an offense that is committed on or after September 1, 1991. For the purposes of this section, an offense is committed on or after September 1, 1991, if any element of that offense occurs on or after that date.

Georgia

Code of Georgia

§ 17-10-30. Procedure for imposition of death penalty generally.

(b) In all cases of other offenses for which the death penalty may be authorized, the judge shall consider, or he shall include in his instructions to the jury for it to consider, any mitigating circumstances or aggravating circumstances otherwise authorized by law and any of the following statutory aggravating circumstances which may be supported by the evidence:

(1) The offense of murder, rape, armed robbery, or kidnapping was committed by a person with a prior record of conviction for a capital felony;

(2) The offense of murder, rape, armed robbery, or kidnapping was committed while the offender was engaged in the commission of another capital felony or aggravated battery, or the offense of murder was committed while the offender was engaged in the commission of burglary or arson in the first degree;

(3) The offender, by his act of murder, armed robbery, or kidnapping, knowingly created a great risk of death to more than one person in a public place by means of a weapon or device which would normally be hazardous to the lives of more than one person;

(4) The offender committed the offense of murder for himself or another, for the purpose of receiving money or any other thing of monetary value;

(5) The murder of a judicial officer, former judicial officer, district attorney or solicitor-general, or former district attorney, solicitor, or solicitor-general was committed during or because of the exercise of his or her official duties;

(6) The offender caused or directed another to commit murder or committed murder as an agent or employee of another person;

(7) The offense of murder, rape, armed robbery, or kidnapping was outrageously or wantonly vile, horrible, or inhuman in that it involved torture, depravity of mind, or an aggravated battery to the victim;

(8) The offense of murder was committed against any peace officer, corrections employee, or firefighter while engaged in the performance of his official duties;

(9) The offense of murder was committed by a person in, or who has escaped from, the lawful custody of a peace officer or place of lawful confinement;

(10) The murder was committed for the purpose of avoiding, interfering with, or preventing a lawful arrest or custody in a place of lawful confinement, of himself or another; or

Figure 9.1, *continued*

(11) The offense of murder, rape, or kidnapping was committed by a person previously convicted of rape, aggravated sodomy, aggravated child molestation, or aggravated sexual battery.

(c) The statutory instructions as determined by the trial judge to be warranted by the evidence shall be given in charge and in writing to the jury for its deliberation. The jury, if its verdict is a recommendation of death, shall designate in writing, signed by the foreman of the jury, the aggravating circumstance or circumstances which it found beyond a reasonable doubt. In nonjury cases the judge shall make such designation. Except in cases of treason or aircraft hijacking, unless at least one of the statutory aggravating circumstances enumerated in subsection (b) of this Code section is so found, the death penalty shall not be imposed.

Florida

Florida Statutes

§ 921.141. Sentence of death or life imprisonment for capital felonies; further proceedings to determine sentence

(1) Separate proceedings on issue of penalty.—Upon conviction or adjudication of guilt of a defendant of a capital felony, the court shall conduct a separate sentencing proceeding to determine whether the defendant should be sentenced to death or life imprisonment as authorized by s. 775.082. The proceeding shall be conducted by the trial judge before the trial jury as soon as practicable. If, through impossibility or inability, the trial jury is unable to reconvene for a hearing on the issue of penalty, having determined the guilt of the accused, the trial judge may summon a special juror or jurors as provided in chapter 913 to determine the issue of the imposition of the penalty. If the trial jury has been waived, or if the defendant pleaded guilty, the sentencing proceeding shall be conducted before a jury impaneled for that purpose, unless waived by the defendant. In the proceeding, evidence may be presented as to any matter that the court deems relevant to the nature of the crime and the character of the defendant and shall include matters relating to any of the aggravating or mitigating circumstances enumerated in subsections (5) and (6). Any such evidence which the court deems to have probative value may be received, regardless of its admissibility under the exclusionary rules of evidence, provided the defendant is accorded a fair opportunity to rebut any hearsay statements. However, this subsection shall not be construed to authorize the introduction of any evidence secured in violation of the Constitution of the United States or the Constitution of the State of Florida. The state and the defendant or the defendant's counsel shall be permitted to present argument for or against sentence of death.

(2) ADVISORY SENTENCE BY THE JURY.—After hearing all the evidence, the jury shall deliberate and render an advisory sentence to the court, based upon the following matters:

(a) Whether sufficient aggravating circumstances exist as enumerated in subsection (5);

(b) Whether sufficient mitigating circumstances exist which outweigh the aggravating circumstances found to exist; and

Figure 9.1, *continued*

(c) Based on these considerations, whether the defendant should be sentenced to life imprisonment or death.

(3) FINDINGS IN SUPPORT OF SENTENCE OF DEATH.—Notwithstanding the recommendation of a majority of the jury, the court, after weighing the aggravating and mitigating circumstances, shall enter a sentence of life imprisonment or death, but if the court imposes a sentence of death, it shall set forth in writing its findings upon which the sentence of death is based as to the facts:

(a) That sufficient aggravating circumstances exist as enumerated in subsection (5), and

(b) That there are insufficient mitigating circumstances to outweigh the aggravating circumstances.

In each case in which the court imposes the death sentence, the determination of the court shall be supported by specific written findings of fact based upon the circumstances in subsections (5) and (6) and upon the records of the trial and the sentencing proceedings. If the court does not make the findings requiring the death sentence within 30 days after the rendition of the judgment and sentence, the court shall impose sentence of life imprisonment in accordance with s. 775.082.

(4) REVIEW OF JUDGMENT AND SENTENCE.—The judgment of conviction and sentence of death shall be subject to automatic review by the Supreme Court of Florida and disposition rendered within 2 years after the filing of a notice of appeal. Such review by the Supreme Court shall have priority over all other cases and shall be heard in accordance with rules promulgated by the Supreme Court.

(5) AGGRAVATING CIRCUMSTANCES.—Aggravating circumstances shall be limited to the following:

(a) The capital felony was committed by a person previously convicted of a felony and under sentence of imprisonment or placed on community control or on felony probation.

(b) The defendant was previously convicted of another capital felony or of a felony involving the use or threat of violence to the person.

(c) The defendant knowingly created a great risk of death to many persons.

(d) The capital felony was committed while the defendant was engaged, or was an accomplice, in the commission of, or an attempt to commit, or flight after committing or attempting to commit, any: robbery; sexual battery; aggravated child abuse; abuse of an elderly person or disabled adult resulting in great bodily harm, permanent disability, or permanent disfigurement; arson; burglary; kidnapping; aircraft piracy; or unlawful throwing, placing, or discharging of a destructive device or bomb.

(e) The capital felony was committed for the purpose of avoiding or preventing a lawful arrest or effecting an escape from custody.

(f) The capital felony was committed for pecuniary gain.

(g) The capital felony was committed to disrupt or hinder the lawful exercise of any governmental function or the enforcement of laws.

Figure 9.1, *continued*

(h) The capital felony was especially heinous, atrocious, or cruel.

(i) The capital felony was a homicide and was committed in a cold, calculated, and premeditated manner without any pretense of moral or legal justification.

(j) The victim of the capital felony was a law enforcement officer engaged in the performance of his or her official duties.

(k) The victim of the capital felony was an elected or appointed public official engaged in the performance of his or her official duties if the motive for the capital felony was related, in whole or in part, to the victim's official capacity.

(l) The victim of the capital felony was a person less than 12 years of age.

(m) The victim of the capital felony was particularly vulnerable due to advanced age or disability, or because the defendant stood in a position of familial or custodial authority over the victim.

(n) The capital felony was committed by a criminal street gang member, as defined in s. 874.03.

(o) The capital felony was committed by a person designated as a sexual predator pursuant to s. 775.21 or a person previously designated as a sexual predator who had the sexual predator designation removed.

(6) MITIGATING CIRCUMSTANCES.—Mitigating circumstances shall be the following:

(a) The defendant has no significant history of prior criminal activity.

(b) The capital felony was committed while the defendant was under the influence of extreme mental or emotional disturbance.

(c) The victim was a participant in the defendant's conduct or consented to the act.

(d) The defendant was an accomplice in the capital felony committed by another person and his or her participation was relatively minor.

(e) The defendant acted under extreme duress or under the substantial domination of another person.

(f) The capacity of the defendant to appreciate the criminality of his or her conduct or to conform his or her conduct to the requirements of law was substantially impaired.

(g) The age of the defendant at the time of the crime.

(h) The existence of any other factors in the defendant's background that would mitigate against imposition of the death penalty.

(7) VICTIM IMPACT EVIDENCE.—Once the prosecution has provided evidence of the existence of one or more aggravating circumstances as described in subsection (5), the prosecution may introduce, and subsequently argue, victim impact evidence. Such evidence shall be designed to demonstrate the victim's uniqueness as an individual human being and the resultant loss to the community's members by the victim's death. Characterizations and opinions about the crime, the defendant, and the appropriate sentence shall not be permitted as a part of victim impact evidence.

(8) APPLICABILITY.—This section does not apply to a person convicted or adjudicated guilty of a capital drug trafficking felony under s. 893.135.

Although aggravating and mitigating factors have been included in death penalty procedures in the United States since they were established in *Gregg v. Georgia* (1976), serious issues have been raised regarding their implementation. Many capital cases heard by the Supreme Court have revolved around procedural and statutory issues involving aggravating and mitigating circumstances. These cases and what the Supreme Court has said over the years regarding aggravating and mitigating circumstances are discussed in the following two sections.

III. Aggravating Factors

A. General Procedural Requirements

In *Gregg v. Georgia* (1976),[14] the Supreme Court required that statutes adequately narrow the range of cases in which the death penalty may be imposed and that the jury's sentencing discretion be sufficiently guided by the consideration of aggravating factors. The Court also maintained that these aggravating factors must be stated and defined in a manner that is not overly vague or broad so as to adequately inform the jury of the specific factors guiding their decision. Although the Supreme Court, in *Gregg v. Georgia*, laid down these broad requirements pertaining to aggravating factors and their role in capital trials, specific processes for implementing these requirements were not prescribed by the Court. In the years that followed, the Supreme Court elaborated on and clarified these requirements.

Early on in the years following *Gregg*, the Supreme Court reaffirmed the requirement of aggravating circumstances. In *Presnell v. Georgia* (1978),[15] the Court held that at least one statutory aggravating circumstance must be found to exist beyond a reasonable doubt in order for the death penalty to be imposed. Furthermore, unanimity is generally required in a jury's determination of aggravating factors. The ultimate sentencing decision is not limited only to those unanimously found to be aggravating circumstances listed in the state's statute, however. In *Barclay v. Florida* (1983),[16] the Supreme Court established that when at least one statutory aggravating circumstance is found beyond a reasonable doubt, any aggravating factor, statutory and non-statutory, can be considered in sentencing a capital defendant.

Although a statutory aggravating factor is required for the imposition of the death penalty, it does not mandate that the death penalty be imposed. A jury may find aggravating circumstances in a trial but still decide against the death penalty. As we will see later in the chapter, one reason for not imposing the death penalty may be a jury finding that mitigating factors are present. But even where jurors find no mitigating circumstances, their determination that aggravating factors are present usually does not preclude them from giving a sentence less than death. However, in *Blystone v. Pennsylvania* (1990),[17] the Supreme Court upheld Pennsylvania's statute mandating a death sentence when at least one aggravating factor and no mitigating factors are found. Although seemingly contradicting its previously strong stance against any form of mandatory death penalty,[18] the Supreme Court concluded that sufficient individualization in the sentencing decision exists under such statutes. As seen in the next section, however, even in cases in which such mandates do not exist, jurors are often left to believe that they must impose the death penalty in such circumstances.

B. Vagueness and Guided (or Unguided) Discretion

The cases that came later to the Supreme Court dealt more with the substance and clarity of aggravating factors. A central concern of the Court in *Gregg* was that aggravating factors not be overly broad or vague so as to apply to virtually all murder cases and leave the jury with unbridled discretion and a lack of real guidance. Georgia's statute provided the following aggravating factor: "[if the murder was] outrageously wanton or vile, horrible or inhuman in that it involved torture, depravity of mind or an aggravated battery to the victim."[19] Although the Court upheld Georgia's death penalty statute, it warned that such aggravating factors and the language used were too broad and vague but left it to Georgia and other states to adequately specify aggravating factors that would appropriately narrow death penalty eligibility and guide capital juries' decisions. The Court again warned against vague language in *Godfrey v. Georgia* (1980),[20] holding that the meaning of statutory aggravating circumstances must be adequately clarified and applied independently to the facts of the particular case. Nevertheless, concerns were raised about vague and overly broad wording in aggravating factors and the fact that juries were not being given adequate guidance when considering aggravating factors in capital cases. Many death penalty statutes include some variation of the Georgia statute's wording, about which the Supreme Court expressed such concern. The Supreme Court has decided numerous cases addressing claims of overly broad and vague aggravating factors, but these decisions have not been all that clear or consistent.

In spite of the Supreme Court's rejection of overly broad and vague aggravating factors and its call for sentencing schemes that "suitably direct and limit" sentencing discretion to minimize the arbitrariness and capriciousness of the application of the death sentence, its later decisions exhibited what many consider a loosening of such standards. In *Lewis v. Jeffers* (1990),[21] the Court held that the phrase "especially heinous, cruel or depraved manner" was not unconstitutionally vague and sufficiently guided the sentencing authority. In spite of extant research raising concerns about juror confusion[22] and the proclaimed need for guidance in capital cases, the Supreme Court went on to approve increasingly vague descriptions of aggravating factors and refused to require increased clarification in the process of capital trials. In *Arave v. Creech* (1993),[23] the Court held that the phrase "utter disregard for human life" used as a statutory aggravating factor sufficiently limited sentencing discretion and therefore was deemed not to be in violation of Eighth and Fourteenth Amendment rights. The Court further upheld, in *Tuilaepa v. California* (1994),[24] factors such as the circumstances of the crime, the defendant's history of violent crime, and the defendant's age as not overly broad or vague and therefore constitutional as factors considered in the sentencing phase of a capital trial.

The Court has increasingly approved the inclusion of more and more aggravating factors in the sentencing phase of capital trials, many of which may be characterized as vague. However, the guidance a jury receives in considering aggravating factors, a notion emphasized in *Gregg v. Georgia*, has been the most recent casualty of the Supreme Court's jurisprudence on aggravating factors in capital cases. In *Tuilaepa v. California* (1994),[25] the Court held that capital juries need not be given instructions on how to weigh the various sentencing factors presented. In *Weeks v. Angelone* (2000)[26] the Court determined that upon request by the jury, the judge is not required to further clarify sentencing requirements beyond reference to the actual words of the jury instructions (The actual instructions used had previously been approved by the Supreme Court in *Buchanan v. Angelone*, 1998).[27] In *Weeks* the jury mistakenly believed that the presence of one of two aggravating circumstances required the jury to impose a death sentence, when in fact the law stated that the presence of such a factor only indicated that the death penalty was appropriate. After indicating their confusion to the judge and the fact that they were basing their decision on misunderstood instructions, the jurors received only a re-reading of the instructions about which they were confused. Research has shown that such confusion and misperception on the part of capital jurors are not isolated occurrences.[28] Nevertheless, the Supreme Court has consistently supported states' refusals to clarify the actual law so that jurors adequately understand their duties and responsibilities in capital sentencing.

C. *The Special Case of Victim Impact Statements*

The role of victims in capital cases has changed significantly in the past decade. Traditionally, victims were virtually absent from capital trials. Their role was often relegated to that of observers in court and in some instances they were allowed to prepare a written victim impact statement that would be presented to the judge along with a pre-sentencing report. Because in a majority of capital cases juries decided the sentence, the voice of victims often went unheard and had no impact on sentencing. The Supreme Court played a direct role in keeping it this way. In the late 1980s, the Supreme Court decided two cases regarding victim impact statements, condemning their use in both. In *Booth v. Maryland* (1987),[29] the Court declared that the introduction of victim impact statements violated the defendant's Eighth Amendment protections from cruel and unusual punishment. In *South Carolina v. Gathers* (1989),[30] the Court was more specific and held that the prosecution's reading of a prayer found in the victim's possession and statements regarding personal characteristics of the victim violated the Eighth Amendment.

This all changed with the Supreme Court's landmark decision in *Payne v. Tennessee* (1991).[31] Overruling, in part, both the *Booth* and *Gathers* decisions, The Court held that the admission of victim impact statements in the sentencing phase of a capital trial does not constitute an Eighth Amendment violation as long as the information presented does not violate principles of fundamental fairness for the defendant. The Court qualified its decision, stating that only statements regarding characteristics of the victim and the emotional impact of the crime on the victim's family are permissible during the sentencing phase of capital trials. Statements characterizing the crime or the defendant would not be allowed.

The *Payne* decision caused extensive controversy about the appropriate role of victim impact evidence in capital trials. Although some applaud it for bringing the victims' voices into the capital sentencing process and as a step toward victim-focused justice, many have criticized it as further inflaming jurors and thus leading to death sentences based on emotional reactions as opposed to neutral and objective reasoning.[32]

Opponents of the inclusion of victim impact statements in capital cases are not insensitive to the needs of victims of such horrible crimes, however, and do not wish them to be removed from the criminal justice process altogether. On the contrary, many have noted that victim impact statements and other victim impact evidence do not, in fact, serve the interests of victims and victims' survivors well. One legal scholar argues that "[a]lthough such testimony invariably serves the prosecution's goal of procuring a death sentence, the opportunity to testify does not address most of the needs of the survivors of murder that could be met by the criminal justice process."[33]

D. The Special Case of Future Dangerousness

A final issue, and one that plays a central role in many capital cases, relates to the future dangerousness of the defendant or the likelihood that he or she will pose a violent threat to the public in the future. Although research has shown that the ability of psychiatrists and psychologists to predict future dangerousness is generally no better than chance,[34] death sentences often hinge on such "expert" determinations of this aggravating factor. In fact, in Texas and Oregon, the key question on which the jury's sentencing decision relies is whether the defendant is likely to present a future danger to society.[35] It was a Texas case that brought the issue of future dangerousness to the forefront of the jurisprudential landscape.

In *Barefoot v. Estelle* (1983), the Supreme Court addressed Texas's sentencing scheme, which required a jury to unanimously answer "yes" to a question asking "whether there is a probability that the defendant would commit criminal acts of violence that would constitute a continuing threat to society."[36] The case centered around the role of psychiatric and psychological experts in making these determinations and the admissibility of the associated evidence of future dangerousness. In spite of research findings[37], amicus briefs filed by the American Psychiatric Association contesting the accuracy of such predictions, and the Court's own admission that "[p]sychiatrists simply have no expertise in predicting long-term future dangerousness,"[38] the Supreme Court held that psychiatric evidence on the prediction of future dangerousness is admissible at the sentencing phase of a capital case.

Barefoot v. Estelle has proved to be the final word on the admissibility of testimony about future dangerousness. To this day, death sentences are often determined primarily based on testimony regarding, and jurors' perceptions of, the future dangerousness of the defendant.[39] Some scholars have pointed out that whether explicitly provided by statute or simply argued by the prosecution, future dangerousness is "always at issue" in capital cases.[40] The role of experts in determining and testifying to future dangerousness has become increasingly central to a state's ability to evoke death sentences. In Texas for example, one psychiatrist, Dr. Grigson, came to be known as "Dr. Death" because he testified for the state in more than 100 capital cases in which he pronounced the defendant a future threat to society, often declaring with 100 percent (and in some cases 1000 percent!) certainty that the defendant would kill again. In 1995, Dr. Grigson was expelled from the American Psychiatric Association for arriving at these conclusions without actually examining the defendants.[41]

IV. Mitigating Factors

In addition to the presence of aggravating factors, jurors' decisions in capital cases are guided further by consideration of mitigating circumstances or factors that may warrant mercy or leniency in the determination of whether the defendant will receive the death penalty. The inclusion of mitigating factors in capital sentencing furthers the goal set forth in *Gregg* of guiding capital juries' discretion and narrowing the use of the death penalty only on those deemed most deserving. Mitigating factors in capital trials exist solely in the sentencing phase, with specific focus on the defendant and whether he or she should receive the death penalty. These factors often revolve around personal history, such as whether the defendant experienced abuse as a child or experienced other trauma as a result of an adverse environment. Specific characteristics may also come into play—age, cognitive deficits, and mental illness are common mitigating factors. Finally, predictions of the future are also often presented as mitigating factors. The defendant's ability to adapt to institutional life and lack of threat of future violence may be raised in mitigation. As with aggravating factors, the Supreme Court has spent a great deal of time considering the appropriate procedural requirements and substance of mitigating factors in capital trials.

A. General Procedural Requirements

Although the Supreme Court in *Gregg* said that the sentencing authority in capital cases must consider mitigating factors before determining the sentence, little guidance has been given as to specific requirements. In a pair of Ohio cases (*Lockett v. Ohio*, 1978[42]; *Bell v. Ohio*, 1978[43]) decided two years after *Gregg*, the Supreme Court declared that both statutory and non-statutory mitigating circumstances may be presented by the defense and all presented mitigating factors must be considered in the sentencing phase of trial. This was an important advance from the general provision of mitigating factors indicated in *Gregg*. In *Hitchcock v. Dugger* (1987),[44] the Supreme Court reaffirmed *Lockett* and *Bell*, stating that jurors may not refuse to consider any relevant mitigating evidence—they must consider all statutory and non-statutory mitigating circumstances appropriately presented. In *Parker v. Dugger* (1991),[45] the Court extended this to judges who either make the final sentencing decision or override a jury's recommendation of a sentence less than death. It was held that all sentencing authorities (judges or panels of judges in addition to juries) must consider all statutory and non-statutory mitigating evidence previously presented.

A decade later, in *Mills v. Maryland* (1988)[46] and *McKoy v. North Carolina* (1990),[47] the Court held that the jury does not need to be unanimous in determining the presence of mitigating circumstances and that sentencing instructions requiring unanimity on the presence of a mitigating circumstance are unconstitutional. Although such unanimity is not required for individual jurors to consider particular mitigating circumstances in weighing factors toward their decision, states are allowed to require some level of agreement among jurors regarding the presence of mitigating factors. For example, Texas law requires that 10 of the 12 jurors agree that mitigating factors warrant a life sentence rather than a sentence of death.[48]

B. Evidence Allowed

The Supreme Court has generally held that just about any relevant mitigating factors must be allowed to be presented and accordingly considered by the sentencing authority (usually the jury). The Court has periodically been confronted by statutes and trial procedures that deny this right. In *Eddings v. Oklahoma* (1982),[49] the Court held that refusal to allow family history as a mitigating factor in the sentencing phase of a capital trial is unconstitutional. This watershed case opened the door to a wide array of information and evidence that could be presented as mitigating evidence in capital trials. History of abuse, neglect, and childhood trauma are now mainstays of mitigation in the sentencing phase of capital trials. In *Penry v. Lynaugh* (1989),[50] the Court further specified that a defendant's mental retardation and child abuse victimization must be considered, if presented, as mitigating factors and that a trial court's refusal to instruct the jury to this effect is unconstitutional.

In *Skipper v. South Carolina* (1986),[51] the Court addressed a different form of mitigating evidence—that relating to current and future circumstances. As mentioned previously, future dangerousness is a key element in many capital cases, usually presented as an aggravating factor that justifies imposing the death penalty. In *Skipper*, however, the Court considered whether evidence that the defendant had adjusted well to incarceration (i.e., was not violent or likely to be violent in jail or prison) was admissible as a mitigating factor in the sentencing phase of a capital trial. In line with its general inclination to allow all relevant mitigating factors, the Court proclaimed that, in accordance with *Lockett* (1978), it was admissible. This presented a potential counter-point to the commonly used aggravating factor of future dangerousness, the argument being that if the interest of public safety is just as well served by incarceration, then the death penalty for that individual is unnecessary.

Recently, the Court has been a bit more reluctant to take the "anything goes" perspective on what mitigating evidence may be allowed during the sentencing phase of capital trials. In *Oregon v. Guzek* (2006)[52] the Supreme Court addressed the specific issue of whether evidence of innocence can be presented as mitigating evidence during the sentencing phase of a capital trial. Guzek had been found guilty and sentenced to death initially and then again after the state supreme court overturned his original sentence. The question before the Court concerned whether Guzek could present evidence of innocence (specifically, an alibi) that was not presented during the original trial. Oregon law restricts the presentation of innocence-related evidence during sentencing or re-sentencing hearings to that presented at the original guilt phase of the capital trial. The United States Supreme Court held that Oregon's requirement does not violate the Constitution and thus the defendant does not have a right to present new evidence of innocence at a sentencing or re-sentencing hearing in capital cases.[53] This is one of the few restrictions on allowable mitigating evidence that has been deemed acceptable by the Supreme Court. This is also one of several recent cases that seem to indicate an increasing deference to states by the Court.

C. Jury Instructions

Another major issue that arose as the Supreme Court fine-tuned its decisions on mitigating factors in capital cases was that of jury instructions. Although issues regarding jury instructions were presented in Chapter 6, they warrant attention here as they relate to mitigating factors. Jury instructions are central to the role of mitigating factors in capital trials. One of the primary concerns in *Gregg* (1976) was that juries be adequately guided in their sentencing decision. For this guidance to be effective, jury instructions must be clear and informative enough to provide the jury with adequate understanding of the meaning and function of mitigating factors in the capital sentencing process.

Although the Court has generally held that most relevant mitigating factors must be allowed at the sentencing phase of capital trials, it has been more equivocal about the associated jury instructions. Again, in spite of research indicating that capital jurors are often confused about the meaning and applicability of mitigating circumstances in their sentencing decision,[54] the Supreme Court has, over the years, consistently resisted imposing specific requirements on state trial courts regarding jury instructions about mitigating factors. In 1993, the Supreme Court handed down two decisions pertaining to jury instructions about mitigating factors in capital cases. In *Johnson v. Texas* (1993),[55] the Court held that specific instructions to consider the defendant's youth as a mitigating factor were not required and in *Delo v. Lashley* (1993),[56] it proclaimed that courts are not required to instruct juries to consider mitigating circumstances when supporting evidence has not been adequately presented (in this case lack of prior criminal history). In 1998, the Court declared its broadest decision related to jury instructions about mitigating factors. In *Buchanan v. Angelone* (1998),[57] it held that the failure to instruct a jury as to the specific meaning of the mitigating circumstances it is to consider, or give explicit guidance in regard to such mitigating circumstances, was not a violation of the Eighth or Fourteenth Amendments. The Court contended that the judge's instruction to consider "all the evidence" was sufficient. The Court continued its approval of seemingly ambiguous instructions regarding mitigating factors in the case of *Ayers v. Belmontes* (2006).[58] In this case, the California trial judge had instructed the jury to consider 11 mitigating factors (factors *a* through *k*). Included among these was a catch-all factor ("factor *k*") telling jurors to consider "[a]ny other circumstances which extenuate the gravity of the crime even though it is not a legal excuse for the crime."[59] Belmontes appealed his death sentence on the grounds that this factor was ambiguous and led to possible confusion over whether the jury should or should not consider mitigating factors not related to the crime. The Court upheld the factor (k) instruction holding that it was sufficient to inform the jury that they must consider all relevant mitigating factors including non-crime-related factors.

Some of the Supreme Court's most recent decisions, however, give some indication of a new direction in the requirements for jury instructions about mitigating factors in capital cases. A series of Texas cases have presented the Court with ample opportunity to define appropriate guidance regarding jury instructions about mitigating evidence. In *Smith v. Texas* (2004),[60] the Court held that Texas's failure to instruct juries about the appropriate consideration of mitigating factors (in this case, low IQ, a troubled family background, and a history of learning disabilities) violated the Eighth Amendment. Nevertheless, the Texas Court of Criminal Appeals re-sentenced Smith to death, contending that the error made in the jury instructions did not constitute "egregious harm" in the original sentencing of Smith.[61] In the follow-up case (*Smith v. Texas*, 2007[62]) the United States Supreme Court rejected Texas's re-sentencing of Smith, holding that the Texas court's standard of requiring Smith to show "egregious harm" was invalid and that corrective instructions were not sufficient to undo the original error.[63] The pair of *Smith* cases have been followed by another pair of 2007 Texas cases (consolidated as companion cases): *Abdul-Kabir v. Quarterman* (2007)[64] and *Brewer v. Quarterman* (2007).[65] In these cases, the Texas capital sentencing statute was challenged in that it was being used to disallow jury instructions directing jurors to consider all mitigating evidence presented during the sentencing hearing. Instead, the trial judge instructed the jury to only consider the two special issues stated explicitly in the statute: that the defendant caused the death of the victim and that the defendant presented a continuing threat of violence to society. The United States Supreme Court decided that jury instructions limited to Texas's two special issues were not sufficient to give full consideration and effect to mitigating factors in a capital trial. Juries must be informed about their duty to consider all relevant mitigating evidence. Although suggesting a change toward stricter requirements and detail in instructing juries about the consideration of mitigating factors in capital cases, it remains to be seen what the broader impact of these decisions will be.

V. In Summary, What Do these Cases Say?

In *Gregg v. Georgia* (1976)[66] the Supreme Court not only reinstated the death penalty, it also set the standards for modern-day death penalty procedure. Central to this procedure was the consideration of aggravating and mitigating factors at the sentencing stage of capital trials. The Court maintained that in order to ensure that the death penalty is reserved for only the most serious and severe cases and that individual factors and circumstances are thoroughly considered, factors about the crime, defendant, and victim may be presented and considered prior to sentencing. Aggravating factors are those that elevate a crime to death penalty status, usually referring to factors that make the death penalty particularly appropriate. These factors are often about the particularly heinous nature of the offense, the future danger the defendant poses, and even the impact of the crime on the victim's family. Mitigating factors, on the other hand, are those that may warrant the mercy of the jury. Often these factors focus on characteristics of the defendant, such as diminished mental capacity or a history of child abuse or circumstances of the offense that might attenuate culpability. By considering and weighing these factors, capital juries must come to a decision about whether a defendant deserves to live or die.

Although approving varying state approaches to the consideration of aggravating and mitigating factors in capital cases, the Supreme Court has established some relatively clear guidelines. First, a jury must be unanimous in its determination of the presence of an aggravating factor in order for that factor to weigh in its decision. On the other hand, unanimity is not required for a mitigating factor to be considered. Second, at least one statutory aggravating circumstance must be found in order for the death penalty to be imposed. States may or may not specifically provide statutory mitigating factors in their death penalty statutes, but the Supreme Court has generally held that any mitigating factors supported by evidence must be allowed to be considered by the jury and that jury instructions must provide sufficient guidance in this regard. Where the Court has been less willing to intervene is in the *nature* of jury instructions regarding the consideration of mitigating factors.

Some of the most significant Supreme Court decisions on aggravating and mitigating circumstances are about specific forms of testimony and evidence. In *Barefoot v. Estelle* (1983)[67] the Court upheld psychiatric testimony about the future dangerousness of the defendant as an aggravating factor justifying the sentence of death. To this day, such testimony plays an important role in securing death sentences in many states. On the other hand, in *Skipper v. South Carolina* (1986),[68] the Court held that evidence suggesting that a defendant is not a future danger was admissible as a mitigating factor in the sentencing phase of capital trials. In *Payne v. Tennessee* (1991),[69] the Court said that testimony about the victim and the impact of the crime on the victim's family is admissible as an aggravating factor in capital cases. Through these and other related decisions, the Supreme Court has molded the intricate workings of death penalty procedure and ensured that all relevant factors are considered in the implementation of this most extreme form of punishment.

VI. Conclusion

The Supreme Court has proclaimed that "this most irrevocable of sanctions should be reserved for a small number of extreme cases."[70] The Court has called for a complex set of requirements revolving around aggravating and mitigating factors in death penalty cases. Aggravating factors serve to narrow the range of offenses eligible for the death penalty and guide individualized consideration in capital cases. Mitigating factors ensure that juries have the option to show mercy to particular defendants.

The Supreme Court has been clear on the requirements for aggravating circumstances in capital cases. At least one aggravating circumstance must be unanimously found by the jury in order for the death penalty to be considered. Aggravating factors must be guided by the court to ensure that they are not overly broad or vague. However, in recent cases the Court has loosely interpreted the standards for such guidance and clarification. Once an aggravating factor is found to be present, almost any other aggravating factors can be presented by the prosecutor. There are some restrictions, however. Although the Supreme Court decided that victim impact statements are admissible in the sentencing phase of a capital trial, it limited this to statements about the character of the victim and the emotional impact of the crime. The Court prohibits victim impact statements characterizing the offender or the offense. Finally, statutory aggravating factors must be adequately clarified and appropriately applied to the facts of the case in the judge's instructions to the jury.

The Supreme Court requires that all relevant mitigating circumstances presented by the defense be considered in the sentencing phase of a capital case. The Court has applied this requirement to both statutory and non-statutory mitigating factors. The Court has generally held that virtually anything can be admitted as a mitigating factor and that such factors must be considered by the sentencing authority at any stage of the process. It has also held that juries must be given adequate guidance via jury instructions pertaining to their duty to consider all relevant mitigating evidence. The Court has been less willing, however, to infringe on *how* states choose to inform juries about their consideration of these mitigating factors. Jury unanimity in regard to specific mitigating circumstances is not required; however, mitigating circumstances must be supported by evidence.

The decisions in *Furman* and *Gregg* ushered in a new era. In line with the notion that "death is different," statutes must now ensure that the specific circumstances of a case are thoroughly considered before a decision is made to impose death. The Supreme Court has consistently required that this extreme and irrevocable punishment be characterized by rigorous scrutiny to ensure that it is used only for extreme cases. Consideration of aggravating and mitigating factors in the capital sentencing process is the mechanism by which this is accomplished.

Cases Briefed in Chapter 9

Case	Issue	Holding
Woodson v. North Carolina 428 U.S. 280 (1976)	Do mandatory death penalty statutes violate Eighth and Fourteenth Amendment rights?	Statutes making death sentences mandatory violate the Eighth and Fourteenth Amendments because they fail to take into consideration the individual aspects of the criminal and crime and the particular circumstances of the case.
Lockett v. Ohio 438 U.S. 586 (1978)	Must mitigating factors be considered in the sentencing of capital defendants?	Death penalty statutes must allow for consideration of mitigating factors regarding the character or history of a defendant as well as the circumstances of the offense.
Presnell v. Georgia 439 U.S. 14 (1978)	Is it constitutional to sentence a defendant to death in the absence of any aggravating circumstances?	It is a violation of due process to sentence a defendant to death if no aggravating circumstances required for a death sentence is found by the jury to be present.

Cases Briefed in Chapter 9, *continued*

Case	Issue	Holding
Barefoot v. Estelle 463 U.S. 880 (1983)	Does the Constitution prohibit psychiatric testimony offering predictions of future dangerousness in capital trials?	Psychiatric testimony regarding future dangerousness is admissible during the sentencing phase of capital trials.
Lewis v. Jeffers 497 U.S. 764 (1990)	Is the aggravating circumstance that a crime is "especially heinous, cruel or depraved" unconstitutional vague or overly broad?	The aggravating circumstance that the crime was "especially heinous, cruel or depraved" is not unconstitutionally vague or overly broad.
McKoy v. North Carolina 494 U.S. 433 (1990)	Does a statute requiring a unanimous finding by the jury for a mitigating circumstance to be considered during sentencing violate the standard set in *Mills v. Maryland* (1988)?	North Carolina's death penalty statute requiring unanimity among capital jurors regarding mitigating factors violates the United States Supreme Court's prior decision in *Mills v. Maryland*.
Payne v. Tennessee 501 U.S. 808 (1991)	Does the Eighth Amendment prohibit victim impact statements from being presented at the sentencing phase of a capital trial?	Victim impact statements pertaining to characteristics of the victim and the emotional impact of the crime on the victim's family do not violate the Eighth Amendment and are admissible in the sentencing phase of trial.
Kansas v. Marsh 548 U.S. 163 (2006)	Is it Constitutional to impose the death penalty when aggravating and mitigating factors are unanimously found to be equal?	It is Constitutional to impose the death penalty when a unanimous jury finds aggravating and mitigating factors to be equal.
Brewer v. Quarterman 550 U.S. ___ (2007)	Can a state's capital sentencing statute prevent a jury from giving, or being instructed to give, meaningful consideration to constitutionally relevant mitigating factors and evidence?	It is unconstitutional for a state's capital sentencing statute to restrict the jury's consideration of relevant mitigating evidence. Such statutes must allow for the full consideration of mitigating factors by the jury and jury instructions should reflect this.

Case Briefs

Woodson v. North Carolina
428 U.S. 280 (1976)

CAPSULE: Mandatory death penalty statutes are unconstitutional.

FACTS: Woodson and three accomplices were convicted of armed robbery of a convenience store in which a cashier was killed and a customer was seriously wounded. Two of Woodson's accomplices made plea agreements, testifying against Woodson in exchange for pleading guilty to lesser offenses. Woodson maintained that he was coerced by accomplices and therefore innocent. He was found guilty on all charges and, in accordance with North Carolina law, was automatically sentenced to death upon conviction of felony murder. The state Supreme Court affirmed the verdict. The United States Supreme Court granted certiorari to consider whether North Carolina's death penalty statute, mandating automatic imposition of the sentence of death upon conviction of first degree murder, was constitutional.

ISSUE: Do mandatory death penalty statutes violate Eighth and Fourteenth Amendment rights? YES.

HOLDING: Statutes making death sentences mandatory violate the Eighth and Fourteenth Amendments because they fail to take into consideration the individual aspects of the criminal and crime and the particular circumstances of the case.

REASON: "The North Carolina statute fails to provide a constitutionally tolerable response to Furman's rejection of unbridled jury discretion in the imposition of capital sentences. Central to the limited holding in that case was the conviction that vesting a jury with standardless sentencing power violated the Eighth and Fourteenth Amendments, yet that constitutional deficiency is not eliminated by the mere formal removal of all sentencing power from juries in capital cases. In view of the historic record, it may reasonably be assumed that many juries under mandatory statutes will continue to consider the grave consequences of a conviction in reaching a verdict. But the North Carolina statute provides no standards to guide the jury in determining which murderers shall live and which shall die.

"The respect for human dignity underlying the Eighth Amendment requires consideration of aspects of the character of the individual offender and the circumstances of the particular offense as a constitutionally indispensable part of the process of imposing the ultimate punishment of death. The North Carolina statute impermissibly treats all persons convicted of a designated offense not as uniquely individual human beings, but as members of a faceless, undifferentiated mass to be subjected to the blind infliction of the death penalty."

CASE SIGNIFICANCE: In *Gregg v. Georgia*, 428 U.S. 153 (1976), the Supreme Court reinstated the death penalty. But the Court also declared the form that death penalty statutes must take in order to be constitutional. The Court approved "guided discretion" statutes, or statutes that allowed the sentencing authority to consider individual case circumstances in determining the appropriate sentence. At the same time as the decision in *Gregg*, the Supreme Court also considered a different form of death penalty statute: those making the death penalty mandatory upon conviction of capital murder. In this case, the Court declared such statutes unconstitutional and thus added to the emphasis made in *Gregg* on individual case consideration. Although mandatory death penalty statutes certainly avoid the arbitrary, discriminatory, and disproportionate application of the death penalty, such statutes do not allow for the individual consideration needed in death penalty cases. As the Supreme Court has stated, "death is different." The Court's decision in *Woodson* reinforced this notion and stressed that statutes not providing adequate procedural safeguards and individualized consideration of the circumstances are unacceptable.

Presnell v. Georgia
439 U.S. 14 (1978)

CAPSULE: The death penalty cannot be imposed unless at least one aggravating circumstance is found to be present by the jury.

FACTS: Presnell was indicted for three capital offenses: rape, kidnapping with bodily injury, and murder with malice aforethought. The jury convicted him of all three offenses. Georgia law provides that a jury may sentence a defendant to death if at least one of 10 aggravating circumstances is present. One of the aggravating factors enumerated in Georgia's statute was that an offender could be sentenced to death if the capital offense was committed during the commission of another capital felony. The jury concluded that each offense was committed during the commission of other capital offenses and sentenced Presnell to three death sentences.

The Georgia Supreme Court overruled the death sentences for the rape and kidnapping charges as it determined that both sentences depended upon Presnell having committed forcible rape. The jury had not established this because the jury actually only convicted Presnell of statutory rape, not forcible rape. As the kidnapping with bodily injury depended upon the act of sodomy associated with forcible rape, this conviction was also thrown out. In spite of establishing that neither of the other capital felonies was valid, and that the death sentence for murder depended upon the aggravating factor of being committed during the commission of another capital offense, the Georgia Supreme Court nonetheless upheld the third death penalty.

ISSUE: Is it constitutional to sentence a defendant to death in the absence of any aggravating circumstances? NO.

HOLDING: It is a violation of due process to sentence a defendant to death if no aggravating circumstances required for a death sentence are found by the jury to be present.

REASON: "Under due process principles of procedural fairness, a state-court, jury-imposed death sentence for murder with malice aforethought—based on the aggravating circumstance that the offense was committed while the defendant was engaged in the commission of "kidnapping with bodily injury, aggravated sodomy"—cannot stand, where (1) the state's highest court had vacated the defendant's conviction on another count for rape, along with death penalties on counts involving the rape, on the ground that the jury had not properly convicted the defendant of "forcible" rape (required for a death sentence), because the jury had been instructed both on forcible and statutory rape but had not specified in its verdict which offense it had found [and] (2) the state's highest court had also held that the state could not rely upon sodomy as constituting the bodily injury associated with the kidnapping . . ."

CASE SIGNIFICANCE: In one of the earliest cases to follow the landmark decision in *Gregg v. Georgia* (1976),[71] the Court made the first of many decisions regarding the specific requirements of the procedural safeguards. In *Gregg*, the Court stated that the death penalty should be reserved only for those cases that are extreme or "aggravated" in some way. The Court left it to the states to determine what is sufficiently aggravating to elevate an offense to death sentence eligibility. But the Court made it clear that such aggravating circumstances were necessary for the death penalty to be imposed. In this case, the defendant was originally convicted of three felonies, thus triggering the aggravating factor of having committed murder in the act of other felonies. However, two of the felonies were found to be unsubstantiated and were thus removed by the trial court. Nevertheless, the trial court imposed the previously applied death penalty. The Court ruled the death penalty invalid in this case due to the absence of any remaining aggravating factors upon which a death sentence must rest. This is an important decision because it underscored the need for aggravating circumstances in sentencing a defendant to death. It also stresses the Court's requirement that the death penalty be reserved only for the most extreme cases.

Lockett v. Ohio
438 U.S. 586 (1978)

CAPSULE: Death penalty statutes must allow for the consideration of mitigating factors.

FACTS: Lockett was convicted of aggravated murder after taking part in the planning and carrying out of the robbery of a pawnshop in which the shop owner was killed. Although she had not entered the pawnshop with her accomplices and did not have a direct role in the murder of the owner, Lockett was found guilty by the jury for her role in the crime. Upon conviction, the Ohio death penalty statute required the judge to impose a death sentence unless he or she found the presence of any of three factors that mitigated the defendant's culpability: (1) whether the victim induced or facilitated the offense; (2) whether the defendant committed the offense under duress, coercion, or strong provocation; and (3) whether the offense was a result of the defendant's psychosis or mental deficiency. The judge concluded that the offense was not a result of mental deficiency or psychosis and, without specifically addressing the other two statutory mitigating factors, sentenced Lockett to death.

ISSUE: Must mitigating factors be considered in the sentencing of capital defendants? YES.

HOLDING: Death penalty statutes must allow for consideration of mitigating factors regarding the character or history of a defendant, as well as the circumstances of the offense.

REASON: "The Eighth and Fourteenth Amendments require that the sentencer, in all but the rarest kind of capital case, not be precluded from considering as a mitigating factor, any aspect of a defendant's character or record and any of the circumstances of the offense that the defendant proffers as a basis for a sentence less than death.

"The need for treating each defendant in a capital case with the degree of respect due the uniqueness of the individual is far more important than in noncapital cases, particularly in view of the unavailability with respect to an executed capital sentence of such post-conviction mechanisms in noncapital cases as probation, parole, and work furloughs.

"A statute that prevents the sentencer in capital cases from giving independent mitigating weight to aspects of the defendant's character and record and to the circumstances of the offense proffered in mitigation creates the risk that the death penalty will be imposed in spite of factors that may call for a less severe penalty, and when the choice is between life and death, such risk is unacceptable and incompatible with the commands of the Eighth and Fourteenth Amendments."

CASE SIGNIFICANCE: In *Presnell v. Georgia* (1978),[72] the Supreme Court held that aggravating circumstances must be present for the death penalty to be imposed. In this case, the Court reinforced that other side to the "guided discretion" set forth in *Gregg v. Georgia*, 428 U.S. 153 (1976):[73] mitigating circumstances. The consideration of aggravating and mitigating circumstances has become almost sacred in death penalty cases. This case said that mitigating circumstances must be adequately considered in the sentencing phase of the trial. Moreover, the Court said that consideration of mitigating circumstances should not be overly limited and should include factors about the defendant's character and history and the circumstances of the crime. This set a broad standard of what mitigating circumstances may be considered in the sentencing phase of capital trials. There are very few restrictions placed on the mitigating factors the sentencing authority is allowed to consider in deciding whether to impose the death penalty.

Barefoot v. Estelle
463 U.S. 880 (1983)

CAPSULE: Testimony regarding a defendant's future dangerousness is admissible during the sentencing phase of capital trials.

FACTS: Barefoot was convicted of capital murder for the killing of a police officer in Bell County, Texas. During the sentencing phase of the trial, the jury, under Texas law, was asked two questions: (1) whether the defendant deliberately killed the victim or acted with "reasonable expectation that the death of the deceased or another would result" and (2) whether "there is a probability that the defendant would commit criminal acts of violence that would constitute a continuing threat to society." Texas law required that the death penalty be imposed if a jury answered "yes" to both questions. In pursuit of the latter question, the prosecution called two psychiatrists who testified that Barefoot "would probably commit further acts of violence and represent a continuing threat to society." Barefoot contended, on appeal, that the psychiatrists' testimony regarding future dangerousness was unconstitutional due to their inability to accurately predict future dangerousness and the fact that both had made their conclusions without actually examining the defendant. The Texas Court of Criminal Appeals rejected his arguments and affirmed the conviction and death sentence.

ISSUE: Does the Constitution prohibit psychiatric testimony offering predictions of future dangerousness in capital trials? NO.

HOLDING: Psychiatric testimony regarding future dangerousness is admissible during the sentencing phase of capital trials. A psychiatrist need not actually interview or examine a defendant in person in order for his or her testimony and predictions to be admissible.

REASON: "There is no merit to petitioner's argument that psychiatrists, individually and as a group, are incompetent to predict with an acceptable degree of reliability that a particular criminal will commit other crimes in the future and so represent a danger to the community. To accept such an argument would call into question predictions of future behavior that are constantly made in other contexts. Moreover, under the generally applicable rules of evidence covering the admission and weight of unprivileged evidence, psychiatric testimony predicting dangerousness may be countered not only as erroneous in a particular case but also as generally so unreliable that it should be ignored. Nor, despite the view of the American Psychiatric Association supporting petitioner's view, is there any convincing evidence that such testimony is almost entirely unreliable and that the factfinder and the adversary system will not be competent to uncover, recognize, and take due account of its shortcomings."

CASE SIGNIFICANCE: Future dangerousness is a common aggravating circumstance in death penalty statutes and is explicitly required in Texas and Oregon. This case centered on the admissibility of psychiatric predictions of future dangerousness. In spite of protest from the American Psychiatric Association and research indicating that psychiatrists' predictions of future dangerousness are inherently unreliable, the Court concluded that such testimony is allowed as aggravating evidence in the sentencing phase of capital trials. Playing on the fears of jurors that the defendant will likely be a violent threat in the future, evidence of future dangerousness is powerful and has arguably been responsible for a substantial number of death sentences. The Court in this case said that such testimony would be admissible and that standard remains intact to this day. Interestingly, expert testimony that the defendant is not a future danger is becoming increasingly used as mitigation in capital trials. In spite of serious questions regarding the reliability of such predictions and conclusions, future dangerousness remains a central consideration in death penalty sentencing.

Lewis v. Jeffers
497 U.S. 764 (1990)

CAPSULE: The aggravating circumstance that the crime was "especially heinous, cruel or depraved" is not unconstitutionally vague or overly broad.

FACTS: In May of 1976, Jeffers and his girlfriend, Penelope Cheney, were arrested on charges of possession of narcotics and receipt of stolen property. Jeffers posted bond for Cheney but was unable to do the same for himself. While in jail, Jeffers found out that Cheney was cooperating with police and providing them with information against Jeffers. He wrote a note offering another inmate money to kill Cheney. The officer who was to deliver the note read it without delivering it. Later that year, after being released from jail,

Jeffers met up with Cheney to provide her with heroin. He injected her with, in his words to a witness, "enough shit to kill a horse." While she was still alive, Jeffers choked Cheney with her own belt and then with his own hands until she was dead.

Jeffers was convicted of first-degree murder. The trial court found two aggravating circumstances and no mitigating circumstances. In accordance with Arizona law, Jeffers was sentenced to death. On appeal, Jeffers contended that the aggravating factor of the crime being "especially heinous, cruel or depraved" was unconstitutionally vague and broad. The Arizona Supreme Court rejected his claims and upheld the conviction and death sentence.

ISSUE: Is the aggravating circumstance that a crime is "especially heinous, cruel or depraved" unconstitutional vague or overly broad? NO.

HOLDING: The aggravating circumstance that the crime was "especially heinous, cruel or depraved" is not unconstitutionally vague or overly broad.

REASON: " . . . [I]f a State has adopted a constitutionally narrow construction of a facially vague aggravating circumstance, and if the State has applied that construction to the facts of the particular case, then the 'fundamental constitutional requirement' of 'channeling and limiting . . . the sentencer's discretion in imposing the death penalty,' *Cartwright*, 486 U.S. at 362, has been satisfied."

"In light of the Arizona Supreme Court's narrowing construction of the 'especially heinous . . . or depraved' aggravating circumstance, the Arizona Supreme Court could reasonably have concluded that respondent committed the murder in an 'especially heinous . . . or depraved manner.'"

CASE SIGNIFICANCE: In *Gregg v. Georgia* (1976),[74] guided discretion statutes were approved. These are statutes in which the sentencing decision is channeled and limited to ensure that only the most extreme cases result in death sentences. In this case, the aggravating factor upon which the death sentence rested was whether the crime was "especially heinous, cruel or depraved." The defendant argued that this was too vague and broad to sufficiently limit the application of the death penalty. The Supreme Court disagreed and held that such an aggravating factor was valid. In a prior case (*Godfrey v. Georgia,* 1980[75]), the Court had held that aggravating circumstances must be adequately clarified and that their meaning must be applied independently to the facts of the case. The Court believed that the aggravating factor in this case was clear and relevant as applied. Many other statutes include aggravating factors that characterize the offense in similarly broad and vague terms. For example, in *Arave v. Creech* (1993),[76] the Court upheld an aggravating factor that the crime showed an "utter disregard for human life." Some have suggested that such sweeping phrases and characterizations could be applied to virtually any murder case, and thus do not limit or channel the sentencing decision in any meaningful way. Nevertheless, the Court set a standard in this case that exists to this day—such imprecise aggravating factors remain common in state death penalty statutes.

McKoy v. North Carolina
494 U.S. 433 (1990)

CAPSULE: Capital juries need not be unanimous in their finding of mitigating circumstances.

FACTS: McKoy was convicted of first-degree murder. In the sentencing phase of the trial, the jury was, in accordance with North Carolina's death penalty statute, required to unanimously agree on the presence of mitigating factors in order for those factors to be considered in their sentencing decision. The jury unanimously found both the presence of aggravating and mitigating factors. They were then asked whether they unanimously agreed that the previously unanimously agreed-upon mitigating factors were insufficient to outweigh the aggravating factors. They answered yes and subsequently sentenced McKoy to death. McKoy challenged the death sentence, claiming the statute violated *Mills v. Maryland* (1988), which had previously held that jurors need not be unanimous in their finding of mitigating factors for those factors to be considered in sentencing. North Carolina's supreme court upheld the sentence.

ISSUE: Does a statute requiring a unanimous finding by the jury for a mitigating circumstance to be considered during sentencing violate the standard set in *Mills v. Maryland* (1988)? YES.

HOLDING: North Carolina's death penalty statute requiring unanimity among capital jurors regarding mitigating factors violates the United States Supreme Court's prior decision in *Mills v. Maryland*.

REASON: "Despite the state court's inventive attempts to distinguish *Mills*, our decision there clearly governs this case. First, North Carolina's Issue Four does not ameliorate the constitutional infirmity created by the unanimity requirement. Issue Four, like Issue Three, allows the jury to consider only mitigating factors that it unanimously finds under Issue Two. Although the jury may opt for life imprisonment even where it fails unanimously to find any mitigating circumstances, the fact remains that the jury is required to make its decision based only on those circumstances it unanimously finds. The unanimity requirement thus allows one holdout juror to prevent the others from giving effect to evidence that they believe calls for a 'sentence less than death' *Eddings v. Oklahoma*, 455 U.S. 104, 110 (1982). Moreover, even if all 12 jurors agree that there are some mitigating circumstances, North Carolina's scheme prevents them from giving effect to evidence supporting any of those circumstances in their deliberations under Issues Three and Four unless they unanimously find the existence of the same circumstance. This is the precise defect that compelled us to strike down the Maryland scheme in *Mills*. Our decision in *Mills* was not limited to cases in which the jury is required to impose the death penalty if it finds that aggravating circumstances outweigh mitigating circumstances or that no mitigating circumstances exist at all. Rather, we held that it would be the 'height of arbitrariness to allow or require the imposition of the death penalty' where 1 juror was able to prevent the other 11 from giving effect to mitigating evidence."

CASE SIGNIFICANCE: In *Mills v. Maryland* (1990),[77] the Supreme Court held that unanimity cannot be required for jurors to consider any particular mitigating circumstances. In that case, the issue was with jury instructions that implied that unanimity was required. In this case, the North Carolina instructions similarly indicated that unanimity was required for a mitigating circumstance to be considered in the sentencing decision. Unlike the instructions in *Mills*, however, the North Carolina jury instructions allow the jury the option of rejecting the death penalty even if they do not unanimously find mitigating factors. The United States Supreme Court held the instructions to be in violation of the principles in *Mills* that each juror be allowed to consider the mitigating evidence as he or she sees fit. The Supreme Court ruled that North Carolina's instructions prevented individual jurors from appropriately assessing mitigating evidence and whether it should influence their sentencing decision. The Supreme Court reiterated that each juror should be given the opportunity to conclude on their own whether mitigating circumstances were present, regardless of the conclusions of other jurors.

Payne v. Tennessee
501 U.S. 808 (1991)

CAPSULE: Victim impact statements are admissible during the sentencing phase of capital trials.

FACTS: Payne was convicted of two counts of capital murder for killing Charisse Christopher and her two-year-old daughter, Lacie. He was also convicted of assault with intent to murder for his failed attack on Charisse's three-year-old son Nicholas. At the sentencing phase of trial, Payne called four witnesses: his mother and father, Dr. John T. Hutson, a clinical psychologist, and a friend he met at church, Bobbie Thomas. Each testified as to various mitigating factors regarding his capacity to commit such a crime. The prosecution called Nicholas' grandmother who testified to the impact the murders had on Nicholas and the rest of the family. The prosecution's closing arguments commented on the impact of the murders on the surviving family members. The jury sentenced Payne to death.

Payne argued that the admission of victim impact testimony violated his Eighth Amendment rights. He based his argument on the previous rulings in *Booth v. Maryland* (1987) and *South Carolina v. Gathers* (1989), which held that victim impact testimony was inadmissible in capital cases. The Tennessee Supreme Court disagreed.

ISSUE: Does the Eighth Amendment prohibit victim impact statements from being presented at the sentencing phase of a capital trial? NO.

HOLDING: The admission of victim impact statements in the sentencing phase of trial does not constitute an Eighth Amendment violation as long as the information presented does not violate principles of fundamental fairness for the defendant. This applies only to statements regarding characteristics of the victim and the emotional impact of the crime on the victim's family, not to statements characterizing the crime or the defendant.

REASON: "There are numerous infirmities in the rule created by *Booth* and *Gathers*. Those cases were based on two premises: that evidence relating to a particular victim or to the harm caused a victim's family does not in general reflect on the defendant's 'blameworthiness,' and that only evidence of 'blameworthiness' is relevant to the capital sentencing decision. However, assessment of the harm caused by the defendant has long been an important factor in determining the appropriate punishment, and victim impact evidence is simply another method of informing the sentencing authority about such harm."

"Such evidence is not generally offered to encourage comparative judgments of this kind, but is designed to show instead each victim's uniqueness as an individual human being. In the event that victim impact evidence is introduced that is so unduly prejudicial that it renders the trial fundamentally unfair, the Fourteenth Amendment's Due Process Clause provides a mechanism for relief. Thus, a State may properly conclude that for the jury to assess meaningfully the defendant's moral culpability and blameworthiness, it should have before it at the sentencing phase victim impact evidence."

CASE SIGNIFICANCE: This case virtually overrules *Booth v. Maryland*, [482 U.S. 496] (1987), which held that victim impact statements (which typically describe a victim's characteristics and the effect of the crime on the victim's family) are not admissible in death penalty cases. The Court said that although the doctrine of stare decisis (adherence to decided cases) is usually the best policy, it is "not an inexorable command," particularly in cases in which the decisions are "unworkable or badly reasoned." Decided only four years earlier, the Court considered the rule in *Booth* to be unworkable and badly reasoned, and overruled that part of the decision. The Court said that the *Booth* decision was based on two premises: "that evidence relating to a particular victim or to the harm caused a victim's family does not in general reflect on the defendant's 'blameworthiness,' and that only evidence of 'blameworthiness' is relevant to the capital sentencing decision." The Court rejected these statements, saying that "assessment of the harm caused by the defendant has long been an important factor in determining the appropriate punishment, and victim impact evidence is simply another method of informing the sentencing authority about such harm."

Decided by a six-to-three vote, this decision reflects the definite imprint of a conservative Court that has shown willingness to allow into the sentencing phase evidence that previously was considered inadmissible. The Court rejected the concept that such evidence must be kept out of death penalty cases because a capital defendant must be treated as a "uniquely individual human being," saying that because there are virtually no limits placed on the relevant mitigating evidence that may be introduced for the defendant in a capital offense, the same should be true with aggravating circumstances as well. The Court seeks to place the prosecution and the defense on the same level in the introduction of evidence in the sentencing phase, even in death penalty cases.[78]

Kansas v. Marsh
548 U.S. 163 (2006)

CAPSULE: It is constitutional to impose the death penalty when aggravating and mitigating factors are found to be equal.

FACTS: Marsh was convicted of capital murder for the multiple-victim killing of a mother and her young child. During the sentencing phase of the trial, the jury found that mitigating and aggravating factors were exactly equal in weight (i.e., in "equipoise"). The Kansas death penalty statute stated that in such a circumstance, death was to be imposed. Accordingly, Marsh was sentenced to death. On appeal, Marsh challenged the Kansas death penalty statute, specifically section 21-4624(e), which reads: "If, by unanimous vote, the jury finds beyond a reasonable doubt that one or more of the aggravating circumstances enumerated in K.S.A. 21-4625 . . . exist and, further, that the existence of such aggravating circumstances is not outweighed by any mitigating circumstances which are found to exist, the defendant shall be sentenced to death; otherwise the defendant shall be sentenced as provided by law." Marsh contended that the phrase "shall be sentenced to death" presents a presumption in favor of death when aggravating and mitigating factors are in equipoise and thus is unconstitutional. The Kansas Supreme Court agreed, holding that the statute was in violation of the Eighth and Fourteenth Amendments due to the fact that death becomes the default, required sentence in such circumstances.

ISSUE: Is it constitutional to impose the death penalty when aggravating and mitigating factors are unanimously found to be equal? YES.

HOLDING: It is constitutional to impose the death penalty when a unanimous jury finds aggravating and mitigating factors to be equal.

REASON: "Kansas' death penalty statute satisfies the constitutional mandates of *Furman* and its progeny because it rationally narrows the class of death-eligible defendants and permits a jury to consider any mitigating evidence relevant to its sentencing determination. The State's weighing equation merely channels a jury's discretion by providing criteria by which the jury may determine whether life or death is appropriate. Its system provides the kind of guided discretion sanctioned in, e.g., *Walton*. Contrary to Marsh's argument, § 21-4624(e) does not create a general presumption in favor of the death penalty. A life sentence must be imposed if the State fails to demonstrate the existence of an aggravating circumstance beyond a reasonable doubt, if the State cannot prove beyond a reasonable doubt that aggravating circumstances are not outweighed by mitigating circumstances, or if the jury is unable to reach a unanimous decision in any respect. Marsh's contentions that an equipoise determination reflects juror confusion or inability to decide between life and death or that the jury may use equipoise as a loophole to shirk its constitutional duty to render a reasoned, moral sentencing decision rest on an implausible characterization of the Kansas statute—that a jury's determination that aggravators and mitigators are in equipoise is not a decision, much less a decision for death. Weighing is not an end, but a means to reaching a decision. Kansas's instructions clearly inform the jury that a determination that the evidence is in equipoise is a decision for death."

CASE SIGNIFICANCE: This was the first time the Supreme Court was confronted with the question of whether death can be the prescribed sentence when aggravating and mitigating factors are determined by the jury to be exactly equivalent or in equipoise. Based on the notion that "death is different," some might conclude that a tie should be decided in a direction less severe than a death sentence. However, the Court decided otherwise, holding that the Kansas statute was not unconstitutional and that when aggravating and mitigating factors are in equipoise, it is appropriate for a death sentence to result. This effectively establishes the standard for imposing death sentences at a point in which *mitigating factors do not outweigh aggravating factors* as opposed to the previously assumed calculus of *aggravating factors outweighing mitigating factors*. The Court determined that this presumption in favor of death was not in violation of constitutional requirements in imposing the death penalty.

Brewer v. Quarterman
550 U.S. ___ (2007)

CAPSULE: Capital juries must be allowed to consider all relevant mitigating factors and jury instructions must adequately direct the jury to this effect.

FACTS: Brewer was convicted of murder in the act of a felony (robbery). At sentencing, Brewer introduced a variety of different mitigating factors. Among these was evidence of a prior history of depression and drug abuse, domination and manipulation by his co-defendant, prior abuse at the hands of his father, and the witnessing of his father's abuse of his mother. At part of his counsel's trial strategy, no expert psychological or psychiatric testimony was presented. When the sentencing hearing concluded, Brewer submitted several proposed jury instructions pertaining to the mitigating evidence that was presented. The trial judge rejected Brewer's requested instructions instead instructing the jury to only consider two particular issues in determinging Brewer's sentence. These were the two special issues noted in the Texas statute: (1) that the defendant caused the death of the victim, and (2) that there is a probability, beyond a reasonable doubt, that the defendant would constitute a continuing violent threat to society. The prosecutor, in his closing argument, noted that Brewer's violent response to his father's abuse supported the fact that he was a future danger to society and argued that any mitigating effect was irrelevant to the jury's decision as to whether they should sentence Brewer to death. Brewer was sentenced to death and the conviction and sentence were affirmed on direct appeal.

ISSUE: Can a state's capital sentencing statute prevent a jury from giving, or being instructed to give, meaningful consideration to constitutionally relevant mitigating factors and evidence? NO.

HOLDING: It is unconstitutional for a state's capital sentencing statute to restrict the jury's consideration of relevant mitigating evidence. Such statutes must allow for the full consideration of mitigating factors by the jury and jury instructions should reflect this.

REASON: "Brewer's trial was infected with the same constitutional error that occurred in *Penry* I, where the Court held that jury instructions that merely articulated the Texas special issues, without directing the sentencing jury 'to consider fully Penry's mitigating evidence as it bears on his personal culpability,' did not provide an adequate opportunity for the jury to decide whether that evidence might provide a legitimate basis for imposing a sentence other than death. The Court characterized Penry's mental-retardation and childhood-abuse evidence as a 'two-edged sword' that 'diminish[ed] his blameworthiness for his crime even as it indicat[ed] a probability' of future dangerousness. Brewer's mitigating evidence similarly served as a 'two-edged sword.' Even if his evidence was less compelling than Penry's, that does not justify the CCA's refusal to apply *Penry* I here. It is reasonably likely the jurors accepted the prosecutor's argument to limit their decision to whether Brewer had acted deliberately and was likely a future danger, disregarding any independent concern that his troubled background might make him undeserving of death."

"Under the narrowest possible reading of *Penry* I, Texas' special issues do not provide for adequate jury consideration of mitigating evidence that functions as a 'two-edged sword.' The Fifth Circuit's mischaracterization of the law as demanding only that such evidence be given 'sufficient mitigating effect,' and improperly equating 'sufficient effect' with 'full effect,' is not consistent with the reasoning of *Penry v. Johnson* (*Penry* II), which issued after Penry's resentencing (and before the Fifth Circuit's opinion in this case). Like the 'constitutional relevance' standard rejected in *Tennard*, a 'sufficient effect' standard has 'no foundation' in this Court's decisions. For the reasons explained in this case and in *Abdul-Kabir*, the Circuit's conclusions that Brewer's mental-illness and substance-abuse evidence could not constitute a *Penry* violation, and that troubled-childhood evidence may, because of its temporary character, fall sufficiently within the special issues ambit, fail to heed this Court's repeated warnings about the extent to which the jury must be allowed not only to consider mitigating evidence, or to have such evidence before it, but to respond to it in a reasoned, moral manner and assign it weight in deciding whether a defendant truly deserves death."

CASE SIGNIFICANCE: This case represents an ongoing conflict between the United States Supreme Court and the Texas capital sentencing procedure regarding jury instructions. Although the decision in this case (and its companion case, *Abdul-Kabir v. Quarterman*) is likely limited to the unique nature of the Texas statute and circumstances of capital sentencing in Texas, the Court reiterates the constitutional requirement that juries be given sufficient opportunity to fully consider all relevant mitigating factors and that they be instructed accordingly. Specifically, the Court re-emphasizes that capital juries be allowed to give "full effect" to all mitigating evidence and that a standard of "sufficient effect" is not enough. From the Court's perspective, this requires that jury instructions specifically inform the jury of their duty to fully consider all relevant mitigating factors and not to resort to a verbatim reading of limited special issues such as those in the Texas statute.

Internet Resources

Capital Sentencing Guide
http://supreme.state.az.us/courtserv/CrtProj/capsentguid/Intro.htm

Conducting the Penalty Phase of a Capital Case
www.flcourts.org/gen_public/courted/bin/2001outlineWTOC.pdf

Texas Defender Service's Report on Future Dangerousness in Capital Trials
http://www.texasdefender.org/DEADLYSP.PDF

"Dr. Death" Obituary and Web Discussion
http://www.blogofdeath.com/archives/001032.html

Barefoot in Quicksand: The Future of Future Dangerousness Predictions
www.uakron.edu/law/docs/regnier37.3.pdf

Victim Impact Statements in Capital Trials: A Selected Bibliography
lsr.nellco.org/cgi/viewcontent.cgi?article=1005&context=cornell/clsops

States that Allow Victim Impact Statements
http://www.deathpenaltyinfo.org/article.php?did=575&scid=62

Notes

1. *Gregg v. Georgia*, 428 U.S. 153 (1976).

2. *Roberts v. Louisiana*, 431 U.S. 633 (1977).

3. *Woodson v. North Carolina*, 428 U.S. 280 (1976).

4. Although the term "circumstances" is often used, it is somewhat limiting in its connotation. The term "factors" is used here because it more broadly applies to all forms of aggravating circumstances and evidence, whether that pertains to the circumstances of the crime or other factors or characteristics of the defendant or victim.

5. *Furman v. Georgia*, 408 U.S. 238 (1972).

6. *McGautha v. California*, 402 U.S. 183, 190 (1971).

7. James R. Acker and Charles S. Lanier, *Beyond Human Ability? The Rise and Fall of Death Penalty Legislation*. In JAMES R. ACKER, ROBERT M. BOHM, & CHARLES S. LANIER (EDS.), AMERICA'S EXPERIMENT WITH CAPITAL PUNISHMENT: REFLECTIONS ON THE PAST, PRESENT, AND FUTURE OF THE ULTIMATE PENAL SANCTION 77 (1998).

8. VA. CODE ANN. § 18.2-31

9. ROBERT M. BOHM, DEATHQUEST II: AN INTRODUCTION TO THE THEORY AND PRACTICE OF CAPITAL PUNISHMENT IN THE UNITED STATES (2003).

10. For an answer of "no" to the first two questions to be valid, 10 of the 12 jurors must answer "no"; for an answer of "yes" to the mitigation question to be valid, 10 of 12 jurors must answer "yes."

11. *Brewer v. Quarterman*, 550 U.S. ___ (2007); *Abdul v. Quarterman*, 550 U.S. ___ (2007).

12. *Kansas v. Marsh*, 548 U.S. 163 (2006).

13. *Id.*

14. *Gregg v. Georgia, supra.*

15. *Presnell v. Georgia*, 439 U.S. 14 (1978).

16. *Barclay v. Florida*, 463 U.S. 939 (1983).

17. *Blystone v. Pennsylvania*, 494 U.S. 299 (1990).

18. *Roberts v. Louisiana, supra; Woodson v. North Carolina, supra.*

19. O.C.G.A. § 17-10-30(b)(7).

20. *Godfrey v. Georgia*, 446 U.S. 420 (1980).

21. *Lewis v. Jeffers*, 497 U.S. 764 (1990).

22. Ursula Bentele and William J. Bowers, *How Jurors Decide on Death: Guilt is Overwhelming; Aggravation Requires Death; and Mitigation Is No Excuse*, 66 BROOKLYN L. REV. 1011 (2001).

23. *Arave v. Creech*, 507 U.S. 463 (1993).

24. *Tuilaepa v. California*, 512 U.S. 967 (1994).

25. *Id.*

26. *Weeks v. Angelone*, 528 U.S. 225 (2000).

27. *Buchanan v. Angelone*, 522 U.S. 269 (1998).

28. Bentele and Bowers, *supra.*

29. *Booth v. Maryland*, 482 U.S. 496 (1987).

30. *South Carolina v. Gathers*, 490 U.S. 805 (1989).

31. *Payne v. Tennessee*, 501 U.S. 808 (1991).

32. AUSTIN SARAT, WHEN THE STATE KILLS: CAPITAL PUNISHMENT AND THE AMERICAN CONDITION (2001).

33. Richard Burr, *Litigating with Victim Impact Testimony: The Serendipity that Has Come from* Payne v. Tennessee, 88 CORNELL L. REV. 517 (2003).

34. JOHN MONAHAN, PREDICTING VIOLENT BEHAVIOR: AN ASSESSMENT OF CLINICAL TECHNIQUES (1981); Christopher Slobogin, Dangerousness and Expertise, 133 U. PA. L. REV. 97 (1984); Randy K. Otto, *On the Ability of Mental Health Professionals to Predict Dangerousness: A Commentary on Interpretations of the Dangerousness Literature*, 18 L. & PSYCHOLOG. REV. 43 (1994).

35. John F. Edens, John Petrila, and Jacqueline Buffington-Vollum, *Psychopathy and the Death Penalty: Can the Psychopathy Checklist-Revised Identify Offenders Who Represent "A Continuing Threat to Society"?* 29 J. PSYCHIATRY & L. 433 (2001).

36. *Barefoot v. Estelle*, 463 U.S. 880, 884 (1983).

37. Mitzi Dorland and Daniel Krauss, *The Danger of Dangerousness in Capital Sentencing: Exacerbating the Problem of Arbitrary and Capricious Decision-Making*, 29 LAW & PSYCHOL. REV. 63 (2005).

38. Id. at 921.

39. Mark D. Cunningham and Thomas J. Reidy, *Integrating Base Rate Data in Violence Risk Assessments at Capital Sentencing*, 16 BEH. SCI. & THE LAW 71 (1998).

40. John H. Blume, Stephen P. Garvey and Sheri Lynn Johnson, *Future Dangerousness in Capital Cases: Always "At Issue,"* 86 CORNELL L. REV. 397 (2001).

41. Texas Defender Service, A State of Denial: Texas Justice and the Death Penalty (2000).

42. *Lockett v. Ohio*, 438 U.S. 586 (1978).

43. *Bell v. Ohio*, 438 U.S. 637 (1978).

44. *Hitchcock v. Dugger*, 481 U.S. 393 (1987).

45. *Parker v. Dugger*, 498 U.S. 308 (1991).

46. *Mills v. Maryland*, 486 U.S. 367 (1988).

47. *McKoy v. North Carolina*, 494 U.S. 433 (1990).

48. Tex. Code Crim. Proc., Art. 37.071 § 2g(2).

49. *Eddings v. Oklahoma*, 455 U.S. 104 (1982).

50. *Penry v. Lynaugh*, 492 U.S. 302 (1989).

51. *Skipper v. South Carolina*, 476 U.S. 1 (1986).

52. *Oregon v. Guzek*, 546 U.S. ___ (2006).

53. *Id.*

54. Craig Haney, Lorelei Sontag, and Sally Costanzo, *Deciding to Take a Life: Capital Juries, Sentencing Instructions, and the Jurisprudence of Death*, 50 J. Soc. Issues 149 (1994).

55. *Johnson v. Texas*, 509 U.S. 350 (1993).

56. *Delo v. Lashley*, 507 U.S. 272 (1993).

57. *Buchanan v. Angelone, supra.*

58. *Ayers v. Belmontes*, 549 U.S. ___ (2006).

59. *Id.*

60. *Smith v. Texas*, 543 U.S. 37 (2004).

61. *Smith v. Texas*, 550 U.S. ___ (2007).

62. *Id.*

63. *Id.*

64. *Abdul-Kabir v. Quarterman*, 550 U.S. ___ (2007).

65. *Brewer v. Quarterman*, 550 U.S. ___ (2007).

66. *Gregg v. Georgia, supra.*

67. *Barefoot v. Estelle, supra.*

68. *Skipper v. South Carolina, supra.*

69. *Payne v. Tennessee, supra.*

70. *Id.* at 182.

71. *Gregg v. Georgia, supra.*

72. *Presnell v. Georgia, supra.*

73. *Gregg v. Georgia, supra.*

74. *Id.*

75. *Godfrey v. Georgia, supra.*

76. *Arave v. Creech, supra.*

77. *Mills v. Maryland, supra.*

78. This case significance is taken from ROLANDO V. DEL CARMEN, SUSAN E. RITTER, AND BETSY A. WITT, BRIEFS OF LEADING CASES IN CORRECTIONS (5th ed. 2008).

Chapter Outline

I. **Introduction**

II. **The Appellate Process**

III. **The Great Writ**
   A. History
   B. The Battle over Successive Petitions and the Road to the AEDPA
      1. The Good Faith/Bad Faith Rule
      2. New-Claim Successive Petitions Rule
      3. The Impact of *Gregg* on Successive Petitions
   C. The AEDPA

IV. **Current Consequences of the AEDPA**
   A. Retroactivity
   B. Statute of Limitations and Actual Innocence
      1. Statute of Limitations
      2. Actual Innocence

V. **The Use of Habeas Corpus to Determine the Constitutionality of Methods of Execution**

VI. **In Summary, What Do these Cases Say?**

VII. **Conclusion**

Cases Briefed in Chapter 10

Case Briefs
   Rose v. Lundy, 455 U.S. 509 (1982)
   McCleskey v. Zant, 499 U.S. 467 (1991)
   Sawyer v. Whitley, 505 U.S. 333 (1992)
   Herrera v. Collins, 506 U.S. 390 (1993)
   Felker v. Turpin, 518 U.S. 651 (1996)
   Nelson v. Campbell, 541 U.S. 637 (2004)
   House v. Bell, 547 U.S. ___ (2007)
   Lawrence v. Florida, 549 U.S. ___ (2007)

Internet Resources

Notes

Chapter 10

Appeals, Habeas Corpus, and the Death Penalty

I. Introduction

Appealing the decision of a trial court is a necessary component of our system of justice. Appeals serve to insulate innocent offenders from a wrongful conviction or protect those who have been subjected to a harmful error.[1] An appeal must be filed shortly after the termination of a criminal trial because the privilege to file an appeal is subject to a statute of limitations.

An appeal is filed to reverse a conviction. It generally progresses through a legal hierarchical maze as defendants, unsatisfied with the outcome of a conviction or the decision of a lower court, seek relief from a higher court. If a defendant is convicted by a state court, an appeal is first filed with the state appellate court, followed by an appeal to the state supreme court. For a capital offender, the process of filing an appeal is similar—except that in some states appeals are made directly to the highest state court, thus bypassing lower appellate courts. Capital defendants can be involved in a lengthy appellate process that can take them to the United States Supreme Court.[2]

Capital defendants who have exhausted their appeals have another legal recourse that may halt execution or lead to a new trial. This is through a petition called a writ of habeas corpus. Unlike an appeal, which is based on state law, a writ of habeas corpus is provided for in the suspension clause of the Constitution (Article 1, Section 9 [2]) and is a constitutional right. One writer summarizes the differences between an appeal and habeas corpus proceedings as follows:

Figure 10.1

Differences Between Appeals and Habeas Corpus

Appeals	Habeas Corpus
1. A direct attack on the conviction	1. A collateral attack, meaning a separate case from the criminal conviction
2. Part of a criminal proceeding	2. A civil proceeding
3. Purpose is to reverse conviction	3. Purpose is to secure release from prison
4. Filed only after conviction	4. May be filed any time a person is deprived of freedom illegally by a public officer, before or after conviction
5. Accused has been convicted but may be free on bail	5. Person is serving time or is detained illegally; cannot be filed if person is free
6. Based on any type of error during the trial	6. Based on a violation of a constitutional right, usually during the trial
7. Must be undertaken within a certain period after conviction, otherwise the right of action lapses	7. Right of action may be filed even when person is serving time in prison
8. All issues must be raised from the trial record	8. New testimony may be presented

Source: Rolando V. del Carmen, *Criminal Procedure: Law and Practice*, Seventh Edition (2007). Wadsworth, a part of Cengage Learning, Inc. Reproduced by permission. www.cengage.com/permissions.

A writ of habeas corpus is filed for the sole purpose of seeking release from prison. Therefore, it is usually filed after a capital offender begins serving his or her sentence. The writ must contain evidence that the capital offender is being held illegally or unconstitutionally. However, because a writ of habeas corpus must be filed with the court that originally tried the offender, a successful habeas corpus petition is a rarity.[3] In addition, federal legislation, such as the Antiterrorism and Effective Death Penalty Act of 1996 (AEDPA) severely limits the right of capital offenders to file successive petitions and thus weakens their repeated attempts to seek release from prison through a habeas proceeding.

This chapter first presents a brief overview of the appellate process, with special emphasis on capital defendants. Then it will discuss the writ of habeas corpus. The origins of the writ are explored from its use in England and its adaptation by the American colonists. This chapter also presents the limitations that both the legislative and judicial branches of government have placed on an inmate's ability to file a writ of habeas corpus, particularly those involving same-claim successive petitions and new-claim successive petitions. Finally, a brief overview of the Antiterrorism and Effective Death Penalty Act (AEDPA) will be presented and its overall impact on the ability of inmates to file habeas petitions will be explored.

II. The Appellate Process

An appeal may be defined as an attempt, through intervention by a higher court, to seek a different court or jury decision. This happens when a defendant, dissatisfied with a lower court's decision, seeks reversal of a conviction based on a harmful legal or constitutional error. Generally, an appeal is filed shortly after the conclusion of a trial, although a special type of appeal called an interlocutory appeal may be filed during trial and before a verdict has been issued against a defendant. Although there are rights given to criminal defendants in the Constitution, the right to appeal is not a constitutional right. Nonetheless, the right to appeal a decision of a lower court has been firmly embedded in our system of justice through state and federal laws.

There are two characteristics of an appeal. The first is that a defendant's initial appeal cannot be denied, meaning that the court has no discretionary authority to refuse to hear the appeal. The second characteristic however, restricts the number of times a defendant may appeal. For instance, defendants are only permitted one appeal. A defendant, dissatisfied with the appellate court's ruling, may file subsequent appeals with higher courts. However, such appeals are discretionary, meaning that the appellate courts may refuse to hear the appeal.[4] For capital defendants, appeals are usually filed directly with the state supreme court. Because it is the defendant's first appeal, the state supreme court cannot deny review.

Appellate courts, even in death penalty cases, do not review the facts of the case to determine whether the defendant is truly guilty or not. Instead, appellate courts review any legal or constitutional errors that may have occurred during the trial or sentencing. Appellate courts recognize two types of errors that may occur during trial or sentencing: harmless error and harmful error. A harmless error, also called a non-constitutional error, does not warrant the reversal of a conviction because it does not affect the outcome of the trial. In other words, the error does not affect the finding of guilt by a judge or jury.[5] A decision by an appellate court to recognize an error as harmless generally occurs when there is enough evidence, without the error, to uphold the conviction. In *Kotteakos v. United States* (1946),[6] the Supreme Court created the following test for harmless errors: "If one cannot say, with fair assurance, after pondering all that happened without stripping the erroneous action from the whole, that the judgment was not substantially swayed by the error, it is impossible to conclude that substantial rights were not affected."

By contrast, harmful errors, also called constitutional errors, require the reversal of a conviction because the error involved a serious violation of constitutional rights, which prejudiced the verdict. Examples of harmful errors are denial of counsel and racial discrimination in the selection of a jury.

A reversal of a conviction does not mean that the capital defendant will not be tried again. The Court considers the defendant's decision to appeal as a waiver of her Fifth Amendment privilege against double jeopardy.

Accordingly, the defendant may be granted a trial de novo (new trial). Another consequence of an appeal may be a reverse-and-remand decision whereby a defendant's conviction is reversed by the appellate court. However, the case is remanded or sent back to the lower court, usually for a new trial. If the defendant is dissatisfied with the decision of the lower court, he or she may appeal again. Such appeals are discretionary and must proceed through the same hierarchical court process, which again may reach the jurisdiction of the Supreme Court of the United States.

III. The Great Writ

A. History

Habeas corpus is a Latin term that means "you have the body." It is a judicial order directed at those detaining any person to bring the detainee to court and explain the reasons for detention. The writ of habeas corpus protects against the most arbitrary type of injustice—illegal detention or confinement—and is often referred to as the Great Writ. There are several reasons why the writ of habeas corpus is viewed with such reverence, but one reason stands out: the writ is a remedy for individuals who have been illegally, unjustifiably, and unconstitutionally confined and thus deprived of freedom.[7] The Great Writ thus "secures justice for those who at any particular moment find themselves execrated by the dominant force in society."[8] It is a protective means or a "safety valve"[9] that bars abusive and arbitrary government action by providing a legal avenue for seeking release from injustice.

As with many of our legal traditions, habeas corpus has underpinnings in English law. Originating in England after the Norman Conquest of 1066, habeas corpus was a common law judicial procedure that required all criminal defendants to be brought before the judge for an inquiry regarding the legality of their detention. During the sixteenth century, the writ became an invaluable tool for those detained or imprisoned for voicing their displeasure against the monarchy.[10] In 1679, after much contention between parliament and the English Crown, the writ was firmly and formally established as a legal right.

In view of the need to protect against illegal confinements, the writ of habeas corpus was quickly adopted by the colonists. The writ was so significant that infringements against it were barred at the time of the writing of the Constitution. The delegates at the Philadelphia Convention debated whether there were any legitimate instances in which the writ should be suspended. The Federalists argued that a rebellion or invasion of the territory of the United States may require a brief suspension of the writ. Conversely, the anti-Federalists were concerned that allowing the government such authority could lead to abuse of power and serve as a means to oppress the citizenry. In the end, the delegates agreed to preserve the writ and allow its suspension only in rare instances.[11] As incorporated in the Constitution, Article I, Section 9(2) (known as the suspension clause), the delegates concurred that "the privileges of the Writ of Habeas Corpus shall not be suspended, unless when in cases of rebellion or invasion the public safety may require it."

Article I, Section 9(2) of the Constitution does not indicate which branch of government is vested with the authority to suspend the writ. Some legal scholars have inferred that the inclusion of the suspension clause in Article I indicated that Congress was vested with the sole authority to make such decision. However, during the Civil War, President Lincoln assumed authority to suspend the writ and since then Congress has legitimized the power of the executive to suspend the writ of habeas corpus in times of war or rebellion.[12]

As with all rights and privileges adopted by the delegates at the Philadelphia Convention, the writ of habeas corpus was exclusively a federal privilege. Accordingly, only federal inmates had the opportunity to use the writ to seek release from prison. In the Federal Habeas Corpus Act of 1867, Congress extended the right to petition courts using habeas corpus to any individual detained or incarcerated in violation of the Constitution. Habeas corpus was therefore extended to state prison inmates. Congress's decision to open a federal legal avenue to state prisoners was not well received by federal judges, who worried that their caseload would significantly increase as a result.[13] In *Ex parte Royall* (1886),[14] the Supreme Court eased such worries by ruling that judges had the discretion to deny state prisoners, who had not exhausted state habeas corpus relief, from seeking relief in federal court.

As is evident in this early ruling, there are two types of habeas corpus proceedings—state-level proceedings and federal-level proceedings. Since 1886, the Supreme Court ruled that an inmate must first file a writ of habeas corpus in a state court (the court that originally convicted the inmate) before proceeding with a habeas petition at the federal level. Also, in *Ex parte Royall* (1886), the Court declared that any inmate seeking review in federal court must first exhaust state court habeas corpus remedies. Thus, the inmate must proceed through a court hierarchy where a denial of a habeas petition by the state district court must be appealed to a state appellate court, followed by an appeal to the state supreme court. If the inmate wants to proceed to the federal level, a petition must be filed in the hierarchy of federal courts, starting with the federal district court, federal circuit courts, and then the U.S. Supreme Court. A federal inmate seeking habeas review, however, need not file a petition at the state level, but instead may directly file review with the federal district court that originally heard the case. Since 1886, the issue of the proper state and federal procedures to follow when filing habeas petitions has occupied much attention in both the legislative and judicial branches of government.

B. The Battle over Successive Petitions and the Road to the AEDPA

1. The Good Faith/Bad Faith Rule

With the exception of the ruling in *Ex parte Royall* in 1886, habeas corpus remained the most significant way, and perhaps the only way, in which state prison inmates, confined in violation of the Constitution, could have their confinement reviewed by the federal courts.[15] Until the early twentieth century, the Great Writ remained unaltered and inmates were allowed to file successive petitions even for claims or issues already litigated (known as same-claim successive petitions) as well as successive petitions for claims not previously litigated (known as new-claim successive petitions). However, beginning in 1924, both the Supreme Court and Congress initiated actions that curtailed the freedom of prison inmates to file same-claim successive habeas corpus petitions. Curtailment of the use of the Great Writ by both the judicial and legislative branches of government was precipitated by the writ being used to delay the carrying out of state court decisions imposing the death penalty.[16]

In 1924, the Court was struck with two instances of blatant abuses of the Great Writ. Although not ready to believe that these two cases were representative of all petitions filed in federal courts, the Court nonetheless marveled at the ease with which inmates could manipulate the justice system. In *Salinger v. Loisel* (1924),[17] the Court created a discretionary rule that authorized federal judges to dismiss successive habeas corpus petitions based on the good faith or bad faith of the inmate's intention in filing such petitions. In other words, the Court allowed federal judges to deny habeas corpus relief to any inmate whom they believed may have filed such petition for disingenuous reasons, such as to impede the imposition of a sentence. In *Wong Doo v. United States* (1924),[18] the Court reiterated its subjective good faith/bad faith directive as a justification for denying successive petitions when it realized that the petitioner in this case had successfully managed to delay the imposition of a court sentence for almost four years through the use of the writ.

2. New-Claim Successive Petitions Rule

In 1948, Congress reacted to the Court's decisions in *Salinger* and *Wong Doo* and codified its good faith/bad faith directive into law in the Judicial Code and Judiciary Act. The act permitted federal courts to "deny a successive federal habeas corpus petition if its claims had been previously presented and rejected and if the new petition presents no new ground not therefore presented and determined, and the judge or court is satisfied that the ends of justice will not be served by such inquiry."[19] The Court in *Sanders v. United States* (1963)[20] placed further limitations on both same-claim and new-claim successive petitions. As for same-claim petitions, the Court again refused to permit inmates from manipulating the justice system by ruling that unless the ends of justice warrant an inquiry, dismissal of such claims was within the discretionary authority of the federal courts. For new claims not previously litigated, the Supreme Court ruled that federal courts may also dismiss or refuse to hear such petitions when the inmate had deliberately and strategically chosen not to include new issues in previous habeas petitions for the purpose of stalling or impeding a state court decision. The Court then said that if evidence was discovered at the time of an initial habeas corpus petition but was not filed in order to create another opportunity to seek the review of a court at a later date, the inmate's right to file such new claim was rescinded. In response to the Court's decision in *Sanders*, Congress revised its habeas corpus statutes in 1966 to include the high court's new rule on new-claim successive petitions.[21]

3. The Impact of *Gregg* on Successive Petitions

After the Supreme Court's decision in *Gregg v. Georgia* (1976),[22] the legal landscape for filing successive petitions, especially for death row inmates, changed to some extent. *Gregg* signified the Court's desire to ensure that death penalty statutes and practices are constitutional. The "death is different" jurisprudence initiated in *Gregg* meant that "capital litigation was not considered final until all available state and federal post-conviction review had been completed. The new prototype for capital litigation was a nine-step process that almost always included petitions for a writ of habeas corpus in federal court."[23] The Court's subsequent rulings on the death penalty after *Gregg* created new constitutional issues that only served to provide capital offenders with more opportunities to file new-claim successive habeas corpus petitions in federal court. Although the Court in *Gregg* ended capricious and arbitrary death penalty sentencing schemes, it significantly increased the caseload for federal judges. This came about despite the Court not having created a federal constitutional right to counsel for capital offenders in state and federal habeas corpus proceedings. This oversight by the Court meant that most lawyers willing to represent capital offenders were overburdened and in some instances had to resort to filing habeas corpus petitions just hours before an execution was scheduled to take place.[24]

The last-minute attempts to halt executions, coupled with the volume of cases filed in federal court, prompted the Supreme Court to seek remedies. In *Rose v. Lundy* (1982),[25] the Court opined that state prison inmates must exhaust state court remedies before filing a writ of habeas corpus in federal court or else the privilege to file in federal court would be revoked. Although the ruling in this case was strikingly similar to one issued almost 100 years before in *Ex parte Royall*, the Court specifically addressed "mixed petitions." A mixed petition was one in which the inmate filed a habeas petition in the state court with two or more claims of illegal or unconstitutional confinement. However, when filing the same habeas petition in federal court, the inmate would include additional claims not previously litigated at the state level. In

Rose v. Lundy, the Court barred inmates from filing mixed petitions because it was a violation of the intent of the Great Writ and federal law.

The mixed-petition rule as well as the new-claim successive petition rule adopted by both the Supreme Court and Congress supplemented another rule created in 1977—the procedural default rule. According to the Court, a state prison inmate who failed to comply with procedural rules may not address issues of habeas relief in federal court because his or her petition was procedurally flawed and was therefore a defaulted petition. Failure to comply with procedural rules, either at trial, during appeal, or in a post-conviction proceeding, virtually barred an inmate from filing a habeas corpus petition. The only way to circumvent this rule was if the inmate met the cause and prejudice test. The cause and prejudice test contains two opportunities to bypass the procedural default rule. For instance, the cause portion of the test required the inmate to demonstrate actual cause for failing to follow procedural rules, such as failure to follow procedures due to ineffective assistance of counsel. The inmate could also circumvent this rule by relying on the prejudice portion of the test. Thus, he or she could demonstrate that some other cause external to the defense (such as a constitutional violation) may have prejudiced the imposition of the sentence or created a miscarriage of justice.[26]

In 1988, Chief Justice Rehnquist created the Ad Hoc Committee on Federal Habeas Corpus in Capital Cases to investigate ways to limit the filing of habeas corpus petitions. Justice Powell, who was appointed chair of the committee, noted that:

> In some cases last-minute habeas corpus petitions have resulted from the unavailability of counsel at an earlier time. But in other cases attorneys appear to have intentionally delayed filing until time pressures were severe. In most cases, successive petitions are meritless, and we believe many are filed at the eleventh hour seeking nothing more than delay.[27]

The Ad Hoc Committee agreed with the observation and recommended the passage of a congressional act that would severely limit successive petitions. However, the recommendations were not adopted by Congress. Because Congress refused to act, the Supreme Court proceeded to curtail successive petitions anyway. In *McCleskey v. Zant* (1991),[28] the Court held that the petitioner must prove that the failure to raise a claim during a prior habeas corpus petition was not an attempt to circumvent a court sentence. Thus, the petitioner must prove that the new claim was based on an objective factor external to the defense that necessitated the court's attention because it was prejudicial to the sentence imposed or would result in a miscarriage of justice. In essence, the petitioner had to provide factual evidence that the petition for habeas corpus was worthy of proceeding through the maze of post-conviction review by either: (1) presenting new evidence that raised sufficient doubt about his or her guilt or (2) showing that a constitutional violation had resulted when the sentence of death was imposed because the petitioner was "actually innocent" of a death sentence.

C. The AEDPA

The Antiterrorism and Effective Death Penalty Act of 1996 (AEDPA) signaled a new era in habeas corpus petitions and provided new rules meant to limit the filing of successive petitions. The AEDPA was passed by Congress in the wake of the Oklahoma City bombing and was primarily designed to protect the country from future domestic terroristic threats. However, the act also contains explicit restrictions on habeas corpus petitions. Although much legal debate has surfaced regarding the connection between the tragic event in Oklahoma and habeas corpus petitions,[29] the AEDPA represents the most restrictive piece of legislation that affects the ability of inmates to use the Great Writ. It has created an even more complicated and elaborate maze of legal technicalities than those previously imposed. To date, the Supreme Court has upheld the constitutionality of the provisions of the AEDPA and has narrowly interpreted its provisions to preserve the goals of the Act. Figure 10.2 briefly outlines the significant provisions of the AEDPA.

Figure 10.2
Provisions of the Antiterrorism and Effective Death Penalty Act of 1996

- Sets a statute of limitations for filing an initial habeas corpus petition. A petitioner who fails to file within the specified time (one year) may be granted review only if the failure to file was: (1) the result of a state action, (2) the result of the Supreme Court's decision to apply a ruling retroactively, or (3) when evidence could not have been discovered through due diligence in time to file.

- Limits federal review of state convictions unless a petitioner can prove that the state court's decision wa:s (1) "contrary to, or involved an unreasonable application of federal law, or (2) was based on an unreasonable determination of facts in light of evidence presented in state court.

- Requires a petitioner to file a certificate of appealability before filing a second or successive petition of a previously unlitigated claim.

The first significant provision of the AEDPA is the statute of limitations for filing an initial habeas petition with the state court that originally prosecuted the inmate. The AEDPA sets a one-year statute of limitations for the filing of any initial habeas corpus petition. A statute of limitations is a legal rule that places a limit on the amount of time that an inmate is allowed to file a habeas petition. In essence, a statute of limitations is an "expiration date" that the court observes when considering hearing a petition. Generally, the one-year statute of limitations begins after the inmate has exhausted his or her state remedies. An inmate who fails to file within the specified time limit may be granted review only if the failure to file was: (1) the result of a state action, (2) the result of the Court's decision to apply a ruling retroactively, or (3) when evidence could not have been discovered through due diligence in time to file within the one-year time frame.

Another significant provision of the AEDPA limits federal review of state convictions unless the petitioner can prove that the state court decision was "contrary to, or involved an unreasonable application of, clearly established federal law, as determined by the Supreme Court or . . . was based on an unreasonable determination of facts in light of the evidence presented in the state court proceeding."[30] This provision, found in § 2254(d) of the AEDPA, gives significant deference to state courts. This deference was echoed by the Court in *Williams v. Taylor* (2000),[31] in which it held that an "unreasonable application" of law was not synonymous with a harmless error or a decision that was incorrect yet reasonable. The Court supplemented Congress's provision by creating a stringent standard for petitions where not even a reasonable though incorrect state decision would pass AEDPA's requirements. *Williams v. Taylor* reflected the Court's attempt to achieve some sense of finality with regard to state decisions, rather than prolonging the imposition of a state decision due to lengthy post-conviction review.

Perhaps the most restrictive provision of the AEDPA applies to successive petitions. The AEDPA prohibits same-claim successive petitions, but allows successive petitions for previously unlitigated claims. The Act requires inmates to obtain a certificate of appealability (COA) before filing a second or successive petition of a previously unlitigated claim. A COA must be obtained from a panel of three circuit court judges before the inmate is allowed to file the petition with the federal district court. Accordingly, the inmate must present evidence that a new rule, created by the Court, applies retroactively to the petitioner's case or must demonstrate that he or she, through due diligence, has discovered new evidence (a constitutional error or violation) that was previously unavailable during the first petition. The petitioner must demonstrate through clear and convincing evidence that, absent a constitutional error, he or she would have been found not guilty of the crime.

The decision to apply the ruling of one case retroactively to other cases is the exclusive domain of the Supreme Court. Traditionally, when the Court issues a ruling in one case, that ruling becomes controlling precedent for future cases only. Generally, automatic retroactivity is associated with appeals and not habeas corpus decisions. Habeas decisions issued by the Court may or may not apply retroactively. Under § 2244(b)(2)(A) of the AEDPA, an inmate cannot file a successive petition on the basis of "a new rule of constitutional law . . . that was previously unavailable," unless it has been "made retroactively to cases on collateral review by the Supreme Court."[32] Prior to the AEDPA, the Court had already explained the retroactivity rule in habeas decisions. In *Teague v. Lane* (1989),[33] the Court held that unless an inmate's claims are based on precedent made retroactive by the Court, he or she cannot use the writ of habeas corpus to seek review. Thus, claims that would result in a new ruling, thereby creating new law, were impermissible under habeas corpus. The essence of *Teague* was incorporated by Congress into the AEDPA. In 2001, the Court was asked to rule on the constitutionality of the AEDPA's "new rule" provision, and in *Tyler v. Cain* (2001),[34] the Court held that the AEDPA's provision was constitutional.

In 2005, the Supreme Court, in *Rhines v. Weber,*[35] addressed the issue of mixed petitions once again but this time clarified the role of the AEDPA and the statute of limitations for such petitions. Consistent with its ruling in *Rose v. Lundy,*[36] the Court confirmed that the AEDPA favors a "total exhaustion" of state court remedies before filing a habeas appeal in federal court. However, because *Lundy* was decided before the passage of the AEDPA, the Court acknowledged that "petitioners who come to federal court with mixed petitions run the risk of forever losing their opportunity for any federal review of the unexhausted claims" if the one-year statute of limitations expires.[37] Therefore, the Court noted that the statute does not bar federal district courts from practicing what is known as "stay-and-abeyance" of petitions. Under the practice of "stay-and-abeyance," a district court may "stay the petition and hold it in abeyance while the petitioner returns to state court to exhaust his previously unexhausted claims. Once the petitioner exhausts his state remedies, the district court will lift the stay and allow the petitioner to proceed in federal court."[38]

Although the Court's decision in *Rhines v. Weber* seemingly relaxes the stringent rules of the AEDPA, the Court noted that the practice of "stay-and-abeyance" should be employed only in the rarest of circumstances, available only in limited circumstances, and should not be used to stay a petition indefinitely because otherwise it may encourage inmates to delay the resolution of their federal proceedings. Thus, both the AEDPA and the Court's decisions are stringent attempts to limit habeas corpus in an effort to accomplish three main goals: "a desire to promote 'comity' between state and federal systems; the need for finality in criminal convictions; and the goal of decreasing the burdens on federal court dockets."[39] In its totality, the AEDPA is massive piece of legislation that severely restricts the original purpose of the Great Writ of habeas corpus. The Great Writ was originally intended to be unfettered and suspension issued only in times of war. The AEDPA seriously undermines the original purpose of the writ. Some argue that the AEDPA violates the suspension clause because it suspends or inhibits confined individuals from seeking to have their petitions heard by state and federal courts. The Court in *Felker v. Turpin* (1996)[40] responded by saying that the AEDPA does not violate the Constitution's suspension clause. Despite the Court's decision, the AEDPA has had several unintended consequences. For example, its legal maze of technicalities has added procedural rules, such as the certificate of appealability, with which inmates must comply with before filing a petition. This has imposed an additional layer to the process and increased the caseload of the circuit courts.

IV. Current Consequences of the AEDPA

A. Retroactivity

The AEDPA limits the capacity of inmates to use the writ, especially when the Court refuses to apply its decision retroactively or when the statute of limitations has expired. This creates significant problems for death row inmates. For example, because of the retroactivity rule, a death row inmate cannot file a writ if it involves a new constitutional issue not previously heard by the Court or not yet applied retroactively by the Court. As noted in Justice Breyer's dissenting opinion in *Tyler*,[41] the AEDPA and the Court have created an absurdity with regard to retroactivity because the Court does not always specify which decisions are retroactive. Thus, an inmate who wishes to benefit from the Court's previous ruling in another case must use the first or initial writ of habeas corpus to petition to have a previous ruling applied retroactively on collateral review. If this fails, the inmate cannot file a same-claim successive petition.[42] For death row inmates "whose stay of execution depends upon filing a successive petition will be unable to do so, and may well be executed, because the Supreme Court has not yet issued a decision announcing the retroactivity of a newly announced rule that renders the prisoner's conviction or sentence unconstitutional."[43]

B. Statute of Limitations and Actual Innocence

1. Statute of Limitations

Also important for death row inmates is the statute of limitations. As noted, a statute of limitation is a legal rule that places a limit on the amount of time that an inmate is allowed to file a habeas petition. The AEDPA, for example, places a one-year time-frame during which to file an initial habeas petition. Ironically, a small category of death row inmates, particularly those who file mental incompetence claims, were originally barred from filing habeas petitions because of the statute of limitations. Incompetent-to-be-executed claims can only be filed shortly before an execution, which means that such claims do not become ripe for petition until an inmate gets closer to his or her execution date. Such habeas petitions also do not become ripe until a death warrant, which specifies the date of execution, has been issued by the court. A death warrant can be issued after the statute of limitations has expired.[44]

In *Stewart v. Martinez-Villareal* (1998),[45] the issues of incompetent-to-be-executed as well as the ripeness to file a habeas petition were addressed by the Court. When capital death row inmate Martinez-Villareal filed his claim of incompetency, the state of Arizona argued that because a death warrant had not been issued, Martinez-Villareal should be barred from filing a habeas petition for this claim. The state district court agreed and denied the petition. After the death warrant was issued, the state argued that the statute of limitations had expired, therefore also barring the petition. The state also argued that if the statute of limitations was to be set aside, the matter had to be decided by a circuit court, under a certificate of appealability (COA). The Ninth Circuit Court, which heard the COA, ruled that a petition that is premature for filing does not bar the inmate from filing such petition even after the statute of limitations has expired. The Supreme Court agreed with the Ninth Circuit Court and assured that the statute of limitations would be suspended only when an issue of incompetency was dismissed on grounds of prematurity. The Court also held that the subsequent filing of this petition did not violate the AEDPA's successive petition rule. Although the Court clarified the issue of ripeness, it did not address instances in which failure to file did not involve prematurity. Some federal circuit courts have strictly interpreted the AEDPA and have barred such claims if they violate the statute of limitations.

In 2006, the Court heard oral arguments to determine whether the AEDPA's one-year statute of limitations is suspended or "tolled" while a state court reviews an inmate's application for state post-conviction relief. The AEDPA "tolls" the statute of limitations while a state prisoner seeks post-conviction relief in state court. Tolling, as defined in the AEDPA, is:

> The time during which a properly filed application for state post-conviction or other collateral review with respect to the pertinent judgment or claim is pending . . . and this time shall not be counted toward any period of limitation under the AEDPA.[46]

In *Lawrence v. Florida*,[47] a death row inmate filed for state post-conviction relief 364 days after his conviction became final. The trial court denied relief as did the state supreme court and later the U.S. Supreme Court. However, while the post-conviction petition was pending in the U.S. Supreme Court, Lawrence filed a habeas corpus petition with the U.S. District Court—113 days after the state supreme court's decision in his post-conviction appeal. The Court held that the AEDPA does not suspend or "toll" the one-year statute of limitations if a defendant is awaiting a decision by the U.S. Supreme Court and then files a habeas corpus petition well after such limitation has expired. Thus, the Court reasoned that the statute of limitations may be suspended while an inmate awaits a response or decision by a state court, which is the final court to resolve post-conviction petitions, but not the U.S. Supreme Court because the Court "rarely grants review of state post-conviction proceedings" and is thus not usually the final court to resolve a post-conviction petition.[48] The AEDPA statute of limitations is suspended only to await a decision by a state court.

The strict interpretation of the AEDPA is consistent with the Court's attempt to "balance the societal interests of finality, comity, and conservation of scarce judicial resources" by ensuring that inmates first exhaust all state remedies before filing a habeas petition in federal court and by encouraging inmates to file petitions on a timely basis.[49] According to the Court, allowing inmates to default on the statute of limitations period would motivate them to file petitions as a tactic to delay proceedings, which runs counter to the goal of the AEDPA.

2. Actual Innocence

Another problem with the AEDPA involves claims of actual innocence. Actual innocence includes situations in which the inmate is factually innocent and also situations in which he or she is "innocent" because he or she received a sentence that was not deserved. In the latter case, a sentence may not be deserved due to a constitutional error at trial or when errors affect "the production and thus evaluation, of mitigating evidence at the sentencing stage of a capital trial—the site of the ultimate life/death decision."[50] The concept of actual innocence was first stressed by the Court in *Murray v. Carrier* (1986),[51] when it ruled that although the defendant could not show cause as to why he failed to meet procedural rules (procedural default), it would nonetheless entertain the petition of an inmate who was unjustly incarcerated due to actual innocence because not doing so would be a miscarriage of justice. In *Smith v. Murray* (1986),[52] the Court further acknowledged that innocence may also be claimed because of a constitutional error during sentencing that "precluded the development of true facts or resulted in the admission of false ones." Thus, the Court affirmed that any errors that affect the mitigation of evidence during the sentencing phase of a capital trial could be used to buttress a claim of actual "sentencing" innocence.

In *Sawyer v. Whitley* (1992),[53] the Supreme Court reconsidered its previous decisions when it ruled that capital petitioners must show "by clear and convincing evidence that were it not for a constitutional error, no reasonable juror would have found the petitioner eligible for the death penalty under the applicable state law." Thus, the Court required that a petitioner demonstrate, through clear and convincing evidence, that a constitutional error (proving actual innocence) would nullify his death penalty eligibility because such error would cancel out an aggravating factor used by the jury to elevate the defendant's status to "death eligible." *Sawyer* limited the ability of death row inmates to file a claim of actual innocence. Following this decision, the Court in *Herrera v. Collins* (1993)[54] further restricted claims of actual innocence when it held that:

> Where a defendant has been afforded a fair trial and convicted of the offense for which he was charged, the constitutional presumption of innocence disappears. Federal habeas courts do not sit to correct errors of fact, but to ensure that individuals are not imprisoned in violation of the Constitution. Thus, claims of actual innocence based on newly discovered evidence have never been held to state a ground for federal habeas relief absent an independent constitutional violation occurring in the course of the underlying state criminal proceedings.[55]

Carrier, Murray, Whitley, and *Collins* represent differing concepts of actual innocence articulated by the Court prior to the passage of the AEDPA. As mentioned, a capital defendant may be wrongfully convicted of a crime that she did not commit and thus is innocent of the crime (factually innocent) or a defendant may be "innocent of the death penalty due to a grave constitutional error at trial." The former category of innocence is referred to by the Court as "free-standing" innocence and usually leads to being exonerated of the crime for which she was convicted while the latter category is called "gateway" innocence because a constitutional error at trial creates a gateway for a new trial. In either case, however, the capital defendant must produce evidence of innocence that was not presented at trial. Yet the Court has created various standards of proof for actual innocence claims and in some cases has not fully clarified how much evidence is needed to successfully prove innocence. Figure 10.3 briefly outlines the different categories, their corresponding cases, and the requisite evidence and/or standard set by the Court. The Court has created a much stricter standard for "gateway" claims of innocence.

Figure 10.3
Different Claims of Actual Innocence

	"Free-standing" Innocence	**"Gateway" Innocence**
Murray v. Carrier		✓ Standard: Defendant must show that it is more likely than not that no reasonable juror would have found him/her guilty beyond a reasonable doubt based on the evidence presented at trial and newly discovered evidence (known as the "probability" test)
Smith v. Murray	✓ Standard: Although the Court did not provide a clear standard, it did articulate that a defendant must provide *enough* evidence of a constitutional error during the sentencing phase to mitigate the aggravating factors that led to the imposition of the death penalty	
Sawyer v. Whitley		✓ Standard: Defendant must show by clear and convincing evidence that, but for a constitutional error, no reasonable juror would have found the defendant eligible for the death penalty
Herrera v. Collins	✓ Standard: Although the Court articulated that claims of free-standing innocence, based on newly discovered evidence, do not exist within the purview of a habeas corpus appeal, it noted that if such a claim were to be brought before a state or federal court, the threshold showing for a free-standing innocence claim would be "extraordinarily high."	

If taking the most strict interpretation of the AEDPA, actual innocence claims of any kind are allowed to be filed as long as there is a showing of innocence, the claim is filed before the statute of limitations expires, and such claims are not raised in same-claim successive petitions, which are barred by the act. The actual innocence provision found in the AEDPA was loosely adapted from the Court's ruling in *McCleskey v. Zant* (1991).[56] In *McCleskey*, the Supreme Court held that a court must entertain a defaulted petition when a petitioner could demonstrate that a miscarriage of justice would result if the court did not hear his petition because he was innocent. Although in *McCleskey* the Court ruled that a petitioner did not have to state why his petition failed to meet procedural rules (defaulted petition), Congress in the AEDPA modified this provision. Under the AEDPA, a petitioner must state why the petition was defaulted and also present evidence of actual innocence.

In 2006, the Court revisited the issue of actual innocence in *House v. Bell*.[57] This was a "gateway" case of innocence but also one that involved a defaulted petition because House did not raise his claim of ineffective assistance of counsel in prior post-conviction proceedings. In fact, in his prior post conviction proceeding, which was heard by the U.S. District Court for the Eastern District of Tennessee, the court ruled that House's appeal was in violation of Tennessee law, which states that "claims not raised in prior post-conviction proceedings are presumptively waived." Even though the district court deemed the claim as procedurally defaulted for such reason, the U.S. Supreme Court nonetheless held an evidentiary hearing to determine whether House fell within the purview of the actual innocence exception to procedurally defaulted claims (this exception was previously created by the Court in *Schlup v. Delo)*[58]. After hearing new evidence presented by House as to his innocence, the Court held that House fell within the procedural default exception and that "it is more likely than not that no reasonable juror would have found him guilty beyond a reasonable doubt" had the juror heard the newly discovered evidence. The Court remanded the case to the state court for a new trial. The Court noted, however, that a gateway habeas corpus claim of actual innocence requires the habeas court to consider all evidence presented at the original trial and newly discovered evidence. The Court also clarified the position of the AEDPA under the procedural default exception in actual innocence claims. Because the claim did not involve a violation of the statute of limitations nor involved a same-claim successive petition but rather was only a defaulted claim, the Court held that the AEDPA and the *McCleskey* standard have no bearing on the case.

Although the AEDPA contains a provision allowing for claims of actual innocence, it is silent on whether such claims can ever be allowed if an inmate failed to meet the statute of limitations. Though the AEDPA has a provision to set aside the restrictive statute of limitations when new evidence is discovered that a constitutional (procedural) error had occurred during trial or sentencing, the Court has previously stated that newly discovered evidence does not fall within the purview of habeas corpus review. Congress never addressed this problem in the AEDPA and has yet to enact any exceptions. Some federal circuit courts, such as the Fifth and Sixth Circuits, have narrowly interpreted the AEDPA and have barred such petitions simply because of a violation of the statute of limitations. Although an inmate has recourse other than a habeas petition in seeking a reversal of a conviction based on actual innocence, such as clemency, "clemency . . . has been described as arbitrary, lacking in both systematic rules and appellate review, and subject to the whims of the governor's personal preferences and the political pressures borne by him."[59]

Although an inmate may also seek to file a petition directly with the U.S. Supreme Court under its original habeas corpus jurisdiction (created under the Judiciary Act of 1789), it is unlikely that the Court would hear the petition.

V.   The Use of Habeas Corpus to Determine the Constitutionality of Methods of Execution

In 2004 and again in 2006, the Court was presented with two cases, *Nelson v. Campbell*[60] and *Hill v. McDonough*,[61] respectively, that challenged the constitutionality of two different methods of execution. In *Nelson*, the inmate sought to prevent the state of Alabama (by filing an injunction) from using a "cut-down" procedure, which would require making an incision into the arm or leg to gain access to veins in order to administer the lethal dose of drugs to effectuate his death. Although the standard technique for gaining intravenous access is through the use of a needle, Nelson's years of drug abuse, which severely compromised his veins, prompted the state to use the alternative cut-down procedure. Nelson argued, however, that such procedure would nonetheless cause him "gratuitous and unnecessary pain." In *Hill*, the inmate sought to prevent the state of Florida from using the three-drug lethal injection procedure because such procedure would cause "severe pain." Both cases alleged that the procedures violated the Eighth Amendment's prohibition of cruel and unusual punishment.

Individually, Nelson and Hill filed their claims under the federal statute known as Section 1983 (42 U.S. Code Section 1983). However, because both Nelson and Hill had already filed one unsuccessful habeas application to stay their executions before bringing their Section 1983 lawsuit, district courts in their respective cases dismissed the Section 1983 lawsuits under the belief that the latter lawsuit was the functional equivalent of a second habeas application, which is prohibited by the AEDPA.

As previously mentioned, when an inmate files a habeas corpus petition, he seeks release from prison because the incarceration is illegal or unconstitutional. It is filed after a criminal appeal and the inmate must exhaust state court remedies and follow the provisions of the AEDPA before filing a habeas application in federal court. Conversely, when an inmate files a Section 1983 lawsuit, he seeks to improve or modify the conditions of incarceration and/or seek monetary compensation from prison officials. A Section 1983 lawsuit originates from a federal law passed in 1871. It is part of a larger federal statute, known as the Civil Rights Act of 1871 or the Ku Klux Klan Act of 1871, which sought to protect southern blacks from the Klan by providing a legal remedy to alleged abuse. Section 1983 states:

> Every person who, under color of any statute, ordinance, regulation, custom, or usage, of any state or territory, subjects, or causes to be subjected, any citizen of the United States or other persons within the jurisdiction thereof to the deprivation of any rights, privileges or

immunities secured by the Constitution and laws, shall be liable to the party injured in an action at law, suit in equity, or other proper proceeding for redress.[62]

An inmate who files a Section 1983 lawsuit is therefore claiming that a person, acting under color of statute (meaning any person who has been vested with authority to enforce a law, ordinance, regulation, or custom such as a prison official), violated a constitutional right. To win, the inmate must not only prove that the person who deprived him of rights was acting under color of law, but also that there was in fact a violation of rights. Several writers summarize the difference between habeas corpus and Section 1983 lawsuits as follows:

Figure 10.4
Difference between Habeas Corpus and a Section 1983 Lawsuit

Habeas Corpus	Section 1983
1. Purpose is to seek release from prison or jail	1. Purpose is to improve prison or jail conditions and/or obtain monetary damages from prison or jail officials
2. Need to exhaust state judicial remedies before going to federal court	2. No need to exhaust state judicial remedies; the case may be filed directly in federal court
3. Begins in state court before it goes to federal court	3. Begins in federal court
4. Affects only one prisoner if it succeeds	4. Affects all prisoners if it succeeds
5. Filed by one prisoner seeking release	5. May be filed as a class action suit, meaning by a group of prisoners

Source: Rolando V. del Carmen et al., *Briefs of Leading Cases in Corrections*, Third Edition (2002: 5).

The Court in both *Nelson* and *Hill* was forced to answer whether an inmate who seeks to prevent the state from administering the death penalty due to a procedure that he deems to be cruel and unusual can file under Section 1983 or whether this type of challenge falls within the purview of habeas corpus and the rules that govern this writ under the AEDPA. In *Nelson*, the Court declared that because he was not challenging the constitutionality of the death penalty per se nor challenging the fact of his impending execution but only the method used to administer it, a Section 1983 lawsuit is the appropriate vehicle to use for such a challenge. Thus, the district court erred in classifying the challenge as the functional equivalent of a defaulted habeas corpus application. Furthermore, the Court noted that, although this case "falls within the margins of habeas,"[63] the fact that Nelson's successful Section 1983 lawsuit would only result in a change of the method used to execute him as opposed to preventing the state from executing him, distinguishes this case from a habeas application. However, the Court, fearing that abuse of

Section 1983 would impede the goals of the AEDPA, was quick to point out that the Prison Litigation Reform Act of 1995 which, among other things, establishes rules that inmates must follow when seeking to prevent the state from fully effectuating a court order, such as the particular method of execution, gives significant deference to the state. The Act states that before a court grants an inmate injunctive relief, it must "give substantial weight to any adverse impact on . . . the operation of the criminal justice system caused by the relief."[64] In addition, similar to the provisions of the AEDPA, inmates must exhaust available state administrative remedies prior to filing a Section 1983 lawsuit. The Act also grants courts the ability to dismiss suits that are "frivolous and/or malicious."

In *Hill*, the Court echoed its decision in *Nelson* and held that if an inmate challenges the lawfulness of his death sentence, then habeas corpus and the rules specified by the AEDPA govern such a challenge. However, if an inmate challenges only the method for which he is to be executed and only seeks to temporarily delay such execution, then Section 1983 is the appropriate remedy. It added that a Section 1983 lawsuit does not entitle inmates to permanently delay their execution but may provide them with a temporary delay of their execution to allow the state sufficient time to reconsider the method by which it executes inmates.

VI. In Summary, What Do these Cases Say?

The writ of habeas corpus has been significantly restricted by the Supreme Court. Together with congressional enactments, the various decisions of the Court indicate that inmates do not have an unfettered right to seek habeas review. As early as 1886 in *Ex parte Royall*,[65] the Court established firm jurisprudence with regard to habeas petitions by ruling that judges had the discretion to deny state inmates who had not exhausted state habeas corpus relief from seeking review in federal court. The Court also established the rule that any inmate seeking review in federal court must first exhaust state court habeas corpus remedies.

In the early twentieth century, the Court continued on its path to curtail the ability of inmates to file habeas petitions by creating the two additional rules—one pertaining to new-claim successive petitions and the other to same-claim successive petitions. These rules were created to address the problem of serial petitions, which the Court in *Salinger v. Loisel* (1924)[66] and *Wong Doo v. United States* (1924)[67] found to be abuses of the Great Writ. In these two cases, the Court authorized federal judges to deny successive habeas review to any inmate whom they believed may have filed the petition for disingenuous reasons. In *Sanders v. United States* (1963),[68] the Court placed further limitations on same-claim successive petitions and new-claim successive petitions. With regard to same-claim successive petitions, the Court opined that that unless the ends of justice warrant review, dismissal of such claims was within the discretionary authority of the federal courts. For new-claim successive petitions, the Court held that federal judges may also refuse to hear such petitions if it was discovered that an inmate had deliberately and strategically chosen not to include new claims in previous habeas petitions for the purpose of stalling the imposition of a state court decision. This was later reinforced by the Court in *Rose v. Lundy* (1983)[69] when it addressed mixed petitions.

By 1991, the Court refined its jurisprudence on successive petitions when in *McCleskey v. Zant* (1991)[70] it ruled that an inmate must prove that the failure to raise a claim during a prior habeas petition was not an attempt to abuse the Great Writ. The inmate had to prove that an objective factor external to the defense prejudiced his or her conviction and that the failure of the court to hear the petition would result in a miscarriage of justice. In 1996, the Antiterrorism and Effective Death Penalty Act introduced a new era in habeas corpus petitions by severely limiting the filing of successive petitions. To date, the Court has upheld the constitutionality of the provisions of the AEDPA and has narrowly interpreted its provisions. In *Williams v. Taylor* (2000),[71] for instance, the Court upheld the AEDPA's provision that a state court decision would only by reversed if it was "contrary to, or involved an unreasonable application of federal law . . ." In *Tyler v. Cain* (2001),[72] the Court upheld the AEDPA provision that an inmate cannot file a successive petition on the basis of a new constitutional law. The Court's decisions to uphold the provisions of the AEDPA can be interpreted as an attempt to achieve finality with respect to state court decisions and also an attempt to prevent any abuse of habeas corpus.

The Court's desire for finality and its strict interpretation of the AEDPA has resulted in substantial problems for death row inmates, especially with regard to claims that are filed after the statute of limitations has expired and those that involve actual innocence. Although the Court in *Stewart v. Martinez-Villareal* (1998)[73] held that the statute of limitations would be suspended when an issue, such as incompetency, was dismissed on grounds of prematurity, it has yet to rule on instances when the failure to file does not involve prematurity. Because the AEDPA does not specifically address this issue, some federal appellate courts have barred claims if they violate the statute of limitations. Under the provisions of the AEDPA, an inmate may file a claim of actual innocence as long as there is factual evidence of innocence, the claim is filed before the statute of limitations expires, and the claim is not raised in a same-claim successive petition. However, in *Herrera v. Collins* (1993),[74] the Court had previously prohibited inmates from filing claims of innocence under the purview of habeas corpus by ruling that "claims of actual innocence based on newly discovered evidence have never been held to state a ground for federal habeas relief absent an independent constitutional error . . ." Thus, although the AEDPA recognizes claims of actual innocence, the Court has curtailed the ability to file such claims if it is based on newly discovered evidence and no constitutional error occurred at trial. The Court does allow gateway claims of innocence, but there are varying standards for such claims.

In *Sawyer v. Whitley*, the Court held that defendants must show by clear and convincing evidence that, but for a constitutional error, no reasonable juror would have found the defendant eligible for the death penalty.

VII. Conclusion

Habeas corpus, a constitutional right secured by the Framers of the Constitution in the suspension clause, was intended to ensure that individuals confined in violation of the Constitution or federal laws could petition the courts in order to obtain their freedom. Although the Great Writ remains an important vehicle for those unconstitutionally detained, both the legislative and judicial branches have limited the ability of those detained to file petitions. Those limitations are a response to inmate abuse of the writ. In 1924, the Court began to limit the occasions when inmates could use the writ by implementing a subjective test that allowed judges to decline to hear petitions if such petitions were filed for disingenuous reasons. The Court's decision was followed by congressional enactment that codified the ruling into federal law. In the next several years, the Court and Congress further limited habeas petitions by restricting same-claim successive petitions and new-claim successive petitions. In addition, the Court further restricted habeas corpus when it ruled on mixed petitions and procedural defaults.

In 1996, the Antiterrorism and Effective Death Penalty Act was enacted by Congress, which significantly limits the ability of inmates to file habeas petitions. Provisions that include the statute of limitations, having to obtain a certificate of appealability, the standard of proof to file petitions, and the retroactivity rule have truly hampered granting of habeas corpus petitions. Retroactivity has had the most impact on death row inmates, who cannot file habeas petitions if the resulting court decision would amount to a new constitutional rule. Death row inmates are barred from filing petitions if the Court has not made its previous rulings retroactive on collateral review. Even in actual innocence claims, the law has limited exceptions to the statute of limitations. Although the AEDPA contains a provision that allows claims of actual innocence, it precludes such claims when the statute of limitations has elapsed. The Court has yet to rule on this issue, but some lower courts have refused to hear claims when the statute of limitations has expired. The Court has, however, recently re-emphasized the stringent adherence to the AEDPA's one-year statute of limitations in the case of *Lawrence v. Florida* (2007). In sum, the restrictive provisions of the AEDPA have fared well in court and have changed the playing field and rules for inmates in habeas cases.

Cases Briefed in Chapter 10

Case	Issue	Holding
Rose v. Lundy 455 U.S. 509 (1982)	Does federal law require a federal district court to dismiss a state prisoner's petition for habeas corpus if it contains claims that have not been exhausted in state court?	Under federal law, state prisoners must exhaust state court remedies before filing a writ of habeas corpus in federal court.
McCleskey v. Zant 499 U.S. 467 (1991)	Does the failure to include a claim of a violation of the Sixth Amendment in the first petition for a federal writ of habeas corpus preclude the same claim from being raised in a second habeas petition?	Failure to claim a violation of a constitutional right in the first habeas petition precludes the same claim from being raised in a second habeas corpus petition.
Sawyer v. Whitley 505 U.S. 333 (1992)	Does a claim of actual innocence, filed in a habeas petition, need a showing of clear and convincing evidence that were it not for a constitutional error, no reasonable juror would have found the petitioner eligible for the death penalty?	In claims of actual innocence, a petitioner must show through clear and convincing evidence, that were it not for a constitutional error, no reasonable juror would have found the petitioner eligible for the death penalty.
Herrera v. Collins 506 U.S. 390 (1993)	Is a claim of actual innocence based on newly discovered evidence a ground for habeas corpus relief absent a constitutional error during a criminal proceeding?	A claim of actual innocence based on newly discovered evidence is not a ground for relief in the absence of a constitutional violation in the criminal proceeding.
Felker v. Turpin 518 U.S. 651 (1996)	Does the Antiterrorism and Effective Death Penalty Act of 1996 prohibit a court from accepting an application for habeas corpus relief? Does the Act violate the Constitution's Suspension Clause?	The Antiterrorism and Effective Death Penalty Act of 1996 does not prohibit a court from accepting an application of habeas corpus relief nor does the Act violate the Suspension Clause.
Nelson v. Campbell 541 U.S. 637 (2004)	Can a Section 1983 lawsuit be used by an inmate who wants to challenge only the method by which he will be executed, but not the constitutionality of the death penalty per se and/or his impending execution?	A Section 1983 lawsuit is the appropriate legal remedy to use when seeking to temporarily halt an execution on grounds that the methods used to cause death violate the cruel and unusual punishment clause of the Eighth Amendment.

Cases Briefed in Chapter 10, *continued*

Case	Issue	Holding
House v. Bell 547 U.S. ___ (2007)	Is a petitioner barred from filing a habeas corpus petition on grounds of actual innocence because he failed to raise all claims in prior post-convictions proceedings?	If a petitioner has a defaulted petition due to not raising all issues in prior post-conviction petitions, habeas relief may be granted if the petitioner demonstrates cause for the default and presents new evidence that if shown to the jurors, it is more likely than not that no reasonable juror would have found him guilty beyond a reasonable doubt.
Lawrence v. Florida 549 U.S. ___ (2007)	Is the AEDPA's statute of limitations suspended or "tolled" while a defendant awaits a decision, of a habeas corpus petition, by the U.S. Supreme Court?	Although the statute of limitations may be suspended while an inmate awaits a response or decision by a state court, which is the final court to resolve post-conviction petition, it is not "tolled" when an inmate awaits a decision by the U.S. Supreme Court because the Court is not usually the final court to resolve a post-conviction petition.

Case Briefs

Rose v. Lundy
455 U.S. 509 (1982)

CAPSULE: Under federal law, state prisoners must exhaust state court remedies before filing for a writ of habeas corpus in federal court.

FACTS: Noah Lundy was convicted in Tennessee of rape and crimes against nature and was sent to state prison. The Tennessee Court of Criminal Appeals affirmed his convictions and the Tennessee Supreme Court denied review. Lundy filed a petition for post-conviction relief in state court, which was denied. He then filed a petition for a writ of habeas corpus in federal district court under 28 U.S.C. § 2254, alleging the following: (1) that he had been denied the right to confrontation because the trial court limited the defense counsel's questioning of the victim; (2) that he had been denied the right to a fair trial because the prosecuting attorney stated that the respondent had a violent character; (3) that he had been denied the right to a fair trial because the prosecutor improperly remarked in his closing arguments that the state's evidence was uncontradicted; and (4) that the trial judge improperly instructed the jury that every witness is presumed to swear the truth." The federal district court granted the writ of habeas corpus despite claims (3) and (4) not having been litigated in state court. The court of appeals affirmed the decision of the federal district court; the government appealed.

ISSUE: Does federal law (28 U.S.C. § 2254 [b] and [c]) require a federal district court to dismiss a state prisoner's petition for a writ of habeas corpus that contains claims that have not been exhausted in the state court? YES.

HOLDING: A district court must dismiss "mixed petitions" (meaning petitions that contain claims that have been exhausted and others that have not been exhausted in state court) because such dismissal furthers the purpose underlying the federal habeas corpus statute.

REASON: "The exhaustion doctrine is principally designed to protect the state courts' role in the enforcement of federal law and prevent disruption of state judicial proceedings. Under the federal system, the federal and state 'courts [are] equally bound to guard and protect rights secured by the Constitution.' Because 'it would be unseemly in our dual system of government for a federal district court to upset a state court conviction without an opportunity for the state courts to correct a constitutional violation,' federal courts apply the doctrine of comity, which 'teaches that one court should defer action on causes properly within its jurisdiction until the courts of another sovereignty with concurrent powers, and already cognizant of the litigation, have had an opportunity to pass upon the matter.'

"The facts of the present case underscore the need for a rule encouraging exhaustion of all federal claims. In his opinion, the District Court Judge wrote that 'there is such mixture of violations that one cannot be separated from and considered independently of the others.' Because the two unexhausted claims for relief were intertwined with the exhausted one, the judge apparently considered all of the claims in ruling on the petition. Requiring dismissal of petitions containing both exhausted and unexhausted claims will relieve the district courts of the difficult if not impossible task of deciding when claims are related, and will reduce the temptation to consider unexhausted claims."

CASE SIGNIFICANCE: Despite the absence of a constitutional issue, this case is significant because it makes clear when state prisoners can file habeas corpus petitions in federal courts. Habeas corpus petitions are filed by inmates to gain freedom, alleging that something was wrong with their conviction and therefore they are in prison unconstitutionally. This is the prisoner's last hope of freedom after conviction has been affirmed by the courts. Although habeas corpus cases seldom succeed, they give prisoners another judicial avenue to pursue when they feel they have been wrongly convicted.

The "exhaustion of state court remedies" doctrine provides that remedies in state courts must be exhausted before a case can be heard in federal court. As this case states, "the exhaustion doctrine existed long before its codification by Congress in 1948." Although now codified, the "mixed petition" issue was not addressed in the codification, hence the need to clarify it in this case. The purpose of the exhaustion doctrine is to avoid piecemeal litigation. Its benefits are obvious. In the words of the Court, "[t]o the extent that the exhaustion requirement reduced piecemeal litigation, both the courts and the prisoners should benefit, for as a result the district court will be more likely to review all of the prisoner's claims in a single proceeding, thus providing for a more focused and thorough review."

There are two kinds of habeas corpus proceedings: state habeas corpus and federal habeas corpus. Both are available to prisoners, but this case states that issues brought to federal court on habeas corpus grounds must first be litigated in state court. In this case, the prisoner alleged four grounds for relief; two grounds were litigated in state court and the other two grounds were not litigated. The issue was whether such a "mixed petition" ought to be entertained by the federal court. The Court decided that 28 U.S.C. § 2254 "requires a federal district court to dismiss a petition for a writ of habeas corpus containing any claims that have not been exhausted in the state courts." This is significant because it lengthens the time of potential relief for state prisoners in habeas corpus proceedings. It usually takes a number of years for prisoner habeas corpus cases to be decided in state court. Only after that will the federal forum be available to a state prisoner. This therefore further delays the availability of the federal habeas corpus remedy because state prisoners must first go through state process before taking their case to a federal court, even when some of the allegations have been litigated in state court. It is to be noted, however, that federal prisoners do not have to exhaust state proceedings because they have been convicted under federal law and were tried in federal court.

McCleskey v. Zant
499 U.S. 467 (1991)

CAPSULE: Failure to claim a violation of a constitutional right in a first federal habeas corpus petition precludes the same claim from being raised in a second habeas corpus petition.

FACTS: McCleskey was charged with murder and armed robbery. At his 1978 trial, the state of Georgia called Offie Evans, the occupant of the jail cell next to McCleskey, to rebut the petitioner's alibi defense. Evans testified that McCleskey had admitted to and boasted about the killing. Due to this testimony and other supporting evidence, the jury convicted McCleskey and sentenced him to death. After the Georgia Supreme Court affirmed the trial decision, McCleskey initiated post-conviction proceedings by filing a state habeas corpus petition, McCleskey alleging that his statements to Evans were acquired by the state creating a situation that induced him to make incriminating statements without the assistance of counsel, in violation of the Sixth Amendment. He was denied relief and filed his first federal habeas corpus and second state habeas corpus petitions, which did not contain the Sixth Amendment claim. Both petitions were also denied. He filed a second federal habeas corpus petition in 1987, challenging on Sixth Amendment grounds a 21-page statement that Evans had made to the police. The statement was made available to McCleskey just weeks before he filed his second federal petition. The document not only contained conversations that were consistent with Evans' trial testimony, but also recounted the tactics used by Evans to engage McCleskey in conversation. At the petition hearing, a jailer who was present during McCleskey's pretrial incarceration gave testimony indicating that Evans' cell assignment had been made at the state's behest.

ISSUE: Does the failure to include a claim of a violation of a Sixth Amendment in the first petition for a federal writ of habeas corpus preclude the same claim from being raised in a second habeas petition? YES.

HOLDING: The failure to include a claim of a violation of a constitutional right in the first federal habeas corpus petition precludes a similar claim in the second federal habeas petition. Allowing the prisoner to do so constitutes an abuse of the writ.

REASON: "Much confusion exists as to the proper standard for applying the abuse of the writ doctrine, which refers to a complex and evolving body of equitable principles informed and controlled by historical usage, statutory developments, and judicial decisions. This Court has heretofore defined such abuse in an oblique way, through dicta and denials of certiorari petitions or stay applications and, because of historical changes and the complexity of the subject, has not always followed an unwavering line in its conclusions as to the writ's availability."

"Although this Court's federal habeas decisions do not admit of ready synthesis, a review of these precedents demonstrates that a claim need not have been deliberately abandoned in an earlier petition in order to establish that its inclusion in a subsequent petition constitutes abuse of the writ, *see, e. g., Sanders v. United States*, 373 U.S. 1, 18: that such inclusion constitutes abuse if the claim could have been raised in the first petition, but was omitted through inexcusable neglect . . . and that, because the doctrine of procedural default and abuse of writ implicate nearly identical concerns, the determination of inexcusable neglect in the abuse context should be governed by the same standards used to determine whether to excuse a habeas petitioner's state procedural defaults, see, e.g., *Wainwright v. Sykes*, 433 U.S. 72. Thus, when a prisoner files a second or subsequent habeas petition, the government bears the burden of pleading abuse of writ. This burden is satisfied if the government, with clarity and particularity, notes petitioner's prior writ history, identifies the claims that appear for the first time, and alleges that petitioner has abused the writ. The burden to disprove abuse then shifts to the petitioner. To excuse his failure to raise the claim earlier, he must show cause—e.g., that he was impeded by some objective factor external to the defense, such as governmental interference or the reasonable unavailability of the factual basis for the claim—as well as actual prejudice resulting from the errors of which he complains."

CASE SIGNIFICANCE: This case was decided on procedural grounds, but its implication is far-reaching. Habeas petitions by prisoners seek release on the ground of unconstitutional confinement. Such petitions are first heard in state courts, and, if denied, may be filed in a federal court under the Federal Habeas Corpus Act. The prisoner in this case went twice to state court and then filed a federal habeas corpus proceeding. In his first federal habeas corpus case, however, he failed to allege a violation of his Sixth Amendment rights. Having been turned down, he filed a second federal habeas corpus case, but this time he raised a violation of his Sixth Amendment rights as the basis for his release. The Supreme Court considered this an abuse of the writ and prohibited him from raising it in the second federal habeas corpus case. The Court said that "such inclusion constitutes abuse if the claim could have been raised in the first petition, but was omitted through inexcusable neglect." The Court added that "to excuse his failure to raise the claim earlier, he must show cause—e.g., that he was impeded by some objective factor external to the defense, such as government interference or the reasonable unavailability of the factual basis for the claim—as well as actual prejudice resulting from the errors of which he complains . . ." The prisoner failed to establish this in his second petition, thus the issue could no longer be raised.

The effect of this decision is to reduce successive filings of habeas corpus cases in federal court by state prisoners. In effect, the Supreme Court is saying that petitioners must include all constitutional claims in their first petition and not "serialize" them. Any claim not raised in the first petition cannot be raised in a subsequent petition. The only exception is if a prisoner can show that "a fundamental miscarriage of justice—such as the conviction of an innocent person—would result from a failure to entertain the claim.

Sawyer v. Whitley
505 U.S. 333 (1992)

CAPSULE: In claims of actual innocence, a petitioner must show through clear and convincing evidence that were it not for a constitutional error, no reasonable juror would have found the petitioner eligible for the death penalty under the applicable state law.

FACTS: Petitioner Robert Sawyer was prosecuted and found guilty of committing first-degree murder in the course of committing an aggravated arson. At sentencing, the jury found no statutory mitigating factors, but found three aggravating factors, thus making the petitioner death eligible under Louisiana law. The jury sentenced petitioner Sawyer to death. After having exhausted his state and federal judicial appeals, Sawyer filed his first habeas corpus petition alleging actual innocence. He said he was innocent because crucial mitigating factors (a claim of intoxication at the time of the murder and evidence of a deprived childhood) were deliberately withheld from the jury when making its determination of death eligibility. This was based on his original claim that due to ineffective counsel, such evidence was never fully presented to the jury. Sawyer claimed that, had such mitigating factors been allowed to be reviewed by the jury, he would not have been found death eligible and thus never sentenced to death.

ISSUE: Does a claim of actual innocence, filed in a habeas petition, need a showing of clear and convincing evidence that were it not for a constitutional error, no reasonable juror would have found the petitioner eligible for the death penalty under the applicable state law? YES.

HOLDING: In claims of actual innocence before a habeas court, the petitioner must demonstrate through clear and convincing evidence that, absent a constitutional violation, a reasonable jury would not have found the petitioner death eligible. Petitioner Sawyer failed to meet this burden because he could not prove that mitigating evidence was deliberately withheld from the jury when it considered his death eligibility. Thus, his death sentence was affirmed.

REASON: "The issue before the Court is the standard for determining whether a petitioner bringing a successive, abusive, or defaulted federal habeas claim has shown he is actually innocent of the death penalty to which he has been sentenced, so that the court may reach the merits of the claim . . . We affirm the Court of Appeals, and hold that, to show actual innocence, one must show by clear and convincing evidence that, but for a constitutional error, no reasonable jury would have found the petitioner eligible for the death penalty under the applicable state law . . . Under Louisiana law, petitioner is eligible for the death penalty because he was convicted of first-degree murder—that is, an intentional killing while in the process of committing an aggravated arson—and because, at the sentencing phase, the jury found two valid aggravating circumstances: that the murder was committed in the course of an aggravated arson and that the murder was especially cruel, atrocious, and heinous. The psychological evidence petitioner alleges was kept from the jury due to the ineffective assistance of counsel does not relate to petitioner's guilt or innocence of the crime. Neither does it relate to either of the aggravating factors found by the jury that made the petitioner eligible for the death penalty. Even if this evidence had been before the jury, it cannot be said that a reasonable juror would not have found both of the aggravating factors that make the petitioner eligible for the death penalty. Therefore, as to this evidence, petitioner has not shown that there would be a fundamental miscarriage of justice for the Court to fail to reexamine the merits of this successive claim."

CASE SIGNIFICANCE: This case is significant because it limited the ability of capital petitions to file a claim of actual innocence. It also established a standard for claims of actual innocence, which is as follows: a petitioner must show through clear and convincing evidence that were it not for a constitutional error, no reasonable juror would have found the petitioner eligible for the death penalty under the applicable state law. The rule on claims of actual innocence was first articulated by the Court in *Murray v. Carrier*,[75] when it said that despite the fact that the defendant could not show cause as to why he failed to meet procedural rules, the Court would nonetheless entertain a petition of a inmate who was unjustly incarcerated due to actual innocence because not doing so would be a miscarriage of justice. In *Smith v. Murray*,[76] the Court further acknowledged that innocence may also be claimed because of a constitutional error during sentencing that "precluded the development of true facts or resulted in the admission of false ones." Thus, the Court affirmed that any errors that affect the mitigation of evidence during the sentencing phase of a capital trial could be used to buttress a claim of actual "sentencing" innocence. However, in *Sawyer* the Court reconsidered its previous rulings and instead opined that capital petitioners must show "by clear and convincing evidence that were it not for a constitutional error, no reasonable juror would have found the petitioner eligible for the death penalty under the applicable state law." Thus, the Court now requires that a petitioner demonstrate, through clear and convincing evidence, that a constitutional error (proving actual innocence) would nullify his death penalty eligibility because such error would cancel out an aggravating factor used by the jury when deliberating whether to impose the death penalty.

Herrera v. Collins
506 U.S. 390 (1993)

CAPSULE: A claim of actual innocence based on newly discovered evidence is not a ground for federal habeas relief in the absence of an independent constitutional violation in the criminal proceeding itself.

FACTS: Leonel Torres Herrera was charged with the capital murders of police officers Carrisalez and Rucker in the state of Texas. At his trial in 1982 for the murder of Carrisalez, Herrera was convicted and sentenced to death based on the testimony of two eyewitnesses, a significant amount of circumstantial evidence, and Herrera's handwritten letter admitting his guilt. Later that same year, Herrera pled guilty to the capital murder of Rucker. After filing a series of unsuccessful judicial appeals seeking a reversal of his conviction and sentence, Herrera filed for habeas corpus relief in 1991 on grounds that newly discovered evidence demonstrated that his brother had committed the capital murders. Herrera's claim of actual innocence was denied by the state district court. In 1992, Herrera filed a habeas petition in federal court alleging actual innocence, and thus, that his death sentence was in violation of the Eighth Amendment and Fourteenth Amendment. Although the federal district court dismissed most of Herrera's claims because of its belief that the petition was filed for disingenuous reasons and thus constituted an abuse of the writ of habeas corpus, the court granted a stay of execution so that Herrera could present his newly discovered evidence in state district court. However, the state district court dismissed his claim. On appeal, the Fifth Circuit Court of Appeals held that no evidence existed to exculpate Herrera and determined that the claim of actual innocence was disingenuous and therefore an abuse of the writ of habeas corpus. The court further held that, absent a constitutional error at trial, a claim of actual innocence was not grounds for habeas relief. Herrera appealed to the Supreme Court.

ISSUE: Is a claim of actual innocence based on newly discovered evidence a ground for habeas corpus relief absent a constitutional error during a criminal proceeding? NO.

HOLDING: A defendant's showing of innocence, and a constitutional claim for relief based upon that showing, must be evaluated in light of the previous proceedings. Absent an independent constitutional violation occurring in the state criminal proceeding, claims of actual innocence based on newly discovered evidence are not sufficient to constitute grounds for federal habeas relief.

REASON: "Claims of actual innocence based on newly discovered evidence have never been held to state a ground for federal habeas relief absent an independent constitutional violation occurring in the underlying state criminal proceeding. The rule is grounded in the principle that federal habeas courts sit to ensure that individuals are not imprisoned in violation of the Constitution—not to correct errors of fact. Petitioner is understandably imprecise in describing the sort of federal relief to which a suitable showing of actual innocence would entitle him. In his brief, he states that the federal habeas court should have an important initial opportunity to hear the evidence and resolve the merits of his claim. Acceptance of this view would presumably require the habeas court to hear testimony from the witnesses who testified at trial as well as those who made the statements in the affidavits that the petitioner has presented, and to determine anew whether or not petitioner is guilty of the murders. This is not to say that our habeas jurisprudence casts a blind eye toward innocence. In a series of cases, we have held that a petitioner otherwise subject to defenses of abusive or successive use of the writ may have his federal constitutional claim considered on the merits if he makes a proper showing of actual innocence. But this body of our habeas corpus jurisprudence makes clear that a claim of actual innocence is not itself a constitutional claim, but instead a gateway through which a habeas petitioner must pass to have his otherwise barred constitutional claim considered on the merits. Petitioner in this case is simply not entitled to habeas relief on the reasoning of this line of cases (see e.g., *Sawyer v. Whitley* [505 U.S. 333 (1992); *Smith v. Murray*, 477 U.S. 527 (1986)]. For he does not seek excusal of a procedural error so that he may bring an independent constitutional claim challenging his conviction or sentence, but rather argues that he is entitled to habeas relief because newly discovered evidence shows that his conviction is factually incorrect. The fundamental miscarriage of justice exception is available only where the prisoner supplements his constitutional claim with a colorable showing of factual innocence. We have never held that it extends to freestanding claims of actual innocence. Therefore, the exception is inapplicable here."

CASE SIGNIFICANCE: Claims of actual innocence may be made in habeas proceedings. These claims may include a factual showing that a petitioner is not guilty of the crime for which he or she is being prosecuted or a showing of innocence because of a constitutional error made during the criminal proceeding. However, claims of actual innocence must meet certain procedural rules. For instance, in *Sawyer v. Whitley* [505 U.S. 333 (1992)], the Court said that capital petitioners must show through clear and convincing evidence that had a constitutional error not been committed during trial or sentencing, a jury would have found the petitioner innocent of the crime. *Sawyer v. Whitley* required a showing that a constitutional error was committed during a criminal proceeding.

The significance of this case is the reaffirmation by the Supreme Court that claims of actual innocence, at least for habeas corpus review, must contain evidence that a constitutional error occurring during the trial or sentencing. Absent such showing, the petitioner is barred from using the writ of habeas corpus to file claims of actual innocence. The case is also significant because the Court said that a court in a habeas proceeding is not a trier of fact or one that corrects errors of fact, but rather examines procedural constitutional errors in a criminal proceeding. The Court also reaffirmed its respect for the trial courts' proceedings, saying that, "because the courts have considerable expertise in matters of criminal procedure . . . we have exercised substantial deference to legislative judgments in this area."

Felker v. Turpin
518 U.S. 651 (1996)

CAPSULE: The Antiterrorism and Effective Death Penalty Act of 1996 does not preclude a court from accepting an application for habeas corpus relief nor does the Act violate the Constitution's suspension clause.

FACTS: Felker was convicted of murder and other crimes in Georgia and was sentenced to death in state court. He was denied relief on direct appeal in two state collateral proceedings and in federal habeas corpus proceedings. While he was awaiting execution, the Antiterrorism and Effective Death Penalty Act of 1996 was enacted. It provides for dismissal of a claim presented in a state prisoner's second or successive federal habeas application if the claim was also presented in a prior application or dismissal of a claim that was not presented in a prior federal application, unless certain conditions apply.

Felker asked to file a second federal habeas petition, but his motion was denied by the Eleventh Circuit Court of Appeals on the ground that the claims raised had not been presented in his first petition and did not meet the conditions specified in sections of the Act. He then appealed to the U.S. Supreme Court.

ISSUES:
1. Does the Antiterrorism and Effective Death Penalty Act of 1996 preclude a court from accepting an application for habeas corpus relief? NO.
2. Does the Act violate the Constitution's suspension clause, which provides that the privilege of the writ of habeas corpus shall not be suspended? NO.

HOLDING:
1. The Act does not preclude the Court from entertaining an application for habeas corpus relief, but it does affect the standards governing the granting of such relief.
2. The Act does not violate the Constitution's Suspension Clause.

REASON: "[W]e conclude that Title 1 of the Act has not repealed our authority to entertain original habeas petitions, for reasons similar to those stated in Yerger. No provision of Title 1 mentions our authority to entertain original habeas petitions; in contrast, Section 103 amends the Federal Rules of Appellate Procedure to bar considerations of original habeas petitions in the courts of appeals. Although Section 106(b)(3)(E) precludes us from reviewing, by appeal or petition for certiorari, a judgment on an application for leave to file a second habeas petition in district court, in makes no mention of our authority to hear habeas petitions filed as original matter in this Court.

"The Act requires a habeas petitioner to obtain leave from the court of appeals before filing a second habeas petition in the district court. But this requirement simply transfers from the district court to the court of appeals a screening function which would previously have been performed by the district court as required by 28 U.S. Section 2254 Rule 9(b) . . . In *McCleskey v. Zant*, 499 U.S. 467 (1991), we said that 'the doctrine of abuse of the writ refers to a complex and evolving body of equitable principles informed and controlled by historical usage, statutory developments, and judicial decisions.' The added restrictions which the Act places on second habeas petitions are well within the compass of this evolutionary process, and we hold that they do not amount to a 'suspension' of the writ contrary to Article 1, Section 9."

CASE SIGNIFICANCE: The Effective Death Penalty Act was passed by Congress in 1996 and contains complex provisions. One provision requires the dismissal of any claim in a habeas corpus case that was raised in a prior application by the same petitioner. It also sets tough standards for claims that are presented to the court for the first time in a second petition. These standards provide for the dismissal of the claim unless: (1) the claim relies on a new, previously unavailable rule of constitutional law that has been made retroactive to cases, and (2) the factual basis for the claim could not have been discovered previously through the exercise of due diligence, and if proven, would be sufficient to establish by clear and convincing evidence that were it not for constitutional error no reasonable fact finder would have found the defendant guilty of the offense.

These provisions make it difficult for prisoners to file a second habeas case and were therefore challenged in this case. The Supreme Court concluded that these provisions did not affect the Court's jurisdiction to issue writs of habeas corpus under prior federal law (28 U.S.C. §§ 2241 and 2254); therefore, the Court still exercised jurisdiction over habeas cases. The Court also said that the law does not violate the suspension clause of the Constitution (which provides that the 'privilege of the Writ of Habeas Corpus shall not be suspended") because the law "simply transfers from the district court to the court of appeals a screening function which would previously have been performed by the district court." The Court concluded, however, that the prisoner in this case did not meet the "exception circumstances" standard set by the Antiterrorism and Effective Death Penalty Act and therefore his habeas petition could not succeed.

Nelson v. Campbell
541 U.S. 637 (2004)

CAPSULE: An inmate who challenges the method by which he is to be executed, and not the constitutionality of his death sentence, can use a Section 1983 lawsuit as a legal remedy to temporarily halt his execution.

FACTS: In 2004, with only three days before his impending death by lethal injection in Alabama, Nelson filed a Section 1983 lawsuit to temporarily halt his execution on grounds that the use of a "cut-down" procedure, which required making an incision into his arm or leg in order to gain access to his veins, violated the Eighth Amendment's ban against cruel and unusual punishment. Nelson, who severely compromised his veins with years of drug abuse, claimed that the procedure would cause him unnecessary pain. Because Nelson had already filed a habeas petition that was denied, the district court dismissed his Section 1983 lawsuit, saying it was the functional equivalent of a second or successive habeas appeal, which is prohibited under the AEDPA. The Eleventh Circuit Court of Appeals held that challenges to a method of execution fall under the domain of habeas corpus and because Nelson had already filed an unsuccessful habeas petition, his most recent challenge was barred by the AEDPA.

ISSUE: Can a Section 1983 lawsuit be used by an inmate who wants to challenge only the method by which he will be executed, but not the constitutionality of the death penalty per se and/or his impending execution? YES.

HOLDING: A Section 1983 lawsuit is the appropriate legal remedy to use when seeking to temporarily halt an execution on grounds that the methods used to cause death violate the cruel and unusual punishment clause of the Eighth Amendment.

REASON: "Section 1983 must yield to the federal habeas statute where an inmate seeks injunctive relief challenging the facts of his conviction or the duration of his sentence. Such claims fall within the core of habeas. By contrast, constitutional claims challenging confinement conditions fall outside of that core and may be brought under Section 1983. The Court need not reach here the difficult question of how method of execution claims should be classified generally. Respondents claim that because the cut-down is part of the execution procedure, petitioner is actually challenging the fact of his execution. However, that venous access is a necessary prerequisite to execution does not imply that a particular means of gaining such access is likewise necessary. A fair reading of the complaint leaves no doubt that petitioner sought to enjoin the cut-down, not his execution by lethal injection.

Respondents are incorrect that a reversal here would open the floodgates to all manner of method of execution and last-minute stay requests. Because this Court does not here resolve the question of how to treat method of execution claims generally, the instant holding is extremely limited. And the ability to bring a Section 1983 claim does not free inmates from the substantive and procedural limitations of the Prison Litigation Reform Act of 1995."

CASE SIGNIFICANCE: This case is significant because it was the first time since the 1940s, in *Louisiana ex rel. Francis v. Resweber*, that the Court heard a method of execution case. In addition, it is significant because the Court held that a Section 1983 lawsuit may be used to challenge the manner in which an inmate will be executed, thus seemingly circumventing the rules of habeas corpus and the AEDPA. The Court held that because Nelson was only challenging the cut-down procedure and not the fact or constitutionality of his scheduled execution, a habeas petition would not be the appropriate legal remedy to use.

In anticipation that its decision would open the floodgates to all method of execution claims and pleas for last-minute stays of execution, the Court held that it is uncertain whether all method of execution challenges would fall under the domain of Section 1983 and that its ruling was "extremely limited." It also noted that Section 1983 challenges are not without substantive and procedural prerequisites. The Prison Reform Litigation Act of 1995 establishes rules that inmates must follow when seeking to prevent the state from fully effectuating a court order, such as the particular method of execution, and gives significant deference to the state. The Act states that before a court grants an inmate injunctive relief, it must "give substantial weight to any adverse impact on . . . the operation of the criminal justice system caused by the relief." In addition, similar to the provisions of the AEDPA, inmates must exhaust available state administrative remedies prior to using a Section 1983 lawsuit. The Act also grants courts the ability to dismiss suits that are "frivolous and/or malicious."

In 2006, the Court again heard a method of execution challenge in *Hill v. McDonough*. In *Hill*, the Court echoed its decision in *Nelson* and held that if an inmate challenges the lawfulness of his death sentence, then habeas corpus and the rules specified by the AEDPA govern such challenge. However, it an inmate challenges only the method by which he is to be executed and only seeks to temporarily delay such execution, then Section 1983 is the appropriate remedy. It added that a Section 1983 lawsuit does not entitle inmates to permanently delay their execution, but may provide them with a temporary delay of their execution to allow the state sufficient time to reconsider the method by which it executes inmates.

House v. Bell
547 U.S. ___ (2007)

CAPSULE: A petitioner who fails to raise claims in post-conviction proceedings as to actual innocence is not barred from raising such claims under habeas corpus because they fall within the purview of the actual innocence exception to procedurally defaulted claims and not under the domain of the AEDPA.

FACTS: Paul Gregory House was convicted and sentenced to death for the murder of Carolyn Muncey. At trial, the state presented false statements made by House, FBI tests showing that semen consistent with House's was present on Mrs. Muncey's nightgown and underwear, and tests showing that small bloodstains consistent with Mrs. Muncey's blood type were found on House's jeans. House challenged the semen and bloodstains used at trial and presented other evidence, including an alleged confession that Muncey's husband committed the murder. The district court denied relief, holding that House had not demonstrated actual innocence nor had he presented new evidence that mitigated his death sentence. The Sixth Circuit Court of Appeals granted a certificate of appealability under the provisions of the AEDPA and denied relief because House's claim was procedurally defaulted because he had not raised all his claims (such as ineffective assistance of counsel and actual innocence) in prior post-conviction proceedings. Under Tennessee law, House's claims were barred because claims not raised in prior proceedings are presumptively waived.

ISSUE: Is a petitioner barred from filing a habeas petition on grounds of actual innocence because he failed to raise all claims in prior post-convictions proceedings? NO.

HOLDING: If a petitioner has a defaulted petition due to not raising all issues in prior post-conviction petitions, habeas relief may be granted if the petitioner demonstrates cause for the default and presents new evidence that, if shown to the jurors, it is more likely than not that no reasonable juror would have found him guilty beyond a reasonable doubt.

REASON: "To implement the general principle that comity and finality must yield to the imperative of correction a fundamentally unjust incarceration, this Court has ruled that prisoners asserting innocence as a gateway to defaulted claims must establish that, in light of new evidence, it is more likely than not that no reasonable juror would have found petitioner guilty beyond a reasonable doubt [*Schlup v. Delo*, 513 U.S. 298, (1995)]. Several features of the *Schlup* standard bear emphasis here . . . First, while the gateway claim requires new reliable evidence not presented at trial, the habeas court must assess the likely impact of all the evidence on reasonable jurors. Second, rather than requiring absolute certainty about guilt or innocence, a petitioner's burden at the gateway stage is to demonstrate that more likely than not, in light of the new evidence, no reasonable juror would find him guilty beyond a reasonable doubt. Contrary to the state's arguments, the standard of review in . . . the Antiterrorism and Effective Death Penalty Act of 1996 is inapplicable here."

CASE SIGNIFICANCE: This case is significant because the Court revisited the issue of actual innocence and clarified the gateway standard of proof, which is consistent with the Court's previous ruling in *Schlup v. Delo*. After hearing new evidence presented by House as to his innocence, the Court held that House fell within the procedural default exception and that "it is more likely than not that no reasonable juror would have found him guilty beyond a reasonable doubt." The Court also noted that a gateway habeas corpus claim of actual innocence requires the habeas court to consider all evidence presented at the original trial and newly discovered evidence. The Court further clarified the position of the AEDPA under the procedural default exception in actual innocence claims. Because the claim did not involve a violation of the statute of limitations nor involved a same-claim successive petition but rather was only a defaulted claim, the Court held that the AEDPA had no bearing on the case.

Lawrence v. Florida
549 U.S. ___ (2007)

CAPSULE: The AEDPA does not suspend or "toll" the one-year statute of limitations if a defendant is awaiting a decision by the U.S. Supreme Court and then files a habeas corpus petition well after the statute of limitations has expired.

FACTS: Lawrence, a death row inmate, filed for state post-conviction relief 364 days after his conviction became final. The trial court denied relief as did the state supreme court and later the U.S. Supreme Court. The statute of limitation was "tolled" during the time that the Florida courts heard Lawrence's petitions. However, while the post-conviction petition was pending in the U.S. Supreme Court, Lawrence filed a habeas corpus petition with the U.S. District Court—113 days after the state supreme court's decision in his post-conviction appeal. The district court dismissed the petition on grounds that it was untimely because the statute of limitation, per the provisions of the Antiterrorism and Effective Death Penalty Act of 1996, had expired. The Eleventh Circuit Court of Appeals affirmed the decision of the district court.

ISSUE: Is the AEDPA's statute of limitations suspended or "tolled" while a defendant awaits the decision of a habeas petition by the U.S. Supreme Court? No.

HOLDING: Although the statute of limitations may be suspended while an inmate awaits a response or decision by a state court, which is the final court to resolve post-conviction petitions, it is not "tolled" when an inmate awaits a decision by the U.S. Supreme Court because the Court is not usually the final court to resolve a post-conviction petition.

REASON: "Read naturally, the statute's [AEDPA] text means that the statute of limitations is tolled only while state courts review the application. A state post-conviction application 'remains pending' until the application has achieved final resolution through the state's post-conviction procedures. This Court is not a part of those procedures, which end when the state courts have finally resolved the application. The application is therefore not pending after the state court's post-conviction review is complete. If it were, it is difficult to understand how a state prisoner could exhaust state post-conviction remedies without filing a certiorari petition. Yet state prisoners need not petition for certiorari to exhaust state remedies."

CASE SIGNIFICANCE: This case is significant because the Court clarified the statute of limitations provision of the AEDPA. It held that the AEDPA does not suspend or "toll" the one-year statute of limitations if a defendant is awaiting a decision by the U.S. Supreme Court and then files a habeas corpus petition well after such limitation has expired. Thus, the Court reasoned that the statute of limitations may be suspended while an inmate awaits a response or decision by a state court, which is the final court to resolve post-conviction petitions, but not the U.S. Supreme Court because the Court "rarely grants review of state post-conviction proceedings" and is thus not usually the final court to resolve a post-conviction petition. The AEDPA statute of limitations is suspended only to await a decision by a state court.

The case is also significant because the Court stood by the restrictions of the AEDPA and with its stance to halt tactics to delay proceedings. The strict interpretation is consistent with the Court's enduring attempt to "balance the societal interests of finality, comity, and conservation of scarce judicial resources" by ensuring that inmates first exhaust all state remedies before filing a habeas petition in federal court and by encouraging inmates to file petitions on a timely basis. According to the Court, allowing inmates to default on the statute of limitations period would only motivate them to file petitions as a tactic to delay proceedings, which runs counter to the goal of the AEDPA.

Internet Resources

American Bar Association—Federal Habeas Corpus in a Nutshell
http://www.abanet.org/irr/hr/summer01/yackle.html

The New Speed Up in Habeas Corpus Appeals
http://www.pbs.org/wgbh/pages/frontline/shows/execution/readings/speed.
   html

Federal Habeas Corpus Review: A Brief Overview
http://library.findlaw.com/1999/Jan/1/241464.html

Federal Habeas Corpus
http://www.prisonlaw.com/pdfs/FEDHABEAS.pdf

The Antiterrorism and Effective Death Penalty Act
http://www.treas.gov/offices/enforcement/ofac/legal/statutes/aedpa.pdf

Notes

1. Errors that violate constitutional rights, such as the right to counsel and the right to trial by jury. Harmful errors necessitate a reversal of conviction.

2. The U.S. Supreme Court only considers cases that involve a constitutional or federal issue.

3. ROLANDO DEL CARMEN, CRIMINAL PROCEDURE: LAW AND PRACTICE (6th ed. 2004).

4. JOHN L. WORRALL, CRIMINAL PROCEDURE: FROM FIRST CONTACT TO APPEAL (2004).

5. ROLANDO DEL CARMEN, CRIMINAL PROCEDURE: LAW AND PRACTICE (6th ed. 2004).

6. *Kotteakos v. United States*, 323 U.S. 750, 765 (1946).

7. Peter Hack, *The Roads Less Traveled: Post-Conviction Relief Alternatives and the Antiterrorism and Effective Death Penalty Act of 1996*, 30 AM. J. CRIM. L. 171 (Spring 2003).

8. Eric M. Freedman, *Federal Habeas Corpus in Capital Cases*. In HUGO BEDAU AND PAUL CASSELL (EDS.), DEBATING THE DEATH PENALTY (2004), p. 553.

9. Tara L. Swafford, *Responding to* Herrera v. Collins: *Ensuring That Innocents Are not Executed*, 45 CASE W. RES. L. REV. 603 (1995).

10. J.W. PELTASON AND SUE DAVIS, UNDERSTANDING THE CONSTITUTION (15th ed. 2000).

11. Eric M. Freedman, *Federal Habeas Corpus in Capital Cases*. In HUGO BEDAU AND PAUL CASSELL (EDS.), DEBATING THE DEATH PENALTY (2004), p. 553.

12. J.W. PELTASON AND SUE DAVIS, UNDERSTANDING THE CONSTITUTION (15th ed. 2000).

13. Bryan A. Stevenson, *The Politics of Fear and Death: Successive Problems in Capital Federal Habeas Corpus Cases*, 77 N.Y.U. L. REV. 699 (2002).

14. *Ex parte Royall*, 117 U.S. 241 (1886).

15. Lisa R. Duffett, *Habeas Corpus and Actual Innocence of the Death Sentence after* Sawyer v. Whitley: *Another Nail into the Coffin of State Capital Defendants*, 44 CASE W. RES. L. REV. 121 (1993).

16. Bryan A. Stevenson, *The Politics of Fear and Death: Successive Problems in Capital Federal Habeas Corpus Cases*, 77 N.Y.U. L. REV. 699 (2002).

17. *Salinger v. Loisel*, 265 U.S. 224 (1924).

18. *Wong Doo v. United States*, 265 U.S. 239 (1924).

19. Judicial Code and Judiciary Act § 2244, 62 STAT. at 966 (1948).

20. *Sanders v. United States*, 373 U.S. 1 (1963).

21. Bryan A. Stevenson, *The Politics of Fear and Death: Successive Problems in Capital Federal Habeas Corpus Cases*, 77 N.Y.U. L. REV. 699 (2002).

22. *Gregg v. Georgia*, 428 U.S. 153 (1976)

23. Bryan A. Stevenson, *The Politics of Fear and Death: Successive Problems in Capital Federal Habeas Corpus Cases*, 77 N.Y.U. L. REV. 699, 717 (2002).

24. *Id.*

25. *Rose v. Lundy*, 455 U.S. 509 (1982).

26. *See Wainwright v. Sykes*, 433 U.S. 72 (1977).

27. *Report on Habeas Corpus in Capital Cases*, 45 CRIM. L. REP. 3239, 3240 (1989).

28. *McCleskey v. Zant*, 499 U.S. 467 (1991).

29. JOHN L. WORRALL, CRIMINAL PROCEDURE: FROM FIRST CONTACT TO APPEAL (2004).

30. 28 U.S.C. § 2254(d) (2000).

31. *Williams v. Taylor*, 529 U.S. 362 (2000).

32. 28 U.S.C. § 2244(b)(2)(A) (2000).

33. *Teague v. Lane*, 489 U.S. 288 (1989).

34. *Tyler v. Cain*, 533 U.S. 970 (2001).

35. *Rhines v. Weber*, 544 U.S. 269 (2005).

36. *Rose v. Lundy*, 455 U.S. 509 (1982).

37. *Rhines v. Weber*, 544 U.S. 269, 272 (2005)

38. *Id.*

39. Tara L. Swafford, *Responding to* Herrera v. Collins: *Ensuring That Innocents are not Executed*, 45 CASE WESTERN L. REV. 603, 606 (1995).

40. *Felker v. Turpin*, 518 U.S. 651 (1996).

41. *Tyler v. Cain*, 533 U.S. 970 (2001).

42. Bryan A. Stevenson, *The Politics of Fear and Death: Successive Problems in Capital Federal Habeas Corpus Cases*, 77 N.Y.U. L. REV. 699 (2002).

43. *Id.* at 761.

44. Jake Sussman, *Unlimited Innocence: Recognizing an Actual Innocence Exception to AEDPA's Statute of Limitations*, 27 N.Y.U. REV. L. &SOC. CHANGE 343 (2001–2002).

45. *Stewart v. Martinez-Villareal*, 523 U.S. 637 (1998).

46. 28 U.S.C. § 2244(d)(1)

47. *Lawrence v. Florida*, 459 U.S. ___ (2007).

48. *Id.*

49. *Id.*

50. Lisa R. Duffett, *Habeas Corpus and Actual Innocence of the Death Sentence after* Sawyer v. Whitley: *Another Nail into the Coffin of State Capital Defendants*, 44 CASE W. RES. L. REV. 121, 136 (1993).

51. *Murray v. Carrier*, 477 U.S. 478 (1986).

52. *Smith v. Murray*, 477 U.S. 527, 538 (1986).

53. *Sawyer v. Whitley*, 505 U.S. 333 (1992).

54. *Herrera v. Collins*, 506 U.S. 390 (1993).

55. *Id.* at 400.

56. *McCleskey v. Zant*, 499 U.S. 467 (1991).

57. *House v. Bell*, 547 U.S. ___ (2007).

58. *Schlup v. Delo*, 513 U.S. 298 (1995).

59. Jake Sussman, *Unlimited Innocence: Recognizing an Actual Innocence Exception to AEDPA's Statute of Limitations*, 27 N.Y.U. REV. L. & SOC. CHANGE 343, 368 (2001–2002).

60. *Nelson v. Campbell*, 541 U.S. 637 (2004).

61. *Hill v. McDonough*, 126 S. Ct. 1189 (2006).

62. 42 U.S.C. § 1983.

63. *Nelson v. Campbell*, 541 U.S. 637, 645 (2004).

64. *Id.* at 647.

65. *Ex parte Royall*, 117 U.S. 241 (1886).

66. *Salinger v. Loisel*, 265 U.S. 224 (1924).

67. *Wong Doo v. United States*, 265 U.S. 239 (1924).

68. *Sanders v. United States*, 373 U.S. 1 (1963).

69. *Rose v. Lundy*, 455 U.S. 509 (1982).

70. *McCleskey v. Zant*, 499 U.S. 467 (1991).

71. *Williams v. Taylor*, 529 U.S. 362 (2000).

72. *Tyler v. Cain*, 533 U.S. 970 (2001).

73. *Stewart v. Martinez-Villareal*, 523 U.S. 637 (1998).

74. *Herrera v. Collins*, 506 U.S. 390 (1993).

75. *Murray v. Carrier*, 477 U.S. 478 (1986).

76. *Smith v. Murray*, 477 U.S. 527 (1986).

Chapter Outline

I. **Introduction**

II. **Methods of Execution**

III. **Proportionality of Punishment**
   A. Types of Crimes
   B. Degree of Involvement in Killing
   C. Proportionality Review

IV. **The Role of Public Opinion and National Consensus**

V. **International Perspectives**

VI. **In Summary, What Do these Cases Say?**

VII. **Conclusion**

Cases Briefed in Chapter 11

Case Briefs
   Pulley v. Harris, 465 U.S. 37 (1984)
   Tison v. Arizona, 481 U.S. 137 (1987)
   Baze v. Rees, 553 U.S. ___ (2008)
   Kennedy v. Louisiana, 554 U.S. ___ (2008)

Internet Resources

Notes

Chapter 11

Evolving Standards of Decency and the Eighth Amendment's Ban on Cruel and Unusual Punishment

I. Introduction

Probably the oldest and most persistent constitutional issue raised in regard to the death penalty is the Eighth Amendment's ban on cruel and unusual punishment. Since its rise in the United States, the death penalty has faced challenges of being excessively cruel and unusual, evoking the use of such adjectives as "wanton," "freakish," "arbitrary," and "capricious."[1] Concern was initially focused on the method of execution. Early death penalty cases challenged firing squads, electrocution, and hanging as violating the Eighth Amendment's ban on cruel and unusual punishment. The Supreme Court decided that each of these methods was constitutionally permissible. Later cases were more concerned with the proportionality of the death penalty when compared to the offense for which it was imposed. Anything less than murder (life for life) has historically been deemed unacceptable. The Court has recently reiterated this limitation by declaring that it is unconstitutional to impose the death penalty for the rape of a child when the victim is not killed. There has also been much recent concern over particular offenders for whom the death penalty may be excessive, including those who are mentally retarded, mentally ill, or juveniles at the time of the offense. Some of the most recent attention, however, has been focused again on the method of execution, with lethal injection being challenged as cruel and unusual punishment.

In this chapter, the Eighth Amendment's ban on cruel and unusual punishment as it applies to the death penalty will be discussed. The chapter begins by considering the role the Eighth Amendment played in early death penalty cases that questioned the methods of execution. The issue of proportionality in the application of the death penalty will be considered in light of the *Furman* and *Gregg* decisions in the 1970s. Finally, the concept of "evolving standards of decency," a standard used to determine what constitutes cruel and unusual punishment, will be analyzed. The Supreme Court in *Trop v. Dulles* (1958) stated that "[t]he Amendment must draw its meaning from the evolving standards of decency that mark the progress of a maturing society."[2] In this chapter, two primary factors in the contemporary assessment of this notion will be considered: public opinion and international law. Both play increasingly important roles in shaping the ever-changing notion of "evolving standards of decency" and our understanding of what might constitute cruel and unusual punishment.

II. Methods of Execution

The Supreme Court has historically refused to authoritatively consider whether particular execution methods are cruel and unusual and thus violate the Eighth Amendment. In two of the earliest death penalty cases heard by the Supreme Court, the Court deferred to state legislatures in the determination of appropriate execution methods. Figure 11.1 indicates the different execution methods used in states that have the death penalty. The Court upheld statutes that provided for executions by shooting (*Wilkerson v. Utah*, 1878[3]), electrocution (*In re Kemmler*, 1890[4]), and hanging (*Andres v. United States*, 1948[5]) as permissible methods. Although refraining from a determination of whether particular methods might violate the Eighth Amendment, the Court did state that such punishments as "burning at the stake, crucifixion, breaking on the wheel, or the like"[6] are cruel and unusual.

Figure 11.1
Methods of Execution by State

STATE:	Lethal Injection	Electrocution	Gas Chamber	Hanging	Firing Squad
Alabama	X	X			
Arizona	X		X		
Arkansas	X	X			
California	X		X		
Colorado	X				
Connecticut	X				
Delaware	X				
Florida	X	X			

Figure 11.1, *continued*

STATE:	Lethal Injection	Electrocution	Gas Chamber	Hanging	Firing Squad
Georgia	X				
Idaho	X				X
Illinois	X	x			
Indiana	X				
Kansas	X				
Kentucky	X	X			
Louisiana	X				
Maryland	X		X		
Mississippi	X				
Missouri	X		X		
Montana	X				
Nebraska*					
Nevada	X				
New Hampshire	X			X	
New Mexico	X				
North Carolina	X				
Ohio	X				
Oklahoma	X	x			X
Oregon	X				
Pennsylvania	X				
South Carolina	X	X			
South Dakota	X				
Tennessee	X	X			
Texas	X				
Utah	X				X

Figure 11.1, *continued*

STATE:	Lethal Injection	Electrocution	Gas Chamber	Hanging	Firing Squad
Virginia	X	X			
Washington	X			X	
Wyoming	X		x		

NOTE: A lowercase x indicates that the method is only approved if the current execution method is ever held to be unconstitutional.

* Electrocution was held to be in violation of Nebraska's state constitution by the state supreme court in February of 2008. No other method has been indicated as a replacement.

Source: Death Penalty Information Center (2008). Available at: http://www.deathpenaltyinfo.org/article.php?scid=8&did=245

Recently, questions concerning methods of execution have re-emerged.[7] Members of the Supreme Court have expressed interest in considering the constitutionality of electrocution[8] and the Ninth Circuit Court of Appeals' decision in *Fierro v. Gomez* (9th Cir. 1996) held that lethal gas was an unconstitutional method of execution.[9] Most recently, lethal injection, long considered to be the ultimate accomplishment in humane executions, has come under fire. It is reported that the three-drug protocol commonly used in executions by lethal injection (see Figure 11.2 for a description of the typical lethal injection process) is a protocol that is prohibited in the euthanization of dogs and cats under animal welfare laws because it has the potential to cause excessive pain and suffering.[10] Although several stays had been granted because of these issues, in 2003, the Supreme Court refused to hear at least six separate appeals claiming that lethal injection was cruel and unusual in violation of the Eighth Amendment.[11] It was not until 2006 that the Court finally entertained the issue of the constitutionality of lethal injection. In *Hill v. McDonough* (2006)[12] the issue of constitutional challenges to lethal injection as a method of execution finally arose to the purview of the Supreme Court. Although lethal injection as an allowable method was not the central issue in *Hill v. McDonough*, the Court expressed increased willingness to consider the issue.[13] The decision in *Hill v. McDonough* stated that condemned inmates could challenge a state's method of execution (primarily lethal injection) under 42 U.S.C. Section 1983 in addition to seeking habeas corpus appeals. The Court finally decided to consider the constitutionality of lethal injection as an execution method in 2007 when it agreed to hear the case of *Baze v. Rees*.[14] From this point until the case was decided in April 2008, executions came to a virtual standstill as condemned inmates continued to challenge lethal injection as cruel and unusual punishment and as states awaited the Court's decision.[15] Furthermore, some states altered their statutes to allow other methods in the event that lethal injection was deemed unconstitutional (see Figure 11.1).

The Court's decision in *Baze v. Rees* (2008),[16] a lengthy and fractured decision comprising seven different Justices' opinions, was that the three-drug lethal injection method under question (see procedure in Figure 11.2), which is used by 30 of the 36 death penalty states, is not cruel and unusual and is thus constitutionally permissible. Upholding the most common execution method, the Court cleared the way for executions to resume across the United States. Although this decision seems to close the door on the debate about the constitutionality of execution by lethal injection, the Court noted some potential standards regarding what might make an execution cruel and unusual and thus a violation of the Eighth Amendment. Chief Justice Roberts, delivering the plurality opinion, noted that the mere risk of pain is not enough to violate the Eighth Amendment's prohibition on cruel and unusual punishment. Rather, the "wanton exposure to objectively intolerable risk" of pain is necessary to show such a violation.[17] Justice Thomas, in his own concurring opinion, went further, suggesting that an execution method is cruel and unusual "only if it is deliberately designed to inflict pain."1[18] In the end, this was a relatively narrow decision applying only to the constitutionality of one particular execution method. Several Justices were quick to note that this was not a case about the constitutionality of the death penalty itself, but there seemed to be a suggestion by some that this broader issue was one they might be willing to consider in the future.

Figure 11.2
Texas Lethal Injection Procedure

Lethal Injection Consists of:

    Sodium Thiopental (sedates person)

    Pancuronium Bromide (muscle relaxant—collapses diaphragm and lungs)

    Potassium Chloride (stops heartbeat)

The offender is usually pronounced dead approximately seven minutes after the lethal injection begins.

Cost per execution for drugs used:$86.08

Source: *Death Row Facts*. Texas Department of Criminal Justice (2007).

Claims of cruel and unusual punishment in light of failed or botched executions have generally been rejected by the Supreme Court.[19] In *Louisiana ex rel. Francis v. Resweber* (1947),[20] after the first attempt at electrocution did not kill the condemned Francis, his execution was postponed to a later date. The Supreme Court declared that this was not a violation of the Eighth Amendment, calling the botched execution "an unforeseeable accident"[21] and "an innocent misadventure."[22]

Horror stories of botched executions remain today. The well-publicized botched execution by electrocution of Pedro Medina in 1997, in which the condemned's head burst into flames, spelled the end of electrocution as the most common method of execution.[23] Medina's was not an isolated case when it comes to botched executions. Numerous other incidents have been documented in the use of the electric chair, as well as horrific "misadventures" (as the Court expressed it in *Resweber*) with hanging, lethal injection, and lethal gas.[24] Some have pointed to these incidents as proof that execution is equivalent to torture and thus constitutes cruel and unusual punishment. Others support the death penalty despite such occurrences and have even used botched executions to strengthen the legitimacy of the death penalty. For example, Robert Butterworth, the Attorney General of Florida, made the following comment following a botched electrocution in which the condemned individual caught fire: "People who wish to commit murder, they better not do it in the state of Florida because we may have a problem with our electric chair."[25]

Most politicians and policymakers, however, do not highlight the horror of such execution incidents. Rather, attempts are made to "sanitize" executions and make them less dramatic, thus producing an "illusion of humaneness."[26] Stories of botched executions only serve to horrify the public and heighten concerns about the constitutionality of the death penalty under the cruel and unusual punishment clause of the Eighth Amendment. Steps have been taken to avoid this by using technology to effect increasingly "humane" methods of execution.[27]

III. Proportionality of Punishment

Although the Eighth Amendment's prohibition against cruel and unusual punishment has historically been applied primarily to the mode of punishment, the proportionality of punishment has also been invoked. In *Weems v. United States* (1910)[28] the Supreme Court interpreted the cruel and unusual punishment clause to include a proportionality requirement. The Court claimed that "it is a precept of justice that punishment for crime should be graduated and proportioned to the offense."[29] Proportionality has been a recurring concern in questions of constitutionality of punishment. In *Furman v. Georgia* (1972),[30] one of the primary factors that led to the temporary abolition of the death penalty was that it was applied "arbitrarily and capriciously" with little consideration of the particular crime for which it was being imposed. In 1976, when the Supreme Court considered statutes effectively reinstating the death penalty, it rejected mandatory death penalty statutes,[31] saying that the death penalty should only be imposed in response to the most extreme crimes because this most extreme punishment is only proportional to the most extreme crimes. The Court approved only "guided discretion" statutes that contained several procedural safeguards to ensure heightened standards of reliability in the application of the death penalty.[32] One of these safeguards was a review process to ensure proportionality.

In this section, several aspects of proportionality in the context of the death penalty are considered in light of Supreme Court decisions. First, the crimes for which the death penalty has been deemed appropriate (proportional) are considered. Second, the defendant's degree of involvement in the capital murder and eligibility for the death penalty are considered. Third, the issue of proportionality review, a procedural safeguard among those suggested in *Gregg v. Georgia* (1976), is discussed. A fourth area of proportionality issues in death penalty jurisprudence will not be discussed here: this is the issue of the type of offender for which the death penalty is appropriate. The Supreme Court has held the death penalty to be cruel and unusual when used on the mentally retarded and mentally ill, as well was for juveniles under a certain age. These issues are addressed in other chapters of this book.

A. Types of Crimes

The earliest post-*Furman* cases to deal with proportionality of the death penalty followed closely after *Gregg* and focused on the types of crimes for which the death penalty was an appropriate punishment. Prior to *Furman*, the death penalty had been imposed for a variety of crimes, including rape, kidnapping, espionage, and treason.[33] Although some states today have statutes allowing the death penalty for crimes other than murder, no executions have been carried out for such crimes since the death penalty was reinstated.[34] Since *Gregg*, the Supreme Court has continued to maintain that the death penalty should be reserved only for murder, with the Court's strongest statement in this regard coming in their most recent decision in *Kennedy v. Louisiana* (2008).[35]

In a pair of cases decided in 1977, the Supreme Court ruled that the death penalty was disproportionate and thus violated the Eighth Amendment's prohibition of cruel and unusual punishment for the crimes of rape (*Coker v. Georgia*, 1977)[36] and kidnapping (*Eberheart v. Georgia*, 1977).[37] Coker had escaped from prison where he was serving multiple life sentences for murder, rape, kidnapping, and aggravated assault. Subsequent to his escape he raped a woman during the commission of a robbery. Under Georgia's statute, rape was a capital crime if committed by a person with previous felony convictions or during the commission of another felony. Coker was sentenced to death. The Supreme Court held that Georgia's statutory allowance of the death penalty for crimes other than murder was excessive and in violation of the Eighth Amendment. Coker's death sentence was overturned. The Court applied the same rationale in *Eberheart*, in which it struck down the death sentence for the crime of kidnapping. More recently, the Court has acknowledged that "[a]rmed robbery is a serious offense, but one for which the penalty of death is plainly excessive; the imposition of the death penalty for robbery, therefore, violates the Eighth and Fourteenth Amendments."[38]

The 30-year precedent that the death penalty be reserved only for murder was recently challenged in the pending case of *Kennedy v. Louisiana* (2008).[39] Amidst increasing public outcry for harsher punishment of sex offenders and the movement in several states to amend death penalty statutes to allow for the death penalty for the rape of a child, the Court considered whether the death penalty is constitutional in such cases in the victim is not killed. Kennedy had committed a particularly brutal rape against his then-8-year-old stepdaughter and, under Louisiana's statute allowing the death penalty for the rape of a child under 12 years old, was sentenced to death. The United States Supreme Court, in a 5-4 decision, held that Louisiana's statute violated the Eighth Amendment, that the death penalty could not be extended to crimes against persons in which the victim was not killed. Relying on the original notions of proportionality and limiting the use of the death penalty to only the most severe cases of murder as expressed in *Gregg* as well as the national consensus against using the death penalty for the crime of rape (it was reported that only six states have laws allowing this), the Court made its strongest statement yet that the death penalty be reserved only for cases of murder.

B. Degree of Involvement in Killing

In addition to being limited only to the crime of murder, the Supreme Court has considered the degree of a defendant's involvement and responsibility (meaning culpability) as important to ensuring that the death penalty is applied proportionally. In *Enmund v. Florida* (1982),[40] The Supreme Court held that the death penalty is disproportionate (and therefore in violation of the Eighth Amendment) for offenders who do not do the actual killing in the commission of a murder (such as those who only aid and abet in the commission of the murder). Again, the Supreme Court adhered to the position that the death penalty is only proportionate and therefore constitutional when imposed on a defendant who killed someone.

However, in *Tison v. Arizona* (1987),[41] the Court retreated slightly from this stance, holding that it is constitutional to impose the death penalty on an individual who participated in a major way in the commission of a felony that resulted in murder and who acted with reckless indifference to human life. The case involved two brothers who assisted their father in his and his cellmate's escape from prison and subsequent armed robbery and murder of a family. Although the brothers did not directly participate in the actual killing of the family, their participation in the felony that led to the murder resulted in death sentences for them.

Most recently, the Court, in *Bradshaw v. Richey* (2005)[42] has held that a defendant may be given the death penalty in cases in which he fails to kill his intended victim but instead causes the death of an unintended victim. This flows logically from the *Tison* decision, in that such a defendant would be causing the death of another in the process of committing a felony. The Court noted that "transferred intent" applied in this case and thus the defendant was eligible for the death penalty.[43] Citing the state death penalty statute, which states that aggravated murder requires that the defendant "intended to cause the death of *another*"[44] (emphasis added), the Court held that the intent to kill was present and thus the fact that the actual victim was not the intended victim did not reduce the murder to a non-capital one.[45]

C. Proportionality Review

In *Weems v. United States* (1910),[46] the Supreme Court interpreted the cruel and unusual punishment clause to include the notion of proportionality of punishment in regard to the gravity of the crime. Proportionality was of primary concern to the Court when approving the new death penalty statutes in 1976. One of the important safeguards approved in *Gregg v. Georgia* (1976)[47] was proportionality review. Proportionality review constitutes the systematic review of a death sentence by comparing the particular case and its characteristics and circumstances to other similar capital cases to determine whether similar sentences were applied. The objective of such proportionality review is to ensure that like cases receive like penalties and that the death penalty is not being discriminatorily or arbitrarily imposed. Similar cases should have similar results.

In *Pulley v. Harris* (1984),[48] the Supreme Court ruled that proportionality of this form is not constitutionally mandated. The Court said that the proportionality review requested by Harris was infeasible, unnecessary, and beyond that required by the Eighth Amendment. The Court held that the more common concept of whether the punishment is appropriate for the crime, in general, is sufficient to satisfy the proportionality requirement. The Court explained the apparent contradiction of *Gregg* by noting that "[proportionality review] was considered an additional safeguard against arbitrary or capricious sentencing . . . [w]hile . . . some form of meaningful appellate review is required . . . those Justices did not declare that comparative review was so critical that without it the Georgia statute would not have passed constitutional muster."[49] The Court then concluded that *Gregg* and the Eighth Amendment did not require proportionality review in capital cases.

IV. The Role of Public Opinion and National Consensus

In *Weems v. United States* (1910), the Supreme Court suggested that what constitutes "cruel and unusual punishment" evolves "as public opinion becomes enlightened by a humane justice"[50] More than 60 years later, in the landmark case of *Furman v. Georgia* (1972), Justice Brennan stated: "A severe punishment must not be unacceptable to contemporary society. Rejection by society, of course, is a strong indication that a severe punishment does not comport with human dignity."[51] Justice Marshall elaborated: "Where a punishment is not excessive and serves a valid legislative purpose, it still may be invalid if popular sentiment abhors it."[52] The cruel and unusual punishment clause of the Eighth Amendment is unique from other constitutional rights and mandates, in that it rests on mutable standards that are representative of the population at a given time. Thus, what we deem cruel and unusual punishment changes over time. Moreover, the Supreme Court's determination of what constitutes cruel and unusual punishment at any time depends upon some sense of a national consensus, a notion driven in large part by public opinion. Indeed, since *Furman*, public support has consistently been used as marker of evolving standards of decency and the legitimacy of capital punishment in the United States.

Since the 1970s, a majority of Americans have been in favor of capital punishment.[53] Public opinion polls have repeatedly found that more than 60 percent of Americans support the death penalty for the crime of murder.[54] However, attitudes about the death penalty are not as cut-and-dried as such numbers might suggest.[55] Research has found that the public is much more conflicted about this most extreme form of punishment than once thought. Although supporting the death penalty, in general, the public is less likely to support its use on juvenile or mentally retarded offenders.[56] Furthermore, support tends to diminish rapidly as people are confronted with certain realities of the death penalty system.[57] The increasing availability of sentences of life without parole (LWOP) has added another dimension to public opinion about the death penalty. One recent study reveals that when given the alternative of LWOP, only 47 percent of Americans support the death penalty for the crime of murder. Forty-eight percent select LWOP as the more desired option.[58]

As stories of the exoneration of innocent people sentenced to death, botched executions, incompetent lawyers, and other failures of the system become more and more publicized, the public will likely become more ambivalent and conflicted about the death penalty. A recent study of Texans, arguably the staunchest supporters of capital punishment, reveals that a majority support a moratorium on the death penalty so that the system can be studied for potential flaws.[59] Indeed, talk of moratoriums on executions is spreading across the United States.[60] In the wake of Illinois' Governor Ryan first imposing a moratorium and then commuting all death sentences to life in prison,[61] other states are starting to look at the flaws in their death penalty systems and consider their own moratoriums. Two states, New York and New Jersey, have recently abolished the death penalty. In spite of some ambivalence, however, the fact remains that a majority of Americans continue to support the death penalty in principle, if not in practice. And this support remains a statement about standards of decency in our society, providing some foundation for Eighth Amendment jurisprudence regarding the death penalty.

In spite of the role of public opinion in Eighth Amendment jurisprudence, the Supreme Court has generally rejected public opinion polls as the benchmarks for a national consensus. The Court has opted instead for the use of state and federal legislation as indicators of what the public perceives and values.[62] The thought is that legislators act on behalf of the populace in voting for and enacting legislation, thus such legislation is an extension of public will. It follows, then, that given that a majority of states have laws allowing for the death penalty (36 out of 50) there is a consensus that the death penalty is neither cruel nor unusual and thus does not violate the Eighth Amendment. This same logic has recently led the Court to declare the execution of mentally retarded (see Chapter 4) and juvenile (see Chapter 5) offenders to be cruel and unusual punishment.

V. International Perspectives

If we take the notion of evolving standards of decency beyond our borders to the realm of international law and opinion, a different view emerges. The measurement of evolving standards of decency and what constitutes cruel and unusual punishment today plays out in an increasingly global context. The policies and practices of the United States can no longer remain restricted to the purview of those within the United States. With the increasingly potent global emphasis on international law and international treaties and the added political and economic presence of coalitions like the European Union, international perspectives on actions occurring within the United States can no longer be ignored.

The United States executes the fifth highest number of people in the world, trailing China, Iran, Saudi Arabia, and Pakistan, in the number of executions in 2007.[63] Eighty-eight percent of all executions in the world were carried out in these five countries.[64] As the international trend moves towards the abolition of the death penalty (see Figure 11.3), the United States, over the last several decades, increased its use to some of the highest levels in the world.[65] These and other facts have generated a tremendous amount of criticism from human rights groups and other Western countries. In fact, the United States' use of the death penalty has been cited as one of the top international human rights concerns in recent years.[66] The United States' execution of juveniles and foreign nationals has threatened its status in international treaties and in some cases prohibited its inclusion in such treaties altogether.[67] Recently, the International Court of Justice held that the United States had violated the Vienna Convention by failing to allow Mexican nationals charged with capital crimes to speak to a Mexican consul.[68]

In 2008, the U.S. Supreme Court decided the case of *Medellin v. Texas*,[69] in which the International Court of Justice (ICJ) had held that the United States had violated international law in accordance with the Vienna Convention by failing to inform foreign nationals—51 of them, including Medellin, a Mexican citizen—of their Vienna Convention rights. Specifically, Medellin argued that he had not been afforded his right to contact the Mexican consulate. The ICJ ordered the United States to review the cases. Texas refused to do so in Medellin's case. Before the U.S. Supreme Court could decide the case, President Bush ordered all states to review the cases as ordered by the ICJ. Texas courts rejected the President's order, maintaining that he had no authority to give such an order. The Supreme Court agreed with the Texas courts, holding that neither the President's order, the ICJ's ruling, nor the Vienna Convention hold authority over states' rights to carry out criminal procedure and, in this case, the death penalty.

In spite of recent decisions supporting U.S. sovereignty in the international arena, factors surrounding international law and opinion appear to have had some, albeit limited, impact on the Supreme Court's consideration of Eighth Amendment issues surrounding the death penalty. In *Trop v. Dulles* (1958), the case in which the Court established the notion of evolving standards of decency, international practices and perspectives were taken into account.[70] More recently, in *Atkins v. Virginia* (2002) and *Roper v. Simmons* (2005), in which the court held that the execution of the mentally retarded and juveniles, respectively, is cruel and unusual, international opinion and trends were cited as support for the contention that the death penalty has become contrary to evolving standards of decency. The dissenting justices rejected international practice or opinion as being irrelevant to the United States' use of the death penalty.[71] It has been opined, however, that as political and economic interests become more global and as more pressure is placed on the United States by the European Union and the international community in general, such factors will become increasingly relevant.[72]

Figure 11.3
Abolitionist and Retentionist Countries (as of May 2008)

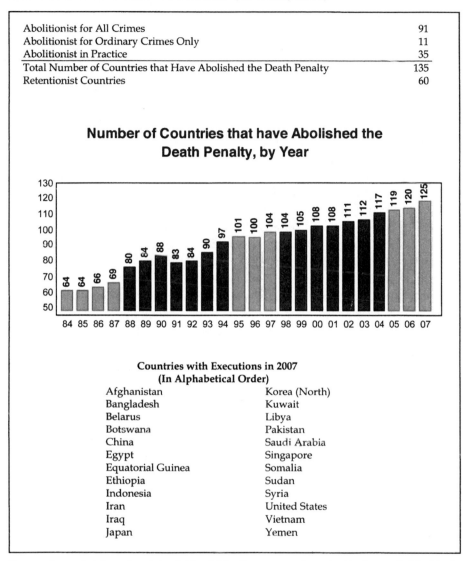

Abolitionist for All Crimes	91
Abolitionist for Ordinary Crimes Only	11
Abolitionist in Practice	35
Total Number of Countries that Have Abolished the Death Penalty	135
Retentionist Countries	60

Number of Countries that have Abolished the Death Penalty, by Year

Countries with Executions in 2007
(In Alphabetical Order)

Afghanistan	Korea (North)
Bangladesh	Kuwait
Belarus	Libya
Botswana	Pakistan
China	Saudi Arabia
Egypt	Singapore
Equatorial Guinea	Somalia
Ethiopia	Sudan
Indonesia	Syria
Iran	United States
Iraq	Vietnam
Japan	Yemen

Source: Amnesty International. Available at: http://www.amnesty.org/en/death-penalty/abolitionist-and-retentionist-countries and http://www.amnestyusa.org/Encourage-Worldwide-Abolition/Death-Penalty-Statistics-2007/page.do?id=1011348&n1=3&n2=28&n3=1277.

VI. In Summary, What Do these Cases Say?

As the Eighth Amendment is inherently malleable, evolving with changing sensibilities and "standards of decency" in American society, the Supreme Court has taken steps to ensure that the death penalty does not violate current sensibilities. In an effort to maintain proportionality of punishment, it has remained steadfast in reserving the death penalty for only the most severe crimes of murder. Less severe crimes of rape, kidnapping, and aggravated robbery traditionally have been flatly rejected by the Court as crimes justifying the death penalty. Indeed, in its most recent case (as of this writing) the Court has once again made a strong statement against using the death penalty for crimes against persons that do not result in the death of the victim, striking down a statute allowing the death penalty for the rape of a child. Finally, the Court has held in several cases that a person may be eligible for the death penalty even if they do not commit the actual act of killing or kill their intended victim but cause these deaths through their commission of or participation in a felony resulting in that murder.

In spite of its concern with proportionality of punishment, the Supreme Court held that proportionality review in which a particular death sentence is systematically compared to sentences in other similar cases is not required by the Constitution. Although the death penalty should be reserved for the most serious crimes of murder, the actual sentence in an individual case is to be determined by the jury and a consideration of the individual facts and circumstances of that particular case. Proportionality of punishment is not guaranteed at this more minute level.

One area involving the Eighth Amendment and "evolving standards of decency" in which the Court has been more "hands-off" is the acceptable method of execution. Hanging, firing squads, electrocution, gas chambers, and lethal injection are all currently permissible methods of execution used in the United States. The Court has not explicitly ruled against any particular method of execution, but has indicated that more torturous methods such as burning, crucifixion, and breaking on the wheel violate standards of decency and thus are prohibited by the Eighth Amendment's prohibition of cruel and unusual punishment. The Court's most recent decision in *Baze v. Rees* (2008) follows in this "hands-off" tradition. The Court, with seven Justices writing their own opinions, held that the currently predominant three-drug lethal injection protocol is constitutionally permissible. Some Justices did, however, add qualifications regarding standards for cruel and unusual punishment when it comes to execution methods. The plurality opinion noted that avoidance of all risk of pain is not required for an execution method to be cruel and unusual; rather, there must be "wanton exposure to an objectively intolerable risk" or a "wanton infliction" of pain and suffering.

VII. Conclusion

Challenges related to the prohibition of cruel and unusual punishment pervade death penalty jurisprudence and to this day continue to face the Supreme Court. The death penalty, the ultimate and most extreme punishment, will always be at the forefront as we contemplate the parameters of "evolving standards of decency." Although we continue to refine the methods of execution, attempting to imbue the death penalty with the appearance of humaneness, stories of botched executions and the unavoidable messiness of killing other human beings always lurk on the periphery of our collective vision. The death penalty, more than any other criminal justice policy, evokes stark images—images of ultimate retribution and of brutality. It has always brought controversy and polarized feelings, often exposing deep contradictions in American culture. The majority of the American public supports the death penalty, but at the same time, calls for moratoriums are surging and support for alternatives such as life in prison without parole is rivalling support for the death penalty. Moreover, the controversy about the death penalty now plays out not only within our borders but in the international arena, as well. We cannot be sure what the future holds for the death penalty, but can be certain that the United States Supreme Court will continue to be confronted with the question of whether the death penalty is cruel and unusual. The Court will continue to define and redefine the evolving standards of decency as they apply to this most extreme of criminal penalties.

Cases Briefed in Chapter 11

Case	Issue	Holding
Pulley v. Harris 465 U.S. 37 (1984)	In capital cases, does the Eighth Amendment require states to implement comparisons of particular sentences to those imposed in other similar cases?	The Eighth Amendment does not require that a state compare the sentence in the case before it with the sentence imposed in similar cases even if asked to do so by the prisoner.
Tison v. Arizona 481 U.S. 137 (1987)	Is it constitutional to sentence to death defendants who did not do the actual killing in a capital murder?	Defendants who participate in a major way in a felony-murder, and who act with reckless indifference to human life, even though they do not directly inflict the act of killing may be given the death penalty.
Baze v. Rees 553 U.S. ___ (2008)	Does Kentucky's three-drug protocol for executions by lethal injection violate the Eighth Amendment's prohibition of cruel and unusual punishment?	Kentucky's three-drug lethal injection protocol, also used by 29 other death penalty states, does not constitute cruel and unusual punishment and is thus constitutionally permissible.
Kennedy v. Louisiana 554 U.S. ___ (2008)	Is it Constitutional to impose the death penalty for the crime of sexual assault against a child when the crime does not result in the victim's death?	It is a violation of the Eighth Amendment to sentence a defendant to death for the rape of a child when the crime does not result in the victim's death.

Case Briefs

Pulley v. Harris
465 U.S. 37 (1984)

CAPSULE: Proportionality review is not required in death penalty cases.

FACTS: Harris was convicted in a California court of the kidnapping, robbery, and first-degree murder of two boys. Having been convicted of multiple felonies, including murder, the "special circumstance" required by California law was met and a capital sentencing hearing was held to determine whether Harris would receive a death sentence or life without the possibility of parole. The jury, finding several aggravating factors, sentenced him to death. Harris challenged the sentence, maintaining that the death sentence was unconstitutional due to the fact that no proportionality review had been implemented. He argued that such a review, in which his sentence is compared with those imposed in similar capital cases, was required.

ISSUE: In capital cases, does the Eighth Amendment require states to implement comparisons of particular sentences to those imposed in other, similar cases? NO.

HOLDING: "The Eighth Amendment does not require as an invariable rule in every case, that a state appellate court, before it affirms a death sentence, compare the sentence in the case before it with the sentence imposed in similar cases even if asked to do so by the prisoner."[73]

REASON: "At the outset, we should more clearly identify the issue before us. Traditionally, 'proportionality' has been used with reference to an abstract evaluation of the appropriateness of a sentence for a particular crime. Looking to the gravity of the offense and the severity of the penalty, to sentences imposed for other crimes, and to sentencing practices in other jurisdictions, this Court has occasionally struck down punishments as inherently disproportionate, and therefore cruel and unusual, when imposed for a particular crime or category of crime. The death penalty is not in all cases a disproportionate penalty in this sense.

"In *Gregg*, six Justices concluded that the Georgia system adequately directed and limited the jury's discretion. The bifurcated proceedings, the limited number of capital crimes, the requirement that at least one aggravating circumstance be present, and the consideration of mitigating circumstances minimized the risk of wholly arbitrary, capricious, or freakish sentences. In the opinion announcing the judgment of the Court, three Justices concluded that sentencing discretion under the statute was sufficiently controlled by clear and objective standards. In a separate concurrence, three other Justices found sufficient reason to expect that the death penalty would not be imposed so wantonly, freakishly, or infrequently as to be invalid under Furman.

"Both opinions made much of the statutorily required comparative proportionality review. This was considered an additional safeguard against arbitrary or capricious sentencing. While the opinion of Justices Stewart, Powell, and Stevens suggested that some form of meaningful appellate review is required, those Justices did not declare that comparative review was so critical that without it the Georgia statute would not have passed constitutional muster.

"Any capital sentencing scheme may occasionally produce aberrational outcomes. Such inconsistencies are a far cry from the major systemic defects identified in Furman. As we have acknowledged in the past, 'there can be "no perfect procedure for deciding in which cases governmental authority should be used to impose death." ' As we are presently informed, we cannot say that the California procedures provided Harris inadequate protection against the evil identified in Furman. The Court of Appeals therefore erred in ordering a writ of habeas corpus to issue."

CASE SIGNIFICANCE: "The Supreme Court ruled in this case that state appellate courts are not constitutionally required to provide, upon request by the defendant, a 'proportionality review' of death sentences in which the court would compare the sentence in the case before it with penalties imposed in similar cases in that state. Proportionality reviews are constitutional and are provided for by law or judicial practice in some states, but such reviews are not required by the Constitution. For example, the Court found the Texas death penalty statute to be constitutional even though neither the law nor judicial practice provide for any form of proportionality review. The Court did not completely close the door to a proportionality review, however, in some extreme cases. It said: 'assuming that there could be a capital sentencing scheme so lacking in other checks or arbitrariness that it could not pass constitutional muster without comparative proportionality review, the California statute involved here is not of that sort.'"[74]

Tison v. Arizona
481 U.S. 137 (1987)

CAPSULE: The death penalty may be imposed on a defendant who did not actually kill the victims but participated in a major way in a felony that resulted in their murder.

FACTS: Brothers Ricky and Raymond Tison, along with other family members, planned and effected the escape of their father from prison where he was serving a life sentence. Ricky and Raymond Tison entered the prison with an ice chest filled with guns, and armed their father and another convicted murderer. They later helped to abduct, detain, and rob a family of four, and watched their father and the other convict murder the members of that family with shotguns. Although the brothers later stated they were surprised by the killings, neither of them attempted to help the victims. Instead, they drove away in the victim's car along with the rest of the escape party. Ricky and Raymond Tison received the death penalty under Arizona's felony-murder and accomplice liability statutes. They appealed their death sentences, alleging that the Supreme Court decision in *Enmund v. Florida*, 458 U.S. 782 (1982) required reversal of their sentences because they were merely accomplices and not principals.

ISSUE: Is it constitutional to sentence to death defendants who did not do the actual killing in a capital murder? YES.

HOLDING: Defendants who participate in a major way in a felony-murder, and who act with reckless indifference to human life, even though they do not directly inflict the act of killing, may be given the death penalty.

REASON: "The issue raised by this case is whether the Eighth Amendment prohibits the death penalty in the intermediate case of the defendant whose participation is major and whose mental state is one of reckless indifference to the value of human life. *Enmund* does not specifically address this point.

"Like the *Enmund* Court, we find the state legislatures' judgment as to proportionality in these circumstances relevant to this constitutional inquiry. The largest number of States still fall into the two intermediate categories discussed in *Enmund*. Four States authorize the death penalty in felony-murder cases upon a showing of culpable mental state such as recklessness or extreme indifference to human life. Two jurisdictions require that the defendant's participation be substantial and the statutes of at least six more, including Arizona, take minor participation in the felony expressly into account in mitigation of the murder. These requirements significantly overlap both in this case and in general, for the greater the defendant's participation in the felony murder, the more likely that he acted with reckless indifference to human life. At a minimum, however, it can be said that all these jurisdictions, as well as six States which *Enmund* classified along with Florida as permitting capital punishment for felony murder simpliciter, and the three States which simply require some additional aggravation before imposing the death penalty upon a felony murderer, specifically authorize the death penalty in a felony-murder case where, though the defendant's mental state fell short of intent to kill, the defendant was a major actor in a felony in which he knew death was highly likely to occur."

CASE SIGNIFICANCE: The *Enmund* Court ruled that accomplices to a crime who participated in a minor role and had no prior knowledge that lethal force might be used in the commission of a felony could not be held responsible for that lethal force. It held that punishment by death in such a case is disproportionate to the crime and thus is prohibited by the Eighth Amendment. The Tison brothers attempted to use that ruling to overturn their death sentences, claiming that the death penalty was disproportionate to their participation in the crime committed. The Court disagreed and concluded that the Tison brothers played a major role in the killing of four family members and that their actions during the commission of the crime also suggested a reckless indifference to life. Based on these findings, the Court stated that it could not find fault with the sentences handed down by the trial court and that a survey of other state procedures in similar cases showed that society was also in agreement with severe punishments for accomplices who actively participated in violent crimes.[75]

Baze v. Rees
553 U.S. ___ (2008)

CAPSULE: The currently predominant three-drug protocol for executions by lethal injection, as represented in Kentucky's execution method, does not violate the Eighth Amendment's prohibition of cruel and unusual punishment.

FACTS: Ralph Baze was convicted of a double homicide and sentenced to death under Kentucky's capital murder statute. Baze, joined by Thomas C. Bowling, filed suit against Kentucky contending that the state's lethal injection process constitutes cruel and unusual punishment because it can result in unnecessary pain and suffering. Petitioners did not challenge the constitutionality of the death penalty itself, just the particular method currently used. Specifically, petitioners believed that the current method carried an unnecessary risk of error or improper administration and thus cause severe pain and suffering. They proposed an alternate method of lethal injection— one that had not been yet adopted or tried in any state. The Kentucky Supreme Court upheld the state's execution method and the United States Supreme Court agreed to hear the case.

ISSUE: Does Kentucky's three-drug protocol for executions by lethal injection violate the Eighth Amendment's prohibition of cruel and unusual punishment? NO.

HOLDING: Kentucky's three-drug lethal injection protocol, also used by 29 other death penalty states, does not constitute cruel and unusual punishment and is thus constitutionally permissible.

REASON: "We begin with the principle, settled by *Gregg*, that capital punishment is constitutional. It necessarily follows that there must be a means of carrying it out. Some risk of pain is inherent in any method of execution— no matter how humane—if only from the prospect of error in following the required procedure. It is clear, then, that the Constitution does not demand the avoidance of all risk of pain in carrying out executions . . . Simply because an execution method may result in pain, either by accident or as an inescapable consequence of death, does not establish the sort of 'objectively intolerable risk of harm' that qualifies as cruel and unusual."

"Reasonable people of good faith disagree on the morality and efficacy of capital punishment, and for many who oppose it, no method of execution would ever be acceptable. But as Justice Frankfurter stressed in *Resweber*, '[o]ne must be on guard against finding in personal disapproval a reflection of more or less prevailing condemnation.'[76] This Court has ruled that capital punishment is not prohibited under our Constitution, and that the States may enact laws specifying that sanction. '[T]he power of a State to pass laws means little if the State cannot enforce them'.[77] State efforts to implement capital punishment must certainly comply with the Eighth Amendment, but what that Amendment prohibits is wanton exposure to 'objectively intolerable risk,'[78] not simply the possibility of pain.

Kentucky has adopted a method of execution believed to be the most humane available, one it shares with 35 other States. Petitioners agree that, if administered as intended, that procedure will result in a painless death. The risks of maladministration they have suggested—such as improper mixing of chemicals and improper setting of IVs by trained and experienced personnel—cannot remotely be characterized as 'objectively intolerable.' Kentucky's decision to adhere to its protocol despite these asserted risks, while adopting safeguards to protect against them, cannot be viewed as probative of the wanton infliction of pain under the Eighth Amendment. Finally, the alternative that petitioners belatedly propose has problems of its own, and has never been tried by a single State.

Throughout our history, whenever a method of execution has been challenged in this Court as cruel and unusual, the Court has rejected the challenge. Our society has nonetheless steadily moved to more humane methods of carrying out capital punishment. The firing squad, hanging, the electric chair, and the gas chamber have each in turn given way to more humane methods, culminating in today's consensus on lethal injection. The broad framework of the Eighth Amendment has accommodated this progress toward more humane methods of execution, and our approval of a particular method in the past has not precluded legislatures from taking the steps they deem appropriate, in light of new developments, to ensure humane capital punishment. There is no reason to suppose that today's decision will be any different."

CASE SIGNIFICANCE: In this case, the Court continues a long-standing tradition of refusing to declare any particular execution method in violation of the Eighth Amendment's prohibition of cruel and unusual punishment. Nevertheless, the Court does weigh in on some key standards for assessing the potential cruelty of such methods, noting that they must be "humane" and not exhibit "wanton infliction of pain." This is not groundbreaking but is about as unequivocal a statement from the Court as one can expect in regard to the constitutionality of particular methods of execution. The Court also addresses the "unusual" component of the Eighth Amendment's ban on cruel and unusual punishment, noting that 30 of the 36 states that have the death penalty have determined the method under question to be the preferred and most humane method available.

This case resulted in a lengthy opinion in which seven justices rendered opinions (the decision and holding resting on a plurality opinion penned by Chief Justice Roberts). Most concurring justices agreed that this case should not be interpreted as one about the constitutionality of the death penalty itself but one that is limited to a very specific execution protocol. However, Justice Stevens, in his concurring opinion, took the opportunity to challenge the constitutionality of the death penalty itself as excessive and presenting an unnecessary risk. Others noted the controversial nature and potential risks of the death penalty as well. These statements perhaps open the door for a later consideration of the very constitutionality of the death penalty. At the very least they entertain the validity of such a debate.

Perhaps the greatest significance of this case, however, occurred before it was decided. During the time in which the Court was considering this case, the United States saw what was the functional equivalent of a moratorium on executions—the longest such hiatus since executions resumed after *Gregg*. Moreover, the pending decision drove some states to amend their death penalty statutes to allow for alternate methods of execution in the event lethal injection was declared unconstitutional. In the end, the Court's decision was not as impacting as it might have been. With the Court declaring the currently predominant mode of execution constitutional, executions were allowed to resume as they had in the wake of past challenges based on the Eighth Amendment.

Kennedy v. Louisiana
554 U.S. ___ (2008)

CAPSULE: It is unconstitutional to impose the death penalty for the rape of a child when the crime does not result in the victim's death.

FACTS:[79] On March 2, 1998, Patrick Kennedy called 911 and reported that his stepdaughter had been raped. He told the 911 operator that he had heard her scream and ran outside to find her in the yard. Kennedy reported that two neighbor boys had dragged her from the garage to the yard and had forced her down and raped her. He claimed he saw one of the boys fleeing on a bicycle. When police arrived at the scene, they found the victim on her bed wrapped in a bloody blanket and bleeding profusely from the vaginal area. Kennedy claimed to have carried her in from the yard and to have washed her with a wet cloth. Injuries to the victim were excessive and required emergency surgery.

An expert in pediatric forensic medicine later testified that the injuries were the worst he had seen in a case of sexual assault in his four years of practice.

In the week following the attack, both Kennedy and his victim reported that the assault had been perpetrated by two neighborhood boys. The victim relayed this account several times but also reportedly told a family member that Kennedy was the one who raped her. Additionally, investigators found blood under the victim's mattress indicating that the assault had taken place in the victim's bedroom and not in the yard as reported by Kennedy and the victim. Eight days after the crime, in spite of the victim's continued refusal to implicate Kennedy, Kennedy was arrested for the rape. On June 22, 1998 the victim told her mother that Kennedy was the one who raped her. This accusation was recorded and videotaped much later in an interview at the Child Advocacy Center. She later told authorities that Kennedy had told her to say that the two neighborhood boys had raped her. Kennedy was convicted and sentenced to death for the assault under Louisiana's statute authorizing the death penalty for the rape of a child who is under 12-years-old. The Supreme Court of Louisiana affirmed the death sentence.

ISSUE: Is it Constitutional to impose the death penalty for the crime of sexual assault against a child when the crime does not result in the victim's death? NO.

HOLDING: It is a violation of the Eighth Amendment to sentence a defendant to death for the rape of a child when the crime does not result in the victim's death.

REASON: "44 States have not made child rape a capital offense. As for federal law, Congress in the Federal Death Penalty Act of 1994 expanded the number of federal crimes for which the death penalty is a permissible sentence, including certain nonhomicide offenses; but it did not do the same for child rape or abuse. Under 18 U. S. C. § 2245, an offender is death eligible only when the sexual abuse or exploitation results in the victim's death."

"The evidence of a national consensus with respect to the death penalty for child rapists, as with respect to juveniles, mentally retarded offenders, and vicarious felony murderers, shows divided opinion but, on balance, an opinion against it. Thirty-seven jurisdictions—36 States plus the Federal Government —have the death penalty. As mentioned above, only six of those jurisdictions authorize the death penalty for rape of a child. Though our review of national consensus is not confined to tallying the number of States with applicable death penalty legislation, it is of significance that, in 45 jurisdictions, petitioner could not be executed for child rape of any kind. That number surpasses the 30 States in Atkins and Roper and the 42 States in Enmund that prohibited the death penalty under the circumstances those cases considered."

"There are measures of consensus other than legislation. Statistics about the number of executions may inform the consideration whether capital punishment for the crime of child rape is regarded as unacceptable in our society. These statistics confirm our determination from our review of state statutes that there is a social consensus against the death penalty for the crime of child rape. Nine States—Florida, Georgia, Louisiana, Mississippi, Montana, Oklahoma, South Carolina, Tennessee, and Texas—have permitted capital punishment for adult or child rape for some length of time between the Court's 1972 decision in *Furman* and today. Yet no individual has been executed for the rape of an adult or child since 1964, and no execution for any other nonhomicide offense has been conducted since 1963."

"The constitutional prohibition against excessive or cruel and unusual punishments mandates that the State's power to punish "be exercised within the limits of civilized standards." *Trop*, 356 U. S., at 99, 100 (plurality opinion). Evolving standards of decency that mark the progress of a maturing society counsel us to be most hesitant before interpreting the Eighth Amendment to allow the extension of the death penalty, a hesitation that has special force where no life was taken in the commission of the crime. It is an established principle that decency, in its essence, presumes respect for the individual and thus moderation or restraint in the application of capital punishment."

"The rule of evolving standards of decency with specific marks on the way to full progress and mature judgment means that resort to the penalty must be reserved for the worst of crimes and limited in its instances of application. In most cases justice is not better served by terminating the life of the perpetrator rather than confining him and preserving the possibility that he and the system will find ways to allow him to understand the enormity of his offense. Difficulties in administering the penalty to ensure against its arbitrary and capricious application require adherence to a rule reserving its use, at this stage of evolving standards and in cases of crimes against individuals, for crimes that take the life of the victim."

"Our concern here is limited to crimes against individual persons. We do not address, for example, crimes defining and punishing treason, espionage, terrorism, and drug kingpin activity, which are offenses against the State. As it relates to crimes against individuals, though, the death penalty should not be expanded to instances where the victim's life was not taken."

"Based both on consensus and our own independent judgment, our holding is that a death sentence for one who raped but did not kill a child, and who did not intend to assist another in killing the child, is unconstitutional under the Eighth and Fourteenth Amendments."

CASE SIGNIFICANCE: The Court, in this case, makes one of its strongest statements in limiting the use of the death penalty in line with the Eighth Amendment notion of "evolving standards of decency" and cruel and unusual punishment. This case reiterates the Court's stance that the death penalty be reserved for cases in which the victim is killed by the perpetrator. Relying, as they did in the recent *Roper* and *Atkins* cases, on consensus among the states based on legislation, the Court determined that executing an offender who does not kill his victims counter to "evolving standards of decency." The Court also notes that such a punishment is disproportionate in cases in which the victim does not die and thus is excessive in terms of the Eighth Amendment's prohibition of cruel and unusual punishment.

This case is important in that it communicates the Court's unwillingness to allow any expansion in the use of the death penalty. In spite of the movement of several states to allow the death penalty for sex offenses committed against children as well as growing public support for such measures, the Court refused to open any new doors in the use of the death penalty. In the majority opinion (written by Justice Kennedy), great reluctance was expressed in regard to broadening the scope of crimes for which the death penalty could be imposed with some verbiage even bordering on abhorrence at the idea that the death penalty might become more widely used. Recalling the original notion from *Gregg* that the death penalty be extremely limited in use, the Court has put an ostensible end to attempts to expand the applicability of the death penalty to crimes in which the victim is not killed. The majority was carefull to point out, however, that the decision does not apply to crimes against the state such as treason, espionage, and terrorism thus leaving the death penalty available in such cases.

Internet Resources

The Death Penalty: An International Perspective
http://www.deathpenaltyinfo.org/article.php?did=127&scid=30#ar

Abolitionist and Retentionist Countries
http://www.amnesty.org/en/death-penalty/abolitionist-and-retentionist-countries

Botched Executions
http://www.deathpenaltyinfo.org/article.php?scid=8&did=478

Methods of Execution:
http://www.deathpenaltyinfo.org/article.php?scid=8&did=479
http://deathpenaltycurriculum.org/student/c/about/methods/contents.htm

Execution Tapes
http://www.soundportraits.org/on-air/execution_tapes/

Notes

1. *Furman v. Georgia*, 408 U.S. 238 (1972); *Gregg v. Georgia*, 428 U.S. 153 (1976).

2. *Trop v. Dulles*, 356 U.S. 86, 101 (1958).

3. *Wilkerson v. Utah*, 99 U.S. 130 (1878).

4. *In re Kemmler*, 136 U.S. 436 (1890).

5. *Andres v. United States*, 333 U.S. 740 (1948).

6. *Kemmler, supra* at 446.

7. Deborah W. Denno, *Getting to Death: Are Executions Constitutional?* 82 IOWA L. REV. 319.

8. *Id.*

9. *Fierro v. Gomez*, 77 F.3d 301 (9th Cir. 1996).

10. Susan Levine, *Death Row Appeal Over Method: Injection Is Cruel Punishment, Attorneys for Md. Killer Argue*, WASHINGTON POST, May 15, 2004 at B2.

11. *Id.*

12. *Hill v. McDonough*, 126 S. Ct. 2096 (2006).

13. Megan Greer, *Legal Injection: The Supreme Court Enters the Lethal Injection Debate*, 30 HARV. J.L. & PUB. POL'Y 767 (2007).

14. *Baze v. Rees*, ___ U.S. ___ (2008).

15. Greer, *supra*.

16. *Baze v. Rees, supra*.

17. *Id.*

18. *Id.*

19. Deborah W. Denno, *Execution and the Forgotten Eighth Amendment*. In JAMES R. ACKER, ROBERT M. BOHM, AND CHARLES S. LANIER (EDS.), AMERICA'S EXPERIMENT WITH CAPITAL PUNISHMENT 547–577 (1998).

20. *Louisiana ex rel. Francis v. Resweber*, 329 U.S. 459 (1947).

21. *Id.* at 464.

22. *Id.* at 470.

23. Denno, *supra*.

24. *See* the Death Penalty Information Center at http://www.deathpenaltyinfo.org/article.php?scid=8&did=478.

25. Cited in AUSTIN SARAT, WHEN THE STATE KILLS: CAPITAL PUNISHMENT AND THE AMERICAN CONDITION, at 61 (2001).

26. ROBERT JOHNSON, DEATHWORK: A STUDY OF THE MODERN EXECUTION PROCESS (1998).

27. Sarat, *supra*.

28. *Weems v. United States*, 217 U.S. 349 (1910).

29. *Id.* at 367.

30. *Furman v. Georgia, supra.*

31. *Woodson v. North Carolina*, 428 U.S. 220 (1976); *Roberts v. Louisiana*, 428 U.S. 325 (1976).

32. *Gregg v. Georgia, supra; Jurek v. Texas*, 428 U.S. 262 (1976); *Proffitt v. Florida*, 428 U.S. 242 (1976).

33. ROBERT M. BOHM, DEATHQUEST II: AN INTRODUCTION TO THE THEORY AND PRACTICE OF CAPITAL PUNISHMENT IN THE UNITED STATES (2003).

34. *Id.*

35. Linda Greenhouse, *Justices to Decide if Rape of a Child Merits Death*, THE NEW YORK TIMES, January 5, 2008. Accessed March 1, 2008, www.nytimes.com.

36. *Coker v. Georgia*, 433 U.S. 584 (1977).

37. *Eberheart v. Georgia*, 433 U.S. 917 (1977).

38. *Tison v. Arizona*, 481 U.S. 137, 148 (1987).

39. Greenhouse, *supra.*

40. *Enmund v. Florida*, 458 U.S. 782 (1982).

41. *Tison v. Arizona*, 481 U.S. 137 (1987).

42. *Bradshaw v. Richey*, 546 U.S. ___ (2005).

43. *Id.*

44. OHIO REV. CODE ANN. § 2903.01 (D).

45. *Bradshaw v. Richey, supra.*

46. *Weems v. United States, supra.*

47. *Gregg v. Georgia, supra.*

48. *Pulley v. Harris*, 465 U.S. 37, 45 (1984).

49. *Id.* at 45.

50. *Weems v. United States, supra* at 378.

51. *Furman v. Georgia, supra* at 277.

52. *Id.* at 332.

53. Bohm, *supra.*

54. Phoebe C. Ellsworth and Samuel R. Gross, *Hardening of the Attitudes: Americans' Views of the Death Penalty*, 50 J. SOC. ISSUES 19 (1994). See also Jeffrey M. Jones, *Two in Three Favor Death Penalty for the Convicted Murderers: Public Divided over Death Penalty or Life Imprisonment as Better Punishment*, Gallup News Service (June 1, 2006).

55. Robert M. Bohm, Louise J. Clark and Adrian F. Aveni, *Knowledge and Death Penalty Opinion: A Test of the Marshall Hypotheses*, 28 J. RES. IN CRIME & DELINQUENCY 360 (1991).

56. Ellsworth and Gross, *supra.*

57. Bohm, Clark and Aveni, *supra.*

58. Jeffrey M. Jones, *Two in Three Favor Death Penalty for the Convicted Murderers: Public Divided over Death Penalty or Life Imprisonment as Better Punishment*, Gallup News Service (June 1, 2006).

59. Scott Vollum, Dennis R. Longmire, and Jacqueline Buffington-Vollum, *Confidence in the Death Penalty and Support for Its Use: Exploring the Value-Expressive Dimension of Death Penalty Attitudes*, 21 JUSTICE QUARTERLY 521 (2004).

60. Ronald J. Tabak, *Finality without Fairness: Why We Are Moving Towards Moratoriums on Executions, and the Potential Abolition of Capital Punishment*, 33 CONN. L. REV. 733 (2001).

61. For a good overview of the moratorium and subsequent review of the death penalty in Illinois, *see* SCOTT TUROW, ULTIMATE PUNISHMENT: A LAWYER'S REFLECTIONS ON DEALING WITH THE DEATH PENALTY (2003).

62. Vollum, Longmire, and Buffington-Vollum, *supra*.

63. Amnesty International. *Death Penalty Statistics 2007*. Available at: http://www. amnestyusa.org/Encourage-Worldwide-Abolition/Death-Penalty-Statistics-2007/page.do? id=1011348&n1=3&n2=28&n3=1277.

64. *Id.*

65. ROGER HOOD, THE DEATH PENALTY: A WORLDWIDE PERSPECTIVE (2002).

66. Rebecca Trail, *The Future of Capital Punishment in the United States: Effects of the International Trend toward Abolition of the Death Penalty*, 26 SUFFOLK TRANSNAT'L L. REV. 105 (2002).

67. *Id.*

68. *Mexico v. United States of America*, International Court of Justice (March 31, 2004).

69. *Medellin v. Texas*, 552 U.S. ___ (2008).

70. *Trop v. Dulles*, 356 U.S. 86 (1958).

71. *Atkins v. Virginia*, 536 U.S. 304 (2002).

72. Trail, *supra*.

73. This is taken from ROLANDO V. DEL CARMEN, SUSAN E. RITTER, AND BETSY A. WITT, BRIEFS OF LEADING CASES IN CORRECTIONS (4th ed. 2005) at 210.

74. *Id.* at 211.

75. *Id.* at 216–217.

76. *Louisiana ex rel. Francis v. Resweber*, 329 U.S. 459, 471 (1947).

77. *McCleskey v. Zant*, 499 U.S. 467, 491 (1991).

78. *Farmer v. Brennan*, 511 U.S. 825, 846 (1994).

79. In the U.S. Supreme Court's written opinion, the facts of the case are preceded with the following: "Petitioner's crime was one that cannot be recounted in these pages in a way sufficient to capture in full the hurt and horror inflicted on his victim or to convey the revulsion society, and the jury that represents it, sought to express by sentencing petitioner to death." The facts of the case as relayed in this brief represent only the facts that were included in the written opinion.

Chapter Outline

I.   **Introduction**

II. **Justifications for Punishment and the Death Penalty**
    A. Retribution and the Death Penalty
    B. Deterrence and the Death Penalty
    C. Incapacitation and the Death Penalty
    D. The Absence of a Justification? The Supreme Court's Reasons for the Death Penalty

III. **Flaws in the Administration of the Death Penalty and Moratoria**

IV. **Trends in the Death Penalty**

V.   **The Future**

Internet Resources

Notes

Chapter 12

Other Issues, Trends, and the Future of the Death Penalty

I. Introduction

Public support for the death penalty in the United States has changed over time. From virtually total support in early colonial times to the abolition of its use by several states during the early twentieth century and culminating with the Supreme Court's decision in *Gregg v. Georgia* (1976),[1] the death penalty continues to be an acceptable and constitutional penal sanction. A May 2006 Gallup Poll showed that 65 percent of Americans surveyed supported the death penalty.[2] Issues concerning the constitutionality of the death penalty have been repeatedly addressed by the Court since its seminal decision in *Gregg*. The boundaries of the death penalty have become better defined since then. At present, more than one-half of the states have the death penalty and it is unlikely that this ultimate sanction will be abolished in the United States in the near future. Since 1976, the year the death penalty was reinstated, 1,099 individuals have been executed in the United States, with another 3,350 death row inmates currently awaiting death[3] (see Figure 12.1). By international standards, the United States joins 60 countries around the world that continue to employ this ancient method of punishment and, in 2007, ranked fifth among countries following only China, Iran, Saudi Arabia, and Pakistan in terms of number of executions.[4]

The basic and most prominent legal issues surrounding the death penalty were addressed in the preceding chapters. This concluding chapter presents other issues and trends regarding the continued use of the death penalty in this country. This chapter first explores justifications for punishment, with focus on the death penalty. It then examines the Court's reasons for the continued use of the death penalty. Inherent flaws in the administration of the death penalty will be discussed, including the execution of innocent offenders and wrongful convictions. Finally, future trends in the death penalty are explored.

Figure 12.1
Number of Inmates on Death Row by State (As of January 2008)

State	# of Inmates	State	# of Inmates	State	# of Inmates
California	669	Mississippi	65	Kansas	10
Florida	388	S. Carolina	58	Connecticut	9
Texas	370	Missouri	45	Washington	8
Penn.	228	Kentucky	39	U.S. Military	6
Alabama	201	Arkansas	38	Maryland	5
Ohio	186	Oregon	35	S. Dakota	3
N. Carolina	166	Indiana	20	Montana	2
Arizona	114	Virginia	20	Wyoming	2
Georgia	107	Idaho	19	Colorado	1
Tennessee	96	Delaware	19	New Mexico	1
Louisiana	85	Illinois	13		
Nevada	83	Nebraska	10		
Oklahoma	82	Utah	10		

Source: Death Penalty Information Center. Available at: http://www.deathpenaltyinfo.org/article.
php?scid=9&did=188#state.

II. Justifications for Punishment and the Death Penalty

There are generally four justifications for punishing a person who has committed a crime. These are: retribution, deterrence, incapacitation, and rehabilitation. Only rehabilitation has no bearing on the continued use of the death penalty. The other three justifications have been used to support the death penalty not only in the United States, but also in other countries. Retribution and deterrence constitute the main reasons the death penalty has survived as a form of punishment in the United States. Ironically, although retribution and deterrence are the two justifications that have been used by the Supreme Court to justify the use of the death penalty, some scholars believe that the Court has yet to "fully articulate a satisfactory rationale for the death penalty"[5] and thus, they believe that such omission by the Court makes the imposition of the death penalty arbitrary.[6] Opponents of the death penalty also argue that retribution does not accord with the provisions of the Constitution, particularly the Eighth Amendment. They further contend that the death penalty is not an effective deterrent to crime and also argue that sentencing alternatives such as life without the possibility of parole (LWOP) can have the same incapacitating effect as the death penalty.

A. *Retribution and the Death Penalty*

Retribution is the oldest form of punishment and one of the main reasons for the use of death penalty in ancient times and today. However, retribution is also the most misunderstood form of punishment largely due to conflicting definitions. The traditional definition of retribution contains the element of revenge. This vengeful form of retribution has its origins in the Mosaic Code of the Old Testament and is captured in the idea of lex talionis ("an eye for an eye"). Lex talionis was the foundation of the Code of Hammurabi, which permitted the victim or the victim's family to seek revenge for injurious behavior. Thus, capital punishment, the ultimate form of vengeful retribution, was a private matter between individuals and also a civil matter during the reign of King Hammurabi, approximately 1,900 years B.C.

The evolution of retributive punishment has naturally produced variants from the classic definition. Some legal scholars maintain that retribution is not synonymous with revenge because revenge is "imposed at the whim of the revenger" who derives "pleasure in the suffering of another."[7] Scholars who subscribe to this differentiation between retribution and revenge also contend that retributive punishment restricts the amount of punishment that is imposed and also restricts the justification for its imposition. Thus, they argue that retributive punishment must be proportionate to the amount of harm inflicted by the offender. They also believe that punishments for vengeful purposes have no internal limitation on the amount of pain to be imposed and justifications for its use need not be consistent with the doctrine of proportionality.[8]

Despite scholarly effort to differentiate the notions of revenge and retribution, the merging of these two elements of punishment constitutes the main reason for the continued use of the death penalty in the United States. Although the death penalty is certainly not imposed at the "whim of the revenger" due to constitutional constraints or limits, there is some truth to the notion of deriving pleasure in the suffering or death of an offender. As one source notes, "Indeed, there have been public celebrations outside prisons during executions. The viciousness of some of these displays can hardly be exaggerated."[9] It is not uncommon for relatives of the victim to express their need to witness the execution of the individual in their desire for closure. However, the death penalty is not a private act that allows families to exact revenge on those who inflict harm and thus must be justified under the Constitution.

From a purely legal standpoint, however, justifying the death penalty under the Constitution has caused problems. Some scholars say that despite numerous cases, the Court has yet to fully and explicitly articulate that this ultimate sanction can be imposed for retribution. For instance, in *Furman v. Georgia* (1972),[10] several justices examined the retributive nature of the death penalty, but there was no consensus among the justices that retribution is an acceptable reason for the death penalty. Justice Stewart, who ruled that the death penalty was unconstitutionally imposed on minorities, opined that the retributive nature of the death penalty was not contradictory to the mandates in the Constitution. According to Justice Stewart, states are given the authority to impose the death penalty on the most violent offenders to seek retribution for crimes committed (just deserts), as long as this ultimate sanction was not imposed arbitrarily or capriciously in violation of the equal protection clause of the Fourteenth Amendment. However, Justice Marshall, who also wrote a concurring opinion in Furman, reached a different conclusion about the retributive aspect of the death penalty. He argued that retribution violated the Constitution, specifically the Eighth Amendment. Acknowledging that retribution has been historically used as a justification for the death penalty in the United States, Justice Marshall argued that "retaliation, vengeance, and retribution have been roundly condemned as intolerable aspirations for a government in a free society" and further stated that "the history of the Eighth Amendment supports only the conclusion that retribution for its own sake is improper."[11]

Justice Brennan, who in *Furman* supported the abolition of the death penalty on grounds that it violated the cruel and unusual punishment clause of the Eighth Amendment, abhorred the fact that "naked vengeance"[12] was used by states to justify the death penalty. He also insisted that retribution could not be accepted as a contemporary reason for the continued use of the death penalty. In *Gregg v. Georgia* (1976),[13] only four justices concurred that retribution was an acceptable reason for the death penalty. In *Gregg*, Justice Stewart, who wrote the plurality opinion, reiterated that retribution was acceptable under the provisions of the Constitution. He further clarified that the retributive quality of the death penalty was essential to an ordered society because it reflected society's desire to punish those who engaged in morally outrageous and offensive conduct. He underscored the importance of bestowing upon the government the authority to impose the death penalty and the consequences that would result if this form of punishment was not legally permitted. Reiterating his previous opinion in Furman, Justice Stewart said:

> The instinct for retribution is part of the nature of man, and channeling that instinct in the administration of criminal justice serves an important purpose in promoting the stability of a society governed by law. When people begin to believe that organized society is unwilling or unable to impose upon criminal offenders the punishment they deserve, then there are sown the seeds of anarchy —of self-help . . .[14]

Although Justice Stewart presented a uniquely pragmatic reason for imposing the death penalty based upon the preservation of an ordered society, there is no conclusive evidence that the death penalty significantly contributes to such order or whether the abolition of the death penalty would lead to anarchy. Accordingly, not only does the lack of evidence discredit arguments for the death penalty based on the notion of retribution, but also brings into disrepute arguments about the deterrent effect of the death penalty.

B. Deterrence and the Death Penalty

In *Gregg*, Justice Stewart noted that one of the social purposes of the death penalty is to permit society to exact retribution on those who engage in the most serious offenses. However, he also conceded that the death penalty was a useful method of deterring the behavior of potential offenders. Deterrence, which is a derivative of eighteenth-century classical criminology, is a sentencing goal or a crime prevention strategy that seeks to inhibit criminal behavior in either the offender (specific deterrence) or in others (general deterrence) by using punishment or the threat of punishment to outweigh any beneficial or profitable outcomes that may result from the commission of a crime. Theoretically, deterrence is based on the notion that offenders, or would-be offenders, rationally consider the consequences of their actions and will be dissuaded if punishment or the threat of punishment is more costly or painful than law-abiding behavior. Deterrence is also based on the premise that punishments must be administered by the legal system with swiftness and certainty, as well as administered to the degree that is proportional to the crime committed.

Deterrence represents the most logical reason for imposing this ultimate sanction on those who commit the most serious crimes in our society. Because "potential offenders are aware of the death penalty and regard it as a more severe sanction than imprisonment . . . murder is discouraged because the threat of one's own death presumably outweighs the rewards gained from killing another."[15] However, this argument, used by proponents of the death penalty, may be flawed in several respects. First, some criminologists argue that offenders may not rationally consider the consequences of their actions. Specifically for the crime of first-degree murder, some criminologists maintain that premeditation does not generally precede the commission of this capital crime because most murders of this degree are committed out of anger or passion[16] rather than after a rational consideration of the legal penalties likely to be imposed if one is convicted.

Second, for the death penalty to be an effective deterrent, it must be administered with swiftness and certainty—two elements that do not characterize our current system of criminal justice, especially with the numerous appeals that are available to capital offenders. Additionally, as noted by Justice Brennan in *Furman*, the infrequency with which the death penalty is imposed conflicts with the basic tenets of deterrence theory. According to Justice Brennan, when the death penalty is inflicted arbitrarily on minority members of our society, the deterrent effect of this sanction becomes a moot issue.

A third flaw of deterrence theory and the death penalty is the so-called brutalization effect—or the notion that the death penalty cannot deter the killing of human beings because state-authorized executions "demonstrate that it is correct and appropriate to kill those who have gravely offended us."[17] Opponents of the death penalty challenge its deterrent effect by stating that the continued use of the death penalty sends conflicting messages about the authority of government to exact revenge on those who commit crimes while at the same time attempting to deter the same vengeful behavior in members of society. Finally, another significant flaw of the belief in the deterrent effect of the death penalty is the lack of empirical evidence to support the contention that this ultimate sanction decreases the number of crimes committed. Although extensive empirical research has been undertaken to determine whether the death penalty has any deterrent effect, only a few studies have demonstrated a marginal deterrent effect.

The value of the death penalty as a deterrent for crime is yet to be conclusively ascertained. Despite the non-proven link between deterrence and the death penalty, the Court continues to believe there might be some possibility that capital punishment deters others from committing crime. In *Spaziano v. Florida* (1984), Justice White noted that:

> the majority of the Court has concluded that the general deterrence rationale adequately justifies the imposition of capital punishment at least for certain classes of offenses for which the legislature may reasonably conclude that the death penalty has a deterrent effect.[18]

C. Incapacitation and the Death Penalty

Incapacitation is the third justification for punishment and is not often associated with the death penalty. The death penalty however, is the ultimate form of incapacitation, because it permanently prevents an offender from engaging in future criminal behavior. Advocates of the death penalty quickly use incapacitation to justify the death penalty, pointing to how effective the death penalty is in incapacitating those who inflict the most harm on society.[19] But opponents of the death penalty are also quick to indicate that incapacitation, particularly in the form of a life sentence, is just as effective at preventing even the most serious offenders from committing crime. Thus, they argue that the death penalty has become an obsolete form of punishment.

Life imprisonment has been used as an alternative to the death penalty in many countries, including the United States. However, for some, a life sentence has not been a sufficiently appealing alternative to the death penalty. Admittedly, incapacitation in the form of a life sentence at times does not fully incapacitate an offender from engaging in future criminal behavior because he or she may be released from prison after serving only a portion of a life sentence. Unless specified by statute, a life sentence does not necessarily mean that the capital offender will remain in prison until death. Under an indeterminate sentencing scheme, an inmate sentenced to life may have his or her sentence reduced depending on good time credit and evidence of rehabilitation while in prison. However, under a mandatory sentencing scheme, life imprisonment without the possibility of parole (LWOP) may be as effective in incapacitating capital offenders. At present, out of the 36 states plus the federal government that continue to use the death penalty, 35 states allow juries to impose life sentences without the possibility of parole (see Figure 12.2). In a May 2006 Gallup Poll, 48 percent of those surveyed indicated that if given a choice, they would support life without the possibility of parole as opposed to 47 percent who would favor the death penalty.[20]

Figure 12.2
Death Penalty States Offering Life without Parole

Alabama	Kentucky	Oklahoma
Arizona	Louisiana	Oregon
Arkansas	Maryland	Pennsylvania
California	Mississippi	South Carolina
Colorado	Missouri	South Dakota
Connecticut	Montana	Tennessee
Delaware	Nebraska	Texas
Florida	Nevada	Utah
Georgia	New Hampshire	Virginia
Idaho	North Carolina	Washington
Illinois	New Jersey	Wyoming
Indiana	Ohio	
Kansas		

Source: Death Penalty Information Center. Available at: http://www.deathpenaltyinfo.org/article. php?did=555&scid=59.

D. The Absence of a Justification? The Supreme Court's Reasons for the Death Penalty

Among the three reasons for the continued use of the death penalty, incapacitation is the weakest. Retribution is the most controversial because the execution of a capital offender is justified on the basis that the offender deserves to die because of the crime committed. However, it remains one of the prime reasons for the continued use of the death penalty. Deterrence is the other equally justifiable reason for the continued use of the death penalty, although empirical research has failed to conclusively demonstrate its deterrent effect.

Among these three reasons or justifications for the death penalty, the Supreme Court has explicitly commented on two—retribution and deterrence. As noted, some legal scholars say that the Court has yet to reach an agreement as to the constitutional justification for the death penalty. The Court's vacillation between retribution and deterrence and, at times, complacency in indicating whether retribution or deterrence (or both) are constitutionally permissible as justifications for the death penalty, has led some critics to argue that the failure or unwillingness of the Court to articulate a reason for the continued use of the death penalty makes such a sanction arbitrary. Other critics contend that "the Court has never undertaken any systematic review of the legitimate constitutional rationale justifying the death penalty . . . and in the absence of a legitimate purpose for capital punishment, imposing the death penalty is irrational and unconstitutionally arbitrary."[21]

Although it is true that the Court has not reached a definitive conclusion about the justifications for the death penalty, critics of the Court's death penalty jurisprudence are doubtless cognizant of the counterarguments. It starts with the reality that the Court, as the judicial enforcer of the provisions of the Constitution, must adhere to principles of federalism that allow states, through the legislature, to decide issues regarding the appropriateness and legitimacy of penal sanctions. Because matters of criminal justice, including the imposition of proportionate sanctions, are issues that primarily concern the states, the Court must respect the decisions of legislatures and the people they represent. As noted by Justices Powell, Blackmun, and Rehnquist in *Furman v. Georgia* (1972),

> The designation of punishments for crimes is a matter peculiarly within the sphere of the state and federal legislative bodies. When asked to encroach on the legislative prerogative we are well counseled to proceed with the utmost reticence. The review of legislative choices, in the performance of our duty to enforce the Constitution, has been characterized as the gravest and most delicate duty of the Court.[22]

The Court is conscious of its duty and is generally unwilling to interfere in state matters, but it has set aside states' rights when state sanctions are capriciously, freakishly, and wantonly imposed.[23] But it has done so on a case-by-case basis and has not overturned the legislative judgments of all the states that continue to use the death penalty.

III.   Flaws in the Administration of the Death Penalty and Moratoria

As has been expressed by the Court, the death penalty is different from any other penal sanction that can be imposed on criminal offenders because, unlike any other form of punishment, death is final and irreversible. This reality necessitates that all means must be employed to avoid executing an innocent offender or wrongfully convicting the innocent. However, as noted by Justice Marshall in *Furman*, "no matter how careful courts are, the possibility of perjured testimony, mistaken honest testimony, and human error remain all too real." Justice Marshall further states that "we have no way of judging how many innocent persons have been executed, but we can be certain there were some."[24] This statement, however, cannot be factually supported because "no capital jurisdiction in this country has ever admitted to executing an innocent person in this century . . . Obviously, the government's failure or refusal to acknowledge that an innocent defendant has been executed is hardly evidence that none have been executed."[25]

Since Marshall's opinion in *Furman*, several studies have looked into the number of innocent offenders who have been executed or wrongfully convicted. In an early preliminary study conducted by researchers Bedau and Radelet, evidence of 23 innocent offenders executed between 1900 and 1990 was uncovered.[26] Bedau and Radelet have further discovered that 400 individuals had been wrongfully convicted in capital cases.[27] The American Civil Liberties Union also reports that as of June of 2003, 108 people had been released from death row in 25 states due to innocence.[28] The Death Penalty Information Center reports that, as of May 1, 2008, there have been 129 exonerations in 26 different states (see Figure 12.3). Had these executions occurred, an innocent person would have died.

Figure 12.3
Exonerations by States as of May 1, 2008

Florida	22	Massachusetts	3
Illinois	18	Missouri	3
Louisiana	8	Mississippi	3
Texas	8	South Carolina	2
Arizona	8	Indiana	2
Oklahoma	8	Kentucky	1
North Carolina	8	Maryland	1
Pennsylvania	6	Idaho	1
Georgia	5	Nebraska	1
Alabama	5	Nevada	1
Ohio	5	Tennessee	1
New Mexico	4	Virginia	1
California	3	Washington	1

Source: Death Penalty Information Center. Available at http://www.deathpenaltyinfo.org/FactSheet.pdf.

According to Bedau and Radelet, reasons for error in death penalty cases include perjury by prosecution witnesses, mistaken testimony, and careless police work. Additional research has indicated that errors in such cases may be attributable to heightened publicity and its influence on the opinion of prospective jurors; death-qualified juries eager to impose the penalty of death; and limited resources or ineffective counsel for the defense of alleged capital offenders.[29] Critics claim that "some prosecutors place so much importance on securing a conviction that doubts about the person's guilt or innocence become secondary."[30] Instances of blatant prosecutorial misconduct have also surfaced as reasons for error in death penalty cases (see Figure 12.4). In the recent case of *Banks v. Dretke* (2004),[31] for example, the Court reversed the

Fifth Circuit Court of Appeals' decision to deny petitioner Banks a certificate of appealability on the ground that the prosecution had suppressed an interrogation transcript that revealed that a paid informant of the police was coached to testify against Banks at trial.

Figure 12.4
Examples of Prosecutorial Misconduct

The Case of Randal Dale Adams

In 1977, Adams was sentenced to death for killing a Dallas, Texas police officer during a traffic stop. In 1989, Adams was given a new trial due to evidence that the prosecution had withheld exculpatory evidence (evidence proving that Adams was innocent) from the defense.

The Case of Clarence Brandley

In 1980, Brandley, an African American janitor, was sentenced to death in Texas for the murder of a 16-year-old girl. In 1990, Brandley was given a new trial due to evidence that the prosecution had suppressed exculpatory evidence and used perjured witness testimony.

The Case of Daryl Atkins

In 2002, Daryl Atkins, the defendant in the Virginia case in which the Supreme Court declared the execution of mentally retarded offenders a violation of the United States Constitution, had his sentence reduced from death to life without parole not because of his mental limitations but because it was discovered that prosecutors coaxed a co-defendant to lie about some of the circumstances surrounding the crime.

The realization that the administration of the death penalty is not infallible and that errors may occur has led to the issuance of several moratoriums. A moratorium, which is an order to stop the executions of capital offenders pending further investigation into the administration of the death penalty, was first considered by the Supreme Court in *Furman v. Georgia* (1976).[32] In *Furman*, the Court concluded that there were several flaws in the administration of the death penalty, specifically referring to the arbitrary and capricious nature with which they were imposed. Consequently, the Court issued a moratorium. The halt on all executions as a result of the *Furman* decision lasted until 1976, when in *Gregg v. Georgia*,[33] the Court concluded that the changes to the laws in the state of Georgia had ensured that the death penalty is not imposed in an unconstitutional manner.

Since 1972, there have been no more formal Court-ordered moratoriums on the death penalty. However, several state governors have issued such moratoriums due to errors discovered in the administration of the death penalty. In 2000, then-Governor Ryan of Illinois, a known supporter of the death penalty, issued a moratorium to stop further executions until a thorough assessment of the administration of the death penalty could be conducted. The moratorium was issued to ensure that no innocent individual was put to death. After a lengthy investigation by a committee appointed by the governor, several recommendations to improve or fix the administration of the death penalty were proposed. Some of these recommendations are as follows:

- Custodial interrogations of alleged capital offenders by the police should be videotaped and/or electronically recorded.

- Police must give prosecutors access to all investigatory materials in their possession.

- Police must ensure that lineups are not biased against suspects.

- Police officers working on homicide cases should receive extensive training on matters such as risks of wrongful convictions, and investigation and interrogation methods.

- An independent state forensic laboratory should be created.

- Minimum standards for DNA evidence should be established.

- Development of a DNA database.

- Bar the death penalty in cases in which there is only one eyewitness, an in-custody informant, or testimony from an uncorroborated accomplice.

- After a jury decides to impose a death sentence, the trial judge must also agree that death is an appropriate sentence.

- Ensure that the death sentence is proportionate to the crime committed.[34]

As a result of errors in the administration of justice, Governor Ryan commuted the sentences of all 156 death row inmates. Since the moratorium in Illinois, other states have issued moratoriums. For instance, Maryland Governor Glendening issued a moratorium due to evidence of racial bias in the administration of the death penalty. In 2003, the newly elected Illinois governor extended Governor Ryan's moratorium on executions.

In 2007, the Court agreed to hear arguments about the constitutionality of lethal injection as an execution method in the case of *Baze v. Rees*.[35] Although the Court eventually ruled in *Baze* that lethal injection did not violate the Eighth Amendment's ban on cruel and unusual punishment, anticipation of the court ruling had led to a de facto moratorium on lethal injections throughout the nation. Through judicial action or executive order (order by the state governor), many states temporarily stopped executions. In addition, several states have issued their own moratoriums in recent years. Florida, for instance, issued a moratorium in 2006 to study its lethal injection protocol because an inmate's execution was prolonged for more than the usual 15 minutes it takes for the three drugs to medically cause death. The execution took more than

30 minutes and Florida's medical examiner deemed that the inmate was conscious but paralyzed throughout most of his execution. Nebraska also halted executions because of a concern that its electrocution protocol, which requires the administration of a 20-second 2,450-volt shock followed by a second shock if needed, violates the Eighth Amendment's cruel and unusual punishment provision. Tennessee's governor issued a moratorium to review its method of execution, as did North Carolina.

The case of Michael Angelo Morales in California in 2006 brought to light many of the flaws in the administration of the death penalty. Morales challenged the constitutionality of lethal injections on the grounds that the manner in which it would be administered by California's Department of Corrections and Rehabilitation would cause unnecessary pain and thus violate the Eighth Amendment. Judge Fogel of the U.S. District Court for the Northern District of California issued a moratorium due to "deficiencies" in the administration of the death penalty. Such deficiencies, according to Fogel, were:

1. inconsistent and unreliable screening of execution team members;

2. a lack of meaningful training, supervision, and oversight of the execution team;

3. inconsistent and unreliable recordkeeping;

4. improper mixing, preparation, and administration of sodium thiopental by the execution team; and

5. inadequate lighting, overcrowded conditions, and poorly designed facilities in which the execution team must work.[36]

Despite such problems, Judge Fogel believed that the administration of the death penalty in California could be fixed. Thus, Governor Schwarzenegger ordered an overhaul of the lethal injection protocols and other administrative details in administering the lethal doses of drugs.

IV. Trends in the Death Penalty

Several trends on the use of the death penalty have occurred in recent years. One of the significant trends has been the number of studies conducted by various legislative committees inquiring into the administration of the death penalty as well as the number of moratoriums imposed by judicial decree, executive order, or self-imposed by states awaiting the Court's decision in *Baze v. Rees*.[37] The most significant development could be the willingness of states to admit that errors plague the administration of this ultimate sanction and their resolve to minimize, if not completely eliminate such errors. This high resolve is significant because in the not-too-distant past, states were willing to overlook a few errors (the execution of one or two innocent capital offenders) in order to retain the death penalty. Findings by various legislative and executive committees as well as judicial officers, however, have revealed errors that cannot be easily overlooked. These flaws in the administration of the death penalty have prompted states to pass moratoriums and issue safeguards against their recurrence.

Another significant trend is the use of DNA testing. Although the use of DNA tests have been relied on by the courts in the past to exonerate innocent offenders charged with sexual crimes, there has been a significant increase in the use of these tests in death penalty cases. States that have decided to rid administration of the death penalty of flaws generally include provisions to create DNA laboratories or use DNA results to ensure the guilt of an offender. However, DNA tests are only as good as the evidence left behind at the scene of the crime, and thus not all capital offenders benefit from this technological advance. Because this procedure depends on the effectiveness of the police in gathering information, capital offenders will not have the opportunity to prove their innocence through DNA evidence if the police destroy evidence or fail to collect enough evidence. If the offender was known to the victim and regularly visited the location of the victim's eventual death, DNA evidence would not be able to fully exonerate the offender. The most damaging criticism of DNA tests continues to be the reliability of the crime laboratory that analyzes the DNA. In recent years, much has been learned about careless mistakes committed by DNA analysts throughout the United States. Investigations by the FBI have even indicated that some crime laboratories fabricate DNA results.[38] In 2000, bipartisan legislation was introduced in Congress that would ensure that DNA testing is available to all who make a credible claim of innocence. In 2004, the Innocence Protection Act, which creates a post-conviction DNA testing process to protect innocent defendants, was signed into law by President Bush. It will also provide training funds for attorneys in death penalty cases (see Figure 12.5).

Another trend in the death penalty has come from an unlikely group of individuals—state prosecutors and law enforcement officials. Although often characterized as favoring the death penalty due to political concerns, several prosecutors have expressed the concern that seeking the death penalty is too costly (see Figure 12.6). In San Mateo, California, state prosecutors announced that they would not seek the death penalty because of the millions of dollars it would cost the taxpayers, coupled with the uncertainty of getting a verdict of death. The increasing uncertainty of getting a death sentence from a jury is perhaps the most significant trend in the death penalty. There has been a growing consensus among citizens of this country to bar the execution of juvenile offenders and also a notable decrease in support for the death penalty in general. Additionally, police officers may also be rethinking their stance on the death penalty. A 1995 Hart Research Poll found that police chiefs across the country did not believe that the death penalty is an effective tool to prevent crime.[39] New Jersey's police chief, who served on the New Jersey Death Penalty Commission to investigate abolishing the sentence, believed that the enormous cost in executing inmates could be better used for crime prevention programs.[40]

Figure 12.5
Significant Provisions of the Innocence Protection Act

The Innocence Protection Act
Title I: Exonerating the Innocent through DNA Testing:

A person convicted of a federal crime may apply for a DNA test to support a claim of innocence. The court "must order the DNA test when it determines that (1) the evidence is still in existence and in such a condition that DNA testing may be conducted; (2) the evidence was never previously subjected to DNA testing or to the type of DNA testing requested that may resolve an issue not previously resolved; (3) the proposed testing uses a scientifically valid technique; (4) the proposed testing has the scientific potential to produce new, non-cumulative evidence which is material to the applicant's claim that he or she did not commit the crime and which raises a reasonable probability that the applicant would not have been convicted; and (5) the identity of the perpetrator was or should have been a significant issue in the case."

The court is prohibited from "ordering a DNA test if the government proves by a preponderance of the evidence that the application was made to interfere with the administration or justice rather than to support a claim with respect to production of such new evidence."

Title II: Improving State Systems for Providing Competent Legal Services in Capital Cases

"Directs the Attorney General to make available grants to States for improving the quality of legal representation provided to indigent defendants in State capital cases. Sets forth provisions describing: (1) what constitutes an effective system for providing competent legal representation (including establishment of qualifications for attorneys who may be appointed to represent indigents in capital cases, maintenance of a roster of qualified attorneys, provision of periodic training programs, and monitoring of attorney performance); and (2) factors in determining whether to include or maintain an attorney on the roster (such as whether the attorney has been sanctioned for ethical misconduct in a Federal or State court felony case)."

Source: *Bill Summary and Status for the 107th Congress.* Available at: http://thomas.loc.gov/cgi-bin/bdquery/z?d107:SN00486:@@@L&summ2=m&.

Figure 12.6
The Cost of the Death Penalty

In a study conducted by the state of Kansas (2003) comparing death penalty versus non-death penalty cases, overwhelming statistical evidence indicated that death penalty cases cost taxpayers 70 percent more than non-death penalty cases. The study estimated that the median death penalty case costs $1.26 million as compared to $740,000 for non-death penalty cases. For death penalty cases, pretrial and trial expenses comprise 49 percent of the total cost, followed by appeals, which account for 29 percent of the total cost. Incarceration and execution combined accounted for 22 percent of the total cost.

Source: *Costs of the Death Penalty.* Death Penalty Information Center. Available at: http://www. deathpenaltyinfo.org/article.php?did=108&scid=7.

The unwillingness of abolitionist states to reinstate the death penalty has also been a trend in the death penalty. Michigan, which was one of the first states to abolish the death penalty 1847, recently considered submitting a referendum to state voters that would have reinstated the death penalty. Michigan lawmakers refused to support the referendum.[41] In Minnesota, the governor called for a referendum to allow state voters the opportunity to reinstate the death penalty, but the Minnesota Senate Crime Prevention and Public Safety Committee voted eight to two against it. In 2007, New Jersey became the first state since the death penalty was reinstated in 1976 to abolish the death penalty. Although some lawmakers voted to end executions in the state due to a belief that the "evolving standards of decency" dictated such a change, others voted to abolish it because it would save the state money.

V. The Future

Of the three justifications for imposing a legal sanction on a criminal offender, retribution and deterrence are the primary reasons for the continued use of the death penalty in the United States. Retribution, however, has many variants, one of which includes the element of revenge. Although this would seem inconsistent with the mandates of the Eighth Amendment's proscription against cruel and unusual punishment, members of the Court have used this form of retribution to justify the use of the death penalty. No doubt there are members of society who subscribe to this justification for the most severe form of punishment. There are no conclusive or determinate studies to indicate that the death penalty deters crime.

Despite the justifications for the death penalty, consideration must be given to the inherent flaws in the administration of the death penalty because there appears to be evidence that wrongful convictions and the execution of innocent capital offenders have probably occurred. Thus, efforts are afoot to prevent their recurrence. Although some states have issued moratoriums as they investigate errors or flaws, these states are in the minority. Several states have expressed concern that improving the administration of the death penalty is costly, particularly when it involves the creation of independent DNA laboratories and DNA databases.

It is unlikely that the Supreme Court will abolish the death penalty in the foreseeable future. It is probably here to stay unless public support declines to a level where it becomes clear that the death penalty no longer comports with an "evolving standard of decency that characterizes a civilized society." Only then might the Court rule that the death penalty, as a form of punishment, deserves its own legal death.

Internet Resources

Death Penalty Moratorium Implementation Project
http://www.abanet.org/moratorium/

Fatal Flaws: Innocence and the Death Penalty in the USA
http://web.amnesty.org/library/Index/engAMR510691998

Focus on the Death Penalty
http://justice.uaa.alaska.edu/death/issues.html

Righting Wrongful Convictions
http://www.northwestern.edu/magazine/northwestern/spring99/convictions.
  htm

**The Evolving Role of State Constitutional Law in Death Penalty
  Adjudication**
www.law.nyu.edu/pubs/annualsurvey/documents/59%20N.Y.U.%20Ann.%
  20Surv.%20Am.%20L.%20341%20(2003).pdf

Notes

1. *Gregg v. Georgia*, 428 U.S. 153 (1976).

2. *Facts about the Death Penalty*, Death Penalty Information Center, January 20, 2008. Available at: http://www.deathpenaltyinfo.org/FactSheet.pdf.

3. *Death Row Inmates by State and Size of Death Row by Year*, Death Penalty Information Center, September 20, 2004, pg. 8. Available at: http://www.deathpenaltyinfo.org/article.php?scid=9&did=188#state

4. Amnesty International. *Death Penalty Statistics 2007*. Available at: http://www.amnestyusa.org/Encourage-Worldwide-Abolition/Death-Penalty-Statistics-2007/page.do?id=1011348&n1=3&n2=28&n3=1277

5. Mary Sigler, *Contradiction, Coherence, and Guided Discretion in The Supreme Court's Capital Sentencing Jurisprudence*, 40 AM. CRIM. L. REV. 1177 (2003).

6. *Id.* at 1180.

7. *Id.*

8. *Id.*

9. Margaret Vandiver, *The Impact of the Death Penalty on the Families of Homicide Victims and of Condemned Prisoners.* In JAMES R. ACKER, ROBERT M. BOHM, AND CHARLES S. LANIER (EDS.), AMERICA'S EXPERIMENT WITH CAPITAL PUNISHMENT: REFLECTIONS OF THE PAST, PRESENT, AND FUTURE OF THE ULTIMATE PENAL SANCTION (2003), pp. 613–647.

10. *Furman v. Georgia*, 408 U.S. 238 (1972).

11. *Id.* at 315.

12. *Id.* at 258.

13. *Gregg v. Georgia*, 428 U.S. 153 (1976).

14. *Furman v. Georgia*, 408 U.S. 238, 308 (1972).

15. Ruth D. Peterson and William C. Bailey, *Is Capital Punishment an Effective Deterrent for Murder? An Examination of Social Science Research.* In JAMES R. ACKER, ROBERT M. BOHM, AND CHARLES S. LANIER (EDS.), AMERICA'S EXPERIMENT WITH CAPITAL PUNISHMENT: REFLECTIONS OF THE PAST, PRESENT, AND FUTURE OF THE ULTIMATE PENAL SANCTION (2003), pp. 251–258.

16. Bowers, W.J. and G. Pierce, *Deterrence or Brutalization: What Is the Effect of Executions?* CRIME & DELINQUENCY 26:453–484 (1980).

17. *Id.* at 456.

18. *Spaziano v. Florida*, 468 U.S. 447, 479 (1984).

19. Mary Sigler, *Contradiction, Coherence, and Guided Discretion in the Supreme Court's Capital Sentencing Jurisprudence*, 40 AM. CRIM. L. REV. 1157 (2003).

20. *Facts about the Death Penalty*, Death Penalty Information Center, January 20, 2008. Available at: http://www.deathpenaltyinfo.org/FactSheet.pdf.

21. Mary Sigler, Contradiction, *Coherence, and Guided Discretion in the Supreme Court's Capital Sentencing Jurisprudence*, 40 AM. CRIM. L. REV. 1157 (2003).

22. *Furman v. Georgia*, 408 U.S. 238, 258 (1972).

23. *Gregg v. Georgia*, 428 U.S. 153 (1976).

24. *Furman v. Georgia*, 408 U.S. 238, 367–8 (1972).

25. Michael L. Radelet and Hugo Adam Bedau, *The Execution of the Innocent.* In JAMES R. ACKER, ROBERT M. BOHM, AND CHARLES S. LANIER (EDS.), AMERICA'S EXPERIMENT WITH CAPITAL PUNISHMENT: REFLECTIONS OF THE PAST, PRESENT, AND FUTURE OF THE ULTIMATE PENAL SANCTION (2003), pp. 333.

26. Hugo Bedau and Michael Radelet, *Miscarriages of Justice in Potentially Capital Cases*, 40 STANFORD L. REV. 21 (1987).

27. *Id.*

28. American Civil Liberties Union, *Three Decades Later: Why We Need a Temporary Halt on Executions: Report on The Anniversary of* Furman v. Georgia, September 4, 2004. Available at: http://www.aclu.org/DeathPenalty/DeathPenalty.cfm?ID=13028&c=17.

29. Richard C. Dieter, *Innocence and the Death Penalty: The Increasing Danger of Execution the Innocent*, Death Penalty Information Center, July 28, 2004. Available at: www.deathpenaltyinfo.org/article.php?scid=45&did=292.

30. American Civil Liberties Union, *Three Decades Later: Why We Need a Temporary Halt on Executions: Report on The Anniversary of* Furman v. Georgia, September 4, 2004. Available at: http://www.aclu.org/DeathPenalty/DeathPenalty.cfm?ID=13028&c=17.

31. *Banks v. Dretke*, 540 U.S. 668 (2004).

32. *Furman v. Georgia*, 408 U.S. 238 (1976)

33. *Gregg v. Georgia*, 428 U.S. 153 (1976).

34. State of Illinois. *Report of the Governor's Commission on Capital Punishment, Recommendations Only.* September 20, 2004. Available at: http://www.idoc.state.il.us/ccp/ccp/reports/commission_report/index.html.

35. *Baze v. Rees*, ___ U.S. ___ (2008).

36. State of California Lethal Injection Protocol Review. Available at http://www.deathpenaltyinfo.org/CALethInject.pdf.

37. *Baze v. Rees*, ___ U.S. ___ (2008).

38. American Civil Liberties Union, *Three Decades Later: Why We Need a Temporary Halt on Executions: Report on The Anniversary of* Furman v. Georgia, September 4, 2004. Available at: http://www.aclu.org/DeathPenalty/DeathPenalty.cfm?ID=13028&c=17.

39. Death Penalty Information Center, *Facts about the Death Penalty*, January 20, 2008. Available at: http://www.deathpenaltyinfo.org/FactSheet.pdf.

40. *Less Money, More Pain and Injustice*, Star Telegram.com, January 20, 2008. Available at: http://www.star-telegram.com/245/story/421340.html.

41. Death Penalty Information Center, *Changes in the Death Penalty*, July 15, 2004. Available at: http://www.deathpenaltyinfo.org/article.php?did=236&scid=40.

Index

WITHDRAWN
WILLOW INTERNATIONAL LIBRARY

9 781593 455750